*For Boyd Cooke
with warm regards*

I. J. Galantin

SUBMARINE ADMIRAL

SUBMARINE ADMIRAL

FROM BATTLEWAGONS
TO BALLISTIC MISSILES

ADMIRAL I. J. GALANTIN, USN (Ret.)

UNIVERSITY OF ILLINOIS PRESS   URBANA AND CHICAGO

Library of Congress Cataloging-in-Publication Data
Galantin, I. J., 1910–
Submarine admiral : from battlewagons to ballistic missiles
/ I.J. Galantin
    p.   cm.
Includes index.
ISBN 0-252-02160-6
    1. Galantin, I. J., 1910–   . 2. Admirals—United States—
Biography. 3. United States. Navy—Biography. 4. United
States—History, Naval—20th century. I. Title.
E480.5.G35A3   1995
359'.0092—dc20
[B]   94-42971
CIP
Chapter 23 originally appeared in the United States Naval
Institute's *Proceedings* in April 1985. Used by permission.

CONTENTS

PREFACE

It is almost a hundred years since the United States Navy acquired its first submarine by purchase from the inventor, John P. Holland. It can be said that in that time the evolution of the submarine in the Navy occurred in four phases: (1) trial and error, 1900–1940; (2) proof in combat, 1941–1945; (3) wishful thinking, 1946–1954; and (4) new dimensions, 1955–1979. The end of the cold war has brought a fifth phase, a period of uncertainty as the Navy reorients its mission to partnership in joint operations and littoral warfare.

My career afloat and ashore included all or part of the first four phases. It extended from days when the 629-ton O-boats were still operating, through the era of R- and S-boats, through the bewildering search for an effective "fleet" boat, through combat at sea, to the new age of nuclear-powered 6900-ton attack boats and 8200-ton ballistic missile submarines. The three tours of shore duty in the Pentagon headquarters of the chief of naval operations (OpNav) were each as the head of successively more senior submarine billets. All together, my duties were a unique opportunity to participate in the evolution of the submarine's capabilities and to experience the sometimes painful process of integrating them in our balanced-forced concept.

The story I tell in this memoir is the outgrowth of the abortive oral history I started when Paul Stillwell was head of that program at the U.S. Naval Institute, Annapolis, Maryland. His stimulating questions and patient guidance convinced me that the sifting of memory and assembly of facts required for a meaningful record could be better done in writing.

To tell my story, I have chosen the anecdotal rather than archival format, relying chiefly on entries in an intermittent journal, on personal correspondence, and on memory of significant events when fortified in discussion with principals involved. When not specifically attributed, statements enclosed by quotation marks are either as recorded by me or so vivid in my memory that I can present them as fact.

Among those whose oral or written comments and expertise were of particular benefit to me are: Adm. Harold E. Shear, Vice Adm. Levering Smith, Captains Edward L. Beach, Richard B. Laning, William E. Sims, and Paul R. Schratz, all USN (Ret.).

In addition, Milton Shaw and Capt. James M. Dunford, USN (Ret.) gave me valuable insights from their many years of close association with Adm. Hyman Rickover in the development of nuclear reactors.

Finally, I am greatly indebted to my friend Louis D. Rubin, Jr., who edited my first book, *Take Her Deep!* and who volunteered to help me with this one. With his own fascination for ships and the sea, he encouraged my effort and piloted it to safe harbor around literary rocks and shoals.

SUBMARINE ADMIRAL

BATTLESHIP PRELUDE

"Come down to my cabin so I can kick you in the ass!"

On the quiet, darkened bridge of the battleship USS *New York,* the imperious voice of her commanding officer, Capt. Husband E. Kimmel, was unmistakable.

It was nightfall at sea off the California coast in January 1934. The ships of the U.S. Battle Force were proceeding to anchorage in Pyramid Cove, San Clemente Island, after a few days of tactical exercises. I was an ensign and junior officer-of-the-deck (J.O.O.D.), charged with keeping the O.O.D. informed of the distances to ships in proximity. It was long before the days of shipborne radar; the distance between ships proceeding in formation was determined by stadimeter. This hand-held instrument required matching two points whose vertical distance apart was known, then reading their range in yards from the calibrated dial.

As our ship approached her designated anchorage, Captain Kimmel had come to the bridge and assumed the conn. I was taking ranges to the battleship *Colorado*, which was the ship next ahead. This involved matching her main truck light to her stern light. Having had considerable training under Captain Kimmel, I knew exactly how he wanted officers to do their jobs. In most positive manner I called out the changing range in yards: "One-eight-five-oh, sir," "one-eight-double-oh, sir," and so forth as the range gradually closed or opened.

It became progressively darker as we proceeded slowly to our designated spot. Intent on my job and using a carefully shielded flashlight to read the latest range from my stadimeter, I did not notice when *Colorado* turned out of the formation to proceed to her berth. I began taking ranges on *Maryland*, whose lights had blended with those of *Colorado*. Because she had a different distance between her lights, it would take a different setting on the stadimeter to ensure correct ranges. Naturally, the distances I called out were in error.

By this time it was completely dark, and the bridge was blacked out save for the dim glow at the steering stand and the subdued light escaping from the curtained-off chart desk where the navigator plotted bearings sent in from the gyro repeaters on each wing of the bridge. As on any well-ordered bridge, there was no excess motion, no extra talk, and a passage was always clear for the skipper as he moved from the bridge to either wing for better visibility. Individuals could be recognized only by their voices; what was important was not the person but the function he was performing.

When my ranges went from six-double-oh to five-eight-oh to five-five-oh, Captain Kimmel spoke up in the darkness and demanded, "What did you say?"

Being a Kimmel-trained officer, I immediately responded, very self-assured, "Five-double-oh, sir," because by this time the range had decreased a bit.

The captain boomed, "Man, you're crazy, just plain crazy! Anyone can see that's less than five hundred yards. All back two-thirds!" And, a little later, "Let go!"

Seconds later the order had been telephoned to the fo'c'sle, and the anchor chain was rumbling out the hawsepipe.

After veering the proper scope of chain and letting our ship swing to it, we took the customary round of bearings and found, sure enough, that the skipper was right. Fortunately, we were just about in our desired position, for it was a matter of great pride to every captain to put his ship in exactly the assigned spot. There is no greater humiliation to the skipper of a man-of-war than, in full critical sight of his peers, to have to get underway again, once anchored, to correct his position.

When it had been determined that we would not have to shift, Captain Kimmel's voice demanded in the darkness, "Who gave me that range?"

"I did, sir."

Thus came my invitation to visit his cabin.

$*$ $*$ $*$ $*$

I admired Captain Kimmel as a dynamic, tough-minded officer, a strong leader, and an excellent seaman. He made a great and lasting impression on his junior officers, not for brilliance of mind or elegance of expression but for positive convictions and forthright action. He was something of a martinet, and his thorough Saturday morning Captain's Inspections of his twenty-year-old ship frequently left us annoyed by his brusque manner and sharp scrutiny.

While his wife maintained their home in the East, where their young sons attended school, Captain Kimmel lived a solitary bachelor's life in his shipboard cabin. His almost continuous presence on board did not endear him to officers or enlisted men, but it occasionally gave us closer contact with our stern taskmaster. On some nights, when *New York* swung at anchor off San Pedro or some other West Coast port, he would appear without warning on the quarterdeck, where the J.O.O.D. paced his lonely watch, to talk about his ship or just to reminisce. The loneliness of command was early apparent to us.

$*$ $*$ $*$ $*$

Many years later, with World War II behind us, I would chat again with my respected skipper. The national disaster of Pearl Harbor had been a personal tragedy for the able, dedicated Kimmel. In February 1941, from commander of cruisers in the Battle Force, with the two-star rank of rear admiral, he had been leap-frogged over many more senior admirals to become Commander-in-Chief U.S. Fleet (CinCUS) with the four-star rank of admiral, a fact that inevitably made some working relationships more difficult. In the prewar Navy, slow, orderly progression to high command was the order of the day and became normal practice again following the war. (Two notable postwar exceptions were the early elevations of Arleigh Burke and Elmo Zumwalt to be chiefs of naval operations.)

After Japan's treacherous and devastating attack on Pearl Harbor on December 7, 1941, sinking five battleships and one minelayer and severely damaging several other ships, it was inevitable that Admiral Kimmel and his Army counterpart in Hawaii, Lt. Gen. Walter C. Short, would be relieved of their commands. This was in keeping with politico-military custom following a severe defeat and consistent with the military ethic that with authority and responsibility comes accountability.

Abandoned by his commander-in-chief, President Franklin D. Roosevelt, Kimmel endured the searchings of eight separate inquiries, investigations, and hearings and was placed on the retired list in the rank of rear admiral. He and his wife chose to live in New London, Connecticut. Two of their three sons had entered the submarine service. Lt. Comdr. Manning M. Kimmel was in command of *Robalo* (SS 273) when she struck a mine in the waters of the Philippines in July 1944. He was among the few who were able to swim ashore to Palawan Island. Captured and imprisoned by the Japanese, he died in prison camp. In 1947 his brother, Lt. Comdr. Thomas K. Kimmel, was on duty as an instructor at the Submarine School, New London.

At that time, 1947, I was a commander serving as personnel officer on the staff of Commander Submarine Force, Atlantic Fleet (ComSubLant), headquartered on the submarine base just across the Thames River from New London. As I was driving home from the sub base one evening, I saw Admiral Kimmel walking along New London's Main Street. When I pulled to the curb to offer him a lift, I reminded him that he had been my first skipper.

As I drove the still forceful but embittered and disillusioned former CinCUS to his home, we talked of our days in the old battleship. When he asked about four of my contemporaries and how they had fared in the war, I was struck by a fact that became increasingly evident to me as I progressed through commands of my own: The individuals a skipper remembers most vividly are those who create problems for him. My classmates to whom he referred had pooled their funds and purchased a used car to give them the mobility needed for the twenty-five-mile liberty runs from Long Beach, California, to Los Angeles and Hollywood. As they returned to Long Beach one foggy night, they had an accident in which a civilian was killed. They were absolved, but it was clear that a commanding officer's responsibility for his ship and his men inevitably meant that troubles and problems that come with the leadership of men, with concern for their safety and well-being, will stick in his memory.

✶ ✶ ✶ ✶

When my Naval Academy class of 1933 was graduated on June 1, President Franklin D. Roosevelt had been in office less than three months. He came to Annapolis and delivered an upbeat commencement address extolling the naval career and our future, which would be dedicated to service of our county. But euphoria over completion of four grueling years of academics was short-lived. Our country was still in the throes of the Great Depression, and reduction of the defense budget took precedence over military readiness requirements. This was true in spite of the facts that in January of that year Hitler had gained control of Germany and soon stamped out its struggling democracy; Japan's military-dominated government had taken Manchuria from China; and Italy was in the hands of her Fascist dictator, Mussolini. All three of those governments were bent on expansion by military aggression.

In 1932 Roosevelt's predecessor, President Herbert Hoover, had reduced the Navy's enlisted strength from one hundred thousand to eighty thousand. The law governing officer strength then required a proportionate cut of eight hundred unrestricted line officers. Measures applied to the Class of '33 to help minimize Navy Department expenditures were simple, direct, and painful. We were informed that on graduation:

a. Only those in the upper half of the class, as determined by academic standing, would be commissioned as ensigns of the unrestricted line and retained on active duty;
b. Our commissions would be probationary for two years, after which a new order of relative seniority would be determined, taking into account a special, written examination and our performance of duty to date; and
c. During the two-year period of probation, we were not to be permitted to marry.

Of the 634 midshipmen who composed our class at one time or another, only 250 were commissioned on graduation. We also took the same

15 percent pay cut applied to all the military. However, in recognition of the hardship being imposed on those who would have to seek civilian careers, the Congress authorized granting bachelor of science degrees to all graduates starting with 1933.

✳ ✳ ✳ ✳

New York was making a Fourth of July visit to Santa Barbara, California, when I reported to Captain Kimmel for duty in 1933 after my hot, dirty, transcontinental train ride. I was one of the batch of nine newly commissioned ensigns ordered to her. It was a time when British military analyst Liddell Hart's statement was true: "A battleship to an admiral was like a cathedral to a bishop." Battleships were the dominant element of high-seas fleets, shaping strategic concepts and the tactical dispositions of naval forces. The inconclusive Battle of Jutland between the German and British fleets in 1916 was closely studied in war college and wardroom for lessons in the tactics of bringing the big guns of cruisers and battleships into play against their counterparts.

The United States had not entered the "Great War" – World War I – until 1917, and our Navy was not tested in battle, but five of our battleships, *New York* among them, had operated in the North Sea with the British Grand Fleet. We had undertaken a massive naval shipbuilding program intended to give us the strongest fleet in the world, but in 1921 President Harding initiated a conference to limit the size and number of capital ships that the major naval powers would have. The initial ten-year "battleship holiday" specified by treaty was extended through 1936. As a result, in 1933 the U.S. fleet included fifteen battleships ranging in age from twenty-three years to ten; one had 12" guns, eleven had 14" guns, and only the three newest had 16" guns.

New York, whose keel was laid in 1911, was obsolescent. She displaced twenty-seven thousand tons and was driven by huge, triple-expansion reciprocating steam engines. Built as a coal-burner, she had been converted to oil fuel. She mounted ten 14" 45-caliber guns in five twin turrets and a secondary battery of twenty-one 5" 51-caliber guns. Her wire cage masts had been replaced by steel tripod masts, which supported antennas that were being constantly modified as radio transmission was improved. Four underwater torpedo tubes in her bow had yielded to the reality that they needed a more nimble platform to be effective, and No. 3 turret, high amidships, carried a gunpowder-actuated catapult for launching a float-plane.

There were still many years of important service ahead for *New York*. In World War II she fought in the North Atlantic and in the far Pacific off Iwo Jima and Okinawa. In 1946 she was a target ship in the Bikini atomic tests, and not until 1948 was she finally decommissioned, to be sunk as a gunnery target in her thirty-fourth year.

Here was a fine example that warships, all weapons, are in a state of continuing obsolescence from the time they are introduced; but here too was evidence that in their long lives ships could be continuously modernized to carry the new weapons and equipment that advances in science and technology made possible.[1]

✴   ✴   ✴   ✴

In 1933 the Navy's personnel policy called for all newly commissioned ensigns of the line (seagoing officers qualified for command of ships) to serve two years in surface ships before entering specialized fields such as aviation, submarines, naval construction, civil engineering, and the like. This was an excellent procedure, followed for many years until the exigencies of war and the tyranny of technology, demanding ever deeper specialization, ultimately induced a change. Now the annual crop of officers from the Naval Academy and other sources goes directly to flight training, submarine school, nuclear power training, specific weapons courses, specialized engineer training, or supply school.[2] Regrettably, this procedure contributes to the growth of parochial loyalties, and to a Navy made up of discrete coalitions or "unions" – the air, surface, and submarine communities.

Brief though the old two-year indoctrination period was, it nurtured appreciation of the unique personnel and materiel problems associated with the sea, and it unquestionably contributed to a more responsive naval support establishment. More than thirty years later, as chief of naval material, I saw the benefits of that policy. At that time most of the heads of the specialized, technical support elements of our shore establishment still retained the practical lessons of seagoing experience. Today and in the future, with the Navy so engineering-oriented and technology-dependent, special effort will be needed to maintain essential and intimate collaboration between seagoing operators and their technical support.

* * * *

In 1933 we had escaped from the petty harassments and regimentation of the Naval Academy, but we entered an environment with its own rigid pattern of custom and conformity. Shipboard life in a major warship adhered to the customs, routines, and niceties of behavior, dress, and address inherited from earlier times. An ensign in a battleship was little more than a "passed midshipman," engaged in supplementing his textbook knowledge with the practical lessons of the sea. There were nineteen of us in *New York,* assigned to all the monotonous, repetitive, routine tasks. For two years we would rotate through the ship's various departments, standing watch in engine rooms or topside in turn. There was an endless variety of collateral duties: recorder of courts martial, shore patrol, instructor of enlisted men aspiring to the Naval Academy, boat officer, athletic coach, mess treasurer, and on and on. The only permanent assignment was one's "general quarters," or battle station. Mine was high in the foretop as a secondary battery control officer. It would take almost two years of tedious J.O.O.D. watches on the bridge, assisting in station keeping and tactical maneuvers, before we were adjudged qualified as O.O.D. and entrusted with the ship's safe navigation.

Our ship's main battery of 14" guns received the most painstaking attention in maintenance and training. Our courses at the Naval Academy had placed great emphasis on gunnery. Small wonder that mess room scuttlebutt had it that the brightest, most promising young officers would gravitate to gunnery and, after a postgraduate course in ordnance engineering or related technology, would enter an elite "gun club" from which those destined for high command would be chosen.

But as we stood our watches beneath the silent muzzles of big guns, there were twinges of doubt. More and more junior officers were talking of naval aviation, impatiently awaiting the end of their two-year probation "before the mast." The fact that aviation was still in its infancy, both as an extension of naval power and as a threat to it, was confirmed by the puny 3"- gun antiaircraft (AA) battery and primitive AA fire control system the battleship carried.

There was another branch of the service that received little attention in 1933, but would eventually have much influence upon the way that navies fought. In 1914–18, U-boats came close to putting Great Britain out of the war by their wholesale sinking of merchant ships bearing food and supplies. However, our boats were still struggling with inefficient power plants and the mistaken mission of fleet support. Nevertheless, the day was coming when, equally with air power, our undersea power would revamp the strategy and tactics of warfare.

In 1933 life aboard ship still revolved around the guns, a ceaseless striving for accuracy and rapidity of fire. When not in our own drills or target practices, there was frequent need to embark in other ships to observe and score their gun-firing exercises. The night-firing exercises were particularly time-consuming and onerous. Sometimes we would transfer by boat in the open sea as many as six consecutive nights before weather conditions or visibility would permit an exercise to proceed safely. The frequent fogs along the California coast and the absence of radar meant that we had to depend on eyesight to judge whether our shooting grounds were clear of shipping. And if weather or distance precluded a return to *New York,* it meant spending the night aboard another ship on a cot in a noisy passageway or, if you were lucky and senior enough, in a spare bunk far below decks.

At sea and in port the learning process continued. In the relatively simple ships of those days, there was time and opportunity to learn much of human relations, of men's aspirations and motivations – the elements of leadership. Our formalized junior officers' training course came under the supervision of such splendid officers as Lt. Comdrs. Willard A. Kitts, Daniel Barbey, and Walter S. DeLany, each later to be vice admiral, but much of our learning would come from working under officers who, through determination and ability, had progressed from enlisted status. I found these men – so-called mustangs, usually of lieutenant rank – a mature, stabilizing, and understanding force in the ebb and flow of the ship's training and disciplinary problems. Officers such as Nathan Bard and Floyd Nuber were a main resource of many years' seagoing experience. They were the mainstay of such technical competence as ships of that era required, whether their route to the wardroom had been from the boatswain's locker in the fo'c'sle, from the boiler tender's gauge glasses far below, or the gunner's well-protected, immaculate magazines.

I received more than my share of below-decks wisdom through the circumstances of my living space. Habitability, for both officers and enlisted men, had not yet become the important element of ship design it is today. Most of our batch of newly launched ensigns lived in the junior officers' (J.O.) bunkroom on the starboard side of the armored first deck. Sharing the bunkroom was No. 1 5" 51-caliber gun, and the outboard bulkhead included portable shutters that had to be removed whenever we had gun drill. It was a living space less commodious and comfortable even than the spartan rooms we had occupied as lordly first-classmen in Bancroft Hall at Annapolis. Under its low, pipe and cable-festooned overhead were tiers of sagging bunk springs supporting thin mattresses, a few steel clothes lockers, and a couple of desks. It was not much better than the living quarters of midshipmen in the days of sail. Although living in the bunkroom had some advantage in its modicum of light and air, it was crowded and, in heavy seas, waves beat against the ill-fitting gun shutters to flood the compartment.

Weighing these factors, I chose instead to live inboard, across the passageway, in what had been the band stowage room when *New York* carried Commander Battleship Division One and the division band. The space of some fifty square feet had since been converted to a two-man room, with one upper and one lower bunk, one wardrobe, and two chests of drawers whose hinged fronts served as desk tops. The inner boundary of this space was the rough steel of No. 2 turret's circular barbette, while the outer partition from the passageway was but thin sheet metal and wire, screened by a curtain of painted canvas. The junior officers' w.c. and showers were far forward and down one deck. They were reached through the massive steel door in the armored bulkhead, a journey not to be undertaken lightly nor yet too long deferred.

Lemuel M. (Steve) Stevens, my friend and classmate, shared the comparative privacy of this nook – and we shared as well the problems, wisdom, and philosophy of the enlisted men whose living space was just outside the discreet shield of our canvas screen.

One of the highlights of our final semester at the Naval Academy had been the series of evening lectures by which distinguished senior officers sought to pass on to us key lessons they had learned. In his remarks, Comdr. W. W. Smith made a never-to-be-forgotten point: "There is no ship so large that a good man can't make his presence felt, and no ship so small that a man can't be spared."

Soon afterward, Adm. Frank H. Schofield, then U.S. Fleet commander, made another point: "In treating enlisted men, handle them with care. Remember, it is a high-class product with which you are working."

These precepts came to mind when I inadvertently eavesdropped on our shipmates, but there were times when the "high-class product" strained one's forbearance and understanding. Our enlisted men of those days were not as well educated as are their counterparts today. (The same, of course, could be said of our officer ranks.) Most were men committed for long service. Very few were married; the ship was their home, in port as well as at sea. From backgrounds as diverse as the alleys of Brooklyn and the plains of Wyoming there emerged a crew intensely loyal to their shipmates and their ship. And if "shipmate" did not, in so large a ship, seem to include their officers, there was generally respect, sometimes admiration, and frequently good humor in their evaluation of officers' abilities and characteristics. Pragmatic and worldly wise, they were keen observers of shipboard life and of our comings and goings in port. On these subjects they expressed themselves concisely and vulgarly, but remarkably aptly. It did not take Steve and me long to identify who were meant by appellations that ranged from "Old Fart Face" to "Big Daddy" to "Lover Boy" to "Grandma Cluck Cluck."

When unknown voices beyond our flimsy wall recounted their tour of brothels from Agua Caliente to Seattle and relived al fresco adventures in Golden Gate Park, "Topic A" became a bore. Yet concise testimony to the truth of at least some of what was claimed came one morning as we steamed into San Francisco Bay. As a communications watch officer at the time, I had the vicarious pleasure of routing to Seaman Second Class Varini the radio message sent to him via the naval base: "Same thing, same time, same place. Bring blanket. Mabel."

There was much profanity, but of the healthy, purgative variety that men under stress or when tired would utter. Occasionally, when language became too lurid or loud, Steve or I would step into the passageway with a reprimand and order the culprits to pipe down.

Life on board ship was austere by the standards of habitability and recreation now applicable in our larger ships, but our periods at sea, except for the long cruise to the East Coast and back in 1934 and the annual fleet-scale exercise, were generally brief, a week or two. At times these were followed by port visits to cities up or down the Pacific Coast. All in all, it was a pleasant life for junior officers, especially for bachelors prevented from early marriage by official directive. We had heard with amusement that mothers with marriageable daughters would meet us on the docks, boat hooks in hand, when we visited the coastal ports, so we were a wary bunch at the many social functions for which each ship had to provide its quota of officers.

Over-riding the repetitious monotony of a junior officer's life was the steady accumulation of experience of the sea, of safety and survival in a capricious environment that imposed its own demands on personnel and materiel alike. As midshipmen, our summer cruises had given us inklings of this, but now direct responsibility for men's lives, for their performance under stress, for the safety of the ship, imprinted more deeply certain habits of thought and action that are the hallmark of seamen worldwide. Perhaps these are summarized in two words: responsibility and forehandedness.

It is responsibility not only for one's own actions but also for the actions – or inactions – of those in one's charge. It is a responsibility rooted in the age-old traditions of the sea, wherein with authority or command comes responsibility, not as a superficial, verbal acknowledgment but as a reality ever subject to accountability.

As to forehandedness, the dictionary defines it as "looking or planning ahead." Implicit in this in the military profession is "acting in advance." In the context of the sea, acceptance of responsibility inspires forehandedness, anticipating the vagaries and dangers of the sea and taking action.

The patient acquisition of experience, the slow climb to greater authority, were based on the schooling of the sea and its universal lessons. As the years passed, I would find that the continuity of the sea, unlike the fragmentation and insularity of the land, gave seamen the world over a background of experience that made understanding and rapport easier. A ship does not know whether its keel rides the Red Sea, the Black, the Yellow, or the White; no matter which, there are the same basic environment, the same dangers, the same elemental forces that shape a common understanding. In the ancient sea powers of the Mediterranean, in China and Japan, and in the navies of our European allies, I found a commonality of experience that made it easy to communicate with my opposite numbers.

★ ★ ★ ★

Our fleet, suffering from the depression years' cuts in the defense budget, was concentrated in the Pacific. It had been sent there by President Hoover in 1931 when war in Asia seemed a distinct possibility. In the spring of 1934, to display our naval capabilities as well as to bring some economic benefit to East Coast ports, our new president, Franklin D. Roosevelt, called for a fleet review to be held off New York. Howls of anguish came from the West Coast. With the nation struggling to work out of the Great Depression, the fleet's payroll, the services required, and the purchases made, totaling some $10 million a month, were of very great importance to the economy of the Pacific Coast.

This was my first lesson in the political and economic pressures that bear on military matters. Fearful that Roosevelt might be using the review only as an excuse to move the fleet east permanently, West Coast politicians and their press made much of the ferment in Asia. Exploiting this environment, communist sympathizers attempted to undermine the morale of enlisted men. In ports up and down the Pacific Coast our men were targets of propaganda. One medium, a flimsy newspaper called *Shipmates Voice,* was handed to men ashore and also smuggled aboard by visitors.

This was the regional climate on April 9, 1934, when we sortied from our home ports. *Texas* led the Battle Force and its train of support ships from behind San Pedro's breakwater, out the open roadstead of Long Beach harbor, on the first leg of our fifteen-thousand-mile round trip. When we passed San Diego we were joined by the carriers, destroyers, cruisers, and submarines of the Scouting Force.

As we steamed steadily southward, the days became oppressively warm. What the radio news termed a "leisurely cruise" was, in fact, an arduous period of exercise in every aspect of naval warfare. There were simulated main fleet engagements, air attacks, submarine attacks, and destroyer night torpedo attacks, as well as countless individual ship's exercises.

As we approached the Panama Canal in late April, we had a two-day problem in which the main body was opposed by submarines and four light cruisers acting to prevent our attack on the canal. While the cruisers were detected and turned back, some of the crude, underpowered S-boats reached positions from which their torpedoes could do great damage. It was a thought-provoking glimpse of submarine warfare, but I scarcely thought that seven years later I would be right in that place in one of those same boats defending against a real enemy.

New York was no stranger to exercises focusing on defense of the canal. She had been there in 1923 in Fleet Problem I, the very first fleet-scale exercise of our Navy. Because we had no real aircraft carriers at the time, she and *Oklahoma* were declared to be "constructive" carriers of an enemy fleet seeking to get into position to launch air attacks on Gatun Lake dam. This time, however, our aging battleship did not have to simulate anything other than a dreadnought as she plodded toward the canal.

The fleet now included the aircraft carriers *Langley,* which had been converted from the collier *Jupiter* to become our first carrier in 1922, *Lexington,* and *Saratoga.* These last two were 33,000-ton ships, giants for their day, which had been converted to their new role from their original design as battle cruisers. Few if any in the Navy realized how quickly the role of queen of naval battles would pass to the aircraft carrier.

Following our mock onslaught on the canal, a United Press correspondent embarked in the battleship *Pennsylvania* reported that "The most impressive and important maneuvers ever conducted by the U.S. battle fleet have demonstrated that the Panama Canal can be captured or destroyed by an enemy fleet and that a Japanese-American naval war under present conditions is virtually impossible. In demonstrating that the canal could be taken, it was proven also that the cost would be so terrible as to make it actually impracticable because the attacking nation would be left crippled. It was demonstrated again, also, that the battleship remains the Gibraltar of naval warfare."[3] Not surprisingly, embarked as he was in the fleet flagship, the newsman's oracular words and confused strategic judgment were essentially a paraphrase of the fleet commander's own evaluation. The last sentence revealed the comfortable, uncritical mindset that pervaded the battleship community.

In successive annual fleet exercises, the emphasis was the same: Seek out an enemy fleet advancing on our coast, then maneuver our battleships into position to annihilate the enemy by surprise and superior gunfire. The admiral in tactical command always strove mightily to "cross the enemy's T." This was the favorable position across the enemy's line of advance from which the fire of all big guns could be brought to bear on the enemy, some of whose ships would be inhibited from firing ahead. There was no doubt about the kind of battle for which we were training. We would be ready to fight the Battle of Jutland again.

From the Panama Canal we sailed through the fresher breezes of the Caribbean to Gonaives, Haiti, then on to Guantanamo, Cuba. The days underway were again a series of exercises oriented on the battleships in which other elements searched for them, attacked, or defended them. Sometimes the battleforce divided in two and simulated battle line engagements.

After a few days' rest in Guantanamo Bay, we rode the Gulf Stream up the East Coast while emphasizing spit and polish to ready our ships for the presidential review off Sandy Hook. As we steamed up the New Jersey coast on the morning of May 31, I had the midwatch as junior officer-of-the-deck in *New York*. About 2 A.M. a cold fog enveloped us, and for the rest of the night the whistle of each ship in the invisible armada sounded hoarsely every two minutes. Every captain visited his bridge, gazed anxiously all around, then returned to a night of uneasy rest in his cabin, knowing that his own career could be dependent upon the experience, training, and good judgment he had instilled in his watch officers.

Even to those of us on the bridge, our running lights were barely visible, their red, green, and white glow soaked up and blotted by the thick, soft, atmosphere. Almost blind in the ghostly fog, we relied on extra lookouts in bow and stern, on the bearing and intensity of the repetitious whistle signals, and chiefly on the acute perceptions and good sense of seamen acting within the disciplines of the Rules of the Road.

Steaming in column, 1500 yards apart, at eight knots, the fleet got through the night without accident. But morning brought only a diffused grayness, an even greater sense of moving not on but in and through a sea that had no surface, no horizon, no sky above, but only boundless, all-surrounding space. As the climax of our 6300-mile voyage, the presidential review scheduled for noon, drew nearer there was doubt and confusion. Would it be canceled, or deferred to another day? Would we have to head back out to sea, trying to maintain formation off one of the world's busiest ports while waiting for the fog to lift? Then, as the morning wore on and the fleet jockeyed speed and formation, the fog gradually dissipated, changing to a haze. Finally the signal was passed down the line: The review would commence at 1430 (2:30 P.M.).

The reviewing ship was *Indianapolis,* one of the new treaty-class 8" gun cruisers. That morning she had picked up President Roosevelt and nine members of his cabinet at Manhattan, and she was now anchored twenty-five miles from the Battery, two miles south of Ambrose Lightship. Nearby was anchored *Louisville,* a sister cruiser. In her were many other dignitaries, including the corps of foreign naval attachés. Perhaps the most interested was Capt. M. Kobayashi of Japan.

Led by the flagship, the battleship *Pennsylvania,* the fleet passed in review with rails manned, thirty-five thousand officers and men in full-dress uniform. Thirty-one ships had saluting batteries, and each boomed out its presidential salute of twenty-one guns as it came abreast *Indianapolis.* On the platform erected on her forward gun turret, the constitutional commander-in-chief took the salute, his hair blowing in the wind. For more than an hour, the twelve-mile column of ships filed by, then turned seaward to the east while 185 planes launched by *Saratoga, Lexington,* and *Langley* simulated dive-bombing and torpedo attacks.

When the last ship passed her, *Indianapolis* got underway. Three signal flags whipped from her forward yardarm – YOKE, WILLIAM, XRAY – the Navy's signal for "well done," now the sailor president's terse commendation. Following her up the channel, the long gray line of ships proceeded to anchorages or berths in the Hudson.

For eighteen days the great city entertained us, the number and variety of its free diversions partly compensating for the austerity pay cut we still endured. When we sailed again it was under a new CinCUS; Adm. David F. Sellers had been relieved by the dynamic and colorful Adm. Joseph M. Reeves, not a full-fledged pilot but a "naval aviation observer." Was it a hint that after years of patient development sea-based air power was moving to the fore as the Navy's Sunday punch?

June, July, and August were spent in port visits, with only brief training periods at sea. New York, Newport, Boston, Baltimore, and Norfolk all welcomed us and filled our days and nights with excitement. Some married officers were fortunate to have their wives come from California, but this was not practicable for those with children. For bachelors there was an almost endless round of parties, receptions, or balls in every port. Yet there is a limit even to sailors' appetites for fun on the beach. Thus, when volunteers in proper numbers were not forthcoming, it became standard practice, when publishing each day's social activities, to conclude with the order: "The following officers will attend." If not enthusiastic, our representation was at least adequate. More than one young woman owed her future life as a Navy wife to such a directive.

In September the fleet sortied from Hampton Roads, Virginia, and headed south for the long return voyage. Once more training exercises filled our days and nights, and again the vulnerability of big, heavy ships to surprise attack by air or by small fast units was apparent. One war problem cast our Scouting Force as units of a European power, with the objective of weakening our own fleet by attrition attacks and preventing our control of the Caribbean. They seemed to succeed. With impressive daytime use of the new technique of dive-bombing, which our Navy and Marine aviators had developed, they badly hurt our battleships and carriers. The ensuing night "enemy" destroyers finished them off with torpedo attacks. In the dark, moonless night the fast, maneuverable destroyers were able to close to a thousand yards or less before being detected and caught in the beams of our carbon-arc searchlights for simulated gunfire. The discovery and development of radar would, in just a few years, make such attacks suicidal. Nevertheless, this experience, coming in the wake of the similar one in the Pacific approaches to the canal, prodded my thinking about the future.

∗   ∗   ∗   ∗

On September 19 the fleet problem was concluded and *New York* was released to proceed independently to Bremerton, Washington, for major overhaul in the Puget Sound Navy Yard. It was pleasant to be sailing alone, to be free of keeping position on other ships, and to have an orderly, daily routine of our own. The skipper benefited most of all; the uncertainties and dangers of formation steaming and of high-speed maneuvers were removed. Navy regulations and his own night orders required that he be informed of all contacts and unusual events, but he now enjoyed much more peace of mind. He could generally remain comfortably in his cabin while keeping a clear mental picture of his ship's situation. Years of duty at sea, a background of training and experience common to his own watch-standers, and long practice in visualizing problems of relative motion gave a skipper the uncanny ability to appraise the navigational situation. Even when wakened in the middle of the night by the bridge messenger's rap on his cabin door, he could quickly transpose the cryptic report sent by the officer-of-the-deck into a meaningful picture of what was developing.

After completion of overhaul during Bremerton's rain-soaked winter, *New York* returned to sunny southern California. Early in 1935 we sailed from San Pedro to exercise with other ships en route to San Francisco. It was also the week in which the Class of 1933, fleetwide, took the professional exams that were part of our two-year probation. These were lengthy written examinations in various technical subjects, the questions prepared in the Navy Department and mailed worldwide under tight security to every ship in which we served. The grades we each received would be weighted and averaged with our original class standing as well as with the aptitude (fitness report) grades we had obtained during our brief service afloat. Because of this redetermination of our relative seniority, there was much incentive to do well.

Unfortunately, that week was a stormy one. The passage up the coast under cold, gray skies required the ship to be tightly buttoned-up as she pitched and wallowed in the trough of seas pounding toward the California coast. We sat for our exams in the flag cabin, which was available because the battleship division commander, Rear Adm. Thomas T. Craven, was not embarked, and were conscious of the thud of waves, the creak of the ship's joints, the squeak of bulkheads, and the shudder of the bow as it pitched and sent tons of green water crashing against the forward turrets.

On the day we took our exam in "juice," confined for hours in the stuffy, smoke-filled cabin that was painted an insipid pea green, I took small comfort in the fact that I was not the only one to be seasick. While

I struggled with questions in electrical engineering, both a.c. and d.c., I made abrupt visits to the w.c.; somehow I passed that and all other subjects and managed to retain my same seniority, number forty-one in a class that graduated 431 members.

The exams were little more than a form of mental hazing. They required no analytical or deductive reasoning and were not a test of what we may have learned or a measure of any intellectual growth since we had left the Naval Academy. They were a carryover from the instructional method we had endured in our four years at Annapolis, where our courses were primarily exercises in memorization as we raced through one textbook after another. There were some good professional civilian instructors at the Naval Academy, but few of the naval officer instructors were good at their task. One or two could make navigation or gunnery classes interesting and rewarding, but most were out of their depth in teaching more abstract subjects. Too many of them simply acted as referees, seeing how many problems we could solve at the blackboards or how accurately we could "sketch and describe" some piece of hardware. They were temporary instructors, with no formal training as teachers. They believed, probably correctly, that in being there they were not enhancing their careers. They were eager to complete their two- or three-year shore duty and to get back to sea in pursuit of their primary interest – a ship command.

Happily, this has changed. The Naval Academy now attracts highly qualified civilian professors, and officer instructors are more thoroughly educated and more carefully chosen than in the past. Instead of a standard, rigid curriculum overemphasizing engineering, midshipmen may now choose from many academic majors, most of which are accredited. There is no question that today's graduates have a much better educational base as they join the fleet than did those of my generation.

∗　∗　∗　∗

When we proceeded through the Golden Gate to the calm of the magnificent bay, our depressed spirits were buoyed by sight of the familiar skyline and anticipation of joys awaiting. This was my first visit to San Francisco since ascending to the lofty eminence of president of the junior officers' mess. This meant simply that I was the senior ensign of the eighteen who then made up the J.O. mess separate from the wardroom mess, which was restricted to more senior officers. Ensigns could expect to move up to the more sedate wardroom in their third year on board.

In my role as president I was more or less responsible for the shipboard decorum and orderly conduct of our aggregation of bachelors and was the link in policy and administrative matters between the ship's executive officer and my peers.

The mail, delivered promptly after we had dropped the hook in our assigned berth, brought not only personal correspondence but also the usual flood of advertisements, announcements, and invitations to local events incident to the fleet's visit. Among them, properly addressed to "The President, Junior Officers Mess," was a very correct invitation to "Junior Officers, U.S.S. *New York*" from a Miss Elsie McDonald for cocktails at her address in a fashionable section of the city. I wondered what occasioned the gracious invitation, but it seemed like those that had been received in New York, Newport, Boston, Baltimore, or Norfolk during our East Coast cruise the year before.

At lunch in the mess I announced the invitation. No one acknowledged that he knew Miss McDonald, but to many it seemed a good way to start an evening on the town. A show of hands indicated that nine of our messmates would accept, and I sent word accordingly to Miss McDonald's RSVP.

At breakfast the next morning I asked what the party had been like, and I quickly learned more than I wanted to know. Located in the exclusive Nob Hill area overlooking the bay, 1020 Broadway showed traces of an elegant past. Ushered to a drawing room by a neatly groomed Chinese steward, our J.O.s met Miss McDonald. They were quickly put at ease by the charming, modishly dressed woman of some thirty years and asked to introduce themselves to the attractive young ladies who soon made their appearance. The bar, tended by two Chinese barboys, was well stocked with excellent liquor, still a rare treat so soon after the end of Prohibition, and the hors d'oeuvres were worthy of San Francisco. Soon everyone was on a first-name basis, and the band of sea-weary young men had no objection to escorting the young women to more private quarters topside. Miss McDonald's establishment was, simply put, a bordello, but an elegant and discreet one. It catered to the diplomatic corps, the military, and similar discriminating clientele. Its duenna was a woman of ingenuity whose chutzpah matched a business acumen worthy of her Scots forebears. She was apparently well schooled in the ways of the Navy, no doubt by a client long since graduated to the wardroom. After *New York* she entertained J.O.s of other battleships.

* * * *

In 1935 our two-year probationary service was completed, and my class received permanent commissions as ensigns. This meant, as well, the end of the ban on marriage for two years after graduation from the academy and first commissioning. Although such restrictions on private life would not be tolerated today, all in all it was not a bad rule. Instituted chiefly for economic reasons, it prevented some hasty marriages into which youths who had been cloistered for four years, then suddenly released with an assured income, could easily fall. It gave us time to get our feet on the deck, so to speak, to look around, to make wiser decisions. Ties already formed that were firmly rooted in love and compatibility would withstand the waiting period.

Thus June 1935 was a bumper month for marriages, the participants in which included those who had abided by the rule as well as the few who had earlier married secretly. Among those taking part was Ens. I. J. Galantin, USNA '33, who during the fleet's visit to New York had met, been smitten by, and successfully courted Miss Virginia Jaeckel. Now she had come out to California, and the marriage vows were recited. As of the time of writing this book, fifty-nine years afterward, they still hold good.

* * * *

By 1935 I had been a junior officer in a battleship for two years. I was increasingly restive. Like all other ensigns, I had rotated through the ship's various departments for experience but was continuously assigned to gunnery for my general quarters (battle) station. In our operations we were encountering more and more new ships as the naval augmentation program gathered momentum, and naval aviation was making great progress, attracting many of my peers. I wanted to be free of the dull, repetitious, institutionalized life of the battleship Navy and to be part of a more personalized, more modern, and flexible Navy.

The fitness report form on which our performance was evaluated and regularly submitted to the Navy Department contained a section in which the officer reported upon could list his preferences for next duty, at sea and ashore. There was no need to concern myself about a shore billet, because we would normally spend our first six or seven years at sea. The mechanistic, generally solo operation of aircraft did not appeal to me; I preferred duty involving leadership of a team and the chance of early command. As my first choice I listed submarines.

At sea off the California coast one day in October 1935, the commanding officer of the USS *New York* received from the Bureau of Navigation in Washington the following message: CONTEMPLATE ASSIGNING ENSIGN I. J. GALANTIN NEXT CLASS SUBMARINE INSTRUCTION IF AN APPLICANT AND PHYSICALLY QUALIFIED. PLEASE ADVISE.

Such personalized treatment probably indicated a shortage in numbers of volunteers, but it was in keeping with submarine personnel handling policy and effective in practice. With a check-up from the ship's senior medical officer and the approval of my new skipper, Capt. John S. Abbott, I replied affirmatively.

In December I set off with my bride for Submarine School in New London, Connecticut. The transfer gave us the first of seven transcontinental family journeys. Most subsequent ones would be enlivened by problems and paraphernalia incident to traveling with babies or young children, but this cross-country drive was sheer holiday. It went a long way toward overcoming the trauma of severing ties with my first ship, one that had been home for two and a half years, and leaving surroundings in which I was comfortable and secure, with shipmates who had filled my days with fellowship. But as we drove away from San Pedro and headed east, there was submerged in the excitement of the long trip the vaguely uneasy realization that I was now a mature naval officer, that I had made a critical choice, and that this was to be but the first of many new assignments, the start of an unforeseeable succession of ships and stations around the world.

IN THE BEGINNING

The submarine service of the United States Navy that I was joining in 1936 had its origins well back in our country's history, but as a recognized and accepted part of naval activity it was of very recent vintage. The first use of a submersible vessel in war was in 1776 in the newly declared independent American colonies. A Connecticut Yankee, David Bushnell, had designed and built a "water machine," a one-man, hand-propelled submersible, for the purpose of attacking British warships at anchor in New York harbor. This craft, named *Turtle*, was armed with a watertight oak cask filled with 150 pounds of gunpowder. The plan of attack was to maneuver under HMS *Eagle*, Admiral Howe's flagship, and drive a long screw into her hull by means of a crank operated from inside *Turtle*. A line from the cask, or underwater bomb, was secured to the screw. When cast loose, the bomb's buoyancy would cause it to nestle against the frigate's bottom.

The historic attack was made on the night of September 6. *Turtle*'s volunteer operator, Army Sergeant Ezra Lee, launched his risky operation from the Battery at the foot of Manhattan Island. Coming under his target as planned, Lee tried to affix the screw. It was designed to penetrate the copper sheathing that protected *Eagle*'s bottom against fouling. By bad luck the screw had come up against an iron plate that supported the rudder. Mystified by being unable to pierce the metal, and with dawn breaking, Lee had to abandon his attack. Two subsequent attacks were also unsuccessful, and when the British seized Manhattan *Turtle* had no base suitable for her short range of operation.

Almost ninety years would elapse before the next application of undersea warfare. In the meantime there was little improvement in the design of submersibles, even though Robert Fulton applied his inventive genius to the task. His own enduring fame rests on the steamboat.

It was the Civil War that gave impetus to the submarine and projected naval warfare into the third dimension. Badly hurt by the North's blockade of her ports, the Confederacy turned to the naval innovations of ironclad warships and vehicles for clandestine attack. To attack Union ships in her harbors she built a number of small, low-freeboard, steam-powered launches called "Davids" after the biblical giant-killer. One of them, a coal-burning craft manned by four volunteers, attacked USS *New Ironsides* off Charleston, South Carolina, on the night of October 5, 1863, by ramming a sixty-five-pound spar torpedo against her. Although the blast did not sink the target, it disabled her and encouraged further development of sneak attack.

This took the form of a primitive submarine, named *Hunley* after its inventor. Because she would be operated fully underwater, she could not use a steam engine and was propelled by eight men turning hand cranks on her propellor shaft. During her development trials, she sank several times with much loss of life, and the project was ordered abandoned. When a group of volunteers pressed for a chance to put *Hunley* to use, they were allowed to do so provided she did not submerge but attacked like a David, from an awash condition with her hatch open.

On the night of February 16, 1864, in the first successful use of a submersible in war, the *Hunley* sank USS *Housatonic* while that Union ship lay at anchor off Charleston. She was herself sunk when waves from the blast of her spar torpedo poured down the open hatch and drowned her crew, but *Hunley* had pioneered a form of naval warfare that would be instrumental in drawing the United States into two world wars.

✳   ✳   ✳   ✳

Our Navy did not acquire its first submarine until 1900. This was almost two years to the day after a dynamic, far-seeing assistant secretary of the Navy sent the following letter to his superior, Secretary of the Navy John D. Long:

10 April 1898

My dear Mr. Secretary:

I think that the Holland submarine boat should be purchased. Evidently she has great possibilities in her for harbor defense. Sometimes she doesn't work perfectly, but often she does, and I don't think in the present emergency we can afford to let her slip. I recommend that you authorize me to enter into negotiations for her, or that you authorize the Bureau of Construction to do so, which would be just as well.

Very sincerely yours,
T. Roosevelt

Following two years of extensive trials and some minor modifications, on October 12, 1900, *Holland* became USS *Holland* (SS 1), the first submarine on the Navy list. She was purchased from her inventor and builder, John P. Holland, for $150,000. The boat[1] was 53.3 feet overall, 10.3 feet in diameter, displaced 63 tons, and had an operating depth of seventy-five feet. Her 45-horsepower gasoline engine powered the boat on the surface, and electric storage batteries did when she submerged. She could make speeds up to 6 knots. She had a single torpedo tube, carried three 17.7" Whitehead torpedoes, a topside gun, and a crew of six. She was the sixth submarine designed and built by Holland and was, for her day, quite advanced in performance. At her launching the *New York Times,* not as omniscient as it is today, said she "may or may not play an important part in the navies of the world in the years to come."

The acceptance of *Holland* was a signal milestone in the evolution of the U.S. Navy, but it would be years before the implications of that acquisition would be clear and the full potential of the new weapon vigorously prosecuted by the United States. There were two major problem areas: technology and strategic concept. These were interdependent factors; as in all other military fields, developments or advances in one area would spur progress in the other.

Although the Navy acquired its first submarine eleven years before it bought its first airplane in 1911, it was slow to recognize the implications of undersea warfare to naval operations and to push vigorously to overcome technologic constraints. Further, there was no commercial market or use for submarines that would stimulate industry to improve that vehicle's technology. By contrast, the tantalizing prospect of widespread commercial application initiated the rapid advance in aeronautic science and technology that to this day is so mutually beneficial to both military and commercial aviation.

The greater attractiveness that naval aviation, rather than the submarine, seemed to hold for ambitious young naval personnel is shown in the careers of two men who were pioneers in both: Kenneth Whiting and T. Gordon Ellyson, Naval Academy roommates from 1901 to 1905. In 1908 Ensign Whiting commanded *Porpoise* (SS 7), followed by command of *Tarpon* (SS 14), and Ellyson was skipper of *Shark* (SS 8). Whiting, a far-seeing, energetic, and innovative young officer, soon became dissatisfied with the slow pace of submarine development and its lack of effective central direction and transferred to aviation in 1910, even before the Navy owned an airplane. In his words, "Aviation will be far-reaching and very important, but there is a lot of work to be done under the seas." Ellyson soon followed his friend into aviation, and in July 1911 became naval aviator number 1 after training by Glenn H. Curtiss, the pioneer aircraft builder.

The limitations of early twentieth-century technology constrained operational thinking and kept the submarine in the role of coastal or harbor defense. The technical problems were formidable: unsafe, unreliable engines, inefficient storage batteries, poor communications, inadequate optics, primitive metallurgy, poor construction techniques, and on and on. Few, whether in the Navy or outside it, could foresee the pace of technological development necessary to advance submarine capabilities. John Holland himself had written in 1900: "Larger [more than two hundred feet long] boats will never be feasible unless we discover some better system of storing electricity than exists today – a contingency which is exceedingly doubtful."

Just as limited was the number of naval officers or strategic planners who could envision the consequences of the ability to operate hidden below the surface during war at sea and then argue convincingly for the funds and effort needed to hasten technical progress. There was no school for submariners, no support facilities or bases tailored to the special needs of submarines. Those serving in submarines were preoccupied with the manifold material problems and safety of their craft. No central authority was in place to direct and coordinate the scattered individual efforts. Submarines went through a slow, painful process of evolving into safer, more reliable ships before they could bring a new capability to the fleet. The most important advance was made in 1911, when the F-class *Skipjack* was launched. She was the first U.S. submarine to be powered by diesel engines instead of the gasoline engines that were so dangerous for submarine use.

Adm. Thomas C. Hart, who, as a captain, became the first to be in charge of the total submarine program, has described the early submarine years:

> In all those years there was a great deal of pioneering work being done but little direction in the doing of it. The boats were small and the divisions were extremely small. There was never any centralized authority, no school, no real bases, the only thing in that line afforded being small gunboats, monitors, etc., which went in and out of the service according to the needs of the moment. The boats were big enough for offshore work but the thoughts in those days never went very far from the coast. There was some excellent personnel in the submarines and there was some in them because of family reasons, resulting in a desire to stay close to the beach. In general the submarines just grew like Topsy and the service at large knew very little about them and cared much less.[2]

It was under Hart that U.S. submarines gained their first wartime experience. In 1917, after our entry into World War I, Captain Hart was given command of the subs that were sent to assist the British navy. In all, twenty boats of the E-, K-, L-, and O-classes reached the war zone. To cross the North Atlantic under their own power was itself a major accomplishment for the primitive, crude submersibles. The *E-1*, displacing only 287 tons, with a complement of one officer and nineteen enlisted men, was the smallest submarine to make the passage. The seven L-boats operated out of Bantry Bay, Ireland, and the other boats were based in Ponta Delgada, Azores. The eight O-boats[3] reached the Azores too late to be given wartime tasks; the armistice was signed as they were en route.

Despite the historic American initiatives in undersea warfare, it was

Germany who proved beyond doubt the military worth of the submarine. She had left the early development of the submarine to wealthier nations, and by the start of World War I in August 1914 had only twenty-nine U-boats of various designs. However, she considered the submarine the quickest, cheapest way to counter a more powerful navy like Britain's, which relied on large, surface warships. The proof came quickly; on September 22, 1914, in little more than an hour, one submarine, the *U-9*, sank three old British armored cruisers. Thereafter, all major warships would have to be screened by an escort of destroyers.

In response to Britain's blockade of foodstuffs that might reach her enemy, Germany declared a war zone around Britain and announced that any British or French ship entering it would be sunk without warning. With even neutral ships at risk and the land war at stalemate, it was clear that the war at sea had become a deadly economic struggle affecting the lives of noncombatants on both sides. Although Germany suffered terrible losses (178 boats and 40 percent of submarine personnel), by war's end the U-boats had sunk more than eleven million tons of shipping and damaged almost as much more. Only the most strenuous antisubmarine campaign and the interventions of the United States saved Britain from being starved into submission.

Our boats made no direct contribution to the Allies' cause, but the skippers who took part in the operation came back convinced that the submarine could play a larger role in our future Navy. They benefited from the combat experience of their British counterparts and saw first-hand the Royal Navy's superior submarine design and equipment. At the end of hostilities, when U.S. crews brought six surrendered U-boats to the United States, the lag in our submarine technology was even more apparent.

The lack of central coordinated effort in U.S. submarine development came to an end in 1918, when Hart was recalled to Washington and designated "Director of Submarines." He was the right man for the job. As many of us would learn when be became superintendent of the Naval Academy in 1931, he was an austere, strict disciplinarian, completely dedicated to personal and professional excellence. As he advanced to higher and higher positions, ultimately to Commander-in-Chief Asiatic Fleet, he remained interested in, and influential in, shaping submarine programs. However, in one respect he was too conservative; he held firmly to his judgment that to be effective the submarine had to be small.

When our entry into World War I seemed imminent, the United States had commenced construction of twenty-seven R-boats (570 tons) and fifty-one S-boats (854 tons). Repelled by Germany's use of her boats in indiscriminate attacks on merchant shipping, the United States intended to use these boats in long-range operations coordinated with the surface fleet. Logically, the mission specified for a warship would determine its design characteristics: size, speed, and armament. However, the actual capabilities of the ships, so limited by the primitive American submarine technology, particularly in propulsion, for many years determined the role our boats could play. Instead of the desired high-seas fleet operations, the R- and S-boats were relegated to coastal and harbor defense missions.

The Navy General Board of senior admirals who specified the performance requirements of ships to be built did not heed the obvious lesson of World War I, that the submarine was the deadliest threat to a nation's shipping, and failed to perceive that its influence on the progress of war at sea and on land was totally out of proportion to the investment of men and money the submarine required. Not grasping the strategic implications of this fact, the board continued to stress tactical integration of submarines with fleet units in defense of the battle line rather than independent operations. It emphasized to our submarine designers the sub's role in accompanying the battle fleet and supporting it by scouting reports and opportunistic torpedo attacks on enemy warships.

The Navy's primary contractor for submarine design and construction was the Electric Boat Company (EB) of Groton, Connecticut. The company also produced the New London Ship and Engine Company (NELSECO) diesel engine that would power most of the S-boats. The unreliability of the engine and the inability of the boats to meet the Navy's performance requirements brought years of rancor and resentment to the Navy's relations with EB. Ultimately, the threat of severe financial penalties to the company and intervention by the secretary of the Navy and Congress brought an end to the feud. However it also caused the Navy to develop its own submarine design capability and to establish its own submarine construction capability at Portsmouth Naval Shipyard, Portsmouth, New Hampshire.

In the Navy's new design for three boats of the V-class, the large ships — 342 feet long and 2000 tons — were powered by the more reliable and powerful Busch-Sulzer diesels. These engines were of Swiss design but manufactured in the United States under license. Nevertheless, on completion in the mid-1920s, the *V-1, V-2,* and *V-3* (later named *Barracuda, Bass,* and

Bonita) were disappointing in performance and reliability. The chief culprit was the main engine installation. In striving for fleet speed (twenty-one knots), good sea-keeping, and long endurance, the designers had packed maximum horsepower into the hull. This compounded the classic ship design problem: More horsepower meant more weight and space, more displacement, more fuel, more drag, more spare parts, more men, more cost, and on and on. There seemed no end to the interlocking complications that were frustrating attainment of a reliable fleet submarine.

For the next step in submarine development, the engine chosen was a U.S.-manufactured version of the German M.A.N. diesel, so called because of its developer, Maschinenfabrik Augsberg-Nurnberg. Produced by our Brooklyn Navy Yard, two nine-cylinder engines of 2800 horsepower each would be installed in *V-5* and *V-6* (*Narwhal* and *Nautilus*).

Once again the finished product failed to meet expectations. The very large 371-foot, 2730-ton ships were unwieldy, slow, and unreliable, unable to perform the submarine "cruiser" mission planned. Neither was *V-4* (*Argonaut*) a success. Built as a minelayer, she required more interior space for stowage of mines and received a foreshortened six-cylinder version of the same engine.

By this time, submarine operating officers themselves were more involved in specifying the characteristics required in a successful submarine. A Submarine Officers Conference had been created in 1926. It was a grouping of experienced submariners to advise the chief of naval operations (CNO) and secretary of the Navy (SecNav) on submarine matters. They stressed the importance of long endurance, improved habitability, and good submerged performance rather than high surface speed.

Disenchanted by the brute-force, high-horsepower approach, submarine proponents called for a smaller ship, about 1500 tons, one that could operate independently of the fleet on forward scouting and intelligence missions. This was *V-7* (*Dolphin*). She was followed by *V-8* and *V-9* (*Cachalot* and *Cuttlefish*), which were somewhat smaller.

As before, the boats were unsatisfactory because of main engine problems. Progress was being made in the purely ship construction phase of submarine development and in the fabrication of essential components, but only with a reliable, compact, and more powerful diesel engine could a successful submarine be achieved. For this purpose the Navy funded five of the country's leading diesel engine manufacturers in the development of high-speed, reliable engines of compact design. There was a powerful additional incentive in this competition. If the Navy's specifications could be met, the same engine could likewise hasten the transition of the nation's railroads to diesel propulsion, thus there would be a market not subject to the vagaries of naval appropriations.

From this program came the efficient and ultimately very reliable Winton diesel produced by General Motors. Fairbanks, Morse also proceeded on its own account to develop its opposed-piston diesel. It, too, was highly successful, so that GM and FM engines powered all our World War II fleet submarines. The parallel development of the more sophisticated Hooven, Owens, Rentschler (HOR) engine was not a success; in the eight boats in which it was installed it had to be replaced.

Japan's invasion of Manchuria and her declaration that she would not abide by the naval limitations treaty after 1936, along with Hitler's bellicose diplomacy in Europe, brought to Congress the realization that a larger, more powerful American Navy was essential. An expanded naval building program would, at the same time, contribute substantially to national recovery from the Great Depression.

From this combination – technologic progress plus international and national political pressures – came the P-class submarines, of which *Porpoise* (SS 172) was the lead boat. Launched in June 1935, she was 1300 tons in displacement, 301 feet long, had an operating depth of 250 feet, and had four torpedo tubes forward and two aft. The ten boats of this class performed handily submerged and had good surface performance as well. Although by no means free of bugs, they were a great improvement over their heterogeneous predecessors.

Improved versions quickly followed, boats of 1500 tons with six tubes forward, four aft, an operating depth of 300 feet, and able to make twenty-one knots on the surface. It was the design and construction of *Gato* (SS 212), completed in 1941, that at last produced a class of U.S. submarines suitable for long-range independent combat operations.

3

SCHOOL DAYS

On the frigid morning of January 3, 1936, twenty ensigns and lieutenants (junior grade), myself among them, who had volunteered and been accepted for submarine duty assembled at the Submarine School at New London, Connecticut, to begin a five-month course of instruction.

In point of fact it would have been difficult to choose a spot that was less suitable for submarine training. The unfavorable climate, the frequent fogs, the shallows of rockbound Long Island and Block Island sounds, the treacherous currents, the poor sonar conditions, the distance to the nearest deep water off Montauk Point, and the interference caused by commercial shipping and pleasure craft all created unnecessary hazard and much loss of training time.

The Navy's sluggish awakening to the possibilities of the submarine can be amply observed in the contrast between the schooling provided for potential submariners and that for fledgling aviators. Within three years of buying its first airplane in 1911, the Navy Department established a flight school at Pensacola, Florida. Thereafter it was never short of enthusiastic, determined Navy and Marine Corps officers who integrated aviation ever more effectively into sea power. By contrast, seventeen years of submarine experience accrued before the Navy formally established schools at New London for the training of officers and enlisted men preliminary to their duty in submarines.

It was almost by accident that New London became our first and most important submarine base. The Navy did not choose the site. Anxious to attract a navy yard to its shores, the state of Connecticut acquired land on the east bank of the Thames River, and in 1868 deeded it to the U.S. government for use as a navy yard. For many years the Navy made little use of the unusual site. Initially it was a yard for small craft of the Atlantic Fleet, then a place to moor a few obsolete warships. In 1881 the yard was converted to a coaling station for the few small warships and auxiliaries that were active in the area.

Not until 1915 did submarines come into the picture. In that year *G-1*, *G-2*, *G-3*, and *G-4* arrived with their tender, the monitor *Ozark*. Other submarines and their supporting tenders soon followed, and in 1917 the coaling station was converted to a submarine base. Thereafter, as newer submarines, weapons, and equipment required, the base did not so much develop as just enlarge itself, with successive needs met by improvisation or hurried construction.

The tardy establishment of a submarine school for officers came on January 17, 1917, with Lt. Felix X. Gygax as its first officer-in-charge. He had been skipper of the *G-3* (SS 31). Not until fall of that year, after we had entered World War I, were classes of submarine instruction instituted for enlisted men. Actually, the first class for instruction in submarines convened in July 1916, when twenty-one young officer volunteers were sent to New London. Their course was really a six-month period of self-instruction in which the students' own efforts were assisted by the commanding officers of the few boats based there.

In 1936 the officer-in-charge was Comdr. Scott Umsted. He was a veteran of submarine duty in World War I, having served in *L-2* when she was among the U.S. boats operating from Bantry Bay for fourteen months. Four lieutenants who were experienced submarine officers made up the teaching staff of instructor-lecturers.

✶ ✶ ✶ ✶

One of the first steps of indoctrination into the undersea Navy was training in escape from a sunken submarine, should we be survivors in such a disaster (Appendix B). (Up to this time, eight boats had been lost, carrying most of their crews with them, and the McCann Rescue Chamber was not yet fully developed.) The initial test was exposure to air pressure in a test chamber to experience the effect of flooding a submarine compartment, a necessary step in preparing for escape from a sunken sub because an escape hatch could not be opened until the air pressure within the boat equaled the sea pressure outside. Hardly had we overcome the discomfort and pain of stopped-up nasal passages and ears when we were hustled, clad only in swimming trunks, up a drafty, unheated elevator to the upper stage of the hundred-foot-deep circular escape training water tank.

After shivering in the zero temperature of the elevator, it was a relief to don a Momsen "Lung," enter the escape lock, and have relatively warm water flood quickly around our quivering bodies. One at a time we ducked from the airlock through the submarine-type bulkhead door into the main tank and slid slowly up the escape line some eighteen feet to the surface. We were lifted by our own buoyancy as, with our nostrils clipped shut, we breathed deliberately in and out of the rubber lung, which had been charged with air at the depth of "escape." Ascents from the fifty-foot and hundred-foot depths were voluntary, and most chose to make them in Pearl Harbor's more inviting clime.[1]

One of those participating in this exercise was my 1933 Annapolis classmate Paul Burton, a genial, engaging spirit with a puckish bent of humor. A few years later, for shore duty after serving in submarines at sea, he was assigned to be officer-in-charge of this same escape-training tank. It was he who had life-size mermaids painted on the underwater inner wall of the tank opposite the airlocks at the three training depths: at eighteen feet Paul had a blonde painted, at fifty feet a curvaceous brunette, and at a hundred feet a saucy redhead.

∗   ∗   ∗   ∗

At Sub School, just as at the Naval Academy, instruction was chiefly by the sketch and describe method. Commander Umsted was a scholarly, sometimes impractical officer of vision; ironically, because of a mannerism, he was called "Blinky." Determined to expand our mental horizons, he required that each of us read and submit a report on at least six books concerning submarines. Choice was left to each individual, but not many books on submarine subjects were available. The relative infancy of submarining in our nation was such that to find six suitable books we had to turn to German and British authors as well. Today there is no shortage of American submarine literature; it ranges from the technical, to wartime memoirs, to the highly imaginative by best-selling novelists.

Our course of instruction included diesel engines, storage batteries, torpedoes, submarine operations, communications, and attack procedure. For the latter there were no electromechanical or electronic problem-solvers. We had to rely on two simple, handheld devices – the "IS-WAS," which assisted in determining courses to steer for desired torpedo attack angles, and the "BANJO," which assisted in determining proper gyro angles to set on torpedoes.

Textbook study was supplemented by practical work in the shops on the sub base, as well as by hours spent crawling through submarines, tracing pipe systems, tanks, and wiring. About one day a week was spent underway in the obsolescent R-class boats allocated to the school. These 1918-vintage ships displaced 570 tons on the surface, were 186 feet in length, and had a complement of four officers and thirty-nine enlisted men.

Although past their useful lives as combat submarines, R-boats made good school boats. Submarines of every class, ancient or modern, all must operate in conformance with the same laws of physics. The R-boats were a practical platform on which to learn the fundamentals of submarining.

The submarine, as we soon learned, relies upon and obeys a natural force, that of buoyancy. As long as it can retain or achieve positive buoyancy it can return to the surface. On the contrary, another vehicle that operates fully immersed in a fluid medium – the airplane – must compete with and overcome another natural force, that of gravity. It can support itself only by continuously applying great power. While buoyancy is the ally and safeguard of the submarine, gravity is the antagonist and hazard of the airplane. Should a submarine lose power, it can use the force of positive buoyancy to bring it to the surface. Should an airplane lose power, the force of gravity can bring it to disaster.

The submarine is constructed so that its crew can bring into balance the two opposing forces: gravity (the weight or downward pull of the ship and its contents) and buoyancy (the lift or upward force of the volume of water displaced by the hull).

A surface ship is built to have positive buoyancy; when it loses that through collision, battle damage, or flooding from any cause, it sinks and is no longer operable or habitable. On the other hand, a submarine is built to have variable, controllable buoyancy, one that can be made positive, negative, or neutral at will. In current U.S. designs this is accomplished by building a heavy "pressure" hull to protect crew, machinery, weapons, and certain variable ballast tanks from sea pressure, and outboard of that a light shell of plating subdivided into main ballast tanks (MBT), which are empty (filled with air) when the sub is on the surface. It is the release of the air through the vent valves at the top of each tank that permits sea water to flood the tanks, thus destroying the previous positive buoyancy and causing the sub to sink. By regulating the amount and distribution of water in the inner variable tanks, the crew can attain the degree of buoyancy desired and control the trim, or attitude, of the submarine.

The neutral buoyancy of a sub – the balance of positive and negative forces acting upon it – can be so finely adjusted that merely raising or lowering a periscope a few feet can cause the boat to rise or sink. The slight additional volume of the periscope barrel exposed to the sea increases the sub's displacement and hence makes it more buoyant and causes it to rise. Lowering the periscope does the reverse. Whether in Archimedes' bathtub or in the sea, the principle is the same.

To return to the surface, the sub has only to close the MBT vent valves and use its stored high-pressure air to blow the water out of the main ballast tanks through the flood openings at their bottom. As one wag has pointed out, all ships can dive; only the submarine can surface.

✳   ✳   ✳   ✳

In the shops of the base we learned to prepare torpedoes for firing, to start and control diesel engines, to diagnose their problems, and to care for the all-important electric storage batteries. In our austere, uncomfortable classrooms we listened to our instructors, augmented our textbook knowledge, and took monthly written exams in some subjects. The days spent underway in one of the R-boats were fun but very uncomfortable. Each of us had qualified as a top watch-stander and officer-of-the-deck in our prior surface ship duty, but we had to learn the peculiarities of handling such small ships with the limited horsepower of either diesel or storage battery propulsion. After backing from one of the sub base piers into the Thames River, we'd be carried swiftly downstream amid the day's assortment of ice floes. The boat's tiny bridge was open, unprotected from wind and spray, and the cold-weather clothing of the time was inadequate. As we proceeded to our assigned diving area in Long Island Sound we wished only to be below, out of the biting wind, huddled around an electric heater, and sipping hot coffee until the raucous diving alarm told us we were diving beyond reach of the weather.

* * * *

To graduate from Sub School would be only the first step in a submarine career. To earn the designation "qualified in submarines," and with it the right to wear the gold dolphin insignia, would require a year of satisfactory service in an operating sub, completion of a notebook in which all the ship's systems were sketched and described, demonstration of proficiency in diving the ship and operating its machinery, and the ability to make a successful torpedo attack Then, a year or two later, subject to the CO's recommendation, which would take into account factors of temperament and leadership as well as performance, could come the designation "qualified to command submarines."

Some of us were to find that Commander Umsted carried his intellectual crusade even to that point. When later he became commander of the submarine division in which I served, he required that, as part of our qualification for command, we submit a thesis on some practical aspect of submarine operations such as personnel, training, attack, weapons, or power plants. Qualification for command of submarines, he said, should be analogous to obtaining a Ph.D. degree.

The class standing attained in Sub School determined the order in which individual preferences for area of assignment were granted. In 1936 the submarine force had only forty-nine subs in commission, and of these thirty-six were overaged R-boats and S-boats. They were organized in squadrons based in New London, Coco Solo, San Diego, Pearl Harbor, and Manila.

Even as we were acquiring our first submarine experience in obsolescent R-boats, we eyed enviously the sleek, newly completed "fleet" boats, *Porpoise, Pike, Shark,* and *Tarpon,* which occasionally appeared at the sub base. We knew that most of us would have to endure years of duty in aging, outworn S-boats before being assigned to the slowly growing numbers of modern fleet boats.

I was happy to be given my preference, a boat based at Pearl Harbor, but not with the means of getting to her. In its recurring end-of-fiscal-year fund shortage, the Navy greatly curtailed its use of commercial transportation. If Army or Navy transports were not available, dependents would go overseas by commercial steamer, but officers and enlisted men would be sent to their new duty stations via other naval ships. My wife would travel from San Francisco to Honolulu in the Matson Line's SS *Malolo,* but I was ordered to the submarine *Bass* at San Diego for temporary duty and transportation to Pearl Harbor, where I would join *Argonaut. Bass* and other boats of her squadron were making a summer training cruise to Hawaii.

I was an extra number in *Bass;* I did not expect, nor did I receive, special consideration. *Bass* was not a good submarine. Crammed full of propulsion machinery that was unreliable and difficult to maintain, she was cramped and uncomfortable. My sleeping quarters consisted of a folding canvas cot that was set up nightly in the narrow passageway of the forward torpedo room. The torpedomen snoring in their "racks" suspended from the overhead fared better; they were not jostled by the roving security watch making his rounds on the pitching, rolling platform on which both men and torpedoes reposed. By the time we rounded Diamond Head on the island of Oahu and set course for the sea buoy off Pearl Harbor, my bags were packed and I was eager for quick transfer to *Argonaut.*

4

RUBE GOLDBERG WAS HERE

Since acquisition of *Holland* (SS 1), all subs in our Navy have been consecutively numbered. *Argonaut* was SS 166 but at times was designated *V-4, SM-1* (for submarine minelayer), or *A-1*. She was a freak, the only one of her kind ever built, but I considered myself fortunate in 1936 to start my active submarine career in her. She was a fairly recent product, built by Portsmouth Navy Yard from 1925 to 1928. Being one in the progression of fleet submarine designs, she incorporated relatively advanced, if confused, concepts. As a good example of the technical problems besetting submarine designers and operators of the time, she is worth a closer look.

Trying to maintain and operate a hybrid ship during four

years' duty in *Argonaut* gave me an immense respect for submarine sailors and positive convictions about what a submarine should be – or rather should not try to be. Through hard work in the progression of billets from mine officer to torpedo officer to gunnery officer to first lieutenant, plus assorted collateral duties, I learned the penalties paid for a misbegotten operational concept and for extraneous unreliable equipment.

With an overall length of 381 feet and a surface displacement of 2710 tons, *Argonaut* was the largest submarine in the Navy. In common with *Narwhal* and *Nautilus,* she mounted two 6" 53-caliber guns identical to the armament of light cruisers. She was second in size to only the French *Surcouf;* that monster (for those days) of 2880 tons mounted two 8" guns.

Argonaut was the only submarine minelayer we would ever build. In her bow she had four 21" torpedo tubes from which to launch her load of twelve three-speed torpedoes. The after third of the ship was given over to the stowage and launching of sixty Mark XI mines. Loading the mines on board prior to mine plant exercises was itself a day-long, laborious task. They could not pass through the standard deck hatches, so a large bolted section of pressure hull, called a "soft patch," had to be removed for the loading operation and then carefully reinstalled by our ship's force.

The two mine-launching tubes in the stern were 42" in diameter, and each held four mines at a time. The handling and launching mechanisms were ingenious but crude and very noisy. In her submerged mine-planting, *Argonaut* was no doubt the greatest undersea noise-maker ever conceived. Because the launch of so many heavy mines from the extremity of the ship made trim and depth-keeping difficult, *Argonaut* had special bow and stern buoyancy tanks as well as an internal mine compensating tank.

In spite of her array of armament, *Argonaut* was woefully underpowered in propulsion. In order to make room for the mines, her two main engines were a shortened, six-cylinder version of the nine-cylinder M.A.N.s that *Narwhal* and *Nautilus* (armed only with guns and torpedoes) received. The engines, aptly called "rock crushers" by their attending machinists, produced only 3175 horsepower. As a consequence, when *Argonaut* worked in company with other ships or submarines she was always first to get underway and last to return to port.

Our ship's designers apparently started from the model of a surface minelayer and made the minimum changes necessary to let her duck underwater occasionally. She retained many features superfluous in a submarine and which consumed too many man-hours for maintenance and repair. The topside bristled with offenders, quite apart from the massive 6" guns and their ammunition hoists. Amidships she had a retractable mast, with yardarms for blinker lights and signal flags. On deck forward were a mast and boom for handling the two heavy wood power boats that were stowed in the superstructure. Their launching required the removal of many sections of heavy deck grating. A pressure-proof tank to carry the gasoline required for the boat engines was installed, thoughtfully, outside the pressure hull.

Heavy clearing wires stretched from the A-frames amidships to bow and stern, supposedly to assist in passing through antisubmarine nets or booms. Also in the commodious superstructure – the space between the slatted teakwood deck and the pressure hull – were four torpedo stowage tubes in which additional torpedoes could be carried. However, we never carried spare torpedoes; the tubes were always full of the extra boatswain's gear and tools that experience proved were needed in some emergency. We even carried a full set of canvas awnings, complete with metal stanchions, to be rigged in port if we wished to keep the tropic sun from us. And not until 1939, and the realization that a submarine in wartime needed to be as invisible as possible, did we reluctantly paint the gleaming teakwood topside deck black.

On each bow there hung a patent anchor weighing 4500 pounds, with ninety fathoms of heavy chain in each chain locker. Far forward, to port and starboard, were the extensible arms of the mine cable-cutters. In theory, should the cable of an enemy mine come in contact with the German-silver electrodes on the arms, our storage battery would be shorted across the cable and burn it through.

At the other end of the ship, protruding above the deck like a giant cocktail shaker for Neptune, was the after emergency escape trunk. Finally, as if to show his awareness of the drag and turbulence that all this top-hamper would cause, the designer provided that the six pairs of mooring bitts should be capable of being housed or recessed below the deck. But even this inconsequential bit of streamlining was denied the ship. From years of neglect in warm tropic waters, the bitts were rusted solidly in place.

All this unusual, unsubmarinelike clutter of topside gear meant that to *Argonaut* a boatswain's mate was as important as a torpedoman's mate. In even-tempered, hardworking Jimmy Lane we had one of the best. He and his "deck apes" worked continuously in a hopeless attempt to keep pace with the ravages of the sea on our enormous topside and superstructure.

Among these deck hands was one of our most likable and distinctive characters. John Pideck was a perennial seaman first class because he could not pass the written examination for promotion to coxswain. Swarthy in complexion, short in stature, but tough and hard-muscled, Pideck was a sailor's seaman, doing any job well, standing a good watch, and always ready to help a shipmate, ashore or afloat. One night he confided that he hadn't been home to see his mother in almost ten years, nor had he written to her in that time. Asked why – "Because I don't want her to know her son is a failure."

He had seen new shipmates come on board, pass their exams, and get advanced in rating, all the while he struggled unsuccessfully with his training booklets. At times his frustration erupted. During an all-day dive I found him in the torpedo room encircled by friendly shipmates as he decried the lack of real man-o'-warsmen in the "modern" Navy. Said he, "What does a new sailor look for first? A book, a bunk, and to get seasick when there's work to be done – that's what he wants."

Within our thirty-three-foot-diameter pressure hull were more pitfalls of misdirected technology. Every complex mechanism that our inexperience in submarine warfare seemed to justify was included – and most were inoperative. The German-made control panel for the cable-cutters was out of commission for lack of replacement parts. Unlike later submarine designs, we had three periscopes, two in the conning tower and one in the control room. The any-height, fixed-eyepiece attack periscope copied from the Germans proved unreliable and had to be replaced by a simpler model, but one whose built-in range stadimeter rarely worked. As a consequence, we took ranges the same way the O-, R-, and S-boats did, by "guesstimate" from the telemeter marks scribed in the optics.

An inoperative gyropilot occupied valuable space in the conning tower. Glass eyeports in the two gun access trunks were provided so that we could see the water level before throwing open the pressure-proof doors for the dash to man the guns. They also served to break the monotony of all-day dives. As we peered patiently through the clear, blue-green tropical water we would sometimes see fish curiously inspecting the huge black monster that intruded in their domain.

Unlike fish, we had to be able to come back to the surface under any circumstances, so the rescue and salvage system was more extensive and complex than in any other sub. Its piping ran the length of the ship and had numerous connections passing through the pressure hull. As a consequence, this salvage feature itself endangered the ship. We even had a voice tube that extended from bridge to conning tower to control room. There were too many connections to the sea, all offering the unrelenting pressure of the sea potential access to the ship's interior.

Our ship was a cranky diver. Her three groups of main ballast tanks were fitted with both flood valves and vent valves. These hydraulically operated valves rarely functioned in the smooth sequence desired. In addition, the huge planing surface of the expansive deck and all the top-hamper made it difficult to drive her under should we be heading into the sea or have a following sea. In those cases, to avoid wallowing half awash it was necessary to turn and dive in the trough of the seas – with the swells abeam. The combination of natural and mechanical forces then produced some interesting sidewise dives, with the ship listing far to one side or the other. Should we be having a meal at the time, there would be a frantic grabbing of dishes as everything slid to the low side, culminating in the resounding crash of crockery, cutlery, and curses from crew's mess room, galley, and wardroom alike.

Such a dive generally inspired Lt. Comdr. Charles D. Leffler, skipper when I reported on board, to tell the story of Willie Brown, who was a steward's mate on duty in the officer's mess at the Portsmouth Navy Yard while *Argonaut* was building there. He had seen submarine crews come and go and had determined that he, too, wanted the comradeship and special bond that those men shared. Finally, he succeeded in getting orders to sea duty, to the precommissioning detail being assembled for *Argonaut,* and for a few days experienced the sometimes heavy-handed banter of his new shipmates.

On the day of commissioning, Brown was absent from morning muster, and the chief-of-the-boat asked, "Anyone seen Willie?"

A sailor replied, "All I know is he was in the barracks yesterday mutterin', 'F-4, S-4, V-4. No, sir, not me!'" (The submarines *F-4* and *S-4* had been involved in operational accidents, sinking with heavy loss of life.)[1]

The skipper's story did not seem so funny when it came time for us, following overhaul by Pearl Harbor Navy Yard, to make our deep-dive test. Such a dive to the ship's designed maximum operating depth (in *Argonaut*'s case, three hundred feet) was normally made in an area of known depth not much greater than required and swept by a wire drag to be sure it was free of obstructions. Because all the other boats based at Pearl were S-boats with a two-hundred-foot operating depth, their shallower test area near Molokai was not suitable for us. The newer, deeper-diving boats conducted their tests off Portsmouth or San Francisco.

SUBMARINE ADMIRAL

To save the long trip back to the West Coast, charts of the Hawaiian Islands were studied to see whether there was a suitable area. Just off the windward shore of Maui, near Kahului, was a sea area that seemed right. The submarine rescue vessel *Widgeon* was sent to verify that it was not too shallow, not too deep.

After *Widgeon's* favorable report, *Argonaut* proceeded along the magnificent panorama of mountains and waterfalls that marked the eastern side of the island of Maui and took position, with *Widgeon* standing by as safety vessel. She would warn off shipping and assist as needed.

Early on the morning of March 23, 1937, we slipped beneath the choppy surface, established sonar communication with *Widgeon*, and eased to progressively deeper levels, testing machinery and taking hull compression readings as we went. This was done by means of sliding battens temporarily installed at key points. When we leveled off at three hundred feet, we measured the maximum distortion of our pressure hull to be $\frac{1}{4}$" in the motor room. When *Argonaut* was built, welding of large hulls had not been fully developed, and she had a riveted hull. As we had gone down, the flexing of the hull caused creaks and groans from partitions and platforms throughout the ship. Suddenly we were startled by a great clatter. Some sheet-metal locker doors were sprung open by the distortion, with tools and spare parts spilling on deck.

The maximum keel depth reached was 323 feet, but as we carefully monitored our fathometer during the descent never did we have less than eight hundred feet of water below us! Although we had dived less than our ship's length below the surface, how good it was to be back on the sparkling blue Pacific and see Haleakala's dark crater gathering clouds about it from the fresh trade winds.

We were much more familiar with the waters on the other side of the dormant volcano. *Argonaut* was a frequent visitor to Kealaikahiki Channel. That Hawaiian word, meaning "the road to Tahiti," reminded seamen that this was the route taken by bold Polynesian navigators in centuries past as they sailed up from the southern islands. The wide, deep water between the islands of Maui and Kahoolawe, with only an occasional interisland steamer interfering, was an excellent operating area for submarines, especially for clumsy *Argonaut*. At times we'd remain there for two weeks. In addition to our gun and torpedo practices, we had many mine plants to conduct as we struggled to perfect the Mark XI and our mine-laying technique. The generally calm, clear water was a boon to the submarine rescue vessel that was detailed to recover the mines, including those that sank to the bottom or otherwise malfunctioned. Sometimes, rather than remain underway all night, we dropped anchor in Lahaina Roads. On the western shore of Maui, Lahaina was, in the mid-1800s, the whaling capital of the Pacific. It was here in this same anchorage that ships of the Pacific whaling fleet, from the Bering Sea to Cape Horn, would rendezvous for rest, repair, and carousing ashore and afloat.

Our own carousals were mild. If we went ashore to stretch our legs they generally took us to the two-story wooden Pioneer Hotel, built in 1901, the focal point of Lahaina's social activity. It was operated by a quiet, smiling Japanese couple known to submarine sailors only as "Papa-san" and "Mama-san." There were rumors that Papa-san was actually an officer of the Imperial Japanese Navy, a point that we tried to keep in mind as we sipped cold beer and ate sukiyaki under the fans that stirred the soft Hawaiian evening air.

The few hours we spent ashore were a welcome relief. This was before the days of air conditioning in submarines, and an all-day dive gave an excellent simulation of a sauna in a subway. When our storage batteries discharged at a high rate and required a prolonged recharge, their temperature could rise to as much as 125°F. This was not good for the battery or for the personnel, because the living spaces for officers and enlisted men were directly above the battery wells. As we tried to sleep, we'd lay in our bunks in a pool of sweat. Attempts to get a good night's rest by sleeping on a cot topside were invariably thwarted by the nightly rain shower.

Argonaut carried three types of ordnance – the mine, the torpedo, and the gun. The mine and the torpedo were able to exploit the submarine's stealth by delivering surprise attack on targets in areas not tenable by surface forces. They permitted carrying the offensive into the enemy's home waters or other critical areas denied to surface or air penetration.

Ironically, the most reliable armament that *Argonaut* and all other subs carried was the gun, the one weapon that required them to sacrifice the unique quality and chief safeguard of their operations – concealment. Hand-me-downs from the surface Navy, the guns were the product of many years of development and use by ships of the surface fleet. They were well tested and efficient but poor in accuracy because of the submarine's low freeboard, unstable platform, and limited fire control equipment. Nevertheless, from periscope depth at sixty-four feet, we could surface and get off our first shot in fifty seconds. Loading the 105-pound shells into the chest-high breech of our 6" guns required our two tallest, strongest men, Charlie Cerrinack on our forward gun and Jack McCormick on the after.

The Mark XI mine that *Argonaut* carried was peculiar to her; no other ship would ever employ it. Inadequately tested, limited in production and use, it was a failure. A heavy, 1100-pound moored mine that could be planted in water up to six hundred feet deep, it had both a contact and a magnetic influence exploder. Its chief fault was its unreliable hydrostatic mooring device; a mine's final position could vary from the bottom (failure of the case to separate from its anchor) to the surface (failure of the mooring cable to lock). There was probably more back-breaking labor per unit expended on the Mark XI mine than on any other Navy weapon. For years we submitted reports and corresponded with the Bureau of Ordnance in Washington seeking to introduce modifications and corrections, but to little avail. It was an ominous foretaste of a remote bureaucracy's power over the forces afloat, its inertia, and its stubborn refusal to accept the facts of operational reality.

Fortunately, an improved mine was being developed, and *Argonaut*'s Mark XI was abandoned early in World War II when the sub was hastily converted to carry a Marine assault force. The tactical and strategic advantages of submarine clandestine mine-laying were so great that the Navy developed a mine that could be launched through the same 21" tubes that fired torpedoes. Thus every sub became a potential minelayer capable of planting moored or self-propelled mines of ever-increasing sophistication.

5

SPIES

In our Hawaii time zone in 1939 we were 10½ hours[1] earlier than England; 1:30 P.M. in Honolulu was midnight in London. Our days were filled with radio and newsprint accounts of ominous events in Europe, where Hitler and Mussolini were bent on expansion by military force.

On the other side of the globe, Japan was 19½ hours ahead of us on the clock. She, too, in the hands of a military-controlled government, was using armed force to dominate East Asia. In December 1937 she had bombed and sunk our gunboat *Panay* in the Yangtze River. The United States demanded an apology, reparations, and a promise not to repeat such an act. It was easy for Japan to comply. Emboldened by our mild reaction to her deliberate aggression, she continued her invasion of China and soon controlled all of that coast.

As we followed events in Europe and Asia, there was awareness that our fleet and individual ship exercises had a purpose that might soon be tested. But the question remained, How far had our submarines progressed toward being useful and effective elements of the fleet? The answer would depend on a clear understanding of what the submarine's role should be. There was no doubt that our potential enemy was Japan, but how would our subs be used against her?

Germany had demonstrated in World War I how effective the submarine could be in destroying an enemy's shipping and cutting her overseas lifelines. She had come perilously close to starving out Britain. However, ever since her resort to unrestricted U-boat war against commercial shipping (dramatized by the loss of American lives in the torpedoing of *Lusitania* in 1915) there was revulsion to submarine warfare. The U.S. public considered it barbarous and inhumane. (As usual, public opinion readily attributed all cruelties and barbarities to the enemy alone.) Influenced by this, the United States had signed naval limitation treaties prohibiting submarine attacks on merchant ships. Within the Navy itself there were senior officers who opposed the use of submarines against merchant ships. In 1928 an experienced submarine officer, Capt. Ridley McLean, testified that, "It is inconceivable that submarines of our service would ever be used against merchant ships as was done during the World War."

It was a time when the strategic implications of both aircraft and submarines in navies were only dimly perceived. Our naval planners were more impressed by the submarine's threat to the operations of surface warships. In World War I, the Royal Navy had lost three battleships and three cruisers to the U-boats, and the French lost a cruiser. In turn, the Germans had lost a cruiser to submarine attack, and the Turks lost a battleship. Both the United States and the United Kingdom viewed the submarine as the enemy of their naval power afloat, not as a purposeful, unrestricted extension of that power.

In 1928 the United States supported a British proposal to abolish submarines. Although that plan did not succeed because of French and Japanese opposition, other protocols agreed to would greatly limit the effectiveness of submarines in attacking merchant ships. In fact, in 1930 the United States, Britain, and Japan reaffirmed the impracticable, unenforceable restrictions on submarine warfare first imposed by the Washington Naval Arms Limitation Treaty of 1922. This required that in any offensive against merchant ships, submarines had to conform to the same rules of international law that governed surface warships in their attacks.

This ignored the fact that if it surfaced to halt, examine, or destroy shipping by gunfire, the submarine became extremely vulnerable to counterfire. Its opponent could generally deliver heavier, more accurate fire from a more stable platform. Further, the sub did not have the means to place crew and passengers in positions of safety, as the wishful morality of the major maritime nations decreed, and neither could it provide search teams or prize crews for ships it intercepted. Like the other new attack vehicle rapidly coming to the fore – the airplane – the submarine could sink or destroy but could not capture or control.

So it was not surprising that our official pre-World War II submarine warfare doctrine specified that the primary task of the submarine was to attack enemy heavy ships. It went on to define a heavy ship as a battleship, battle cruiser, or aircraft carrier. Only if authorized by special order could the target list include heavy cruisers, light cruisers, or other types of ships.

The Commander-in-Chief U.S. Fleet estimated that seventy-eight modern long-range boats would be adequate for that primary mission as well as for unspecified "other needs that might arise." Applying the accepted rule of thumb that in a submarine campaign one-third of the boats would be on station, one-third in transit, and one-third in upkeep and training, there could be only twenty-six on station at a time. Against the determined opposition that could be expected from an island nation dependent on overseas transport, such as Japan was, that number could not be adequate for an effective war on shipping.

Between 1937 and 1939 the submarines of the Pacific Fleet were commanded by a nonsubmarine officer. Rear Adm. Charles S. Freeman had served ably in many types of surface ships, including command of two battleships. His reputation as a tough, impatient martinet spread throughout the force, already uneasy about his lack of submarine experience. There was muttering that he had been assigned to ensure that submariners gave primary attention to direct fleet support.

Nevertheless, while the highest echelons of the Navy were becoming more preoccupied with the support role, submariners were becoming more articulate in expressing their views on the most productive use of their craft. It was helpful that Admiral Freeman supported their opinion that their proper use was to operate independently, on the offensive in distant areas not tenable for surface or air forces.

We were fortunate that the fleet-type boat that had evolved from *Porpoise* for long-range, high-speed surface operation was just as capable of seeking out and destroying merchant ships as it was of working with the fleet. Nevertheless, as late as May 1941, the Navy General Board turned down the Naval War College's recommendation that our submarines be used as commerce destroyers should there be war against Japan. The fallacious fleet support doctrine continued to govern our operations. We were to be advance scouts for the battle fleet and would attack enemy heavy warships as opportunity presented. In exercises at sea, our target was always a small fleet unit simulating a larger warship. Never, in my experience, did we practice making torpedo approaches on cargo ships, let alone fire practice torpedoes at such. Neither did we practice torpedo attacks at night on the surface, a tactic that war would prove to be the most profitable.

Our practice targets were generally destroyers, submarine rescue vessels, or even fleet tugs, which would zig-zag from an initial range of ten or twelve miles. Because we could not risk hitting our target with even a water-filled exercise warhead, the "fish" – 21" in diameter, almost twenty-one feet long, about 2500 pounds in weight – had to be set to run at a depth safely below the target's keel. The point where the fish actually crossed the target's track could be roughly determined by projecting forward from the bubble track rising from the torpedo's exhaust. When the torpedo expended its fuel and ended its run, the water would be blown from the yellow-painted exercise head, which thereupon became a buoy supporting the torpedo as it bobbed vertically in the swells. Meanwhile, target ship, submarine, torpedo retriever, and sometimes observing aircraft all sped down the torpedo's wake in search of it.

The loss of a $12,000 torpedo, from whatever cause, was a serious matter for both captain and torpedo officer. Each fish had its own record book detailing its use, care, and performance during the several exercise runs it might have made. Woe betide the torpedo officer who did not personally supervise meticulous performance of all prefiring tests and preparations.

Little did we know then that the Mark XIV torpedoes that fleet boats fired, as well as the Mark X that S-boats fired, ran eleven feet deeper than the depth we set on them, invalidating our guesstimates of "hits" made on our targets. This gross defect was not discovered until we were well into the war, when frustrated, enraged skippers returned from war patrols telling of torpedoes that ran right under their targets.

*   *   *   *

The year 1939 did bring some simple touches of realism into the submarine force. Extraneous top-hamper was removed, and boats were painted a variety of colors to find which was least visible to a searching aircraft. Black was quickly chosen.[2] When *Argonaut* was directed to cover the natural teak of her deck with black paint, we knew something serious was developing. As he went about the task, Boatswain's Mate Jimmy Lane did so with mixed emotions; he was glad to end the work of keeping a spotless deck and sad to surrender the proud symbol of a smart ship.

On September 3, World War II started when Britain and France declared war on Nazi Germany in response to Hitler's invasion of Poland. Meanwhile, on the far side of the Pacific, Japan was extending its domination of East Asia. The United States seemed a timid bystander as President Roosevelt sought to overcome strong isolationist pressures in Congress.

Our submarine exercises took on new meaning. We went on so-called patrol runs of a week or more, cruising off the Hawaiian Island chain, submerged by day and surfaced at night. In another exercise, in October, *Argonaut* accompanied *Nautilus* to French Frigate Shoals, a cluster of tiny islets surrounding a large lagoon some 550 miles northwest of Pearl Harbor. *Nautilus* had part of her main ballast tanks fitted to carry 19,000 gallons of aviation gas with which to refuel seaplanes. As we lay-to on the surface of the lagoon, we watched countless sea birds wheel and dart about La Perouse Rock, whose guano-covered, 135-foot peak glistened white in the hot sun. Soon PBY (Catalina) seaplanes, which had left Pearl Harbor some four hours earlier, swooped down and carved white wakes on the brilliant green lagoon. One by one they taxied to the mooring buoy, where *Nautilus* was headed into the wind, and took aboard the refueling hose from the submarine.[3]

The following spring, in April and May of 1940, the U.S. fleet conducted Fleet Problem XXI and sailed from its bases in southern California to test its ability to find and destroy an enemy fleet threatening the Hawaiian Islands. The scenario obviously had Japan's fleet in mind. Success in intercepting and "destroying" a simulated Japanese fleet gave reassurance to the belief that the islands were safely out of reach for the most likely enemy.

Only one squadron of submarines, a few destroyers, and some support craft were based in Pearl Harbor, but they, too, participated. Slow, clumsy *Argonaut* would be an advance scout for the fleet. In addition, she would simulate shelling "enemy" seaplanes anchored in a lagoon and lay a simulated minefield. As a lookout she was not very successful. Radio transmission and reception in submarines were inefficient, and only after nightfall was there hope of our sending a signal even 650 miles. On conclusion of the problem the fleet anchored in the lochs of Pearl Harbor for a critique of the exercises and a few days of recreation before returning to California.

*   *   *   *

By 1940 I had been four years in *Argonaut* and had served under three different skippers. I had progressed through the shipboard billets for which I was eligible. Friends whom I had seen depart for shore duty in the States were returning for new tours of sea duty. I was pleased to receive orders transferring me to the West Coast, where I would be executive officer of *S-28* based in San Diego.

As the end of another fiscal year approached, it was again a period of stringent economy in the Navy. On applying for transportation to the West Coast I found that my family would sail on board the Matson Line's SS *Mariposa,* but that I would have to make the trip in a ship of the fleet. Then, unexpectedly, it was announced that the fleet would not return to California, but would remain in Hawaii. The reason given was the improved opportunity for advanced training because of Hawaii's ideal weather and sea conditions, but one did not have to consult meteorologic charts to realize that Hawaii was some two thousand miles closer to Japan than is California. With Europe already at war, and with ominous ground swells spreading toward us from Asia as Japan extended her grip on China, President Roosevelt wanted to impress Japan with more than diplomatic representations. Basing the fleet in Hawaii was intended to be a deterrent to further aggression by Japan.[4] Besides, 1940 was an election year; bold action could fortify the president's bid for an unprecedented third term.

The Commander-in-Chief U.S. Fleet, Adm. James O. Richardson, opposed this plan and protested strongly to the president. It was not that Richardson foresaw a grave threat to the fleet should it be based in Pearl Harbor. Rather, he did not believe that the limited training and support facilities available at that forward position were adequate to advance fleet readiness for the wartime operations that both men anticipated. He also pointed out that if the fleet operated in its normal training and support areas, this would not provoke Japan to possible rash action.

President Roosevelt was equally strong-willed. With a lifelong interest in ships and the sea, and seven years' experience as assistant secretary of the Navy, he was confident in his own judgment on naval matters. After he won election to his third term he directed that Admiral Richardson be relieved. As replacement, he personally chose Rear Admiral Kimmel, whom he had favorably observed during his tenure as assistant SecNav.

Thus, in June 1940 no ship of the fleet was returning to the West Coast, and I was allowed to join my wife and two-year-old daughter in *Mariposa*. There was plenty of space in that ship, and I was given the room adjacent to my family. I looked forward to a lazy, luxurious passage.

When we embarked I was met at the gangway by an individual in civilian clothes. He identified himself as Lt. Comdr. M. C. Partello, an intelligence officer of the Fourteenth Naval District. In best cloak-and-dagger style he said it was necessary to speak to me in private. When we reached my cabin he carefully closed the door and explained his mission.

During my four years in Honolulu, the plentiful evidence of Japanese influence on Hawaii's cultural and commercial life left no doubt in Navy circles of Japan's pervasive espionage, probably coordinated by her busy consulate on Nuuanu Street. We accepted as a fact of international life that our readily accessible, easily observable Army and Navy activities in Hawaii were targets. Japanese agents easily blended with the multiracial population of farmers, fishermen, industrial laborers, and businessmen. However, Lieutenant Commander Partello described a more unusual suspect.

A Miss Hedy Schaefer had been the house guest of the commanding officer of a locally based destroyer, and Naval Intelligence had reason to believe that she was using her visit to obtain information on our fleet for an unspecified foreign government. "Now," he said, "you are the only naval officer sailing in this ship, and we have an important task for you."

Miss Schaefer, whom he described as an attractive blonde in her thirties, was also to be a passenger and, "We want you to get to know her well." I was to find out all I could about her, her friends and associates. When I remonstrated that this would be very awkward with my wife and daughter on board, he quickly convinced me that this was "for the flag" and that nothing should be allowed to interfere.

I therefore had the not inconsiderable task of explaining to Ginny that if she did not see as much of me as she would like, or if she saw me paying particular attention to a certain passenger, she would have to accept that I was only doing what duty demanded.

Partello had arranged that I be seated at Miss Schaefer's table. When we went to dinner the first evening shortly after rounding Diamond Head and setting course to the northeast, I found the seating as he had planned. The fact that Miss Schaefer did not appear that evening did not surprise me. The gaiety and excitement of a Honolulu sailing, the almost overpowering scent of flower leis, and the motion of the ship as it headed into the northeast trade winds made many passengers keep to their staterooms. When the next day's breakfast and luncheon also found her missing, a check with the purser brought the distressing news that at the last moment Miss Schaefer had canceled her passage. This fact, which did appear to confirm her interest in our fleet in Hawaii, was all I could report to Naval Intelligence. The turn of events left me disappointed, but it also made the voyage on the sea of matrimony somewhat smoother.

6
HEADING FOR WAR

In the summer of 1940 Great Britain faced a near-desperate war situation. The German land and air forces seemed invincible. They had overrun Poland, Denmark, Belgium, and Holland, had conquered Norway, and had forced France to capitulate. England's forces had been driven off the mainland of Europe; only her control of the sea enabled evacuation of most of her army from Dunkirk in France.

The United States was bound by a series of isolation-motivated Neutrality Acts. These had been enacted following Italy's invasion of Ethiopia and were extended incident to the Spanish civil war and to Hitler's mounting aggressions. In the vain hope of preventing U.S. involvement in world conflicts, the acts prohibited sending arms or granting loans or credits to belligerents. U.S. citizens and ships were forbidden to enter designated combat zones, and the arming of merchant vessels was forbidden.

Although we had historically championed freedom of the seas and the rights of neutral nations, the Neutrality Acts effectively surrendered many of those rights. However, when disaster seemed to be overwhelming Britain, U.S. policy began to change. The Neutrality Acts were eased to allow the purchase of U.S. weapons on a cash-and-carry basis.

President Roosevelt was convinced that our security required keeping open the sea-lanes to England and preventing its defeat. He exercised his powers to the full when, by executive order in September 1940, he transferred to Britain fifty of our overage destroyers in exchange for ninety-nine-year leases on British naval and air bases in the western Atlantic and Caribbean. He also permitted British warships to come to U.S. ports for repairs.

With direct American involvement in the European war becoming more and more apparent, the administration looked for ways to augment our naval forces quickly. For submarines the quickest way was to activate the boats that were then laid up at the sub base in New London and at the Philadelphia Navy Yard. In addition to *Barracuda, Bass,* and *Bonita* there were sixteen S-boats, thirteen R-boats, and eight O-boats. Built as early as 1918, these ships seemed to be more the products of blacksmiths and boilermakers than of shipwrights and machinists. Components were heavy and crude. There was much use of cast iron and brass, and even of wood. Maintenance problems were severe. Fortunately, the boats were simply constructed, and their material condition could be monitored readily.

To provide the experienced enlisted personnel needed for these boats, Rear Adm. Chester W. Nimitz, Chief of the Bureau of Navigation (as the Bureau of Naval Personnel was then known), directed that all physically able men who had at any time been qualified in submarines and whose separation from submarines was not for being temperamentally unfit should be made available from both the surface fleet and the fleet reserve. They would join the few officers and enlisted men who could be diverted from active subs.

I never did reach San Diego and *S-28.* I was sent to New London to help activate the four S-boats laid up there. They were to be placed in-commission-in-reserve awaiting a clearer definition of need and the build-up of personnel. Under Lt. Willard A. (Bill) Saunders, and with the equivalent of one submarine's complement, we had the job of making S-21, S-24, S-26, and S-30 operational. We would man the boats in turn, take them down the river that had become familiar to us during our Sub School days, and dive them briefly in the shallow waters of Long Island Sound.

The chief problem with our old ships was the poor condition of their storage batteries. There were times when we returned to base and there was not enough electric power remaining to permit maneuvering safely alongside one of the finger piers that extended into the swift current of the Thames. It would then be necessary to anchor in the river, and the duty section would remain on board to recharge batteries with our tired NELSECO diesels.

When it came time in late 1940 to place the boats in full commission, we augmented our numbers with officers and enlisted men from the naval reserve. All had to be volunteers. The fleet reserve enlisted men were a motley collection of older men; their years since serving in submarines had been spent as bakers, house painters, plumbers, policemen, machinists, or what-have-you. By weeding out the physically unfit and those unwilling or unable to adjust to their new circumstances, swapping them for volunteers from the sub base, we gradually shaped a crew in which we had confidence.

In S-24 we had a special problem. Among the old hands recalled to active duty was Charles Spritz, a chief torpedoman who had served many years in the boats, chiefly on the China station, some in Panama. He was a deep-sea diver as well. When he "retired on twenty" he stayed in the fleet reserve and worked as a security guard on the Moore-MacCormick Line piers in Brooklyn. I thought he was just the man I needed as chief-of-the-boat to help meld our recalled veterans, fresh-caught volunteers, and few experienced sailors into a smooth-working team. He loved his return to the boats. With no family ties, he spent long days and nights in S-24.

Alas, I had misjudged Charlie's brand of leadership. He didn't lead, he ruled. He was just as tough on our three respected active-duty CPOs as he was on new recruits. Within a few weeks' time I had to report to skipper Bill Saunders that we would have to transfer Spritz; his heavy-handed approach was upsetting our whole crew.

Bill had seen this developing, and we soon had a plan. Spritz was just the man the sub base could use as chief master-at-arms of the enlisted men's barracks. The raw, eager young volunteers flooding into Sub School needed a firm hand to keep peace in their ranks and to indoctrinate them with submarine discipline and obedience.

The CO of the base concurred. Thus was born "Spritz's Navy." The tyranny with which Spritz ruled his domain produced not only order and discipline but also hatred. His busy black eyebrows almost met over his disfigured broken nose, smashed in a brawl with U.S. Marines in Tsing-tao. His hard, dark eyes, his powerful jaw and bull neck, his harsh, loud voice, as compelling as a diving alarm, all struck fear and brought quick response from submarine recruits.

Soon, as his young graduates spread throughout the submarine force, tales from Spritz's Navy were a favorite topic in every boat's mess room. And today every reunion of submarine veterans hears new stories of hardships endured, discipline enforced, punishments assigned in Spritz's Navy. In their telling is a blend of personal pride in torments endured and a grudging respect for the man who left his mark on young sailors.

✶ ✶ ✶ ✶

By the spring of 1941 our squadron of eight recommissioned S-boats was ready for its first deployment. We were sent to Bermuda to advance our own training, to provide target services to our air and surface anti-submarine warfare (ASW) forces, and to demonstrate U.S. readiness to defend the former British overseas bases.

The accelerating tempo of our training, the deepening crisis in Britain's situation, and the debates in Congress had created a quasi-war atmosphere in New London as we sailed on an overseas deployment whose outcome could not be foreseen. There were last-minute goodbyes on the dock, some tears from wives and girl friends, and much good-natured joshing from buddies on the sleek new fleet boat moored just across the pier. The greatest send-off belonged to Nate Dogan, our hard-working, powerful black steward's mate, much liked by all. Once a taxi driver in Chicago, by force of personality and character he was virtually the unofficial mayor of the black community in New London as he served uncomplainingly in the rating generally reserved for blacks in the Navy.

At 2 in the afternoon the word was passed, "Take in all lines," and with an ear-splitting, prolonged blast of our air whistle we backed into the Thames to be carried swiftly downstream by the strong current even as our screws and rudder were used to twist our bow down river.

After we passed Race Rock and its tide rips, the word was passed, "Secure the maneuvering watch. Station the regular sea detail, third section on watch." As we headed to the southeast, I took a round of bearings through the periscope, calling out familiar landmarks to McCormick, our seasoned quartermaster. This was more accurate piloting than the primitive bearing circles mounted on both sides of the crammed bridge could provide. Soon the low hills of Connecticut and Rhode Island grew fuzzy on the horizon to the north. We passed Montauk Point and reached the open sea.

As we began to roll to the cold, gray North Atlantic swells, we sensed that our submarining would never again be the same. Everyone was subdued and quiet, settling into sea routine and wartime cruising procedure just as though we were already in enemy waters. Most men turned in early. On the bridge, just a few feet above the surface, the officer-of-the-deck and his two lookouts tried to duck the cold, flying spray. Our squadron was in a loose formation of two columns, and never were all ships in sight at once. They kept disappearing behind the swells that rose high above our bridge.

At midnight we changed course to adjust for the set we were encountering. The seas that had overtaken us on our starboard quarter and run along the light plating of the superstructure with a deep-throated rumble now slapped more sharply on our side. Sailors whose heads rested just a few inches from the curved steel hull stirred as they adjusted to the new rhythm of their private planet throbbing through the darkness. The quickened motion of the ship kept time for the creak of taut bunk springs, the muted slap of clothing hung on stanchions, and the ocean tones the Atlantic played on our resonant hull.

We steamed steadily southward and next day found our scattered formation in the Gulf Stream, its vivid blue stained with brown gulf weed. As the temperature mounted with each watch, our heavy clothing was stowed. After the many chilly days at sea during training off New England it now seemed oppressively warm. There were many volunteers for lookout watches among men whose normal duties below made them eager to get topside for fresh air by day or night. After intensive coaching in the duties and responsibilities of a lookout, so important in a ship living by stealth, a few would be allowed short tricks topside as relief of a regular lookout.

How to scan an assigned sector, the phraseology to use in reporting, the importance of dark adaptation, the need to wear red goggles for thirty minutes before taking the watch at night, the extra sensitivity gained by not straining directly toward a faint light sensed in the gloom, but of catching it from the corner of one's eye – all these had to be learned. To them was added a stern warning, "And don't bang your glasses around. They're hard to get, and we need every pair. Whatever you do, don't drop them over the side. If you do, the Old Man'll skin ya alive!" This was no idle threat. The pace of recommissionings, of new construction, of transfers to foreign navies was such that there was a shortage of even the simplest navigational equipment.

Approaching Bermuda, we made our landfall on St. Catherine's Point, then stood eastward for the sea buoy of St. George. When we settled on the course of the swept channel, we identified ourselves to the harbor entrance control point and were given clearance to enter the almost completely land-locked St. George Harbor.

There were no support facilities at the dilapidated dock on Ordnance Island, but the Navy's recently acquired passenger ship, SS *St. John*, renamed *Antaeus* for her new role of submarine "accommodation vessel," was awaiting our arrival. As we moored alongside, our division commander, H. L. Challenger, looked on approvingly. This was none other than the man we had dubbed "Our Pal, Chall" for the friendly guidance he had given my Naval Academy class during our plebe summer in 1929. Now, twelve years later, he was portly and florid but still a relaxed, good-humored mentor. On the first day we operated in the new waters, he sent all boats the message, "Permission granted to blow heads on Challenger Bank."[1] Although the water around Bermuda is generally very deep, just to the southwest is an area that shoals to some twenty fathoms. It is named Challenger Bank.

The White Horse Tavern on the square at dockside in St. George became the nightly rendezvous for sub sailors, skippers at one table, their officers at others. In an adjacent room enlisted men congregated until the expiration of their liberty, one hour earlier than for officers.

I was beginning to look on my shipmates through different eyes, often with admiration, sometimes with secret amusement. Although we were not officially at war, censorship of outgoing personal mail was in force, and as executive officer I was chief censor. At times I felt as though I was peeping through keyholes at the private lives of my comrades. I could vicariously imagine the girls whose letters inspired some of the return effusions, and, for one Casanova I had to keep two in mind.

After a few weeks of realistic exercises in the excellent operating area, we returned to New London. We were satisfied with our ability to deploy overseas when needed and knew that our aged ships could still be useful.

S-24 received a new skipper, John Corbus, a quiet intellectual, taking over from the dynamic, gregarious Charles H. (Herb) Andrews, who moved up to the force commander's staff as engineering officer. Johnny was the seventh skipper under whom I had served in submarines since I reported to *Bass* in 1936. Each had his own style of leadership, emphasized different facets of submarining, and each left enduring impressions on his junior officers in traits to avoid or qualities to emulate. It was from Herb Andrews that I learned most about how to be an effective submarine skipper.

✳   ✳   ✳   ✳

As the summer of 1941 drew to a close, the war news from Europe was grim. Britain's plight was grave. The United States had occupied Greenland and shared in the occupation of Iceland so as to enhance our "Neutrality Patrol" in defense of our shipping. That would also keep German forces from establishing bases so close to North America. In August, President Roosevelt and Prime Minister Churchill met on board the battleship *Prince of Wales,* anchored off Argentia, Newfoundland. The Atlantic Charter they enunciated was merely a lofty statement of Western ideals, but it served notice of the increasingly close collaboration between the United States and Great Britain. We were still officially neutral, but Roosevelt ordered the use of our Navy in ways that amounted to undeclared war against Germany. Our destroyers were escorting ships bound for the United Kingdom from American ports to a midocean rendezvous with British ships who would be escorts for the rest of the voyage. Our first Navy casualties in this participation in the Battle of the Atlantic came when eleven sailors died in the destroyer *Kearney,* torpedoed by a Nazi U-boat. Two weeks later another ancient four-stacker, the *Reuben James,* was blown apart by a torpedo from *U-552;* 115 men were lost.

While Navy surface and air units were playing a significant part in the Atlantic, our submarines were used to provide realistic target services to our struggling ASW forces and to advance our own attack training. When *S-24* sailed in September from New London to enter overhaul in the Philadelphia Navy Yard, official U.S. entry into the war seemed only to be awaiting some climactic event. As we stripped our ship to lay her bare for what seemed obscene handling by shipyard workmen, we could see in an adjacent dry dock the British cruiser *Liverpool,* a gaping hole in her underbody. The one torpedo hit she took in the Mediterranean put *Liverpool* out of action for twelve months.

This was my first direct view of the work of a torpedo warshot. Sailors had died within that tangle of torn and twisted metal, but I felt no horror or revulsion, only the realization that this was the kind of work for which I was being trained. War at sea is impersonal; it is ships that fight each other, and it is their survival that counts.

It was Sunday, December 7, as I listened to an afternoon radio news program in Philadelphia. A local announcer was reporting what sounded like a war game, a simulated attack on Pearl Harbor like those in which I had taken part. He seemed to be embellishing the exercise with imaginary accounts of fires and explosions before saying, "Now we switch to Honolulu for a direct report from the scene."

When the voice of the speaker five thousand miles away came, it was charged with excitement. Suddenly I realized that this was Webley Edwards describing events that were real. This was no war game! During four years in Hawaii I had many times observed Edwards's popular radio program, "Hawaii Calls," where it originated at the Moana Hotel on Honolulu's Waikiki Beach. As his anguished voice described familiar places burning and billowing smoke, the reality of disaster became clear. Japanese planes had swept in from north of Oahu in complete surprise to bomb and torpedo our battle fleet moored placidly in Pearl Harbor.

Disbelief gave way to shock, and shock to bewilderment. Stunning shock came from the unexpected treacherous attack and its dreadful toll of men killed and ships sunk – just how dreadful the public was not to be told until later. Duty in Pearl Harbor had made me mindful of the danger of Japanese espionage and sabotage, but I had shared the general, shipboard-level view that direct attack on Pearl Harbor was neither likely nor even possible. We were unaware, too, of the detailed, timely, and foreboding intelligence being gathered from our breaking of Japanese naval and diplomatic codes, information that should have been alerting top Army and Navy commands to impending attack. We believed that only enemy submarines could reach Hawaii without detection.

It had been easy to get in that complacent state of mind. Successive fleet exercises had simulated a Japanese fleet advancing toward Hawaii, followed by its interception and defeat in a battle of annihilation. What was lacking was the imagination to foresee the long-range striking power that carrier-based aircraft brought to the fleet, and the bold way it could be applied. Furthermore, was not defense of the Hawaiian Island bastion and protection of the fleet when in port in the capable hands of the Army's Hawaiian Department, assisted by the Navy's Fourteenth Naval District shore command? The Army commander was Lt. Gen. Walter C. Short, and the Navy commander was the well-regarded Rear Adm. Claude C. Bloch, who had been one of Admiral Kimmel's predecessors as fleet commander-in-chief.

Bewilderment came from my knowledge of officers in the U.S. fleet's top command. How could Admiral Kimmel have been so taken by surprise? As a junior officer under his command in *New York* I had seen his insistence on perfection, attention to detail, thorough planning, and forceful leadership. He had chosen as key members of his staff outstanding officers who had been my shipmates and mentors in the old battleship. Capt. Willard A. Kitts was fleet gunnery officer; Capt. Walter S. DeLany was fleet operations officer. Two other exceptional officers by whom I had been influenced at the Naval Academy were Chief of Staff Capt. William W. Smith and War Plans Officer Capt. C. H. McMorris. How could such capable, diligent, and dedicated men, under so able and experienced a leader, prove so collectively ineffective?

Our Navy strategy to defeat Japan was War Plan Orange, which emphasized advance of our battleships across the Pacific to engage the Japanese fleet in a decisive battle. Fortunately, the Japanese high command had the same fixation about the worth of the battleship in modern warfare as did ours. To preempt our strategy, Japan concentrated air and midget submarine attacks on our moored battleships. No aircraft carriers were in port at the time. While Japanese tactics were brilliantly successful, their strategy was wrong. Had they destroyed the logistic support facilities ashore and the few submarines in port, our counterattack would have been delayed many months, with incalculable effect on progress of the war worldwide.

But the night of December 7 was no time for a critique of U.S. or Japanese actions. The fleet in general knew very little of what really happened at Pearl Harbor – or why. In whatever information was released, the extent of damage was minimized to avoid further alarming the public and to prevent giving useful information to Japan.

Meanwhile, wherever we were, it was our duty to get our ships and ourselves in readiness for combat as quickly as possible. The skipper and I hurried to the navy yard, strengthened our security watch, and made plans to speed our overhaul and departure. As we went about the business of readying S-24 for deployment, I knew that something had gone terribly wrong for Admiral Kimmel to be so victimized by fate.

In years to come, as official information was released and scores of independent investigators explored every possible theory as to cause of the disaster, it would become clear that in both Army and Navy commands in Hawaii there had been complacency and inadequate attention to some indicators of imminent attack. In Washington there was even more reason to be on guard. From our own code-breaking and from foreign intelligence sources, the president and his top Army and Navy advisors knew that war in the Pacific was certain. However, like their commanders in the field, they did not imagine that the fleet in Pearl Harbor, so far from Japan, would be the target. Doubt persists that Kimmel and Short were given all the intelligence that would have been useful to them and that was available in Washington.

To assuage the national trauma and fury over the staggering defeat, the blame was loaded on Admiral Kimmel and General Short. The poorly coordinated separate intelligence sources, the jockeying for power and influence within the Navy headquarters in Washington, and the politically influenced judgments of Admiral Harold R. Stark and General George Marshall were also at fault. And, in a particularly glaring example of political expediency, the inexplicable ineptitude of General Douglas MacArthur in the Philippines was not exposed. He had been given several warnings that attack on the Philippines was expected, yet even eight hours after notification of the attack on Pearl Harbor he had neither gone on the offensive nor disposed his forces to minimize loss. As at Pearl Harbor, Japanese air attack caught his forces off guard and destroyed most of his air force on the ground. The resulting early loss of the Philippines as a base for U.S. counterattack was of greater strategic consequence than the damage to ships in Pearl Harbor.

Nor was the Japanese onslaught confined to the United States and its territories and possessions. On December 9 the British battleships *Prince of Wales* and *Repulse,* operating out of Singapore, were attacked by Japanese high-level bombers and then by torpedo-bombers. Defended solely by their on-board antiaircraft guns, both ships were quickly sunk.

The destruction of battleships moored in port, of aircraft caught on the ground, and of battleships maneuvering freely at sea was convincing evidence that the swift, powerful, long-range attack capability of the airplane had ended the supremacy of the battlewagons. The lesson was clear: The big guns were no longer relevant; the aircraft carrier was queen of battles at sea. Surface forces needed more than antiaircraft guns for protection; they needed active, efficient air cover. While remaining useful for some bombardment and ground support missions, the battleship's main role was to be defender of fast carrier task groups. As for the submarines – their role, too, would now be very different, as I and thousands of other undersea sailors were about to find out.

7
LESSONS IN WAR

After hurried completion of shipyard work and test dives in the shallow, dirty waters of Delaware Bay, we provided for the well-being of our families as best we could, and on December 20 sailed for our secret destination. Only the skipper and I knew that we were ordered to Panama. When we sailed out of Delaware Bay and took departure from Cape May, the track I laid down on my navigational chart headed us for Crooked Island Passage through the Bahamas. The chart desk was merely a hinged wooden shelf over the gyro compass that stood in the starboard after-corner of the control room. It received the curious glance of everyone who ducked through the watertight door leading to the after battery compartment. Once the lookouts saw the penciled track on the chart, they didn't need a reminder to keep a sharp watch; they knew that this focal point for shipping could quickly become a happy hunting ground for U-boats.

At this time German submarines had not yet made their appearance off our coast in spite of occasional false alarms, but with Germany's declaration of war on the United States on December 11 it seemed certain that Admiral Karl Doenitz would want to cash in on the dense traffic so loosely guarded by our inefficient ASW forces. It was January 13, 1942, when the first German submarine operations began off the Atlantic Coast in Operation *Paukenschlag* (Drumbeat). Five U-boats, deployed between the St. Lawrence and Cape Hatteras, commenced their attacks. In twenty-five days this puny but potent force sank twenty-five ships totaling more than 150,000 tons. We were fortunate that Doenitz had been ordered by Hitler to divert some of his force to defend Norway against an expected British counterattack, so that only five to eight U-boats could be on station off the U.S. coast at a time.

To counter even that small force, and in spite of the lessons of Britain's two-year-long antisubmarine battle, our ASW forces were unready in organization, numbers, tactics, and training. There had been little prewar consideration of the submarine as a threat to naval or commercial ships, hence there was virtually no planning for the defense against it. Navy strategy had stressed the offensive, and our thinking focused on the battleships and their big guns, which were to seek a climactic engagement with Japan's capital ships.

Our destroyers were not configured or trained to be effective antisubmarine ships; they were general-purpose vessels. Like our prewar submarines, they were used to screen the Battle Force and protect it from enemy surface ship attack by delivering their own torpedo attacks. As a consequence, when the U-boats invaded our coastal waters our ASW force was a hodge-podge of old destroyers (DD), patrol craft (PC), subchasers (SC), Coast Guard cutters, and hastily acquired, sketchily trained private yachts commissioned in the Navy as PCs. The air search and attack so essential to ASW was left to inadequate numbers of Navy patrol planes and such numbers of Army Air Force planes as could be spared for that duty assisted by the newly formed, enthusiastic, but inexperienced Civil Air Patrol.

The enormous effort required to cope with even small numbers of submarines is shown by the expansion in the U.S. forces deployed in 1942 against the U-boats operating in the western Atlantic. In January, 173 ASW surface craft and 268 aircraft were used against 19 U-boats. By December of 1942, the numbers had grown to 403 surface craft, 686 aircraft, and 50 U-boats.[1]

Even in the days of sail, long before the development of the submarine, the convoy system had been used in the defense of shipping. Instead of allowing ships carrying valuable cargo to sail independently, easy prey for an enemy, they were often assembled in groups and sailed in company, shepherded by warships. In World War I, when the submarine came into play, Germany's U-boats almost severed Britain's vital supply lines. In their four years of off-again, on-again campaigns, U-boats sank more than four thousand ships, totaling eleven million tons. This appalling toll was taken by some 140 boats, of which only about fifty could be on patrol at a time. The small, relatively cheap, mass-produced submarine with a crew of thirty was the most effective weapon ever brought to bear on shipping.

Yet it was not until the spring of 1917, when she was well on the way to being isolated and starved out, that Britain instituted the convoy system. Its worth was convincingly demonstrated. Out of 84,000 ships that sailed in convoy, U-boats sank only 257. In the same period, 2616 ships were sunk while sailing independently.[2] Consequently, when World War II brought an even greater U-boat challenge, Britain promptly resorted to convoying.

Despite these examples, the United States was slow to prepare and train a convoy system. It is true that convoying did have some disadvantages. It caused port congestion and delay both in loading and discharge and prevented optimum use of available ships. It limited the speed of transit to that of the slowest ship. It increased the risk of collision between ships that had different propulsion and maneuvering ability and operated in relatively close proximity. Merchant ship skippers resisted sailing in convoy; used to sailing independently, they did not like the constraints and hazards of steaming in formation under direction of a military commander.

Yet the drawbacks were far outweighed by the benefits. U-boats were denied a steady stream of unescorted targets, all straining to reach port in minimum time. Submarines could make contact with convoys only after long periods of search, and to attack they had to penetrate a ring of convoy escorts. In addition, the convoy system made possible much better use of the excellent intelligence of U-boat positions and movements that the British and later the United States gained from their remarkable cryptanalysis of Germany's naval operations codes and the radio direction-finding of the U-boats' frequent transmissions. Finally, the morale of merchant seamen was enhanced by the presence of warships that could fend off attack or provide rescue.

All this experience and information was available to us, but the United States was slow to change its comfortable peacetime routine to the austere controls demanded by war at our very coastline. Inhabitants of the East Coast were closer to the scene of battle action than were our soldiers overseas.[3] Even so, lighthouses and navigational beacons continued to shine. Coastal cities and towns were not blacked out; even night baseball games were not forsworn. The tourist and entertainment industries wanted business as usual. Not only did this help U-boats fix their position at night, but the glow from shore also silhouetted ships as they plodded up or down the coast. Moreover, such antisubmarine patrols as we mounted sailed on repetitive, predictable routes.

U-boats, often operating on the surface in shallow waters that provided little freedom for submerged operations, were quick to exploit the exceptional advantage these conditions offered. In the first four months of 1942 they massacred shipping along the East Coast, sinking eighty-two ships of almost five hundred thousand tons. Targets were so plentiful, so easily sunk, and U.S. antisubmarine action so ineffective, that U-boat captains in retrospect called it the "happy time."

The only weapons with which to attack a submerged submarine were the depth charge and depth bomb, both of them dumb, brute force weapons that required as much luck as skill to be effective. It seems incredible, but in the quarter century since U-boats had last terrorized Atlantic shipping, neither Britain nor the United States had seen the need to develop a more effective weapon and enlisted the efforts of their top scientists and engineers in securing it. After the war, Vannevar Bush, who had been the wartime director of the U.S. Office of Scientific Research and Development, berated naval officers of all countries for failing to insist on the development of homing torpedoes in the period after World War I and thus being ready for the submarine campaigns of World War II.[4]

Fortunately, there was time to develop and produce the necessary weapons concurrent with the gradual increase in enemy submarine capabilities. As the number of German subs off our coast grew slowly to sixteen, then eighteen, deployed from Cape Sable to Key West with a few others attacking the tanker routes in the Caribbean, American ASW gradually improved. By midsummer the convoy system was adopted; blackout was instituted; air and surface patrols were augmented; and new equipment and tactics, largely the result of scientific analysis and development, were introduced. But in the six months before these measures became effective, the U-boats sank 397 ships in western Atlantic waters patrolled by the U.S. Navy. Only then, after the loss of just five of his submarines, did Doenitz redeploy his boats to concentrate attacks on convoys in the North Atlantic.

Strict censorship kept the public and the Navy at large ignorant of the sorry state of our antisubmarine effort. Adm. Ernest J. King, who had been designated both Commander-in-Chief U.S. Fleet (CominCh) and chief of naval operations (CNO) after Pearl Harbor, insisted on keeping operational control of all ASW forces in his own hands instead of prescribing an antisubmarine strategy for the Atlantic Fleet commander to pursue. Hard-driving, brilliant, and autocratic, King would tolerate no intrusion into his command and control, and he declined to accept Britain's vastly greater experience in ASW as applicable to U.S. effort. Neither would he deviate from his conviction that it was better for a convoy to sail unescorted than to assign it an inadequate weak escort. He did not believe in far-ranging offensive ASW search and attack as a way to reduce the threat to convoys, but insisted that the best tactic was defense by strong forces in the vicinity of the convoy. As in most matters, he believed that he knew best and insisted that the Navy, kept free of outside interference, would end the submarine menace once it had sufficient forces available.

Only after continuing severe losses in the Atlantic and heavy pressure from the British, from Secretary of War Henry L. Stimson, Army Chief of Staff General George Marshall, the president's chief of staff, Adm. William D. Leahy, and from the president himself did King consent to change his organization to give ASW the emphasis and priority needed if the Battle of the Atlantic were not to be lost. In May 1943 he established the Tenth Fleet, still under his direct command, as the organization specifically charged with the Navy's ASW effort. Rear Adm. Francis S. (Frog) Low, a submariner (and one of the first class of trainees in 1916), was designated chief of staff in that fleet and was, in effect, Mr. ASW. He ably provided the central authority to promulgate doctrine and to coordinate all aspects of our antisubmarine war, including the overdue acceptance of scientists and operational analysts into ASW strategy and doctrine.

∗ ∗ ∗ ∗

In the period of confusion and uncertainty that marked the opening weeks of war, S-24 made her way southward. Her two NELSECO diesels could push her against the Gulf Stream only at ten knots as we plodded uncomfortably on the surface in rough wintry seas. We dived briefly each day to adjust our trim and for the training needed after our months in the yard. Christmas Day in the Caribbean was warm, with bright sunlight sparkling off the calm blue sea. It gave us a welcome chance to get down on deck to repair storm damage and to clean and dry out our sodden ship.

At Coco Solo in the Canal Zone a couple of days later, we joined the other boats of our squadron who had preceded us, and the six S-boats of SubRon 3 that had already been based there before the war. The first three boats of the V-class, the 2000-ton *Barracuda, Bass,* and *Bonita,* unreliable as ever, were also ordered to this duty, demoted from more demanding operations in the Atlantic.

Most dependent personnel had been evacuated from the various Navy activities in the Zone, and the large modern apartment houses stared blankly at us. Each boat was assigned one of the vacant apartments to use as officers' sleeping quarters. Although we slept on cots or on mattresses spread on cement floors, the change from our cramped, damp, stifling bunkrooms in the boat was a luxury. Our forty-two-man crew felt the same way about the cool, breezy barracks, where all except a duty section slept.

The job of our hastily deployed squadron was to form a defensive screen guarding the Pacific approaches to the canal. After the success of the Japanese attack on Pearl Harbor, a carrier strike against the vital canal was not ruled out, nor, in spite of the vast distance from Japan, would surface or submarine raiders be unlikely to prey on the steady stream of shipping to and from the canal.[5]

Our submarine patrols were augmented by the air patrols of Army Air Force B-17 (Flying Fortress) bombers and Navy PBY (Catalina) patrol planes. We soon learned that these planes and the hastily mobilized, sketchily trained Navy surface craft escorts were our chief source of danger through mistaken identity or faulty ship handling. The handheld Aldis lamp we had for signaling was not steady or powerful enough for daytime communications. We had to use our 12" searchlight and, on occasion, even semaphore flags to send slow, laborious identification signals to ominously circling planes.

The time-coded, pronounceable, three-letter groups of challenge and response came from code books that the British Admiralty furnished to our Navy. (We had so much to learn about fighting a war.) We kept the recognition signal in effect for each watch chalked in large letters on the bridge windscreen. One series of challenge and response amused us. It was:

COM   FUD

MUJ   ERK

and was thereafter referred to as the private signal of Comdr. Charles F. Erck, our division commander, who generally wore a worried frown as he clucked over us like a mother hen. When out of earshot he was referred to as "Ma Erck." His final injunction to Johnny and me as we left on each patrol was, "Remember eternal vigilance is the price of safety."

Our submarine base was at Coco Solo on the Atlantic side of Panama, placed there in 1916 when the most likely threat to the canal was deemed to be from a European power, specifically Germany. As a result, each patrol we made, averaging about twenty days, required a round-trip transit of the canal. The day of sailing was always arduous. Roused from sleep at 0430, Johnny Corbus and I would be on our feet until about 2100. Underway before dawn in company with one or more sister ships, we'd pick up a canal pilot for the seven-hour transit through the "big ditch" and its locks. We had to be constantly on guard to prevent damage to our projecting stern planes, rudder, and screws, but the civilian pilots of the Panama Canal Zone Company quickly learned the peculiarities of handling our craft, so ungainly on the surface. They liked the quick response that the use of battery power gave in tight maneuvering conditions.

Once safely through the canal we were led through the Army's controlled minefield that guarded the approach to Balboa Harbor. Leaving that astern, we picked up our surface escort, either a small patrol craft or a converted private yacht, to be led past San Jose Island in the Gulf of Panama to our point of departure for the open Pacific.

After our terse message – "Thanks. Proceed independently." – was flashed to the escort by blinker tube, we sailed on alone with no lights showing. We had only to ensure an alert watch as we steamed through the pitch darkness, wary of blacked-out merchant ships belching gouts of smoke as they scurried to or from Balboa. The day of return to base would be no better.

The first dive in the Pacific quickly demonstrated the varying salinity of the oceans. The Atlantic is saltier than the Pacific. Our eight-hundred-ton ship had to be lightened by four tons of ballast water to be in diving trim. There was so much we didn't know about fighting a war with submarines. With our sister subs we were ordered to take position on a line some eight hundred miles west of the canal and to maintain a submerged patrol. In keeping with classic coast defense doctrine, we were to give warning of enemy ships and to attack if feasible.

Our visual search, through periscopes exposed only a few feet above choppy seas, was very inefficient, and the primitive sonars of the time were of little help. Compounding the difficulties of maintaining an effective barrier patrol was the problem of position-keeping. We had to rely solely on celestial navigation in waters of unknown currents during a season of prolonged heavy overcast and frequent rain squalls. Surface patrol would have made our visual search vastly more efficient, but it would be some months before a few aggressive skippers in the far western Pacific would demonstrate that.

In the confused, early weeks of war, being submerged did, at least, spare us from impetuous bombings by overeager young pilots of Army Air Force or Navy planes on long-range patrol missions. We lived with this hazard throughout the war, but in spite of several such incidents none of the "friendly" bombings definitely caused the loss of a submarine. In only one case, that of *Dorado,* lost in the Atlantic in October 1943, was this a likelihood.

We returned from our first patrol on January 24, 1942. We had sighted no enemy; our only contacts had been with inquisitive, friendly patrol planes that we eyed uneasily as they circled overhead. (On her first patrol in this area *S-44* had been bombed by such a "friendly" plane.) We had, at least, carried out a wartime operation and kept our ship in fighting condition despite frequent machinery casualties requiring much hard work and improvisation.

After leaving San Jose Island abeam to port, we headed for Balboa in the gloom of a dark, overcast night. Just outside the harbor we met *S-21, S-26, S-29,* and *S-44.* They had just transited the canal and were lying-to, awaiting our brief rendezvous before proceeding to their patrol stations. Their escort was a converted yacht now bearing its Navy number, *PC 460.* We went close alongside *S-26* to exchange information. Johnny Corbus spoke with his fellow skipper, Earl C. (Droop) Hawk, while I chatted with my opposite number, Thomas V. Peters. Tommy Peters was my classmate at both the Naval Academy and at Sub School.

Johnny and I were eager for news of the war, for what had transpired while we were at sea, and for what changes of duty might be in the offing. In return we gave whatever information might be useful to our friends on their own patrol. In a few minutes we called out "Good luck, Droop,"

"So long, Tommy," and proceeded on our opposite way as *PC 460* led our friends seaward. When we reached Gatun Lock on our nighttime transit we were shocked by the report that *S-26* was on the bottom, sunk with all hands. Following the friendly exchange just a few hours before, the news of disaster hit us like a blow to the solar plexus.

Not until we moored at Coco Solo did we learn what had happened. After *PC 460* sent a visual signal to her covey of S-boats that she was leaving formation to proceed on duty assigned, she turned to starboard. Only *S-21* received the message. Instead of steadying on a course clear of the formation, for some reason *PC 460* continued in a circular turn to the right in the pitch-black night. Suddenly, on her original course, *S-26* loomed up dead ahead. With no time for either ship to take avoiding action, *S-26* was rammed in the starboard side of her torpedo room. In seconds she plunged to the bottom in water more than three hundred feet deep. Only three men survived, Captain Hawk, Lt. Bob Ward, and Seaman J. B. Hurst, all of whom had been on the bridge.

Less than a month later, submarine disaster came again off Panama, and once more at the hands of friends. The giant French submarine *Surcouf*, which had recently been overhauled by our navy yard in Portsmouth, New Hampshire, was en route to Panama when, on February 18, she radioed her position and reported that she would reach Colon the following day. She never arrived. The U.S. freighter *Thompson Lykes* reported that on the night of the eighteenth she had struck a low-lying object some eighty miles east of the canal. The freighter's bow was damaged. In all probability, the object she had struck was the blacked-out *Surcouf*, which had disappeared with all hands.

The loss of two submarines in a few weeks due to negligent seamanship and faulty ship-routing procedures was tragic, not for the loss of two decrepit subs, but for the waste of trained submariners. Forty-five men died in *S-26*, 129 in *Surcouf*.

After four fruitless patrols in which our accomplishment was keeping our twenty-two-year-old boat operating by dint of constant hard work and much ingenuity on the part of our machinist's mates and electrician's mates, *S-24* was ordered back to New London. We were to train a British submarine crew, then transfer our boat to them for operations in the Atlantic.

All hands were elated. Aside from reunion with loved ones, this was like being called up from the minor leagues to the majors. There would be a change of duty for each of us, and everyone hoped for assignment to one of the new boats being built in Groton or Portsmouth, or, better still, to a fleet boat already operating in the Pacific.

In May we warily headed northward, picking our way by sextant and periscope through Windward Passage and Crooked Island Passage. Hardly had we cleared the latter when the diving alarm startled all hands, its unexpectedness adding urgency to its absolute command. Sounding the second blast of the raucous horn from the switch in the conning tower, Tom Raywood, quartermaster of the watch, waited, lanyard in hand, to slam shut the conning tower hatch over the head of Lt. (jg) Gerald L. Cameron. Jerry was from the University of Washington Naval ROTC and was typical of the bright, eager, young reserve officers attracted to submarine duty.

As O.O.D., Jerry would be the last to leave the bridge. The lookouts had leaped below at his electrifying shout, "Clear the bridge! Two blasts! Take 'er down!"

Jerry followed, almost on their shoulders, and slid down the ladder to the control room. Just as he reached his post at the diving station, the captain got to the control room from his tiny cubicle.

"Green board," reported Chief Yelliott, who had jumped to his diving station at the flood and vent control manifold.

"Pressure in the boat. Secure the air!" said Jerry. "Hard dive. Take her to one hundred feet."

The deck slanted forward beneath our feet, and we could feel the thrust of the screws as Electrician's Mate English at the control panel just abaft the diving station sent a surge of power from the storage batteries to the main motors. For a long instant the ship seemed to hang on the surface like a gigantic needle upheld by surface tension, but soon the pointer on the depth gauge crept past the mark that indicated the highest point of the ship. S-24 settled faster and faster, freer and freer, into her proper element.

Only then did the skipper speak up. "What is it, Jerry? Why did we dive?"

Still watching his gauges and bubbles intently, and first ordering, "Ease your planes. Pump from forward trim to sea," the shaken young officer replied, "It was a periscope, captain. About broad on the starboard bow, only a few hundred yards out. I only got a quick look at it."

"Stay at one hundred feet! Come right to zero-five-zero! Slow down as soon as you can. Sound, search carefully from bow to bow and report everything you hear." Johnny spoke quickly and precisely.

As we went to battle stations, torpedo, Jerry was relieved as diving officer by Frank Lynch, our six-foot-four-inch engineer officer. Now free to enlarge on his sighting, Jerry described what he had caught sight of in the choppy seas – a length of periscope and what was probably the top of a U-boat's periscope shears. Close to the surface as she tracked us through her periscope, the rough seas probably caused her to lose depth control briefly. Was she just watching our movements, wondering whether we were worth a torpedo that might be better spent on a tanker or freighter, or was she getting into firing position? At any rate, we groped blindly for her with our inefficient passive sound search equipment, which yielded only mushy sounds different from familiar sea noises. Even if we detected and tracked the U-boat by sound, we would have no way to tell how deep she was, how deep to set the running depth of our torpedoes. Not for years would we have acoustic homing torpedoes. Submarine-versus-submarine was not yet a practicable mode of warfare unless one should catch the other on the surface.

We continued our search until sundown, then surfaced and transmitted a report of our contact. Perhaps the position we reported would be of help to the thin ASW forces guarding our sea frontier. Our first brush with the enemy was sobering and useful. Commander Erck was right; all hands now knew what it took to stay alive.

* * * *

In New London, Comdr. Peter Webb, RN, and his crew quickly learned the peculiarities of *S-24*, her weapons and equipment, but not without sharing our envious inspections of the trim, new-construction boats on the ways at the Electric Boat Company or fitting out at the sub base. Most of Webb's officers and men were veterans of more than two years of war in their own boats, but a few were novices.

Shoreside and underway instruction were completed in August, and all hands, British and American, mustered on the pier alongside our ship. With our flag hauled down and the Union Jack raised, on August 10, 1942, *USS S-24* became *HMS P-555*.

Of the nine boats transferred to Britain, six, including *S-24*, survived and were returned after the war. *R-3* was lost as a result of perils of the sea, and *R-19* was rammed and sunk by HMCS *Georgian* in the western Atlantic. *S-25* was manned by the Polish navy and operated under British orders. She had been renamed *Jastrzab* and was sunk by mistake by Allied convoy escorts off Norway.

From *S-24* I went to command of *R-11* in Key West, Florida. She was older and more primitive than *S-24*. Built in 1919, the 570-ton boat was one of several whose mission was to provide target services for the training at sea of Fleet Sonar School students embarked in destroyers or patrol craft. At the same time, we gave preliminary training and screening for the Submarine School to young reserve ensigns who had volunteered for submarine duty.

The thrill of attaining my first command was tempered by disappointment over not proceeding to combat in the western Pacific. Still, no event can be more meaningful in the career of a naval officer than his first command, humble though it may be. It is the culmination of his years of preparation. It is realization that, as commanding officer, captain, skipper, or "old man," he has total responsibility for a ship and her men, their training and readiness to cope with perils of the sea or of combat. No other man on board is so privileged – or held so accountable. And, perhaps for the first time, young Navy wives would wonder, "Does he love his ship more than me?" Answering the insistent ringing of the telephone, they'd hear, "Honey, collect the children; put up the shutters. A hurricane is coming and I've got to take the ship to sea."

✳ ✳ ✳ ✳

Duty as a tame-target submarine brought months of lengthy, monotonous, sweat-soaked dives in the Gulf Stream. We had no air-conditioning or dehumidification. Soon after submerging we stripped to shorts and sandals. To avoid losing training time when sonar trainees lost contact with their small, elusive target, we towed a floating buoy to mark our underwater position.

After six months of this, orders to Prospective Commanding Officers (PCO) School in New London were most welcome, a step toward a command in the Pacific war zone. The four-week course emphasized torpedo attack tactics, weapons, and communications, taught by experienced skippers returned from the war zone. There were seven in the class, all lieutenant-commanders. I was junior man. Roderick S. Rooney, with four additional years of experience, was senior man. On completion of the course we envied Rod; he was the only one to be given command of a brand-new boat.[6] The rest of us were sent to Pearl Harbor, Brisbane, or Perth for further assignment by the Submarine Force commanders. It was policy that unless the prospective CO had experience in a submarine on war patrol he must make an indoctrination patrol under a combat-experienced skipper before getting his own command.

We did not learn much from our three instructors; between them they had made only one successful attack, sinking a three-thousand-ton ship. We respected them for having done their best when plunged into a war for which doctrine and training had not prepared them, but they could impart little useful combat experience. They were products of an unrealistic peacetime operations and training system whose insidious effect was not recognized until the realities of combat disclosed it.

To a greater degree than in any other type of warship, the success of a submarine depends on the actions and attitude of her commanding officer. When the war started, the average age of skippers was thirty-seven. They had all survived the rigorous screening that preceded command. They had progressed through most shipboard billets from "George" (most junior officer and jack-of-all-trades) to executive officer and had served about seven years each in subs before attaining their coveted first command.

In the environment of peace, however, a submarine skipper's record, and hence his chances for promotion, was enhanced more by his administrative skills than by proficiency and daring in torpedo attacks. There was no reward proffered for risk-taking. It was foolhardy for a skipper to risk the loss of a periscope or more severe damage to his ship by demonstrating aggressiveness or permitting his officers to do so. The cleanliness and material condition of his boat, the smart appearance and disciplinary record of his crew, the reenlistment rate in his ship, and the accuracy and timeliness of his reports were critical factors more apparent to his division commander than the less measurable qualities of aggressiveness and leadership under stress. It was hardly the way to prepare for a form of warfare that demanded utmost initiative and daring.

Thrust suddenly into the unforgiving realities of war, many skippers suffered the "first time syndrome." Solely responsible for the actions and survival of eighty men and their ship, it was a lonely, frustrating period as they sailed on their solitary missions. There were no ships in company sailing against a common foe, a situation wherein, under a bold leader, the dynamics of visible support, of shared danger, of common action would sweep along even the faint-hearted. No background of combat experience existed from which to evaluate the enemy's capabilities or assess the worth of specific tactics. Deep within enemy-controlled waters, hundreds or even thousands of miles from the nearest friendly forces, the submarine CO had to devise his own tactics as he weighed the chances of his ship against real or imagined enemy countermeasures.

Many of those in command when the war started performed admirably. Skippers like Chester Bruton, Freddy Warder, Chet Smith, Joe Grenfell, Lu Chappell, and others went after the enemy aggressively. Considering the grossly deficient torpedo with which they sailed off to war, their performance must not be judged by the record of ships they sank or damaged. They were an inspiration to their crews and to the younger skippers who followed.

In some other cases there was a lack of aggressiveness, as well as a tendency to credit the Japanese with better antisubmarine tactics and weapons than they had. Among these were some of the skippers whom we had admired in peacetime as most proficient and most likely to succeed in combat. Sadly, most notable among these was Morton C. Mumma, Jr. Highly intelligent and personally attractive, he was a dynamic, self-confident peacetime skipper. His strict, authoritarian handling of his S-boat and crew gave him an enviable reputation: effective in administration and, seemingly, very proficient in torpedo attacks. When *Squalus,* sunk by accident in 1939, was salvaged, refurbished, and renamed *Sailfish,* Mort was singled out to command her in special recognition of his ability.

In December 1941, on his first war patrol, a routine Japanese depth-charging in the Philippine area unnerved Mumma. But even in the shattering crisis of a brilliant career, Mort showed good sense and moral courage. He turned over command to his exec and kept to his stateroom. He was the first skipper to be relieved for cause. Numerous others, less notable, followed. Some were relieved for inadequate performance, and some, acknowledging inadequacy, voluntarily requested a change of duty.

A happier example of moral courage came in late 1943. My classmate and close friend Joseph F. Enright was skipper of the new submarine *Dace* on her first war patrol. Off Japan, in an area that presented numerous cargo and warship contacts, Joe got no results, not even when an Ultra message alerted him to the course of the aircraft carrier *Shokaku.* Feeling that he had let his ship and shipmates down, on his return to Midway after forty-nine days at sea, Enright requested to be relieved. "I feel I was responsible for the unproductive patrol and request to be relieved by an officer who can perform more satisfactorily."[7]

Taken at his word, Joe served for almost a year in submarine staff assignments ashore. When he requested another chance he was given command of *Archerfish,* and the rest is history. On the night of November 28,

1944, patrolling off Tokyo Bay, Enright waylaid the new, huge, secretly built aircraft carrier *Shinano* and sank her. At 71,890 tons she was the largest ship ever sunk by submarine.

The lesson is clear: skills of management and administration do not translate to success in combat. It is leadership and daring, combined with experience, imagination, and reliable weapons, that count in the sudden, unpredictable demands of warfare.

For me, the most valuable lessons for success in submarine combat came from poring over the war patrol reports that each CO had to submit immediately on return to port. These were a detailed account of a submarine's actions and experiences on its patrol. All important factors were covered: materiel, personnel, health, communications, and torpedo attack, as well as enemy countermeasures. By this time, early 1943, many more boats were on patrol, and younger officers had been given command of some. Benefiting from patrol experiences under their former skippers, they were eager to put their own theories into practice. Soon their patrol reports began detailing innovative, more daring, search and attack procedures whose results clearly showed the value of the submarine's keeping the initiative. Evidence was also accumulating that Japanese ASW tactics were generally inept and lacking in persistence, with equipment inferior to that used by British and American forces against the U-boats. A glaring weakness was their lack of the hunter-killer teams of light aircraft carrier and surface forces that were giving the Western allies the upper hand in the Battle of the Atlantic.

It was becoming apparent that, depending on the area and weather conditions, the most productive submarines were those that dared to spend more and more time on the surface in search of targets and pressed home their attacks at night.

Along with all the good information being gleaned from the patrol reports, there was a disquieting, recurring complaint – poor torpedo performance. Too often, fish that had every chance to hit their targets when launched exploded prematurely or not at all. Soon I would be victimized by the same faults and have a part in their solution, as will be described later.

Our S-boats used the 21" Mark X torpedo, which had a range of 3500 yards at its thirty-six-knot speed. It carried a TNT warhead of 497 pounds. The newer fleet boats used the dual-speed Mark XIV, also 21" in diameter. Its range was 4500 yards at forty-six knots, or 9000 yards at thirty-one knots. Its warhead was 650 pounds of Torpex, an explosive somewhat more powerful than TNT. Neither torpedo had been subjected to realistic live-firing tests. This omission, partly for economy, partly from complacency, proved to be tremendously costly in U.S. lives and the prolongation of the war.

Because the lower-speed, long-range shot required more accurate target data as to course, speed, and range and gave the target more time to evade, it was rarely used. As a consequence, to accelerate production of torpedoes and replace the thousands being expended, many uselessly, the low-speed feature of the Mark XIV was eliminated. The resulting fish was designated Mark XXIII.

All Marks were propelled by an alcohol-fueled steam turbine that produced a smoky bubble track that pointed to the submarine's firing position. To eliminate the detectable exhaust trail, an electric torpedo, Mark XVIII, was developed by Westinghouse Electric Company during the war, following the example of a captured German model. In spite of its slower speed (about seventeen knots) and more demanding maintenance, the Mark XVIII became the weapon of choice during the last year of war.

In contrast to our torpedo problems, Japanese torpedoes were very efficient. The Type 95, Mod. 1 used by submarines was 21" in diameter. It had a wakeless oxygen-fueled engine and carried a 900-pound warhead to 10,000 yards at forty-nine knots, or 13,000 yards at forty-five knots. Most important, it had been extensively tested against actual ships. Our torpedoes had not.

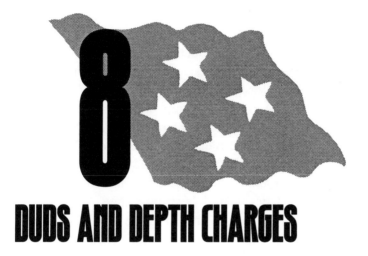

DUDS AND DEPTH CHARGES

By the spring of 1943 the confusion that existed in the organization and command of our submarines at the start of the war was pretty well overcome. At the time of the attack on Pearl Harbor there were 111 submarines in commission: 60 were in Submarines Atlantic Fleet (SubLant), with headquarters in New London; 22 were part of the Pacific Fleet that was based in Pearl Harbor; and 29 were attached to the Asiatic Fleet based in Manila. About a year later, submarines of the Pacific Fleet were designated a force of their own, becoming SubPac. Meanwhile, after their retreat to Australia, subs of the Asiatic Fleet were designated Submarines Southwest Pacific (SubSoWesPac).

Each of the three submarine groups was separately administered and operated independently of the others, so there was no submarine strategy common to all. Such commonality of doctrine and strategy as was achieved came from the cooperative efforts of the autonomous commanders. The mutually satisfactory relationship worked well, largely because of the common background of experience and friendship in the small, close-knit prewar submarine force. Nevertheless, the operations of the three components – Atlantic, Pacific, and Southwest Pacific – were influenced by the command styles and idiosyncrasies of the officers at their head.

The subs based in Pearl Harbor (SubPac) were under command of Rear Adm. Thomas Withers, Jr., a man of normally mild, soft-spoken demeanor. When only a commander in 1930, Withers was one of the first to advocate freeing the submarines from their ties to the battle fleet so that they could operate independently on the offensive. When he became ComSubPac in 1941 he made training practices somewhat more realistic and stressed the need for aggressive action, but the conservative mind-set and cautious procedures ingrained in his skippers by years of unrealistic peacetime routine were not easily overcome.

After the attack on Pearl Harbor, the prompt declaration of unrestricted submarine warfare (even before war was formally declared) freed submarines from their ill-conceived mission of fleet defense, opening the way for aggressive individual action. However, when most skippers of the early patrols returned with poor results, Withers belied his normal manner and soundly criticized their tactics and lack of aggressiveness.

In May 1942, Rear Adm. Robert H. English relieved Withers. Responsible for waging a form of undersea warfare very different from peacetime planning, he was not an inspiring, imaginative, or bold wartime leader and did not have the confidence or high regard of his skippers. After only eight months, he died in an airplane crash.

In Australia Rear Adm. Charles A. Lockwood, Jr., was Commander Submarines Southwest Pacific. His subordinate operational commanders were Capt. James (Jimmy) Fife at Fremantle and Capt. Ralph W. Christie at Brisbane. Jimmy Fife was an intense, dedicated workaholic who did not like to delegate authority. On the other hand, fun-loving Ralph Christie, although a more likable personality, was to be remembered chiefly as the torpedo expert who for so long stubbornly refused to accept the fact that his pet Mark VI magnetic exploder and Mark XIV torpedo were defective.

In January 1943, after Admiral English was killed, Lockwood was recalled from Australia to be ComSubPac. Aside from Admiral Nimitz, he was our most experienced submariner. (While still a midshipman at the Naval Academy, Nimitz had ridden our first submarine, *Holland* [SS 1], and his first command was *Plunger* [SS 2] in 1909.) Lockwood's first submarine duty came in 1914, and his own first command, while still an ensign, was the 123-ton *Adder* (SS 3). Their shared roots in the beginnings of our submarine service tightened the bonds of respect and confidence between the two men.

From Lockwood's many years of submarine duty, he carried an air of casual but effective command that put his juniors at ease and inspired their best efforts. His warm, genial personality was quickly felt in SubPac. He received the wholehearted support and admiration of his skippers, to whom he was "Uncle Charlie," the understanding, kindly critic and taskmaster of their lonely commands.

Patrols made off Panama did not count as combat experience, so ComSubPac assigned me to *Sculpin* (SS 191) for my PCO run. She would be making her seventh war patrol. Her skipper for all of them was Comdr. Lucius H. Chappell. When the war started on December 8, 1941 (Philippine time), *Sculpin* was one of the first boats to sail from Cavite Naval Base to patrol east of Luzon. In successive patrols Lu Chappell realized that something was drastically wrong with his torpedoes and added his voice to the angry protests coming from other skippers. When they saw their fish run right to and under their targets without exploding, they had no doubt that the torpedoes were running deeper than set. Moreover, no small number of them were exploding prematurely before nearing their targets.

In Washington the Bureau of Ordnance (BuOrd), the agency responsible for overseeing the development, testing, and production of torpedoes, did not agree. When it would not take action to verify and correct deep-running, Lockwood and Fife improvised tests in Australia that would prove that the Mark XIV ran deeper than it was set to do. A fishnet was rigged submerged across a calm inlet, and torpedoes were fired through it. The holes showed that the fish ran eleven feet deeper than set, and in July 1942 the boats were directed to adjust settings accordingly. They were still required, however, to use the magnetic Mark VI exploder.

The Mark VI had been developed by our Naval Torpedo Station in Newport, Rhode Island, and thereafter held in such secrecy that most submarine personnel did not know of its existence until war was upon us. It was designed to make the torpedo more lethal by detonating its warhead beneath the target rather than against its side as a contact exploder would. In 1940 in Pearl Harbor, a carefully controlled few officers (and no enlisted men) were introduced to the device. It was just a passing acquaintance; we were given only a look at a sample and a brief explanation of its principle of operation before it was replaced in its box. It had not undergone adequate live-fire tests, and there was no fleet experience in its maintenance, installation, or use.

Early in their war we had offered the Mark VI to the British, but they turned it down. Perhaps the Mark VI was the weapon system described in one of their reports: "The extreme ingenuity of this instrument rather blinds one to its utter uselessness."

Unfortunately, we persisted in its use. It was expected that setting the fish to run at the proper depth – five feet beneath the keel of the target – would bring it into the stronger part of the ship's magnetic field and result in more reliable actuation of the exploder. However, this did not solve the premature explosion problem. So disgusted were they with the Mark VI that, once in their patrol areas, some skippers inactivated it on their own authority.

Again it was the forces afloat who had to devise tests to find the cause. They demonstrated that the undulations of the torpedo as it sought to maintain set depth on its way to the target, along with the perturbations induced by rough seas, produced magnetic influence enough to activate the exploder. When presented this fact in July 1943, Admiral Nimitz ordered that the Mark VI be discarded in all boats of his Pacific Fleet command. However, Rear Admiral Christie, in Australia and not under Admiral Nimitz's command, had been instrumental in the development and production of the magnetic exploder. He required his boats to use it for almost a year more and gave up on it only reluctantly when so ordered by his superior in the Southwest Pacific Fleet, Adm. Thomas C. Kinkaid, Commander Seventh Fleet.

Once again, isolation of a fault failed to result in a completely reliable weapon. There were actually three defects: (1) running too deep; (2) premature firing or failure of the magnetic exploder; and (3) unreliable action of the contact exploder.

Lu Chappell was one of those who took matters into their own hands. The area assigned *Sculpin* for her seventh war patrol in May 1943, on which I was aboard as an observer, was the two-hundred-mile strip of ocean extending up the east coast of Honshu from Inubo Saki, the cape just east of Tokyo. She found plenty of targets. In five separate attacks, nineteen fish were expended, but time and again we watched in frustration as one or more torpedoes exploded prematurely, alerting their targets and allowing them to evade, or else ran to their targets and failed to explode. Even after Lu ordered the magnetic exploders inactivated we got no hits. We returned from patrol empty-handed save for two small picket boats destroyed by the only reliable weapon we had, the obsolescent 3" deck gun.

My own first war patrol in command likewise brought bitter evidence that all torpedo problems were not solved. On August 12, 1943, I took command of *Halibut* (SS 232) at Midway Island, in relief of Comdr. Philip H. Ross. After a few days' training, at 2 o'clock in the afternoon of August 20 we sailed for Japan in company with *Pompano* (Comdr. W. M. Thomas) and *Searaven* (Comdr. Hiram Cassedy). Overhead a Navy fighter plane searched along our track for possible enemy submarines. At nightfall we parted company, each boat proceeding independently to its assigned areas. *Halibut*'s was off the east coast of Japan's two major islands, Honshu and Hokkaido, and astride the entrance to Tsugaru Strait, which led to the Sea of Japan. *Halibut* was the first boat sent back to these areas since *Pickerel* and *Runner* were lost there from unknown causes.

On August 28, the very first day in our area, we sighted a loaded freighter proceeding northward close inshore, escorted by a *Shigure*-class destroyer. The day was ideal for periscope work. It was a clear, sparkling morning with a fresh breeze laying a pattern of whitecaps on the dark blue water. Up-sun from the destroyer as we were, there was almost no chance that her many lookouts could sight the slender 1.4"-diameter tip of our attack periscope when it was exposed above the wave tops for just the few seconds necessary for intermittent looks.

With the destroyer about two thousand yards to seaward of the freighter, hence between us and the *maru*,[1] it was apparent that we could not get close enough for a good shot at the freighter. However, pressing in, it was clear that we could attack the destroyer at a favorable range.

I maneuvered *Halibut* carefully and precisely into position just as though this was a practice approach on the attack teacher in PCO School. Twenty-four minutes after first sighting our target, we fired a spread of three torpedoes. They had less than 1900 yards to run. With the fish set for a depth of six feet with very small gyro angles on a favorable, almost broadside, track angle, I had every reason to expect a kill on a man-of-war on my very first attack. We were using only contact exploders, and depth was set well within the target's draft.

I followed the bubbles of the torpedo tracks as they sped toward their doomed target, and sonar reported, "All fish running hot, straight, and normal."

Instinctively I gripped more tightly the knurled handles of the attack periscope and braced for the explosions. They did not come! I watched with horrified fascination as the torpedo tracks ran right to the target but could see or hear no explosions.

Betrayed by our own weapons, all surprise lost, we were suddenly in a deadly duel – the fast, maneuverable destroyer with its potent depth charges pitted against the slow, stealthy submarine with torpedoes that didn't work. Close to the enemy shore, in water only 240 feet deep, and with twelve hours of daylight before we dared surface, we were in for a busy day!

Halibut moved cautiously. In the glare of the bright morning sun and with numerous whitecaps hiding our periscope "feather," we were intent on keeping the initiative, ready to fire at the first good opportunity.

Some twenty minutes after our first salvo, the *Shigure,* still not certain where we were, crossed our stern, giving an almost ideal setup to a spread of three torpedoes fired with a zero gyro angle at a range of a thousand yards on a nearly 90° track. Surely this time the destroyer would be done for. In a few seconds the crashing roar of our torpedoes would silence the sharp metallic pinging of her sonar, the thrashing of her propellers.

But no! I was wrong! Once more the fish passed under their target or failed to detonate. And this time the hunter located us. The rest of the day was spent evading counterattacks; we received forty-three depth charges but came safely to the surface after dark.

Time after time I reviewed the actions of our two unsuccessful attacks but could find no serious flaws in our tactics. In future attacks, in patrols that followed, never again would I attain so favorable a firing position or fire with such accurate target data. Why didn't we hit, or, if we did, why didn't the warheads explode?

The next day, off the southeast tip of Hokkaido, near the steel-producing city of Muroran, we sank *Taibun Maru,* a 6600-ton freighter, with a salvo of three torpedoes fired at 1200 yards. The first hit near the bridge with a very satisfying explosion; the other two, spread to cover possible errors in estimating target course and spread, passed harmlessly ahead and stern of the target.

In evading the counterattack by the two escorts, we went deep and headed for the open sea. While still in the relatively shallow water of Iburi Wan, we brushed against the mooring cable of a mine. As agonizing seconds ticked by, the cable or chain slide along our side, its mine floating above us undisturbed.

A few days later we attacked another freighter. The first spread of three fish at 650 yards gave no explosion. Reducing the depth setting to eight feet, we sent three more, this time at a range of 950 yards. Again no explosion. To miss on these attacks was incredible. At short range, the use of radar, sonar, and visual bearings had given perfect fire control data. One or more of the fish must certainly have hit.

By this time we had fired fifteen of our twenty-four torpedoes against three different ships. The sole explosion had sunk one ship. My men needed to hear warheads exploding to know that we were doing all right and to reassure them that their blind imprisonment was productive.

At dawn on September 6 we found another target, the cargo ship *Shogen Maru* of 3400 tons. With perfect target data a spread of two torpedoes was enough. At the correct time of torpedo run I saw a mound of water at her side, but I could see no sign of damage. Puzzled and angry by the continued poor performance of our torpedoes, I fired two more. At once I wanted them back. The *maru* was settling by the stern and listing toward us. The first two fish had hit, probably punching 21" holes in her rusty side. The mound of water may have been caused by rupture of a torpedo's high-pressure air flask.

Unquestionably our fish had holed their target, but we had seen and heard no explosion. Certainly a 2500-pound torpedo moving at forty-five knots, hitting squarely, could punch a hole in a freighter's rusted side. But why didn't the warheads explode? Had we really missed on all those earlier attacks, or had we been victimized by our contact exploders? If *Halibut*'s experience on just one patrol in 1943 was typical, what a shameful waste of ships and men to date!

Late that night, on a pitch-black sea, radar made contact on a high-speed target, closing fast. Diving to radar depth, we got a perfect solution of target's course and speed, 112° at 21½ knots. From her dim outline, I thought the target was a destroyer and ordered a depth setting of six feet.

Fifteen minutes after making contact we fired four stern tubes at a range of two thousand yards on an ideal track. In our patrol report I said, "At predicted time of hitting, the set-up was still checking perfectly on the TDC and both sound heads tracked torpedoes to the target. No explosions were heard in the conning tower, but men below reported a dull thud similar to the sound of this morning's hit and felt a slight tremor."

When we surfaced there was no trace of an enemy destroyer. The postattack noises we had heard were not conclusive of a sinking; all we could claim was another dud hit with damage to an enemy warship. With only one fish remaining, we headed eastward to clear the coast and head for home, but we did so reluctantly. We were familiar with all parts of our area, and it was yielding at least one contact a day. If only we had torpedoes that worked! Maybe the one we were taking back with us would yield a clue.

Ten days later, after we had logged seven thousand miles from Midway to Japan and back, we moored at the sub base in Pearl Harbor, and Admiral Lockwood came on board. "Welcome back, skipper. Congratulations on a good job."

Seated in our wardroom, sipping iced coffee and reviewing the highlights of our patrol, I told him how pleased I was with my crew but how bitter over the terrible performance of our torpedoes. Of the twenty-three fish fired, only one hit with a normal explosion, and three others hit as duds. Four were positively tracked to enemy ships with no result observable, and two others probably ran deep as well. Of the remaining thirteen fired, the tracks could not be observed.

"I think we finally know what's wrong, Pete," Lockwood said. "By the time you go out again we should have the fix."

A sad, grim postscript to our report of action came a month later when *Pompano* was declared overdue and presumed lost. She had been assigned the area along Honshu's east coast just south of ours. After *Halibut* vacated the area, "*Pompano* was informed by dispatch that the area to the north of her own was open. Since that area was considered more productive of sinkings than the one she was in, it is quite possible that she moved into it. Both the one between Honshu and Hokkaido, and the one east of northern Honshu are known to have been mined by the enemy, with the greatest concentration of mines in the northern area. In view of the evidence given, it is considered probable that *Pompano* met her end by an enemy mine."[2] Could it have been the minefield that *Halibut* scraped through? After the war I would read Admiral Lockwood's words: "These northern areas were the toughest in enemy waters and we finally shut them down for a few months because of our losses."[3]

✶ ✶ ✶ ✶

Admiral Lockwood's confidence in finding a solution to our torpedo problems came from tests he had directed. Loyal to his frustrated, irate skippers, he would tolerate no more bureaucratic delay. If the Bureau of Ordnance couldn't find the cause of warhead duds and cure it, the forces afloat would.

The first step was to have the submarine *Muskallunge* fire live torpedoes against the underwater face of a cliff on the deserted Hawaiian island of Kahoolawe until a dud occurred. The first two torpedoes exploded properly; the third was a dud. Divers recovered the crushed warhead. When the exploder was extricated, it was found that its firing pin had traveled only part way up its guide posts en route to contact with the fulminate of mercury firing caps that would, in turn, actuate the warhead-detonating charge.

With this major clue, dry-land tests proceeded swiftly. A tall crane was set up on the parade ground in front of the enlisted men's barracks at the sub base. From the crane's ninety-foot height, dummy warheads fitted with actual exploders were dropped onto a steel plate, simulating the impact of a Mark XIV torpedo striking the hull of a target.

These tests showed that warheads that hit squarely, at a right angle to the plate, resulted in duds. By slanting the plate to the line of impact, however, fewer duds occurred. In other words, a perfectly directed attack, one that gave its torpedoes the benefit of maximum broadside target length, was less likely to produce a sinking than an attack that could deliver only a glancing blow at a foreshortened target! The firing pin spring was not strong enough to overcome the friction and distortion of guideposts caused by the impact of a solid hit.

Perhaps because we had had such terrible luck with our torpedoes, on completion of our two-week recuperation period at the Royal Hawaiian Hotel *Halibut* was given ten war shots, all fitted with locally modified exploders. I was directed to repeat the test that *Muskallunge* had made with the official Bureau of Ordnance exploders. Because of the danger of an erratic or circular-running torpedo coming back to hit us, all fish were fired from stern tubes, with *Halibut* on the surface. We kept our bow pointing to seaward and, with all four main engines on the line, were ready to maneuver at high speed if necessary.

At a thousand yards from the island's sheer cliff, each torpedo was set to run with a zero gyro angle for a hit as close to a 90° track on the underwater rock face as we could manage. Six consecutive shots each yielded a high-order explosion. The seventh was a dud. We returned to Pearl knowing that progress had been made but that complete reliability still eluded us.

In what can be described only as a "torpedo scandal," our submarines had been sent to war for twenty-one months with a defective weapon. It was September 1943, with almost 4000 torpedoes expended in combat, before the Mark XIV's faults were corrected, and that chiefly by the operational forces.

There was culpable negligence in the shore establishment (the Bureau of Ordnance and Naval Torpedo Station Newport) responsible for the design, production, and testing of torpedoes, yet no one was held accountable. Most at fault was NTS Newport, which evaluated and tested its own product and declared it ready for service use. It resented and rebuffed criticism by the operating forces, considering itself the final authority and sole repository of torpedo expertise. It attributed the lack of sinkings to inept attack by submarine skippers.

There was small comfort in the fact that at the outset of war in the Atlantic in 1939, Germany's U-boats had suffered almost the identical problems in their torpedoes. However, the opposing naval high command took very different action. In Germany, evidence of faulty torpedoes was quickly followed by the court martial and punishment of naval officers and civilians in their equivalent of NTS Newport.

In the United States, no disciplinary action was taken against those responsible for the improper performance of our torpedoes. What a contrast to the summary relief of command of submarine COs whose performance in combat was considered inadequate! In some cases their lack of effectiveness was, in large measure, induced by the defective weapon with which they were sent in harm's way. There should have been punishment of those responsible for the torpedo debacle. That would have sent a clear signal to all materiel agencies and given assurance to frontline operators that they were being given utmost support.

★ ★ ★ ★

U.S. submarine operating personnel were not entirely free of blame for the situation. Almost to the very start of war in 1941, submarine operators were preoccupied with improving their vehicle, making it safer, and giving it the reliability and long endurance required if it were to fulfill its mission of fleet support. They finally succeeded in this, with the consistent support of the Bureau of Ships (BuShips) and its commercial contractors. However, "total system" reliability, which included consideration of the submarine's primary weapon, received little attention. Prewar torpedo performance and lack of realistic testing were not challenged. The "in-house" Navy monopoly of torpedo development, testing, and production was not recognized as the serious deficiency it was. It was uncritical, self-satisfied, and smug, aloof from the real world of its operational customers, be they submariners, destroyer sailors, or naval aviators. NTS Newport's assurance that its product was fully ready was accepted.

Aside from Christie, whom Admiral Lockwood called "the godfather of the magnetic exploder," few submarine officers wished to be involved in the development and production of torpedoes in a bureaucracy dominated by the "gun club." Thus, when Admiral Lockwood complained of BuOrd's failure to acknowledge and correct torpedo problems, the respected chief of the bureau, Rear Adm. W. H. P. Blandy, responded that submariners were all too ready to stand on the sidelines and criticize but unwilling to get on board and help find solutions. Thereafter, experienced submarine skippers were placed in appropriate billets ashore.

The lack of emphasis on the military effectiveness of the submarine was partly due to uncertainty as to the submarine's proper role in the Navy. Whereas it was quickly recognized that the airplane would be of critical importance to the fleet in both defense and offense, the submarine's utility in the fleet was questionable. By 1914 Navy aircraft had received their first exposure to enemy fire when planes were used for battlefield reconnaissance at Vera Cruz, Mexico. Thereafter, with the great infusion of funding during World War I and the use of aircraft both at sea and shore, enthusiastic, innovative young Navy and Marine aviators rapidly developed tactics and techniques such as dive-bombing, torpedo attack, and sea surveillance that would weave aviation ever more tightly into fleet operations. By 1921, just ten years after acquisition of its first plane, the Navy established a separate bureau – the Bureau of Aeronautics – to monitor and improve all materiel factors of naval aviation. Five years later, the post of assistant secretary of the Navy for aeronautics was established.

These facts are cited not in envy or criticism but in realistic appreciation that in spite of its ten-year head start over naval aviation the submarine had severe technical problems to overcome before it could bring a significant new capability to the fleet. Even when the basic "platform" problems were overcome, the submarine would still lack the flexibility and utility required for the Navy's multiple missions worldwide. It remains a ship, albeit a unique one, the only one that can operate within – not on – the sea. There is no need for a separate Bureau of Submarines.

9

CRESCENDO

Until October 1943 all our boats operated singly, free to roam independently and attack whatever targets they could find in the area assigned them. In the spring of that year the commander-in-chief, Admiral King, no doubt influenced by the immense success of German U-boat wolf-pack attacks on convoys, directed ComSubPac to develop our own wolf-pack tactics.[1] Admiral Lockwood was aware of the advantages and disadvantages of wolf-packing and sought to devise a system more suited to the conditions of the war in the Pacific.

From his own experience in command of a submarine in World War I, Admiral Doenitz knew that submarines operating singly spent much time in fruitless search of open-ocean areas, only to be overwhelmed by contact with large numbers of freighters and tankers escorted by a variety of small warships. When the U-boat closed for attack, it was limited by its small number of torpedoes and inability to sustain the level of attack so rich a target warranted.

To overcome this problem and exploit a fundamental principle of successful warfare – concentration of force – Doenitz evolved his "group tactics." When a convoy was detected by reconnaissance aircraft, submarine search, cryptanalysis, or any other means, a group of U-boats would be vectored by the shore-based headquarters to intercept and attack. A pack of fifteen to twenty U-boats, each carrying at least fourteen torpedoes, could ravage any convoy. Given an adequate number of boats to cover likely convoy routes, and in view of the state of the art of Allied ASW at the time, the campaign against convoys could have been decisive in winning the Battle of the Atlantic, starving out Britain, and permitting Hitler to turn his full power eastward against Russia. Doenitz had estimated that a force of three hundred boats would do this. As it was, Germany's land-oriented high command started the war with only fifty-seven.

Aside from requiring a large number of submarines, the flaw in the Doenitz scheme was its reliance on central tactical direction by a remote land-based headquarters. This required much easily detected radio transmission, from first location of a convoy, to tactical disposition of U-boats, to postattack reports, as well as from boat to boat. High-frequency direction-finding (HF-DF, or Huff-Duff) of such transmissions and the operational pattern they disclosed was of great assistance to Allied ASW forces.

In the Pacific, Japan did not use convoys of great size that would warrant coverage by a large number of submarines. Where convoys of fifty or more ships were used in the Atlantic, rarely would we see even twelve or fifteen at a time. Moreover, the escorting forces of Japanese convoys were not as numerous, as well trained, or as well equipped as those of the United States and United Kingdom. It was more profitable to deploy the small number of U.S. boats available to operate individually at focal points of Japan's shipping.[2] Besides, unlike Germany, Japan had gone to war with a well-developed surface fleet, strong in battleships and aircraft carriers. While our own shattered battle fleet was being restored and expanded, our target list gave top priority to battleships and carriers.

An important consideration was the lack of secure, reliable communications between submarines, making operations in close proximity hazardous, especially when submerged. This risk was even less acceptable in training exercises. It was after improved high-frequency radio and surface-search radar made intership communication more reliable and less susceptible to intercept that wolf-pack tactics became practicable for us.

The system developed by ComSubPac at Pearl Harbor called for three boats to operate as a search-and-attack team. By coordinating their search, they could do a better job than a single boat looking for traffic in the great expanse of the Pacific. Embarked in one of the boats would be a submarine division or squadron commander to coordinate the group's movements. He was not there to exercise combat direction, but to assist in bringing all boats into action, with each skipper using his own attack procedures. The only function of ComSubPac headquarters was to furnish by one-way radio transmissions any intelligence or other information that might be useful.

On October 1, 1943, the first U.S. wolf pack (a better term being "coordinated attack group") sailed from Midway Island for the East China Sea. It included *Cero, Shad,* and *Grayback,* with ComSubRon 2, the resourceful Capt. C. B. (Swede) Momsen, embarked in *Cero.* Results were disappointing; only three sinkings were confirmed.

The second group, *Harder, Snook,* and *Pargo,* left Midway on November 3 for the Marianas Island region. On board *Pargo* as its aggressive, greatly respected division commander was Freddy Warder. Seven ships were sunk, but again the skippers of the boats were not enthusiastic about the system, particularly the lack of reliable communications within the group. Freddy Warder saw no benefit in having a separate, senior officer riding along in tactical command.

The third wolf pack, *Tullibee, Haddock,* and *Halibut,* was sent out in December to test group tactics with the senior skipper, Charles F. Brindupke of *Tullibee,* acting as officer in tactical command (OTC). We were assigned the vast area covering the routes converging on Truk and Rabaul from the Marianas and Japan.

We quickly discovered the disadvantage of a small number of boats operating in a huge open-ocean area. To search effectively, our group had to operate on the surface as much as possible. When we did make contact, either by our own efforts or when alerted by the code-breakers in Pearl, it required much high-speed running as we vainly attempted to close fast warships proceeding to or from Truk. The accelerated expenditure of fuel shortened the time we could stay in the area.

Nevertheless, it seemed that with the help of Ultra, which had broken the enemy's top-secret communications, our three small subs would accomplish in the Pacific what it took many ships and aircraft to do in the Atlantic – find and destroy the enemy's greatest ship. The German battleship *Bismarck* had been hunted down and destroyed in the North Atlantic. In our case, alerted by an Ultra message to guard a certain route from Truk, we did not know that our quarry would be Japan's *Yamato*, one of the two 72,000-ton (full load), 18" gun battleships she had built in utmost secrecy.

Ultra messages were those conveying operational intelligence derived by cryptanalysis and study of Japanese radio traffic. Extreme care was taken to prevent disclosure of U.S. success in breaking Japan's codes. The Ultra messages were always cryptic, never identified the Japanese units involved, and were sent to our submarine or surface forces only if there was a good chance of intercepting important enemy units. The messages were of special value to our submarines because we were the only ones able to maintain continuous presence in enemy waters but needed all the help we could get to extend our limited search radius. It was feared that the frequency with which our boats waylaid important combat or cargo ships would alert the Japanese to the compromise of their codes, but they made no such deduction.

When Brindy received the Ultra from ComSubPac, he disposed the three boats of our group fifteen miles apart across the projected track of an important enemy warship. Using our fully raised periscope in a careful search of the surface, about an hour before sunset on January 11 *Halibut* sighted the massive top-hamper typical of Japan's battleships. At seventeen miles range, only a towering, pagodalike mast could be seen above the horizon. We alerted *Tullibee* and *Haddock* by radio, using the special, very brief (two-letter) wolf-pack code, and tracked the target by visual bearings and a few intermittent pulses of our radar. In the gathering darkness and flat, calm sea, we maneuvered to get dead ahead of her. The range to our target decreased steadily, but we would dive before her lookouts could catch sight of their tiny opponent.

Soon there was no doubt that it was *Yamato*, or her sister, *Musashi*, who was closing on us. It would soon be dark, and I could expect *Tullibee* and *Haddock* to join in night attacks like the ravenous wolves we were. Only *Tullibee* had so far expended any torpedoes, her long-range spread of four having missed a Japanese submarine. Our group still had a total of sixty-eight fish. If one of us could slow *Yamato* with a hit or two, we would keep slinging torpedoes into her until she sank.

With these happy thoughts I called for one more range by radar as the season's early darkness fell, only to have our expert radar technician, Ray Welley, report, "Range opening fast!"

Speeding up, we headed for the target, but her range kept increasing, and soon the target pip faded from the screen. What a bitter disappointment – outwitted by the skipper of Japan's most powerful ship! At the great range at which we held her, he could not have detected our small 1500-ton boats by sight or even by radar, if he had one.[3] Probably he had a simple radar detector that alerted him to the probing of our three high-power radars. With nightfall imminent, he had held course and speed to mislead us. Then, once it was dark, he changed course and quickly ran away. It was a reminder that technologic superiority still yields to tactics generated by the brain. *Yamato* survived until April 7, 1945, when, in her suicidal one-way mission to attack U.S. forces off Okinawa, she was sunk by bombs and torpedoes from relentless waves of U.S. carrier planes.

When boats sailed from Pearl Harbor with the improved contact exploders at the end of September 1943, it was the beginning of the end for the cargo shipping that was essential for Japan to prosecute the war. In 1943 she lost 1.5 million tons to our submarines and could build only eight hundred thousand tons in replacement. In 1944 her losses were almost 2.5 million tons. Replacement by an industry that was itself dependent on import of raw materials was impossible.

Halibut contributed to the carnage. In ten war patrols she sank twelve ships (seven while I commanded, two of them men-of-war) with a total of 45,257 tons and damaged nine others. Only a ship sunk in deep water was out of the war for good, but ships forced into dry dock for repair could not hurt us while they soaked up manpower and money. Two of the ships we damaged were warships, the 13,380-ton heavy cruiser *Nachi* and the 24,140-ton aircraft carrier *Junyo*. *Nachi* was the ship I thought was a destroyer and had hit on the night of September 21. She got to port with one of our dud torpedoes sticking in her side. *Junyo*, hit by three of our puny torpedoes, was heavily damaged as she entered Bungo Channel.[4]

The great success our boats were having in spite of the torpedo fiasco would not have been possible had the Japanese navy given adequate attention to antisubmarine warfare, both before and during the war. It is incomprehensible that an island nation, with the historical example of Britain's near-defeat by U-boats so compelling, could have been so shortsighted.

Like our own Navy, at the outset of war the Japanese navy was not prepared to cope with submarine warfare aimed at shipping, but, unlike our Navy, the Japanese never faced up to the problem. "In a nutshell, Japan failed in ASW largely because her navy disregarded the importance of the problem. . . . The Japanese navy took it for granted that the role to be played by American submarines would be the same as that of Japan's own submarine forces, and slighted the role as raiders of commercial shipping."[5]

Because she lacked an appreciation of the importance of ASW in sustaining both her military power and her civil economy, Japan did not allocate sufficient forces to it or train them properly. "Until 10 April 1942 the Japanese navy had no unit whose duty it was to escort merchant vessels."[6] Not even Japan's warships were given the constant defense of coordinated air and surface ASW that the situation required. And when their ASW screens did detect us and attack, a common fault was lack of tenacity. Instead of harrying us to exhaustion and forcing us to the surface, too often they made impetuous, inefficient attacks and left the scene. Of course, there were isolated, individual ASW actions in which the Japanese were successful, but although they claimed a total of 468 "positive sinkings" of our submarines, we lost only 52 to all causes.

On her last patrol, *Halibut* was almost added to that number. She was in a coordinated attack group comprised of *Haddock, Tuna,* and *Halibut,* which had been deployed across the Japanese fleet's probable line of retreat from the battle for Leyte Gulf.

On October 25, 1944, by monitoring the excited voice transmissions of our carrier dive-bomber pilots as they attacked ships of the Japanese Northern Force, *Halibut* was able to close and attack. Just after dark I fired six torpedoes at the largest of three Japanese warships fleeing from action off Cape Engaño in the Philippines. These were *Ise,* a battleship converted to a hermaphrodite aircraft carrier; *Oyodo,* a light cruiser; and an unknown destroyer. The torpedo explosions we heard as we went deep proved to be against the destroyer, which had turned and come between us and our primary target.

The postwar report of the Joint Army-Navy Assessment Committee (JANAC) was for many years considered the definitive record of Japanese naval losses, and it credited *Halibut* with probably sinking the destroyer *Akitsuki.* From what research I could do after the war, I believed that our victim was the destroyer *Hatsusuki.* More recently, John D. Alden, in the most thoroughly researched compilation of U.S. submarine attacks to date, has identified our target as either *Akitsuki* or *Yamagumo.*[7]

In his account of our attack, the eminent naval historian Samuel Eliot Morison wrote, "An object resembling the hull of a capsizing ship was sighted in the moonlight. Who was the victim? It is still a mystery. Looks like a whale to me."[8]

When another respected historian repeated this canard in 1984 and wrote that "Adm. Samuel E. Morison, dean of American naval historians, pondered all possibilities," I was moved to remonstrate.[9] After all, I was on the scene. In an exchange of letters, I objected to Professor Morison's establishment as an expert in this case and the use of his flippant remark to trivialize the outcome of *Halibut*'s action. I wondered whether Morison had "pondered" these facts:

a. The radar of those days could not detect whales at 12,300 yards (six miles), nor could one be seen at night at that distance.
b. The strength of the radar pip, plus my own and my lookout's observations, showed ship, not whale.
c. JANAC credited *Halibut* with sinking *Akitsuki*.

The issue is of little consequence to the overall record of the Pacific War, but it is a good example of the "fog of war," which is as blinding when viewed through a submarine periscope as through the eyepiece of a Navy dive-bomber screaming through ack-ack toward its target. It can persist and envelope even distinguished historians as they try to put individual actions into context with a battle's broader scope.

✴ ✴ ✴ ✴

For three weeks following the warship encounter *Halibut* patrolled the Luzon Strait area. At that stage of the war, Japanese shipping was hard to come by. It was a dreary time, endless hours and days of fruitless search in stormy weather. We ran surfaced as much as we could, submerged only when we had to, at times wallowing in mountainous seas. When on the surface we took great amounts of water down the conning tower hatch. Frequently soaked to the skin, irritable from constant buffeting and pounding, we did our best to avoid damage to our ship and crew. In the midst of the storm, we sighted a large ship and closed her excitedly. She was not "zigging," and soon I saw why. She was a properly marked hospital ship proceeding toward the Philippines. Dejectedly, we let *Hikawa Maru* pass.

The submarine war had become very complicated. Instead of having large open-ocean areas in which each boat was free to roam, the increasing use of coordinated attack groups (wolf packs) in a combat zone that was contracting around Japan required great care. This was true in working with our own packmates as well as being a concern lest we become entangled with boats in adjacent areas, all pressing to exploit any contact. Still, it was comforting to know there were friends within reach, for on November 14 the war almost ended for *Halibut.*

During the night of November 13 we observed an unusual amount of Japanese air activity and deduced that the area was being swept for some important traffic. Just before noon the next day we heard the pinging of distant sonar. Speeding up and heading for the contact thus disclosed, we made out the tops of a northbound convoy: one large freighter, three smaller ones, and several small escorts. To get close enough for an attack we had to use high submerged speed, a noisy six knots, with only brief looks through the periscope. We would have to fire at long range or not at all. A torpedo run of 3100 yards was the best we could get. This meant that it would take the fish three minutes to reach their target, giving it time to zig once more.

At 1320 we fired four torpedoes at the large freighter when she had a ship in the far column overlapping her. Chief Quartermaster John T. O'Brien, with stopwatch in hand, marked the time of torpedo run. "Mark! They should be there!" But there was no explosion until two more minutes passed, and I saw the freighter in the far column making black smoke and dropping astern.

Suddenly, we heard a strange, loud, fast buzzing noise, unlike any we'd heard on any patrol. Men in the crew's mess reported they heard this sound pass over us four times. In the conning tower, the sound came to me as a fast, low-pitched buzz, increasing in loudness and then decreasing for a total of perhaps thirty seconds. As it faded, a heavy explosion, similar to the hundreds of depth charges we had heard, came close to port. I was puzzled by the strange noise and fearful of a new antisubmarine weapon. "Take her deep! Use negative and full speed!"

Four more heavy explosions detonated close to starboard as we leveled off at 325 feet. For seventeen minutes we ran quietly, trying to slink away, while two escorts could be heard overhead, their sonar echoes bouncing off our hull. Suddenly all hell broke loose! The tremendous concussion of a close depth charge deformed the hull of our conning tower, wrecking the radar transceiver and periscope hoist motor. Glass shattered and gauges broke – the sonar was dead. It was time to abandon the conning tower and seal it behind us.

For two minutes all seemed calm, save for the sharp probing of active sonar beams bouncing off our hull. A few hundred feet overhead, Japanese sonar operators intently watched the greenish blob that denoted our presence or listened carefully to the sharp metallic echoes our hull returned. We had survived many depth chargings in the past and had no doubt we would do so again, but this was a more professional ASW performance than any we'd experienced.

Suddenly, several close depth charges, very loud, shook *Halibut* violently. They were so nearly together that it was not possible to count them. The enormous concussion drove *Halibut* a hundred feet deeper, to 420 feet, 40 percent below its designed operational depth. The interior of the boat was a shambles. There was much damage, with many oil and water leaks. Then came the chilling words, "Chlorine gas in the forward battery!"

This most dreaded of submarine emergencies had to be treated as just another of the serious problems with which we were struggling. Depth charges exploding very close to the hull of the compartment had so distorted the thick steel pressure hull that a pipe from a bank of high-pressure air tanks had ruptured. This released into the battery well, which was under the deck of the living quarters for officers and chief petty officers, air that had been stored at 2500 pounds per square inches of pressure.

The sharp hiss of escaping high-pressure air sounded like water spurting through a crack. Combined with the indefinable odors of sweat, hair tonic, shaving lotion, shoe polish, vinegar, salad oil, coffee, and other things from shattered bottles and containers, it meant to young officers that the hull was ruptured and sea water was reaching the sulphuric acid of the battery electrolyte, creating chlorine gas. When they sealed and abandoned the compartment, its air pressure built up to 52 pounds per square inch.

We were making enough noise with our squealing shafts, singing propellers, topside banging, and internal racket to announce our location and invite more barrages of depth charges. They didn't come. I reasoned that the Japanese, desperately short of shipping as they were, had instructed their ASW commanders not to leave a convoy unguarded and prey to another submarine while they worked over one that was in no position to harm their flock. Whatever the reason for the lack of persistence, the knockout punch was not delivered. We crawled away battered and bleeding, victims of only a technical knockout.

Deep underwater, we struggled slowly upward while all hands worked grimly to control and repair damage. When we surfaced after dark, we were without radio, radar, sonar, or compass, but our marvelous Fairbanks, Morse diesels worked. We proceeded cautiously in search of *Haddock* or *Tuna.* In time we made contact, not with either of them but with *Pintado* from the wolf pack operating north of us. She escorted us 1500 miles to Saipan.

In Saipan, moored outboard of the sub tender *Fulton,* we learned that the strange noise we had heard passing over us came from a large plane flying low, using *jikitanchiki,* the Japanese version of magnetic anomaly detector (MAD). This could detect a submerged submarine directly beneath it at a distance up to five hundred feet. After the plane pin-pointed our position, the ASW escorts delivered the near-fatal depth-charging.

The repairs *Halibut* required were beyond the means of a tender at an advance base. She would never dive again. When she sailed back to Pearl Harbor and its navy yard, experts declared that her repair would be too costly and time-consuming. After I turned over command to my exec, she made her way painfully to New London to serve as an alongside school ship, in effect a floating training aid. Five years after she was launched, *Halibut* was sold for scrap for $23,123.

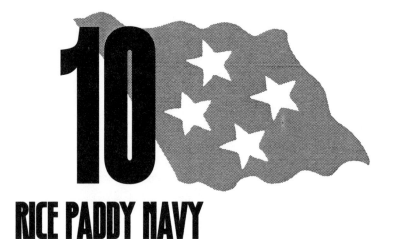

10

RICE PADDY NAVY

The apparent anomaly of a submarine operational billet deep in China's interior in Chungking, more than a thousand miles from the sea and a thousand feet above sea level, came about in 1944 when Admiral Lockwood saw that the most productive period of submarine operations was drawing to a close. With the steady advance of U.S. air and ground forces and the rapid decline of Japanese sea power, the fruitful areas for submarine patrols were shrinking drastically just when his force was reaching peak strength and efficiency. To employ his boats as gainfully as possible, he encouraged air commands, both Navy and Army, to include in their plans the use of our subs in air-sea rescue and as navigational beacons. The great number of Navy fliers already rescued by our "lifeguard" boats proved the worth of the system, and it was not difficult to sell the same service to the Army Air Force.[1]

Consequently, when Capt. Milton E. Miles, Commander Naval Group China (ComNavGruChina) proposed the addition of a submarine officer to his staff, Lockwood acted quickly. He designated Comdr. Walter G. Ebert to be submarine liaison officer (SLO) with a twofold mission: (1) to sift and pass on all intelligence that could be of use to our subs in either offense or defense; and (2) to assist the air commands, specifically the Fourteenth Air Force and the Twentieth Bomber Command, by providing submarine rescue services for their airmen downed at sea.

To this end, when informed by the air headquarters in Kunming or Chengtu of forthcoming strikes on targets in Japan or occupied China, the SLO would alert submarines in the vicinity or direct one or more to specific geographic coordinates. Knowing submarine capabilities and limitations, he could decide whether a request for lifeguard services was reasonable and capable of fulfillment without unduly hazarding the sub. Admiral Lockwood, in Pearl Harbor, delegated authority to the SLO to communicate directly with boats that operated under his ComSubPac command. Characteristically, Admiral Fife, in Perth, Australia, required that all requests for support by his ComSubSoWesPac boats be sent to him for action.

Ebert's assignment to Chungking stemmed from the fact that in March 1943, Admiral Lockwood had embarked in *Scamp*, which Wally commanded, for passage from Pearl Harbor to Midway. Despite Lockwood's constant desire to go on war patrol in one of his boats, Admiral Nimitz would permit him only an occasional short trip outside the actual combat zone. At any rate, impressed by the dynamic, forthright Ebert, ComSubPac chose him for the unique assignment.

In January 1945, in order to get closer to the area of combat operations tightening around Japan, Fleet Admiral Nimitz moved to an advance headquarters on Guam. He took with him from Pearl Harbor only a select planning and operations staff, leaving behind the logistics and administrative sections of his dual commands, Commander-in-Chief Pacific Fleet (CinCPacFlt) and Commander-in-Chief Pacific Ocean Area (CinCPOA). To be near the Big Boss, Vice Admiral Lockwood also moved to Guam, setting up shop on board the submarine tender *Holland* moored in Apra Harbor. He too left most of his staff in Pearl Harbor, taking only his operations and communications sections.

Already at Guam, on board the tender *Sperry,* was Capt. George L.

Russell, ComSubRon 10, to whom I reported as operations officer after leaving my battered *Halibut* in Pearl Harbor. Hardly had I taken up my new duties and become accustomed to the luxury of a commodious stateroom in *Sperry* when Admiral Lockwood informed Captain Russell that I was being ordered to Chungking in relief of Ebert.

✶   ✶   ✶   ✶

NavGruChina was the U.S. element of the Sino-American Cooperative Organization (SACO), which evolved from a directive by Commander-in-Chief Adm. E. J. King. A few weeks after Pearl Harbor he called in then Commander Miles and said, "You are to go to China and set up some bases as soon as you can. The main idea is to prepare the China coast in any way you can for U.S. Navy landings in three or four years. In the meantime, do whatever you can to help the Navy and to heckle the Japanese."

Admiral King was right in sending Miles to China as soon as he did. There was no assurance that our Army could maintain its foothold in China, or that it would have the will and resources to provide the weather data that was important to naval operations. Knowledge of weather fronts moving eastward from the Asiatic mainland was of special interest to aircraft carriers. In effect, accurate prediction of weather to be encountered en route to and over a target translated into the availability of many additional aircraft. Even in my own submarine operations in *Halibut* among the Ryuku Islands and along the coasts of Kyushu, Honshu, and Hokkaido, I had often wished for better knowledge of approaching weather. With such information, better deduction could be made of Japanese shipping movements, and the risks of surface cruising versus the more limited submerged patrolling could be better judged.

The basic premise of the SACO agreement that the Navy negotiated with China was the mutual interest of each nation in defeating their common enemy, Japan. To that end there would be a pooling of assets, each country contributing what it was best qualified to do. The United States would train Chinese guerrillas and saboteurs and provide equipment and training for weather stations, intelligence operations, and radio and radio intercept stations. China would furnish most of the personnel, the bases required and their supply support and security, as well as access to its existing intelligence network.

The quid pro quo arrangement was a pragmatic response to the special circumstances of a unique theater of war. It was one with very limited material resources, but one where centuries-old culture and tradition influenced analysis and action.

The commander of SACO was Gen. Tai Li, and Miles was his deputy commander, with each having a veto on operations. Tai Li had great power as head of the Kuomintang (nationalist force) secret service, an organization euphemistically titled the Bureau of Investigation and Statistics (BIS). Western diplomatic and military intelligence and Western newsmen portrayed Tai Li as a very unsavory character, a ruthless torturer, and the head of China's version of the Gestapo. It was a characterization he vehemently denied. More than once I heard him protest, "I am not Mussolini's Gayda; I am not Hitler's Himmler; I am the Gimo's Tai Li."

Intensely loyal to Generalissimo Chiang Kai-shek, Tai Li was distrustful of westerners in general, the British in particular, and Major General Donovan's Office of Strategic Services (OSS) in detail. However, through his understanding and respect for China and her people, an appreciation gathered during his prewar duty there, Miles won the friendship and support of the enigmatic Tai Li. The men's mutual respect, and Miles's absolute commitment to assist in ending Japan's grip of China, made a reality of Chinese-American cooperation, which ultimately took the form of 2500 Americans from every military service and almost a hundred thousand Chinese from the ranks of police, pirates, fisherman, farmers, and organized guerrillas.

When the Japanese cut the Burma Road, virtually every pound of fuel, ammunition, supplies, and material to support China and our own forces there had to be flown over the "Hump" to Kunming for further distribution by plane, truck, jeep, ox cart, and, finally, coolie. This "Hump tonnage" was controlled by the Army Air Transport Command and was vital to any military effort in China. It was one of two chief sources of contention, even acrimony, between Army and Navy in the China theater.

When SACO was established, it was assigned a Hump tonnage of 150 tons a month out of the total 3500 tons monthly being flown into China. Despite the growth in total tonnage to more than 70,000 a month and a great expansion in NavGruChina's forces and operations, Miles never succeeded in getting his allowance increased. In three and a half years, SACO received a total of about 9000 tons, which was what the U.S. Army, China Theater, was getting in three days as the war was coming to an end.

These figures indicate the austerity and scarcity under with NavGruChina had to operate. Three other separate and often competing elements – Chiang's central government, Lt. Gen. Joseph W. Stilwell's ground forces, and Maj. Gen. Claire Chennault's Fourteenth Air Force – were also dependent on the vital air link to the United States. Probably only Miles knew of the extent to which politics, international and interservice as well as Chinese, dominated all military action in China. Small wonder that NavGruChina, the unloved stepchild of U.S. forces, got short shrift. Our attitude toward the more generously supported, more "regulation" U.S. Army headquarters in Chungking was not resentful but disdainful; it seemed entangled in red tape while in relative opulence.

The second source of interservice dissension was the difference in philosophies of command and operational control. The Army adhered to the general staff concept of a central, supposedly omniscient but highly compartmented, staff that planned, assigned tasks, and allocated resources to forces in the field. It did not approve of combined international forces, nor of irregular special operations outside the recipes of its field manuals.

SACO did not fit into the neat organizational boxes and command lines so dear to general staff planners. There were no staff manuals or standard tables of organization and equipment to which Miles could adhere. He assembled from any source he could the specialists needed for his unconventional operations, and he was a master of extemporaneous action. The intelligence, reconnaiscence, mining, sabotage, rescue, and guerrilla operations he conducted were forerunners of the special operations by elite units that the U.S. Army, Navy, and Air Force would each find useful in future conflicts.

However, SACO was the subject of much controversy and opposition as it carried out guerrilla and intelligence operations behind enemy lines in what historian Barbara Tuchman called "the bewildering confusion of commands and intelligence services that operated in China during the final years of World War II." (Supposedly gathering intelligence were eight different U.S. agencies.) To be sure, with its own command line going directly to the commander-in-chief, Admiral King, in Washington and not being under the theater commander's operational control, NavGru-China contributed to the confusion. But also apparent, with far greater impact on theater operations, was the cleavage within the Army between its ground and air forces and the lack of rapport between the U.S. and Chinese army commands.

The Air Transport Command, the essential link between China and the outside world, was also outside theater jurisdiction, under direct control from Washington. As T. H. White and Annalee Jacoby wrote, "In 1944 the Twentieth Bomber Command of the B-29's, a great hoglike organism that consumed enormous quantities of goods and gasoline, entered the CBI [the China, Burma, India theater]; this command was completely above any control except that of General Arnold in Washington."[2] Under the command of dour, hard-driving Maj. Gen. Curtis Lemay, it mounted long-range raids against Japan from Chengtu, China.

Of all the working relationships Commander Miles had to develop and sustain with the diverse commands in the CBI theater, that with Maj. Gen. Chennault, USA, was best. The men had fine rapport from the start, founded on shared respect for the Chinese and a common understanding of customs and traditions that constrained action in China. Each man was struggling with modest forces, at the end of a tenuous supply line, to inflict all possible damage on the enemy.

When he was retired from the U.S. Army Air Service in 1937, ostensibly for a hearing deficiency but possibly because of his uncompromising insistence on the supremacy of air power, Chennault became the Generalissimmo's adviser on aviation and the supervisor of all China's air-training programs. After Japan invaded north China, he organized the American Volunteer Group, recruited from U.S. Army, Navy, and Marine Corps flyers who were permitted to transfer to U.S. reserve status for this purpose. Called the "Flying Tigers" because of the tiger-shark jaws painted under the noses of their P-40 planes, they were a colorful, hard-fighting, hard-playing outfit. In 1942 Chennault was recalled to active U.S. duty and took command of the Fourteenth Air Force when it was activated in Kunming.

Miles quickly reached agreement with Chennault as to the mutual support their forces could render. The recovery of downed pilots by SACO forces was enthusiastically received, and, for our part, the shipping information and other intelligence derived from Fourteenth Air Force operations along the coast was of interest to our subs.

Soon after taking up my post in Chungking, I flew to Kunming to pay my respects to General Chennault and learn whether we could improve procedures in any way. I was received cordially but found the general eager to tell of exploits by his young pilots and not much interested in submarine operations. Based on the wildly inflated claims of sinkings by his men, he was convinced that given more support his air force could cut the Japanese army's sea and land lines of supply and bring their operations in China to a halt. For my part, I knew what our submarines were accomplishing along the same line.

If the appellation "bird man" was applicable to anyone, it certainly fit

Claire Chennault. His lean, wrinkled, leathery face had the look of eagles. As usual, Winston Churchill said it best; attributed to him is the remark, "Thank God that face is fighting on our side and not against us!"

*   *   *   *

When I arrived in China, I naively expected that years of Japanese rapacity and brutality would have unified the country in a massive effort to oust her invaders. However, neither Chiang Kai-shek, leader of the Kuomintang and head of the government, nor Mao Tse-tung, leader of the Chinese communist movement, was willing to replace years of hostility by a united effort against their common enemy.

Although he gave us the intelligence and weather stations we wanted, there was little doubt that Tai Li's major concern was to keep a wary eye on Mao Tse-tung's communist forces. They had withdrawn to Yenan in the north of China and observed a nominal truce with Chiang Kai-shek's Kuomintang government, ostensibly to resist the Japanese invasion. However, both communist and Kuomintang leaders were more interested in hoarding resources for their inevitable confrontation than in taking aggressive action against Japan's occupying forces. Both wanted to acquire, from whatever source, as many modern arms and as much equipment as possible. The U.S. Army was providing weapons for twenty-six Nationalist divisions, while the communists were receiving arms from Russia.[3] Both Chiang and Mao knew that once the United States turned its full might against their common enemy, Japan's defeat was only a matter of time. Why, then, risk their own manpower and material in needless battle?

In 1945 the only offensives against the Japanese in China were the hit-and-run air attacks by Chennault's Fourteenth Air Force and the continuing sabotage and guerrilla warfare of Tai Li's Loyal Patriotic Army, which received very limited material and technical assistance from SACO's Hump tonnage. The few B-29 bombing raids against Japan proper flown by the Twentieth Bomber Command from Chengtu were a costly waste of effort that contributed virtually nothing to Japan's defeat.

*   *   *   *

The commanding general of the China theater was Lt. Gen. Albert C. Wedemeyer. He was the youngest lieutenant general in the U.S. Army and had been carefully chosen to replace the combative, outspoken "Vinegar

Joe" Stilwell, who could not get along with Chiang. Wedemeyer had a reputation as a brilliant staff officer devoted to detailed staffing and adherence to channels. The general was pressing his case to amend the SACO agreement in a way that the Navy believed inimical to U.S.-China relations. He was a thoroughly conventional, inflexible, bureaucratic planner, more interested in drawing a neat, standard, organizational diagram than in exploiting NavGruChina's special capabilities. Its unorthodox organization and irregular, clandestine operations were anathema to those schooled in traditional warfare concepts: if only NavGruChina could be placed in the proper box on the diagram, the ground war in China could proceed in orderly fashion.

Commodore Miles was summoned to Washington to present the Navy's case before the Joint Chiefs of Staff.[4] At the same time his chief of staff, Capt. Irwin F. Beyerly, was afar afield in eastern China, leaving me in charge. I had to feel my way through the maze of international politics, petty interservice rivalry, and incongruous military operations.

Although I had come from our submarine service, perhaps the most informal element of the Navy, I was amazed and initially distressed by the seeming lack of discipline, the unkempt appearance of personnel, their unmilitary bearing, and the disorderly routine in the "rice paddy navy." However, I quickly came to respect the individuals engaged in that effort, and also Miles's leadership. He trained his men as best he could for their often remote, lonely tasks, specified his general policies, and stated what results he wanted. He freely delegated authority and relied on the initiative, ingenuity, and loyalty of his subordinates, all elements characteristic of his own performance. No resources, none of the precious Hump tonnage, could be wasted on spit-and-polish items; all energy had to be focused on the common tasks shared with our Chinese allies.

I found great similarity between Miles's concept of leadership and command and that which prevailed in the submarine force. Perhaps this was because submarine warfare is much like guerrilla warfare: Operating behind enemy lines, out of direct communication with headquarters, daily facing unforeseeable problems that have to be resolved by the human and material resources at hand, the submarine skipper is assigned a task and left free to do it.

When he left for the Washington conference that was to clarify once and for all the U.S. military command relationship in China, Miles had specified that he wanted his staff to "make friends with the Army staff" in Chungking. He wanted some of them invited to our headquarters "so that they might see just what we are doing." I did what I could on the first count, and there was a congenial, if inconclusive, return visit by several of the Army staff.

At Army headquarters I conferred with Assistant Chief of Staff Brig. Gen. Mervin E. Gross and with his head of clandestine warfare activities (G-5), Col. George Olmstead. I was basically sympathetic to the Army position even before its sanction by the Joint Chiefs of Staff. Its logic was clear: The coordination of all American personnel and material assets in the theater made sense not only from the military command viewpoint but also for economics. Nevertheless, there were practical political factors to consider: how to avoid undermining SACO's valuable special relationship with the Chinese and the Gimo himself, and how to prevent sabotage or strangulation of SACO's productive guerrilla warfare by an Army staff opposed to such operations, especially when conducted by one it considered an interloper. In my judgment, in these aspects the Army staff was obtuse and obstructionist. It would not acknowledge the worth of unorthodox operations conducted on a shoestring by a seemingly ragtag outfit outside Army channels and immune to its staff manuals.

The Army's G-5 section was primarily concerned with material requirements, production, procurement, and civil affairs. To these responsibilities of the able, energetic Olmstead, Wedemeyer had added that of handling clandestine warfare matters. Because the chief practitioner of this mode of warfare in the China theater was SACO, this was clearly designed to bring NavGruChina's operations under the theater commander's supervision and control. This was in accord with the Joint Chiefs of Staff ruling, which Miles reluctantly accepted. That his continual supply problem, dependent on the Hump tonnage quota, was real in the past and would now be exploited openly and officially was revealed in a biography of Olmsted written after he became a highly successful financier:

Olmsted's compromise plan was to allow the Navy group autonomy as far as their day-to-day operations were concerned since the work, mostly behind Japanese lines, entailed unorthodox military methods, but that Wedemeyer would take charge if political or orthodox military problems were created.

Wedemeyer agreed to the basic philosophy and a working settlement was reached although Miles still was somewhat balky. Olmsted, however, held the winning card – the Navy group was dependent on his section for supplies. They could get just what G-5 figured could be afforded. Their dependency made them more pliable and the controversy faded.[5]

While such realpolitik influenced Army-Navy relations, my meetings with Army colleagues were invariably cordial. At my first meeting with General Gross he indicated that he was gravely concerned about U.S. arms that were appearing in Japanese hands around Canton. He said they could come only from U.S. Army or Navy sources through Chinese hands, and that the Army had checked everything they issued and could account for it all. I had no way to dispute this revolutionary development in Army logistics, and the suspicion that Navy-supplied munitions were being diverted and smuggled to the enemy remained a festering sore. Some of our minuscule stock no doubt was lost in guerrilla operations, but an equally likely source was the great quantities issued by the Army and OSS in support of their operations.

Not long after the transition of NavGruChina to Army supervision, as if to affirm his loyalty to SACO and appreciation for Miles's great part in it, the Gimo came to our base in "Happy Valley," some ten miles out of Chungking, to review our forces and to witness demonstrations of the various training activities. He expressed great admiration and pride in the uniquely harmonious Chinese-American organization and in its successes against the common enemy.

But what struck me most on that occasion was the fact that a nation's leader, supposedly on a par with Roosevelt, Churchill, and Stalin, had to concern himself with a detail of supply. In his conversations with me the Gimo brought up the great need for batteries of various kinds to power radios and other field equipment. He asked whether we could use submarines to deliver quantities of them to the coast. This was feasible, of course, just as we had resupplied beleaguered outposts and coast-watchers in various parts of the Pacific, but I was not keen to hazard a submarine on such a mission when it seemed a simple, straightforward operation to fly in an adequate supply. Or it should have been, were it not for the stranglehold Army had on SACO's Hump tonnage. I did not pursue the Gimo's request.

✶ ✶ ✶ ✶

My mission to gather intelligence useful for our submarines required the screening of countless messages coming to headquarters in Happy

Valley from many sources. We had coast-watchers at key points strung all the way from Shanghai south to Swatow. Generally these were U.S. Navy enlisted men, supported and defended by local elements of Tai Li's guerrillas. Also, the Fourteenth Air Force in Kunming passed along information of ship movements that its planes detected. In addition, BIS headquarters gave us information its spies gathered in Japanese headquarters and bases.

The naval intelligence provided by Chinese sources initially gave me much trouble and loss of sleep. The ancient Chinese culture did not match Western civilization's variety and richness of expression concerning modern tools for death and destruction. I was startled by the frequency with which "battleships" were sighted, and in what unlikely waters. To a Chinese guerrilla or peasant, a battleship was any ship, even a boat, mounting a gun. I quickly gained cartographic familiarity with China's long coastline as I plotted ship sightings, trying to validate the information given.

There were a few occasions when NavGruChina's intelligence reports were of direct assistance to our submarine operations. In October and November 1944, while patrolling in *Halibut* off Takao, Formosa, I had made contacts as a result of NKN (Radio Chungking) broadcasts. Other boats had also found targets as a result of those intelligence reports, but few were able to get in position to attack.

The most famous submarine exploit along the China Coast came in January 1945, when *Barb* (under Comdr. Eugene B. Fluckey) went into shallow water in pursuit of a large Japanese convoy that was seeking shelter for the night in Namkwan Harbor. Reassured by a message from Ebert that the area was not mined, Fluckey ran boldly in on the surface. He went nineteen miles inside the twenty-fathom curve on his charts and delivered torpedo attacks that earned him the Congressional Medal of Honor.

Two other events involving our subs had poignant, personal meaning for me. Dick O'Kane, my *Argonaut* shipmate, who had sunk more ships – twenty-four – than any other U.S. skipper, had been lost on his fifth patrol in *Tang*. In his crew were two *Halibut* veterans, Chief Motor Machinist's Mate R. B. MacDonald and Torpedoman Third Class Pete Narowanski. Their ship was sunk on October 24, 1944, when the very last of her twenty-four torpedoes was fired on the surface at night. The fish made a circular run and struck *Tang*. Although we did not know it at the time, nine men, O'Kane among them, survived the sinking of their ship and were picked up by the Japanese.

Tang had gone down in the East China Sea between Formosa and the

China coast. A SACO coast-watcher reported from Pinghai Point near Foochow that Japanese gunboats had been seen circling a spot in the water marked by oil and American bodies. It was deduced that this was where *Tang* had sunk, and because the water was comparatively shallow (180 feet) it was possible that the Japanese might salvage the sub or some of her equipment. Instructing our men to be especially alert for Japanese activity at that spot, I scanned most carefully all messages from Pinghai, but the Japanese made no effort to retrieve what could have been important intelligence for them.

The other event of more than routine interest to me was the sinking of *Awa Maru* on April 1, 1945. Her story started in 1944 when, gravely concerned by the conditions in the prisoner-of-war camps in which the Japanese held American and Allied captives, the United States used the good offices of the Swiss government to alleviate the situation. It was arranged that a ship carrying about 2000 tons of Red Cross relief supplies sent from the United States to Japan via Siberia would be granted safe passage to and from Southeast Asia. The guarantee of safe passage applied regardless of what other cargo the ship carried, what other purposes she served. Taking advantage of this, the Japanese designated *Awa Maru*, a 11,600-ton liner, as the mercy ship. Obviously, the ship was much larger than necessary to carry the modest tonnage of relief supplies. When notified of *Awa Maru*'s schedule and precise track, ComSubPac informed all submarines at sea. This was done by a plain-language message that was broadcast three times on each of three successive nights. In Chungking I read this traffic with interest and no particular concern. I had come across Japanese hospital ships more than once and let them pass unmolested; I could see no danger to a distinctively marked, well-lighted ship passing through a submarine zone on a preannounced track. The frequency with which we sighted Japanese hospital ships seemed excessive, but we had no way of checking their compliance with the Geneva Convention. We could only eye them suspiciously as they passed across our field of periscope view.

In Chungking we received from our numerous intelligence sources detailed information of *Awa Maru*'s movements and cargo, listing arms and ammunition she unloaded as well as raw materials she picked up for return to Japan. Such use of a mercy ship would normally be illegal and the cargo contraband, but in this case the Japanese government had been assured the ship's safe passage.

Among the U.S. subs then on patrol was *Queenfish*, operating in the

East China Sea off the northern tip of Formosa. Her skipper was Comdr. C. Elliott Loughlin, my Naval Academy classmate and warm friend. Elliott had captained the tennis team at the same time I was captain of the fencing team, but our weapons were now more deadly than tennis racquet and dueling sword.

Due to atmospheric conditions as she was en route to her station, *Queenfish* did not receive the original message giving *Awa Maru*'s itinerary, appearance, and guarantee of safe passage. Lacking that, when the second and third messages were received, their significance was missed, and the captain was not properly informed.

Late on the night of April 1, 1945, on the surface in a dense fog, *Queenfish* made radar contact on a single target. Not adequately informed about *Awa Maru* and never sighting his quarry, which he took to be a destroyer, Loughlin closed to less than 1500 yards and fired four torpedoes. They were set to run at shallow depth, consistent with a destroyer's draft. All four fish hit, and the unseen target quickly sank. From the one survivor he was able to pick up, Loughlin learned to his horror that his target had been the ship guaranteed safe passage at highest government level. When he sent a dispatch to ComSubPac reporting what had happened, *Queenfish* was ordered to return to Guam.

On the peremptory order of Admiral King, Loughlin was relieved of command and tried by general court martial. He was found guilty of "negligence in obeying orders" and given a light sentence. But the bizarre chain of events continued. Admiral Nimitz was greatly dissatisfied with the outcome of the trial. He shared Admiral King's view that violation of the guarantee of safe passage was inexcusable and a major embarrassment to the U.S. government. He was also concerned that, in reprisal, the Japanese would barbarously mistreat U.S. POWs, especially submariners. He promptly issued letters of reprimand to the members of the court, a more serious punishment than that given Loughlin.

*   *   *   *

As the war in Europe ground to its bloody finale, U.S. forces in the Pacific had retaken the Philippines and had seized Okinawa as well. Air searches from those bases covered all the sea routes converging on Japan. Aircraft could detect and attack most traffic more quickly than could submariners. In addition, our boats were hampered by the ever more shallow waters into which Japan's few remaining ships were forced. Furthermore, clandestine sources in China were providing almost no intelligence of value to our subs. My work had devolved chiefly into assisting the recovery of airmen shot down or crashed in the vicinity of our coast-watchers or network of camps. For this no submarine officer was required. I recommended to Commodore Miles that the billet of submarine liaison officer be discontinued and that I be returned to the fleet.

✷　✷　✷　✷

When I left China it was with no clear understanding of U.S. policy toward that immense, potentially powerful country. Early in the war our State Department, advised by our embassy in China, had urged Chiang Kai-shek to join forces with the communists to take action against the Japanese. That was a popular notion in the United States. After all, some highly placed foreign service officers and some well-known journalists were calling Mao and his followers "agrarian reformers."

All through the war the United States pressed Chiang to make a deal with Mao, but the Generalissimo resented any contact U.S. diplomats, military, or newsmen had with Mao, believing that would only add legitimacy to his enemy. The question of who lost China is a bitter one and still unresolved. I can only speculate that with its customary concentration on an immediate problem, in this case the military defeat of Japan, the United States neglected to consider the long-term implications should China become communist.

At a SACO reunion in Washington in 1965 I had occasion to recall our gropings over China's future course. I was seated next to Dr. T. F. Tsiang, Free China's ambassador to the United States. Before that post he had been Nationalist China's permanent representative to the United Nations Security Council. During my time in China he had been budget director for Chiang's government.

Dr. Tsiang had lived many years in our country, taking his Ph.D. in history at Columbia University. During dinner the ambassador spoke of the importance of culture in a nation's life and of having a continuity to that culture forged through historical experience. "In my opinion," he said, "the very young United States, with its yet unassimilated ethnic groups, has not established a culture that is uniquely its own."

Sensing an opening, I asked, "Mr. Ambassador, in your opinion what is the communist regime contributing to China's cultural evolution?"

I was impressed by the candor of his reply. "At long last, there seems to be an acceptance of a national authority, of centralized government, instead of just provincial authority or warlord-ism."

My first billet, USS *New York*. (U.S. Navy Historical Center)

Argonaut underway off Pearl Harbor, 1937. Designed as a minelayer, at 2710 tons she was the largest U.S. sub built before World War II. She was sunk by the Japanese in 1943. (National Archives)

S-24 in the Caribbean, Christmas Day, 1941. Cases of canned food are being retrieved from their stowage in the free-flooding superstructure. (Author's photo)

Adm. Husband E. Kimmel, Commander-in-Chief Pacific Fleet, with Capt. W. S. Delany (left) and Capt. William W. Smith, 1941. (U.S. Naval Historical Center)

Vice Adm. Charles A. Lockwood, Commander Submarine Force Pacific Fleet, aboard one of his submarines in 1944. (National Archives)

USS *Halibut* returns to Pearl Harbor, May 15, 1944, after her ninth war patrol off Okinawa. (U.S. Navy photo)

A Chinese soldier guards the headquarters compound of the Sino-American Cooperative Organization (SACO), near Chungking, 1945. (Author's photo)

Generalissimo Chiang Kai-check visits SACO headquarters, April 1945. With him are Commander Charles S. Johnston, USNR, and General Tai Li. (Author's photo)

Fleet Adm. Chester W. Nimitz, Commander-in-Chief Pacific Fleet. (National Archives)

USS *Navasota,* underway off Korea, September 1952. The aircraft carrier USS *Bonnhomme Richard* is in the background. (U.S. Navy photo)

In 1964, a group of former World War II submariners pay their respects to Fleet Admiral Nimitz, who had commanded *Plunger* (SS 3) in 1909. Left to right, standing: Rear Adm. John A. Tyree, Rear Adm. V. L. Lowrance, Nimitz, Rear Adm. E. B. Fluckey, author, and Rear Adm. E. P. Wilkinson. Note the submarine weathervane. (Author's photo)

11
END OF WAR

After reporting "mission accomplished" to CinCPac on Guam, I was returned to the submarine force and assigned as operations officer of Task Group 37.2 at Saipan. This included two squadrons (sixteen boats) and their supporting tender, *Orion*. By this time the seas around Japan seemed crowded. Once only submarines dared these waters; now our surface warships were present, and both Navy and Army Air Force planes passed overhead. Our boats had to be routed and deployed most carefully to avoid mutual interference, and they had to be kept informed of friendly forces moving in their vicinity. *Guardfish* provided a tragic example of what could happen. She had encountered the U.S. salvage tug *Extractor* west of Guam, mistook her for a Japanese I-class sub, and sank her.

As U.S. military might converged on Japan's home islands, the war became increasingly an aviator's war. Tonnage sunk by submarines declined rapidly, while that sunk by aircraft or the mines they sowed in waters not accessible to submarines mounted swiftly. It was clear that, once in position and properly supported, ship- and land-based air could produce a rate of sinkings exceeding that by submarine. The end of the war in six or seven months seemed certain.

On the morning of August 7, we received the news that an atomic bomb had been dropped on Hiroshima the day before, delivered by a B-29 from our neighboring island of Tinian. We had no advance knowledge; not even Admiral Lockwood was informed of the readiness of the new weapon and its imminent use.

Official information was slow in coming. We learned more from reports of newsmen in the Pacific than from official announcements. From Honolulu, Roy Howard, publisher, *New York World-Telegram*, reported:

> That the end of the war must come within a few months is certain. That it may come within weeks is possible. That it will come within days is not impossible.
>
> The time factor must inevitably be governed by the speed with which the Japanese people can grasp the full significance of warfare's latest development. The atomic bomb is destined to change not only the course of this war but of all future wars.
>
> With a single explosion it has made largely obsolescent all previous conceptions of navies, armies and war machinery.

With only sketchy knowledge of nuclear physics, we read unbelievingly of the devastation caused by one bomb dropped from one plane. Our major submarine weapon, the torpedo warhead, carried less than a thousand pounds of TNT. Against the equivalent of the twenty thousand tons carried in one bomb it seemed a puny toy. Suddenly the ample horrors of war could be measured not in ships sent to the bottom but in cities and their populations eradicated. And none of us could foresee that the controlled release of atomic energy would bring to the submarine a more profound expansion of capability than to any other "war machinery."

When the second atomic bomb was exploded over Nagasaki two days later, events moved rapidly to Japan's unconditional surrender on August 14. The most devastating war in history was over. It had been six years since Hitler invaded Poland. Sixteen million soldiers and more than eighteen million civilians had died. In the four years of its involvement the United States lost three hundred thousand soldiers, sailors, and marines.

The war had started when a land power, Germany, overran Poland with blitzkrieg tactics by armored tanks and *stuka* dive-bombers, spread worldwide after Japan's attack on Pearl Harbor, and involved sea power to an extent never possible before. It was a war in which the most significant aspect of naval combat was the extent to which it used the third dimension – the atmosphere and the undersea. Control and effective use of these critical operating zones were essential to sustain the Allied land campaigns in Europe, North Africa, and Asia.

The United States emerged from the war as the mightiest sea power of all time. Morale in the Navy was sky high. It had risen from disaster at Pearl Harbor to become the spearhead of American power relentlessly piercing Japan's successive perimeters of defense. In the Atlantic it had met the challenge of the U-boats and made possible Allied victory over Germany and Italy. Now an awesome symbol of a nation's power rode quietly at anchor in Tokyo Bay as the formal documents of surrender were signed by Japan on board the battleship *Missouri* on September 2, 1945. But would the hard-earned lessons of World War II even be relevant to sea power in the atomic age to follow?

Given time, in its sanctuary behind two ocean ramparts, to marshall its vast industrial capacity, the United States had created a comprehensive but flexible Navy-Marine combat system able to control the three zones, air, surface, and undersea, in which it operated. It demonstrated sea power's ability to play a decisive role on a global basis in a world power struggle. U.S.-British command of the seas kept open the vital lifelines that permitted the industrial and manpower might of America to be deployed where needed. But it did more than ensure the passage of armies and goods through its sea lanes and prevent the enemy from doing the same. The airplane had become an essential, integral component of naval power and gave it new flexibility and extended reach. The fast carrier task force became the Navy's primary means of power projection.

To be sure, the Pacific sea battles, fought with opposing warships never coming in sight of each other, and the threat of land-based air attack required more than close-in protection by the antiaircraft gunfire of screening ships. New formations and compositions of task forces had to be devised to give maximum early warning of air attack and to get in-depth defense. A distant screen of fighter aircraft was essential, and it needed intercept direction from shipborne long-range radar. Fortunately, fleet defense against air attack went hand in hand with the integration of aviation into the fleet.

Continuing improvement in air-search and surface-search radars, in radio communications, in fighter plane performance, and in antiaircraft armament, including the proximity fuse, provided defense adequate for the World War II air threat. However, the severe losses inflicted by Japan's fanatic, suicidal kamikaze pilots portended the much greater threat that supersonic homing missiles would present in a few years. The Navy realized that to remain a credible, viable component of national military power it had to have effective defense against land- and sea-based aircraft and missiles. It was an effort that would take many years of costly development of sophisticated radars and ship and aircraft weapons systems.

Given that defense, naval power no longer had to remain on the margin of land conflict. Its integral, carrier-based aircraft brought a new concentration of power. The war vindicated the Navy's concept that in sea warfare the airplane is only one element or tool of naval power, not a separate entity. The carrier task group makes it possible to bring the airplane to the scene of combat with endurance unimpaired and to operate at short range of its targets.

Teamed with sustained and accurate naval gunfire, the intimate and constant collaboration makes massive amphibious assault possible and confers a strategic flexibility that forces the enemy to fight on distant fronts at times and places not of his choosing. During World War II many of these places were seized solely to permit construction of the landing strips and support bases that land planes required. Until advanced air bases can be established, supported, and defended, the great handicap that land-based air suffers in any distant continuing operation is that it must expend so much endurance in going to and returning from the scene of the action. Nevertheless, in postwar years, the cult of strategic air power enthusiasts who equated destruction by bombing with victory would attack the Navy's carrier task forces as redundant and too costly.

Victory is not gained until control of the ground, of the land on which all power ultimately rests, is assured. The relationship of the three arms of military power in achieving this have nowhere been better stated than by the official historian of the British Royal Flying Corps, writing after World War I, "A country that is conquered must be controlled and administered; a city that surrenders must be occupied. Battles can be won in the air or on the sea, and the mark of victory is this: that the patient infantry, military and civil, can then advance to organize peace."[1]

To improve its own staying power and ability to sustain a high level of action, the Navy refined and extended its system for underway replenishment. The ability to resupply combat ships with fuel, food, ammunition, and supplies while en route to or in their operating areas was of special importance in the vast expanse of the Pacific and to the success of the island-hopping strategy. Fleet oilers of the Service Force, the mobile logistic support element of the fleet, were able to refuel two ships simultaneously as they steamed close aboard on either side. Other specialized ServFor ships did the same with ammunition and food. Repair ships moved farther and farther forward to provide repair and supply facilities. Even floating dry docks large enough to lift a battleship were towed to forward sheltered anchorages to permit prompt repair of battle damage or installation of improved equipment. The lesson well learned, the mobile, sea-based logistic support system gave the Navy ability to maintain forces continuously on station in the Korean and Vietnam wars as well as a forward presence when needed in scores of remote trouble spots.

But of all the maritime lessons that should have been learned in World War II, none was more important than the need for a ready, effective antisubmarine capability. In the Atlantic, where Germany started the war with only fifty-seven U-boats, a small force of submarines, comprising a very small fraction of her military power, came close to forcing Britain out of the war and preventing the defeat of the Axis. British tenacity and innovation enabled her to survive until U.S. ASW effort could augment her own. That U.S. effort was initially inept, almost too little too late. As it was, British ASW, air and surface combined, sank 500 of the 630 U-boats sunk at sea.

On the other hand, Japanese submarines did not pose a severe threat to U.S. shipping in the Pacific. Unlike the U.S. Navy, Japan's sailors clung to the prewar doctrine of supporting the battle force, up to and including a final climactic battle with the U.S. fleet. As a consequence, her boats sank only 171 ships, warships included, totaling fewer than one million tons. Germany's U-boats, admittedly much greater in number and purposefully directed against shipping, sank more than fourteen million tons, and our submarines sank five million.

The U.S. ASW capability, honed in the severe test of the North Atlantic, had little difficulty coping with Japan's misdirected submarine campaign. Our losses to air attacks, including those to the sacrificial, human-guided kamikazes, were more significant.

As for the wartime record of our own submarine force, there was much to be proud of and much to be learned. When the fighting ended, we had 169 fleet-type boats in the Pacific, plus 13 S-boats, which were used to furnish target services to our ASW forces. When the war started there had been a total of 51, including 6 S-boats. The force comprising only 1.6 percent of the Navy's personnel strength sank 55 percent of all Japanese tonnage that the United States sent to the bottom. It sank 201 naval vessels and 1113 merchant ships, for a total tonnage of 5,320,094.[2] This was all the more remarkable for a force whose prewar doctrine and training had not prepared it for the war it actually fought and which for almost two years fought with a grossly defective weapon. The postwar report of the U.S. Strategic Bombing Survey stated that the war against shipping was the single most decisive factor in the collapse of the Japanese economy and the logistic support of her armed forces.

However, it is sobering to remember that if Japanese ASW had been as efficient as the U.S.-U.K. effort in the Atlantic, our losses would have been much higher and our productivity much less. In the Atlantic, the effectiveness of Allied ASW had major influence on outcome of the war. In the Pacific, inefficient Japanese ASW had equally great effect on that war. The Japanese navy, single-minded in its belief that the fleet-versus-fleet action was its sole purpose, neglected the task of protecting its seaborne commerce.

Still, although our submarines had not been up against first-rate opposition, combat operations had proved that the basic design of the fleet boat, although not thoroughly "de-bugged" by war's start, was excellent for operations in the Pacific and permitted incremental improvements as combat urgencies prodded technologic progress. Behind us were the main propulsion problems that had so long constrained full exploitation of the submarine's unique qualities. The General Motors (Winton) and Fairbanks, Morse diesels were marvels of ruggedness and reliability. Pushed time and again in emergencies beyond their design limits, they made all else possible.

We did not have to innovate or make major redesign to the extent the Germans had to with their U-boats. By the summer of 1943 the U-boats were driven from the surface by the coordinated efforts of Allied air and surface forces using very short-wave radar, and the Germans were forced to adopt the snorkel. This was a tube projecting above the surface through which air was drawn to supply the diesel engines while running submerged at shallow depth. A shorter tube served to discharge exhaust gases just below the surface. The Dutch invented the snorkel and used it for battery charging and ventilation of the boat. It was in the spring of 1938 that I saw my first snorkel – in Pearl Harbor on board a Royal Netherlands navy sub of their O-class en route the Netherlands East Indies.

But the snorkel was not protection enough. Along with the introduction of pattern-running and acoustic-homing torpedoes, the Germans had to design boats of greater underwater speed and endurance. These were the Type XXI and Type XXIII. They had conventional diesel-electric propulsion, with snorkel, but emphasized streamlining and greatly enlarged electric storage battery capacity. They were ordered into production on a mass-produced, modular construction basis in July 1943, but the ships were not completed in time to get into combat.

Strenuous efforts were also made to introduce a closed-cycle (non-air-breathing) propulsion system that would eliminate the need for frequent contact with the atmosphere. This was the Walther system, in which hydrogen peroxide was used as the oxidant to burn fuel oil to produce steam for a turbine. Speeds up to twenty-five knots were possible, but the system's severe safety problems and limited endurance frustrated attainment of a useful ship. In the Atlantic the lesson was plain: ASW had made the surface untenable by submarine; in a future war they would need some way to remain submerged all or most of the time.[3]

Considering the success our boats were having, what were necessities for the German U-boats would have been costly, time-wasting mistakes for ours. We were able to concentrate on rapid buildup in numbers of our basic, well-designed fleet submarine. From January 1941 to December 1945, 214 boats were delivered. To achieve this, three additional shipbuilding yards were brought into submarine construction: Manitowoc Shipbuilding Company in Manitowoc, Wisconsin, Cramp Shipbuilding Company in Philadelphia, and the Boston Navy Yard. They joined the old-line submarine yards: Electric Boat Company in Groton, Connecticut, the Portsmouth Navy Yard in New Hampshire, and Mare Island Navy Yard in California.

Manitowoc and Boson had never before built submarines, and Cramp had built only one, *G-4*, in 1912. Manitowoc quickly gained a reputation for building splendid subs, but the boats delivered by Cramp were poorly regarded. Boston was brought into the picture late; her performance was disappointing, and none of her boats was completed in time to serve in the war.

We attained a building rate of nine boats per month, with construction times as short as seven months. But as our submarine campaign wound down, such a pace was not needed. As early as July 1944 a series of cancellations began. All told, the construction of ninety-six boats was canceled.

The foremost submarine material advance we made during the war was the increased operating depth built into the pressure hulls and hull components, commencing with *Balao* (SS 285). Built by Portsmouth Naval Shipyard to a test depth of four hundred feet, its 33 percent increase brought greater assurance of safety when going deep to avoid detection or evade counterattack.

It was commonly accepted that our "thin skin," three-hundred-foot, test-depth boats had a built-in 100 percent safety factor. Many skippers under stress of depth charge attack had voluntarily or otherwise taken their boats to depths far exceeding their design test depth. Admiral Lockwood was aware of this but never officially approved or disapproved the practice. He realized that, given the facts of their boats' construction characteristics, skippers were best left free to operate their boats as their tactical situation warranted.

Tang (SS 306) was built by Mare Island Naval Shipyard as a "thick skin," heavy-hull boat with a test depth of four hundred feet to the centerline of her pressure hull. During her postconstruction trial operations in November 1943, she easily reached that mark. Before leaving the West Coast for Pearl Harbor and war patrol, she deliberately dived to 612 feet and was probably first to thus certify an unofficial new test depth. The significance of the event, as expressed by her skipper, Lt. Comdr. Richard H. O'Kane, was that in subsequent deep excursions made for any reasons they could have "a confidence no submarine could have had before."

Early in the war our boats received an omnidirectional aircraft warning radar, designated "SD." It was not much good, and little relied on for fear it would be a beacon on which enemy planes could home. On the other hand, the surface-search radar, designated "SJ," first deployed in the summer of 1942, was excellent. It greatly extended target acquisition at night or in poor visibility and gave skippers new initiative in night surface attacks. And when the plan position indicator (PPI) scope was added we had a marvelous tool for surface action in a melee of ships or for navigation in confined waters. For submerged attacks, in late 1944 a night periscope with built-in radar, the "ST," was introduced to provide more accurate torpedo fire control.

A major improvement, introduced in new construction boats late in the war, was elimination of noisy, trouble-prone reduction gears and the substitution of slow-speed, direct-drive main motors.

Sonars, in both sonic and supersonic bands, were improved to some degree, chiefly in reliability and mode of presentation, but the vagaries of oceanic sound transmission kept them from being a major factor in attack. A short-range mine detector sonar, designated "QLA," using frequency modulation, was developed and used successfully to penetrate moored minefields.

A new torpedo, the wakeless, electric Mark XVIII, became the most popular weapon by war's end. A small electric acoustic-homing torpedo, the "cutie," was also developed as a means to counterattack small ASW vessels maneuvering overhead.

We had learned, through bitter experience, the truth of General De-Gaulle's statement, "The weapons which a military leader has at his disposal can never be too sharp or too reliable." The lesson was clear: From development to production to testing and support of weapons systems, there must be close effective liaison between the operating forces and their logistic support agencies.

Great as were the increase in numbers and the material improvements, the increase in individual ship performance was more striking. Most important, of course, was the submarine operational and attack competence gained through successful combat. Diffused throughout the submarine force was the cumulative experience of such aggressive, innovative skippers as Dealey, Morton, Ramage, Fluckey, and O'Kane. Morale of our crews, officers and enlisted men alike, was superb. However, in the euphoria of victory to which submarines had contributed so greatly, one aspect of our operations was largely overlooked. The skippers who were most successful were not reluctant to use their ships as submersible torpedo boats, attacking on the surface at night. This was possible because of the technical shortcomings of Japanese ASW, both air and surface, and ineptness in its application.

Thus, we came out of the war with a nagging question: Against a first-rate opponent, one with the technical and operational competence such as the British and U.S. navies had attained, would our boats and personnel be equal to the task? Even more fundamental was the question of whether, in the reshaped power balance of the world and the apparent supremacy of air power, our submarines could make a meaningful contribution to our naval power.

12

LET-DOWN

In 1944 President Roosevelt chose Sen. Harry S Truman to be his running mate in his unprecedented bid for a fourth term. The senator had achieved favorable attention as the watchdog of defense spending. He had established and chaired a committee to investigate fraud, waste, and abuse in every aspect of the military budget. This experience hardened the former captain of field artillery in his freely expressed denigration of most admirals and generals and in his emphasis on reduction of the defense budget.

When Truman succeeded to the presidency in April 1945, after only three months as vice president, World War II was as good as won. Within a month Germany surrendered unconditionally, and, in the Pacific, Japan's days were clearly numbered. The new commander-in-chief presided over the mightiest naval force the world had ever known. From Pearl Harbor to V-J Day, the increase in the number of the fleet's combat ships had been phenomenal:

7 Dec. 1941		14 Aug. 1945
17	Battleships	23
7	Carriers, fleet	28
1	Carrier, escort	71
37	Cruisers	72
171	Destroyers	377
	Frigates	361
112	Submarines	232
135	Mine warfare ships	586
100	Patrol craft	1204
	Amphibious craft	2116
580	Total	6626

Planning for the postwar Navy called for two fleets, one in the Pacific and one in the Atlantic, each with a "ready reserve" fleet capable of swift activation.[1] The active fleets were to be (in addition to various amphibious and auxiliary ships):

U.S. Pacific Fleet (Adm. Raymond A. Spruance)		U.S. Atlantic Fleet (Adm. Jonas H. Ingram)
2	Battleships	2
9	Carriers, fleet	4
9	Carriers, escort	4
20	Cruisers	8
81	Destroyers	54
16	Destroyer escorts	20
39	Submarines	51

This approximate composition of the Navy was reached by July 1947, a reduction of ships from their peak of 6626 to 842.

Political pressure to "get the boys home by Christmas," and the eagerness to resume civilian careers by the personnel who had so rapidly and efficiently augmented the Navy, hastened demobilization in 1945. As a first step for submariners, the boats were quickly divided between the Atlantic and the Pacific submarine forces and assigned ports for leave and recreation while postwar planning continued. My task group, shepherded by its tender *Orion*, proceeded to Tompkinsville, Staten Island, New York. It was an eleven-thousand-mile voyage from Saipan via Pearl Harbor and Panama.

ComSubLant was Rear Adm. Charles W. (Gin) Styer. He had been my squadron commander, headquartered on board the sub tender *Sperry* at Midway Island. Now I joined his staff in New London as personnel officer of a force whose active ships included 54 U.S. submarines, 4 surrendered German U-boats, 4 submarine tenders, and 7 submarine rescue vessels. There were three sub bases in SubLant: the major one at New London, and two others at Balboa in the Canal Zone and at Key West, with a minor shore facility at St. Thomas in the Virgin Islands. By this time the O-, R-, and S-boats that had been pressed into wartime service were all in the process of disposal.

In early 1946 Admiral Nimitz relieved Admiral King as the first postwar chief of naval operations, and King's collateral position of CominCh was discontinued. Because of the near-decisive part German and U.S. submarines had played in the war, and foreseeing the even graver threat of more advanced submarines, Nimitz established the new position of coordinator of undersea warfare (OP 31) on his staff. The flag officer assigned to this billet was limited to a staff of three and would have to oversee both pro- and antisubmarine aspects of undersea warfare. The complexities of each, and their rapidly advancing technology, would justify two separate flag billets, but at least it was a start toward rationalizing the emergency ASW organization that Admiral King had used. Rear Admiral Styer was designated to be the first incumbent of the anomalous position, and in 1946 he reluctantly gave up the foremost submarine operational command to be submerged in the morass of Washington bureaucracy.

"It was the best of times; it was the worst of times" – peacetime, but a time of turmoil for the fleet. When the war ended, the Navy had on active duty 317,000 officers and about 3 million enlisted personnel. To carry out its peacetime mission it planned a force of 52,000 officers and 500,000 enlisted. Appropriations for pay and subsistence were granted for that size force. However, that goal could not be reached in orderly fashion by July 1946, and, to keep within budgetary limits, personnel strength had to be further reduced to 437,000. Demobilization and release of personnel continued unabated throughout 1946, creating a serious imbalance between numbers of ships and their required complements. The surface Navy was particularly hard-hit. Critical shortages, especially in the technical ratings, were so acute in all types of surface ships that barely 70 percent of the Atlantic Fleet's active ships could get underway.

On the other hand, the 50 percent extra pay for hazardous duty and the traditional esprit de corps of the submarine service helped keep our experienced men on board (Appendix B). We were soon the best-manned force in the fleet when it came to qualified technicians. Equally soon, we were being levied upon to provide electrician's mates, motor machinist's mates, radiomen, sonarmen, fire control technicians, and the like to augment the surface Navy's depleted ranks.

It was a trying task to lay quotas as equitably as possible on our squadrons for the transfer of the technical ratings the Commander-in-Chief Atlantic Fleet (CinCLantFlt) called for. It was my sad duty to transfer dedicated volunteer submariners, men who had fought a particularly hazardous war, to duty they didn't want and that would cost them their submarine pay, with consequent impact on family living standards.[2] When many men chose a return to civilian life rather than transfer, thereby compounding our problem, the Navy lost skilled sailors it might otherwise have kept. As my assistant Lt. William M. Calkins, a former enlisted man, would say, "Personnel officers have more fun than people."

When it appeared that loss of key personnel was affecting our submarines' operations to the point that safety might be jeopardized, ComSubLant agreed it was time to present our case to CinCLantFlt. Rear Adm. John Wilkes had relieved his cousin, Gin Styer, as ComSubLant, and his chief of staff was Capt. Chester C. Smith, the quiet, workmanlike submariner who was the first U.S. skipper to sink a Japanese ship. On December 16, 1941, his *Swordfish* sank *Atsutasan Maru* off Hainan Island.

Taking advantage of the fleet flagship *Pocono*'s visit to Boston in the fall of 1946, Chester and I drove there armed with all pertinent personnel statistics. The commander-in-chief was the wizened, ailing Adm. Marc Mitscher of Pacific naval air battle fame, but our conference was with his robust, dynamic chief of staff, Commodore Arleigh Burke.

During the war Arleigh Burke had commanded Destroyer Squadron 23, a group of eight modern destroyers, and had been given the sobriquet "Thirty-one-knot Burke." Generally taken to mean that Burke did everything at full speed, under forced draft, the nickname was actually an ironic reference to the time his squadron was proceeding to a combat station at only thirty-one knots instead of its full thirty-four-knot potential, one of his ships having suffered an engineering casualty. At any rate, under his driving, demanding leadership, DesRon 23 had become the most combat-ready, most attack-minded destroyer outfit in the Navy.

From his brilliant leadership of a front-line combat command, Burke was ordered to be chief of staff to Vice Admiral Mitscher, commander of Task Force 58, the aggregation of four fast carrier task groups that had been built into the Navy's overwhelming knockout punch in the Pacific. When operating under Adm. Raymond A. Spruance in the Fifth Fleet it was TF 58; when under Adm. William F. Halsey in the Third Fleet, the same ships were TF 38.

Embarked in the flagship, the carrier *Lexington,* Burke developed the operation orders and coordinated the battle tactics of the mighty force as it took part in the Battle for Leyte Gulf. It was TF 38 that harried the Japanese fleet off Cape Engaño and drove remnants of its Northern Force toward ambush by our submarines, my own *Halibut* among them. Planes from *Lexington* were among those whose voice transmissions *Halibut* overheard and which we saw going into their bombing attacks preceding our torpedo attack.

The war over, Arleigh Burke was once again chief of staff to the taciturn Marc Mitscher, now Commander-in-Chief Atlantic Fleet. As I followed Chester Smith up the brow to the quarterdeck of *Pocono* in Boston Harbor, I reflected that this was not the first time my actions were being influenced by Thirty-one-knot Burke. I was eager to meet the man who, while still a captain, had become a legend in our Navy for his destroyer battle exploits and relentless drive for perfection in every facet of naval performance. We knew Arleigh's first love was destroyers, a passion all seamen could understand and respect. Then came his great admiration for naval aviation, for its immense contributions to the defeat of Japan in operations he had helped plan and direct. He had had no close contact with our submarine force, and as representatives of that small fraction of the Navy – a force with an uncertain future – we felt like supplicants before the throne.

Led to the chief of staff's cabin by a Marine orderly, Chester and I were greeted courteously but, I felt, a bit aloofly. As I shook hands I was struck by the remarkably youthful, unlined face, the direct gaze of searching blue eyes, and the aura of vitality and energy from the broad-beamed, rather stocky figure that would never be chosen if the problem were to display a uniform smartly. Arleigh Burke's clothes rumpled as easily as his hair tousled, but his mind worked precisely. He was a rather halting speaker, his thought seeming to outrun his command of rhetoric.

Following our statement of our problem, the commodore's questions were pointed, and his review of the fleet situation broad-ranging. In a few years I would have many occasions to meet with Thirty-one-knot Burke in the Pentagon, but this was a useful initiation. My peroration amounted to this: Isn't it better to have at least one element of the fleet efficiently manned than to have all reduced to a least common denominator?

The great sailor eyed me frostily, removed his worn briar pipe from between strong teeth, and said, "That may seem sound from where you sit, young man, but not from the viewpoint of the fleet."

As we drove home, tails between our legs, the only comfort we had was assurance that any case well founded on safety would be carefully considered. Our scrambling continued as we sought to get adequate number of volunteers into Sub School, to keep the pipelines to and from advanced technical school filled, and to distribute shortages fairly.

My task was made no easier when our colleagues in the Pacific Fleet complained, alleging that we were skimming the cream of the crop from Sub School graduates. My friend Lawson P. (Red) Ramage was ComSubPac's personnel officer. He was the first living submariner to win the Congressional Medal of Honor during the war when in command of *Parche* (SS 384). Red never left you in doubt about his feelings, so it took a conference at Mare Island to reestablish our good standing.

By this time, the shortcomings of New London as our primary submarine training site were even more apparent than they had been during my Sub School days. Boats were diving deeper and running faster; surface traffic was greater; weather conditions were as bad as ever. We looked longingly to other locations in the South and to St. Thomas in the Virgin Islands. Unfortunately, because of the major political implications and the huge capital investment required, the idea of relocation had to be dropped. Before long, the advent of nuclear-powered subs and ballistic missiles, requiring still more urgent investment in the sub base at New London, ruled out relocation for good.

John Wilkes, who had relieved Styer as ComSubLant, was himself relieved by Rear Adm. James Fife. When Wilkes was Commander Submarines Asiatic Fleet in 1941, Jimmy Fife had been his chief of staff when the Japanese attacked. Each of these flag officers had his distinctive style of command. Gin Styer was personable and affable. He inspired loyalty and best efforts. John Wilkes, the tough descendant of our early naval explorer Lt. Charles Wilkes, delegated authority freely, demanded performance, and went to bat forcefully for his subordinates when necessary. Jimmy Fife was a difficult person to work for. He involved himself in details to an unusual degree and left little room for subordinates' initiative. Hard-working and intensely dedicated to his profession, he had sacrificed his own family life and left no doubt that, in his book, family life and a successful naval career were not compatible. Not averse to liquor in his early days on the China station, he had become an austere, teetotaling taskmaster. A discolored blotch on his close-cropped head had given him, when out of earshot, the nickname "Hardpatch." Rumor said it was caused when a periscope lowered on him, but years later I would learn from his brother that it was merely a birthmark.

While England still fought alone, Commander Fife had been sent as a naval observer to the British submarine force. His task was to acquire firsthand experience of war operations. This he did in his usual precise and detailed fashion. His observations, based on actual war patrols in the Atlantic and Mediterranean, were valuable to our own yet-untested skippers. This experience, and the daring operations of British boats that came under his command in SubSoWesPac, made Fife an Anglophile. To the amused but guarded annoyance of his staff, he even adopted the accent on the second syllable, sub-*mar*-in-er, rather than the third. To resolve the good-natured impasse, I jokingly suggested to Admiral Fife that the best word to use would be "submarinist," thereby connoting expertise in a specialty.

"Humph. I don't like it," he snorted.

And because the boss didn't buy it, the word never did fly; it took a dive.

Unlike John Wilkes, who took the staff he acquired with the job, Jimmy Fife recast his staff, as he had every right to do. He brought on board officers who had worked for him before and whom, by his count, he was now rewarding. To some this proved a mixed blessing; an unusual number of outstanding officers, evaluated throughout the submarine service as almost certain of selection for flag rank, men like Chester Smith and Karl Hensel, each of whom had been Jimmy's chief of staff, were not selected to be rear admiral.

My own time for a change of duty was near, so I was not distressed to learn I was being ordered to the sub tender *Proteus* as executive officer. This would mean the loss of submarine pay, which our family had enjoyed for eleven years, but it would bring me some useful diversification. My relief as personnel officer would be burly, likable John C. (Jack) Martin, teased throughout the submarine force as one who commanded a boat named in his own image: *Hammerhead.* A large, jovial man, Jack fought well in the Southwest Pacific.

My satisfaction with the new assignment was short-lived. Even before I was detached from the ComSubLant staff came word that *Proteus* would be inactivated. Successive reductions in the defense budget forced progressive changes in the composition of the fleet. *Proteus* and more submarines would have to join the group already moored "in reserve" in New London. This pleased me not at all; I viewed the brief inactivation period as simply marking time.

Just at that time I flew to Washington with Admiral Fife and asked his permission to talk with the Bureau of Naval Personnel about changing my orders. I reasoned that the experienced exec on board could do a better job of inactivation, and that there would be benefit in sending me directly to another sea billet. Reflecting on my views as our DC-3 headed out over the Atlantic, Jimmy at length said, "You can never make a mistake by carrying out your orders."

He was telling me that it was not a particular assignment that mattered; it was what one did with it that counted. I took the advice. Never again did I protest what came. And perhaps that helped in the cordial relations I always had with Jimmy, even when, as vice admiral in the Pentagon and in charge of fleet operations and readiness, he was again my demanding taskmaster.

WHERE DO WE GO FROM HERE?

The early postwar years were a trying time for the Navy. Soviet Russia was becoming increasingly hostile, but Navy strategic planners could make no convincing case for the need for naval strike forces in a possible war with the U.S.S.R. Dramatic, effective, and essential as naval operations had been in the Pacific War, the nature of that arena, and Japan's near-total dependence on overseas transport, would have no counterparts with respect to Russia.

The prospect for our submarine force was particularly bleak. What was its future? Was there a potential enemy for whose defeat submarines would be needed or useful? Our most likely opponent was a land power not dependent on overseas transport.

The Soviet navy was engaged in a massive submarine building program, which she knew was the quickest, cheapest way to counter our naval supremacy. Could we design and equip submarines to be effective in antisubmarine operations? What tactics would we use? There were other questions. Could our boats survive in an era of steadily improving, more sophisticated ASW? Were there other missions or tasks our boats could perform? What weapons would they need?

The Submarine Conference declared that our fleet submarine had become obsolete to a greater degree than any other type ship, and the General Board, with the strong support of Fleet Admiral Nimitz, had recommended to Navy Secretary James V. Forrestal "taking earliest possible advantage of developments of atomic energy for application to submarine main propulsion."[1]

Our World War II subs were built for long-distance surface cruising and could be described as torpedo boats capable of short periods of submerged operation. What we had to strive for in our postwar designs was greatly improved submerged performance as we worked toward the "true" submarine, one that was nuclear-powered and capable of 100 percent submerged operation. This was expected to take ten years. For the interim, the conference chaired by Admiral Styer recommended a program that was approved by the chief of naval operations, Fleet Admiral Nimitz, "as a policy for the guidance of the Navy in planning for submarines."

During the war, submarines were called upon to perform many special tasks for which they were not designed. Drawing on that successful experience, the conference recommended such a variety of projects that it was apparent that the submarine force was groping for a mission. In addition to an orderly replacement program of six new, improved attack submarines a year, it proposed increasing the effectiveness of existing fleet boats by giving them greater submerged speed and endurance through higher-capacity storage batteries and streamlining. (The acronym for this project was GUPPY, for *Greater Underwater Propulsive Power.*) They would have much greater battery power in the existing spaces. In a lead-acid cell this can be achieved only by exposing more lead to the action of the electrolyte, hence requiring more but thinner plates. Instead of lasting six years, such a battery required costly replacement every two years.

Then came an interesting mix of realism and wishful thinking in the proposal for design studies or actual conversions of fleet boats for specialized tasks:

Type	Designation	Function
Picket	SSR	Radar warning and fighter direction
Bombardment	SSB	Gunfire attack
Troop carrier	SSP	Troop transport
Cargo carrier	SSA	Transport material
Antisub	SS-AS	Detect and attack subs (later SSK)
Super picket	SS-R	Anti-guided missiles
Carrier	SSV	Operate suitable aircraft
Super bombardment	SSSB	Guided missile attack (later SSG)
Tanker	SSO	Refuel seaplanes
Minelayer	SSM	Covert minelayer
Ammunition	SSE	Transport ammunition
Assault	SSPA	Deliver Marine assault troops
Service	SSS	Resupply subs on station

Over the next few years the following conversions were made in various numbers and operated successfully: SSR, SSP, SSA, SSK, SSG, and SSO. In addition, several boats were converted to auxiliary status for underwater research and test purposes.

The SSO was *Guavina,* called the "pregnant whale" because of her distended ballast and fuel tanks. She was to deliver fuel to combat beachheads. Later she was further modified to be part of a new weapon system. She was to refuel and give limited support to seaplanes, in effect being a mobile, clandestine air base. The P6M Seamaster, a large, heavy-hull, four-jet seaplane minelayer, was expected to be her chief customer. (The Air Force also expressed some interest in *Guavina* as a possible way to resupply an ice-island station in the Arctic.) Designed to fly at 600 miles per hour and to carry a 30,000-pound payload, Seamaster made its first flight in July 1955. After it exploded in midair in December, the project was abandoned.

Of the 52 boats receiving all or part of the GUPPY conversion, 16 of them had one engine removed to make space for an improved sonar room. The rationale was that the new primary target was the enemy submarine, and efficient sonar was more important than high surface speed.

Pickerel (SS 524) was one of the full GUPPPYs. Under her innovative, daring skipper, Comdr. Paul R. Schratz, she demonstrated the ultimate performance of the snorkel. She was the first GUPPY to be deployed to the Far East, and in returning to Pearl Harbor from Hong Kong she snorkeled all the way, 5194 miles in 505 hours. Although this was only a peace-time exercise, it was a remarkable feat of submarining. It required careful planning, superb engine operation and maintenance, and great physical stamina and determination. Her twenty-one days continuously submerged in 1950 remained a record until 1958, when nuclear-powered *Seawolf* made her sixty-day test.

Ingenuity and humor, two attributes of successful submariners, were not lacking in *Pickerel*. In his report, Paul Schratz said, "The most accurate and reliable vacuum indicator aboard is almost too homely for mention in an official report. To alert the maneuvering room controllerman to stand by to pull clear when the head valve is cycled, the electricians placed a red-painted condom over the mouth of a bottle. As soon as the vacuum increased, the condom stands up rigid, pointing a lurid finger of caution at the controllerman."

Because of the high life-cycle cost of the GUPPYs, 19 fleet boats were given a lesser conversion, called "fleet snorkel," involving chiefly a snorkel and some streamlining. But a better indication of our submarine's progress toward new capabilities and greater worth to the fleet is shown in the new construction projects undertaken in the postwar years and culminating in the world's first "true submarine."

The following ships were built from the resumption of submarine construction in 1949 until 1957 and the decision to build only nuclear-powered submarines thereafter:

No.	Type	Designation	Function
7	Fast attack	SS	Attack surface ships
3	Hunter-killer	SSK	Detect and attack subs
2	Target and training	SST	Low-cost target and training
1	Midget	X-1	Penetrate harbors
1	Test submarine	AGSS	Hydrodynamic research
1	Deep diving	AGSS	Deep research
2	Radar picket	SSR	Warning and fighter direction
2	Guided missile	SSG	Attack with Regulus missile
3	Attack, single screw	SS	Attack surface ships
2	Nuclear-powered	SSN	Attack surface and submarine targets

The fast attack boats were designed to make twenty knots submerged, albeit briefly, but couldn't quite reach that speed. They were somewhat larger than the fleet boats of wartime, but were deeper-diving and snorkel-equipped. They represented the highest state of the art in U.S. submarine design, incorporating lessons learned in our war operations, as well as those culled from the German U-boats acquired after their surrender. The two Type XXI boats, *U-2513* and *U-3008*, which we operated were at that time the most technically advanced submarines in the world.

As in the prewar search for an efficient fleet sub, success of the fast attack class would depend on the diesel engine. General Motors thought it had the answer in its compact "pancake" design – four banks of four radial cylinders stacked around a vertical crankshaft. Each ship required four engines. Hedging its bet on the unproved design, the Bureau of Ships (BuShips) put the General Motors engine into the first four ships of the class, but the last three got conventional in-line Fairbanks, Morse engines.

Tang (SS 563), lead ship of the class, was launched at Portsmouth, New Hampshire, in June 1951, four days after *Trigger* (SS 564) had been launched at Groton, Connecticut. At the time, on my first tour of shore duty, I was in the Pentagon as Head, Submarine Section, Fleet Maintenance.

Command of the long-awaited, exciting new attack submarines was eagerly sought, and two of our most forward-thinking, dynamic young submariners were assigned to them. Ordered as skipper of *Tang* was Comdr. Enders P. Huey, a slow-speaking, no-nonsense Texan. The captain of *Trigger* was Comdr. Edward L. Beach, the brainy, articulate son of another accomplished naval officer. Both Huey and Beach had much combat experience as junior officers in submarine war patrols in the Pacific. Their executive officers were also hand-picked, Lt. Comdr. William R. Anderson for *Tang* and Lt. Comdr. Harold E. Shear for *Trigger*.

There was friendly rivalry between the fast-maturing crews of the two ships, which were being built a hundred miles apart on the New England coast. Each wanted to be first to dive its ship to the new test depth, which would be a record for U.S. submarines. Charged with monitoring construction programs, it was my responsibility to choose between them.

One of the chief satisfactions of my job was the opportunity to escape from Washington and embark in newly completed submarines to witness performance of ship and crew. But in this instance, which ship should it be? It was a difficult choice – one ship built in a government shipyard, one in a private yard, both with superb skippers and excellent crews, all vying for a historic "first." Considering all factors, the chief difference being the somewhat more deliberate training period her building schedule had permitted, I approved *Tang*'s request to go first.

Portsmouth, our oldest navy yard, lay on the rocky shore of the Pis-cataqua River, where its cold waters fed the foggy Atlantic. It was a place full of meaning for submariners. Since 1916 the yard had specialized in the construction and repair of submarines. *Halibut* had been built there, and I felt a special bond to the men of that yard as I recalled *Halibut*'s last war patrol. *Argonaut,* my clumsy, cranky home for four years, was also a product of the yard. Other memories lay off-shore. Near the Isle of Shoals was the swept area for conducting the deep dives that followed comple-tion of construction, conversion, or overhaul. Here it was that *Squalus* sank in 1939. And it was off the Isle of Shoals that another deep dive end-ed in disaster; *o-9,* recommissioned for use as a training ship as we pre-pared for war, was lost with all hands in 1941.

These memories lurked in my mind as, early in the cold, dark morn-ing of April 30, 1952, we backed into the swift, icy currents of the river and stood out to rendezvous with our escort, the submarine rescue vessel *Greenlet.* It would be her job to keep the surface of our deep-dive area clear of shipping and to monitor our descent, maintaining contact by sonar and underwater telephone as we carried out the deliberate, step-by-step op-eration. We would level off at successively deeper depths to make careful inspections of hull fittings, operate pumps and equipment, and take read-ings of the compression of the hull.

Under Captain Huey's cool, sure direction all went according to plan. Without serious incident we reached the goal of our dive, a depth of 713 feet. When *Tang* leveled off there, the repetitious ping of her fathometer told us how much water lay beneath us. Her hull was squeezed by the enormous pressure of all the sea above, 313 pounds pressing inward on each square inch of her skin, or 23 tons on each square foot! After completing our mea-surements and testing pumps and components, we began our slow ascent, retaking compression measurements as we rose. We had made a record dive; the operating depth of the new class submarine was proven.

The increase in operating depth was a major advance for our boats, but once again the main engines proved inadequate. The high-speed, light-weight General Motor diesels were extremely noisy, so deafening in the steel chamber of the engine room that personnel could suffer harm. Special silencing measures were taken, including booths and ear protec-tion for the enginemen. More important, however, the engines were un-reliable, requiring constant attention and repair. In time, all had to be replaced by the less sophisticated Fairbanks, Morse engines. To do that was a major, costly job that required lengthening the ships nine feet.

*   *   *   *

Even as Portsmouth Navy Yard added to its historic record of U.S. submarine progress, it sheltered an earlier history. Moored in the yard was *U-505*, a Type IXc boat, Germany's most successful class of submarines. She was 252 feet long, 1120 tons displacement, a size Admiral Doenitz considered a "big" submarine.

U-505 had been detected and attacked by a U.S. antisubmarine task group in the North Atlantic in June 1944. Forced to the surface, she was abandoned by her crew after they took measures to scuttle her. Quick action by a boarding party from USS *Guadalcanal*, the light carrier in the ASW group, kept the boat from sinking, and she was towed to port. She was the only enemy warship that the United States had captured on the high seas since the War of 1812 against Britain.

Commander of the task group who engineered the capture was Capt. Daniel V. Gallery. He was determined that the historic prize be preserved and displayed for all time in his home city of Chicago. After the war, he lobbied tirelessly to that effect, both in the Navy Department and in the Congress. My desk in OpNav had cognizance of the material condition of the inactive subs in the reserve fleet and of those awaiting disposal. Inspection of *U-505* showed what sorry state she was in. Used during the war on a tour to promote the sale of U.S. war bonds, she had then been laid up and received only enough care to keep her from sinking at her pier. Her topside was battered and rusted; inside she was a dank, corroded hulk. Souvenir hunters had stripped her of many artifacts; missing were many gauges, handwheels, label plates, and sections of pipe. She was so decrepit, and would cost so much to refurbish, that I recommended to my boss, Vice Admiral Francis S. Low, that the transfer to Chicago be disapproved and the ship disposed of. Once initial enthusiasm had waned, I feared that nongovernment funds would not be forthcoming to keep *U-505* presentable as an authentic prize of war, safe for hordes of curious visitors. Before long she would reflect no credit on the U.S. Navy or on the brave men who had fought and nearly died in her.

I was wrong. I underestimated Dan Gallery's determination and thorough planning, which were fortified by the ample political savvy of his two brothers, one a priest, the other a fire chief in Chicago. And "Frog" Low, who had been so instrumental in the war against the U-boats, probably viewed *U-505* as a suitable memorial to the enormously difficult and costly effort required to defeat them.

Today *U-505* is a splendid, carefully restored, well-kept exhibit in the Museum of Science and Industry in Chicago. Far from the sea that she and her sisters came perilously close to dominating, she is one of the museum's major attractions, a tribute to the men who captured her and a mute reminder of blind combat beneath the seas in aptly named "iron coffins."

* * * *

The hunter-killers (SSK) were boats of 765 tons, designed specifically for detecting and destroying enemy subs. There was great difference of opinion, even among submariners, over whether submarines could be used effectively in an antisubmarine role. Out of approximately one hundred attacks they made on Japanese submarines, our boats were credited with sinking twenty-four. In every case but one, the target was proceeding on the surface, so the attacks were virtually no different from those on surface ships. When our submarine *Tautog*, on the surface, did torpedo and sink the submerged Japanese *RO-30*, it was a lucky, one-in-a-million affair. A single torpedo, fired in desperation in the direction of *RO-30*'s periscope, had scored a hit.

The chief proponent of SSKs was the strong-willed but innovative Rear Adm. Charles B. (Swede) Momsen, inventor of the Momsen Lung, the emergency breathing device used for escape from a sunken sub. He had not commanded a submarine during the war but had been in charge of our first wolf pack. Following postwar command of the battleship *South Dakota*, he moved to the Pentagon to relieve Gin Styer as coordinator of undersea warfare. That position, with its dual responsibilities, gave him an influential voice in shaping a concept that seemed to promote both submarine and antisubmarine readiness. Momsen believed that large numbers of single-purpose submarines deployed across enemy transit routes could be an effective counter to the rapidly growing Soviet submarine force. At a time of great fiscal austerity, the concept of simpler, cheaper submarines that could be mass produced was very appealing – assuming that they worked as advertised.

The target and training submarines (SST) were also controversial. They displaced 310 tons and had a crew of only 2 officers and 12 men. They were planned to be low-cost in production and economical in operation for both submarine training and antisubmarine target purposes. Obviously, they could not be very realistic simulators of Soviet high-seas submarines. We got what we paid for – cheap boats and inadequate performance – but they served loyally for twenty years.

The midget submarine (X-1) was a submersible craft of 28 tons, less than half the size of *Holland,* our first submarine. She was a copy of British X-craft, which had been successfully used against the German battleship *Tirpitz* in her Norwegian fjord hideout and against the Japanese heavy cruiser *Takao* at Singapore. The Italians, Japanese, and Germans had also used midget subs during the war, and there had been comments by Admiral King and his CominCh staff that we should do the same. Admiral Lockwood had fought off the idea as not pertinent to our strategy. In every case, the foreign midgets had been built and trained to penetrate specific harbors at relatively short range. We had no such need. Now, however, with Vice Admiral Fife shaping our shipbuilding program, the idea was revived, partly because British X-craft had performed heroically for him during his command of Submarines, Southwest Pacific. When I asked the admiral why we didn't just lease or buy one from the British, he replied that we had to acquire the know-how to build them on our own.

Next to the nuclear-powered ships, *Albacore* (AGSS) was the most significant of the early postwar submarine designs. Displacing 1250 tons and 210 feet long, her length-to-beam ratio of 7.4 was close to the ideal for a totally immersed vehicle. Our wartime fleet boats, built for much surface operation, had a ratio of 11.5 to 1 and were propelled by twin screws. *Albacore* had a clean, streamlined hull of circular cross section, which tapered to her single-propulsion propeller. Naturally enough, her form and proportions were those of an inverted blimp, both vehicles being designed to operate fully enveloped by a fluid medium. The ship had been proposed by the Bureau of Ships as a high-speed, battery-powered, hydrodynamic test vehicle with no military characteristics. Able to make 30 knots submerged, she was the world's fastest sub. She was needed to provide construction and operational experience for future attack submarines, no matter what would be their form of propulsion power. Through subsequent modifications of her propulsion and diving control systems she added greatly to our knowledge of high-speed, submerged maneuvering problems.

The radar pickets (SSR) were designed to support carrier task forces by deploying in advance and providing early warning from their high-powered air-search radars. The sea-air battles of World War II, notably that off Okinawa, had shown the importance of a distant radar screen around our carriers and other task forces, both for detection of enemy aircraft and to assist in direction of our own fighters. The first ships cast in this almost sacrificial role were destroyers, those indispensable jacks-of-all-trades, but their vulnerability to airplane and kamikaze attack forced consideration of other platforms for the special radars required. Before the end of the war some submarines had been fitted out as improved radar picket-fighter directors. Their stealth of deployment and ability to lurk concealed, awaiting need, did give a measure of security that surface pickets lacked.

The guided missile subs, *Grayback* and *Growler* (SSG), were launch and control platforms for Regulus II, the supersonic-speed, surface-to-surface cruise missile. (A cruise missile is an air-breathing missile, as differentiated from a ballistic missile, and is basically an unmanned jet aircraft.) Both ships had been designed as attack boats but modified during construction by insertion of a 42-foot section of hull in which to carry 4 Regulus I's or 2 Regulus II's. We had previously converted two fleet boats, *Tunny* and *Barbero,* to carry 2 Regulus I subsonic missiles in a topside hangar. All four boats had to surface to launch their missiles. Their ability to deliver nuclear warheads to ranges of 500 miles made the submarine a valuable surreptitious supplement to the aircraft delivery systems in both Navy and Air Force. The submarine system quickly gained support in the Congress and the media.

The three attack submarines, *Barbel, Blueback,* and *Bonefish* (SS), were the last diesel-powered boats we would build, save for the deep-diving research submarine *Dolphin.* They were the first application of the *Albacore* hull form and single screw to combatant ships.

There was lively debate in the Ship Characteristics Board (SCB) and in less formal submarine councils over the wisdom of doing this. In war with Japan, our boats had generally operated alone, close to enemy shores, remote from any assistance. Some skippers who had experienced heavy counterattacks on their lonely patrols were reluctant to give up the second screw. My own boat, *Halibut,* had received extensive depth charge damage, but I knew of no case when a boat owed its safe return to having twin props. The speed and submerged maneuver advantages of the *Albacore* design were so great that they would greatly benefit attack boats.

There was similar debate as to the wisdom of removing topside gun armament. The 4" or 5" guns mounted on our World War II boats had been used successfully in surface attacks against small, lightly armed picket boats and sampans. They were also the last resort in defense for a disabled boat, as in the case of *Sculpin*'s loss to a Japanese destroyer. In my own boat, I had been cautious in use of our 4" gun. We shelled an isolated shore facility on one occasion and attacked sampans on two others. With three of our crew wounded by return fire, it was clear that a submarine on the surface, except in special situations, is simply too vulnerable to make the use of its gun a reasonable risk. At any rate, the single-screw, cleanly streamlined attack boats could make more than 30 knots submerged, and they operated very successfully for many years. However, by the time they went to sea in 1959, *Nautilus* and *Seawolf* had demonstrated the overwhelming advantages of nuclear propulsion.

In this period of experimentation and uncertainty over our submarines' military worth, it was recognized that operations in the Arctic Ocean might become necessary. Aircraft were already overflying it; ballistic missiles would not be far behind. Submarines might be the only way to maintain a presence there for early warning, for rescue or research, or to cope with enemy subs that might seek sanctuary immune from aircraft and surface ship attack.

With depths up to 17,000 feet, this fourth-largest ocean area separates the northern margins of Russia from Alaska, Canada, and Greenland, being, in effect, a "Mediterranean Sea" of its own. It is covered not by icebergs but by sea ice, which is relatively thin. It is impossible for sea water to freeze to thickness greater than about twenty-four feet, a thickness that can be penetrated by explosives or other means to create a lake in which a submarine can surface. However, there are also numerous open leads and polynyas in Arctic waters that exist naturally and can be readily located. From summertime flights due north from Point Barrow we learned that the greatest distance between openings in the ice was forty-two miles and the average only fourteen. Even so, the very limited endurance and relatively fragile superstructure of the diesel-powered submarines we sent to learn more of Arctic Ocean operations could do little more than probe its margins. To make proper use of it we would need the unlimited endurance of nuclear power and greatly improved, self-contained navigation systems.

Even before the war and the top-secret, top-priority project to apply the power of atomic fission to bombs, some scientists had foreseen its eventual application to other uses. In 1939 Dr. Ross Gunn of the Naval Research Laboratory had speculated on the use of atomic power for submarines. He induced Dr. Philip H. Abelson, a research scientist engaged in studies of uranium and its isotopes, to work at the lab. After the war Abelson concentrated on the application of atomic energy to propulsion rather than to explosion. In 1946 he put forward a report detailing his concept of a nuclear-powered submarine. He believed that a nuclear submarine could be built in two years, given the highest priority and adequate funds. Other distinguished scientists agreed that the concept of a nuclear-powered submarine was feasible. But few, if any, emphasized the essential realities of material and engineering development, safety engineering, and production controls, all of which needed the practical disciplines and firm management of tough-minded engineers, other highly skilled professionals, and men who understood the hostile environment of the sea and combatant ship operations.

Also in 1946, BuShips formalized its liaison with the Manhattan Engineer District (developer of the A-bomb) and its successor, the Atomic Energy Commission (AEC), in order to keep abreast of atomic energy developments for possible ship propulsion. A team of five officers and three civilian engineers was sent to the Manhattan Project in Oak Ridge, Tennessee. Their mission was to learn all they could of nuclear technology, with a view to its application to Navy requirements.

Rear Adm. Earle W. Mills, Deputy Chief of BuShips (later chief of BuShips with the rank of vice admiral), had long foreseen the potential value of nuclear propulsion to the Navy, especially in submarines. He recalled Capt. Hyman G. Rickover from his postwar administrative assignment in the Pacific Reserve Fleet and designated him to lead the Oak Ridge team in spite of strong opposition to his choice on the part of the upper echelon of BuShips officers. They feared that Rickover would create an empire of his own, and that the bureau's normal methods of handling an important new development would be bypassed. How right they were!

Well aware of Rickover's abrasive style and controversial character, Mills persisted in his choice. He was confident that Rickover was the man who would most quickly and thoroughly develop the information and knowledge that the Navy needed.

When Rickover completed his assignment in Oak Ridge and returned to Washington in 1947, there was no place for him to go. The responsibility for nuclear power development in BuShips, with the title "coordinator of nuclear matters," rested in Capt. Armand Morgan, with another brilliant engineering duty officer (EDO), Capt. Alfred G. Mumma, as his deputy.

There being no Navy nuclear-power project in which to exploit Rickover's brand of hard-driving, impatient management, Mills designated him his special assistant for nuclear matters. The newly established AEC had statutory responsibility for all nuclear-related development programs, but it showed little interest in a reactor for submarine propulsion. Its programs were guided by physicists who were chiefly interested in studies and analyses of alternative approaches to nuclear reactors. They did not understand the urgency of the Navy's need for a submarine propulsion reactor, nor did they share Rickover's view that enough was already known to justify proceeding with engineering development. When Mills and Rickover prodded the AEC into accepting the Navy's need for a submarine reactor, the Nuclear Power Branch of BuShips was established in 1948, with Rickover as its chief.

Rickover occasionally briefed the Submarine Conference about progress being made. At these meetings he spoke with assurance on the technical aspects of nuclear power. It was only three years since he had been sent to Oak Ridge when, in May 1949, he stated flatly, "It [an atomic power plant] is almost entirely an engineering job. That means that when you get it depends on how much effort you put into it."[2] Implicit in that statement was his credo that all effort expended, to be worthy of an individual, had to be one's best and most intense. At this time the world's first nuclear-powered submarine was still in the design stage; her keel was not laid until June 1952. Although as yet unnamed, in Rickover's mind she was already "Nautilus," the realization of Jules Verne's imaginary ship.

The characteristics that the SCB initially specified for the ship defined it as a testbed for the nuclear propulsion plant. The ship's mission would be "to determine the capabilities and limitations of a high-speed nuclear powered attack submarine," and its primary task would be "to develop a means of utilizing nuclear power for submarine propulsion and to evaluate the capabilities and limitations of a submarine so propelled." It was further stated that "initially, there will be no armament in the original ship."[3]

This cautious approach to establishing nuclear propulsion in the Navy's combatant ships did not please Rickover; he wanted no label of experimentation or any possible conflict with other innovative features. He insisted that his test and production procedures would provide a safe, reliable propulsion plant, and that the Navy should take advantage of this opportunity to bring the great advantages of nuclear propulsion directly into an operating unit of the fleet. The General Board and other key officers of the Office of the Chief of Naval Operations (OpNav) agreed. The statement of ship's characteristics was changed to require six torpedo tubes in the bow to give the attack capability a fleet unit required.

However, with no conviction that Rickover could solve in the near term the host of technical problems associated with a mobile nuclear reactor, his BuShips rivals continued design studies and tests of closed-cycle propulsion systems. A closed-cycle system permits operating a combustion power plant when fully submerged and disposing of its exhaust products overboard. Six different systems were under study, one being the German Walther system, which used hydrogen peroxide (H_2O_2) as its oxidant. Chemical catalysts broke the H_2O_2 down into water and oxygen. The oxygen burned the diesel fuel in a combustion chamber. Water sprayed into the chamber became high-pressure steam. The steam and burned gases were led to a turbine, which drove the ship. At war's end we acquired a German 2500-horsepower test plant and began operating it at our Engineering Experiment Station in Annapolis.

The very number of such hybrid systems hampered prompt evaluation and development. Also significant was the fact that BuShips was asking U.S. industry to develop for submarines a poweer plant that had no apparent commercial use. Following the war, industry had turned its development and production efforts to fulfilling the demands of ravenous civilian markets for products that would guarantee years of profitable enterprise. Lacking in the submarine program was the competitive commercial stimulus that had been fruitful in the prewar development of diesels.

Even though the list of six closed-cycle systems was pared to three, their development dragged on for years. In 1950, as part of a group considering new submarine designs, I visited the plant near Niagara Falls that was the chief supplier of hydrogen peroxide. We went to learn what we could of that costly, exotic fuel in case we should have to use it.[4]

No experienced submariner was enthusiastic about closed-cycle propulsion. It was a more complex, dangerous, and inefficient way to gain increased submerged performance. In particular, it was deficient in that it meant the submarine would "run out of gas" when its hydrogen peroxide was expended and it had to revert to being a diesel-electric boat of degraded performance. This was not a feature to appeal to submarine commanders trying to carry out long-range, aggressive operations. Nevertheless, as late as 1954 the closed-cycle alternative was still alive and was not abandoned until the shore-based, pressurized-water nuclear reactor for *Nautilus* was successfully operating in the Idaho desert test site. Not far behind was the prototype reactor for *Seawolf,* which used liquid metal (sodium) as its heat transfer agent and was being tested in a special enclosed facility in West Milton, New York. Meanwhile, the Electric Boat Company in Groton, Connecticut, was proceeding with the construction of the two ships for which Rickover's organization was providing the reactors and propulsion machinery.

On January 17, 1955, *Nautilus* got underway on nuclear power, and a new era in sea power began. That fact was demonstrated in May, when *Nautilus* made her shakedown cruise from New London to San Juan, Puerto Rico. She steamed entirely submerged for 1381 miles at more than fifteen knots. Other record-setting performances followed. At last the submarine was freed from its tie to the atmosphere. It no longer required oxygen to generate its power by combustion. It became a "true submarine" instead of a surface ship capable of brief periods of submergence. It could run fully submerged for as long as it wished at high speed.

Submariners brought up on diesel engines and storage batteries could fully appreciate what this meant. Antisubmarine warfare had been based on one premise: A submarine under water was powered by an electric storage battery that must soon exhaust itself. *Nautilus* destroyed that comforting fact. In the future, our air and surface antisubmarine forces would be denied the ability to make visual or radar contact on their nuclear-powered prey. Submariners' uncertainty over the role of their craft was now replaced by confidence in the great new capabilities it would bring to the fleet.

SEX AND THE SINGLE SERVICE

In early 1949 Hawaii was no longer the languid, tropic paradise we had known before the war. The prewar weekly arrival in Honolulu of a passenger ship from the mainland back then had been virtually a local holiday, but now it was supplanted by daily airplane flights. Debarking passengers were extruded from their planes as though some giant hand was squeezing the massive aluminum tube. They were swept up by tour agents and hotel representatives, who whisked them by bus or auto along busy Nimitz Highway into town. What had been a peaceful two-lane road through pineapple fields was now a roaring four-lane expressway.

The city itself was changing, with homes creeping farther and farther up the hills and valleys that sloped so sharply toward the sea (*makai*) from the Koolau Range of mountains. In town, high-rise buildings were challenging the once-dominant Aloha Tower. The war had brought thousands of workers to Hawaii. Many of them, and many servicemen as well, stayed on, attracted by the friendly multiracial society, the perfect climate, and the opportunities of a booming economy. Housing was in short supply, and most service families lived on their posts or bases in service ghettos. We were a family of five – father, mother, and three daughters – a good example of what I called the "Grady Postulate." The Grady Postulate held that 70 percent of the children of submarine officers were female.

In 1943 my Naval Academy roommate, James B. (Jim) Grady, of Clinton, North Carolina, had made his prospective commanding officer (PCO) run with me in *Halibut* before taking command of *Whale*. Ten years after leaving Bancroft Hall we were roommates once more, sharing the tiny skipper's cabin of a submarine on war patrol.

On this patrol from Pearl Harbor to the Caroline Islands, *Halibut* was in a three-boat wolf pack with *Tullibee* and *Haddock*. It was a most disappointing experience. The few contacts we made as we roamed the vast open-ocean area on the surface were generally Japanese warships proceeding at high speed between Japan and her overseas bases. Rarely could we close to attack, and our wolf pack had a miserable score: *Tullibee* sank a five-hundred-ton net tender, *Haddock* damaged the light aircraft carrier *Unyo,* and, for *Halibut,* zero.

Jim was an expectant father at the time and was always statistically inclined. During the frequent long periods of inactivity common to submarine war patrols, he had tabulated the offspring of submarine officers as best we could recall, and we found that 70 percent were girls. Thus it was no surprise, as we sailed dejectedly homeward, that one of the nightly "family-grams" that ComSubPac broadcast to his boats on patrol brought the good news that Betty Grady and newborn daughter were in excellent condition. After fifty days at sea, during which we had roamed 11,000 miles, an event in faraway New Jersey gave us our only prize. We could paint on the wardroom bulkhead, among the symbols depicting Japanese ships sunk or damaged, the silhouette of a stork, its tiny bundle representing our minuscule tonnage for the patrol.

In 1949 I found vivid confirmation of Jim's pioneering research. Serving in the submarine squadrons based at Pearl Harbor were three of us who were division commanders (Arnold Schade, Antone Gallaher, and I) and the two operations officers (Roy Davenport and William Kinsella). We were contemporaries; all had been married about the same length of time. One Saturday afternoon we were relaxing with our families at the swimming pool of the Sub Base Officers Club, keeping a watchful eye on our jumping, splashing, squealing progeny. Suddenly, we were aware that the ratio of girls to boys was 15 to 1!

"Quick! Get a photographer!" said someone, and we hurried to round up the elusive, improbable evidence of submariners' procreational discrimination.

Only the last-born child of the five couples present was a boy. He was Antone Joseph (Skippy), son of Antone and Mary Gallaher. Tony Gallaher was not only my 1933 classmate, but he and Mary had also been with us in the winter class at Sub School in 1936. After five lovely daughters, they were overjoyed to be blessed with a son. Rumor had it that one week after Skippy's birth Tony was asked who the baby resembled. His reply became legend in the Submarine Force: "I don't know. I haven't looked at his face yet."

In fact, the imbalance of sexes was yet to be compounded: Tony and Mary were to have still another daughter, as did Arnie and Becky Schade. For our particular group of submarine officers, the female-to-male ratio was 17 to 1. This curious fact remained in the back of my mind and was occasionally a topic of humorous discussion on social occasions. It remained only that until 1968, when I read a news story in London to the effect that the children of British frogmen were nearly always girls. No one knew why, so Comdr. Philip A. White, RN, MBE, the father of two girls, attempted to find out. Said he, "I began looking into this when a twelve-man diving team with their wives in Malta produced eleven girls and only one son." In another sample of twenty-five divers, 75 percent of their offspring were girls.

Although Commander White acknowledged the myth that "it depends whether you were facing east at the vital moment," a noted obstetrician at London's Hammersmith Hospital was quoted as saying, "The possible reason that leaps to mind is the effect caused by pressure changes on the body."

As chief of naval material at the time, I was disappointed by so superficial and unscientific analysis of so intriguing a subject. I passed the international evidence to Capt. George F. Bond, Medical Corps. He had been with me in the Fleet Ballistic Missile Program, and in 1968 was assistant for medical effects in the Navy's Deep Submergence Systems Project. He was specially trained in diving medicine and was himself a diver of long experience, a dedicated scientist seeking to extend the ability of humans to do useful work beneath the sea. Of fundamental significance to this effort was his discovery that once a diver's blood has been saturated with breathing gases at a given depth, the time required for decompression is a function only of the depth and not the time the diver remains at that depth.

George's November 4, 1968 reply to my query follows:

Dear Admiral Galantin:

In accord with my reputation for accelerated correspondence, I hasten to reply to your query of many months ago, concerning sex disproportion in siblings of diving personnel.

The obvious time lag results from detailed planning, some field work, and some weeks of bemused consideration of the results of preliminary surveys.

Commander White's remarks, first uttered at a cocktail party last winter in Portsmouth, and repeated in the published enclosure, resulted in a deluge of research proposals from various biological laboratories. The lowest price tag was not inconsiderable. To most of these supplicants, I replied in a negative fashion, by telephone. Meanwhile, I undertook a preliminary investigation – an inquiry which, I hasten to add, will not hold up under careful statistical scrutiny.

Some ten years ago, in conformance with the cyclical nature of these fables, my Escape Training Instructors sought from me verification of the legend of female progeny and sterility amongst the diving fraternity. The fact that the two situations were mutually exclusive did not disturb my co-workers; nor, apparently, did they believe the visual record of our biannual picnic affairs. Nonetheless, I followed through with a rapid survey, which revealed a normal male/female ratio in offspring, and a remarkable degree of fertility. Regrettably, I failed to publish my meager findings, nor did I further pursue the issue.

Some weeks ago, in a completely untruthful session with my colleagues, the question was again raised. One doctor, with a straight face, claimed to have interviewed 218 hard-hat divers, with very sad results. According to this informant, 68.7 percent of his diver informants could not recall the number, sex, names or birthdates of their children. An additional 10.3 percent averred, he said, that because of the hippie influence, they could no longer distinguish sons from daughters, and were not sufficiently interested to pursue the question. The remaining 11.0 (*sic*) percent had been remarried so often as to invalidate their record.

Another colleague, who works with caisson workers, drew a complete blank in his inquiry. He got no responses whatsoever, on the basis that none wished to light off another paternity suit. This would seem to be a singularly unprofitable area of research.

Finally, in careful consideration of CDR White's allegation, our group looked at cause and effect. The consensus was that perhaps the reported female imbalance might merely reflect the desire of a naval rate to volunteer to an escape from an all-female household. This, of course, may be a canard.

In all seriousness, we have instigated a rather careful study of the possibility of disproportionate birth ratios, if for no other reason than to answer the recurrent questions which arise. To this end, my office is initiating research within the Navy of the procreation records of all married aquanauts, a group of median-experienced deep sea divers, instructors at our two Submarine Escape Training Tanks, plus the crews of several Polaris submarines. We cannot ignore the possibility that, if the chaff of superstition be removed, a kernel of truth may be discovered.

The final answer will require more months of investigation; but perhaps the ultimate report may provide an all-time answer to this recurrent headache. You have done us all a great service by forcing the issue.

✳   ✳   ✳   ✳

But all was not fun and games in the Paradise of the Pacific in 1949. Pearl Harbor was the base for SubRons 1 and 5, each comprised of two divisions of four submarines each. My four were commanded by able young skippers who had served as junior officers on war patrols just four years before. The war had taught us that we could not rely on the assurances of distant bureaucracies; there was need for continuing, realistic testing and exercise of our weapons. The cold war with the Soviet Union was in progress, and our training exercises focused on Russia as our most probable future opponent. The Soviet navy had not fought an ASW campaign, and we were confident that we could circumvent their best efforts. However, with no substantial surface fleet to oppose us, what would be the best use of our submarines? We might talk of sub-versus-sub tactics, but it would be years before new sonars and new weapons made that possible.

As in the Atlantic squadrons, our training aimed to exploit the new equipment and modest increases in capabilities that our boats had acquired since the war. To that end, ComSubPac's Rear Adm. John H. Brown, the same "Babe" Brown who had been our wartime training officer at Pearl Harbor, assigned to each of his four squadron commanders the task of concentrating on a special facet of submarine warfare. With guided missiles just coming into play as a significant naval weapon, the submarine force was experimenting in the development of the unique advantages that could come from marrying the stealth of the submarine launching platform to the high-speed, extended range of the cruise missile carrying a nuclear warhead.

Based at San Diego, *Cusk* and *Carbonero* were developing that new form of naval power, using the Loon missile. Loon was an Americanized version of the V-1 "buzz bomb" that the Germans had launched from land platforms in World War II. Before the war ended, the German army had experimented with the launch of short-range bombardment missiles from a submerged U-boat. The concept had advanced to the point of devising schemes for the submerged launch of the next-generation missile, the V-2. However, the flagrant lack of German army-navy cooperation impeded progress, and no operational system resulted.

Cusk and *Carbonero* were in the submarine division commanded by John S. McCain, Jr., son of Adm. J. S. McCain, who had won fame as a fighting air task group commander under Halsey and Spruance. "Junior" McCain was a chip of the old block – small, wiry, colorful, profane, and full of nervous energy. He advanced both his own career and the Navy's cause by making himself the super-salesman of sea power. Before he retired in 1972, he was Commander-in-Chief Pacific. Like his predecessor Adm. U. S. G. Sharp, he would be charged with prosecuting the war in Vietnam, not in the positive, let's-get-the-job-done fashion advocated by military professionals, but in tentative, misguided fashion micro-managed from Washington by Secretary of Defense Robert McNamara.

While Jack and his boats were pioneering a new form of submarine warfare – attack against land targets with an impatient airborne weapon – the task assigned my division concerned "the weapon that waits," the mine. It was our job to improve submarine mine warfare readiness, a task made more meaningful to me by my *Argonaut* mining experience and the wartime torpedo debacle. Through countless loading exercises and many mine plants at sea, we disclosed technical deficiencies and developed improved mine-planting procedures.

The ponderous Mark XI of *Argonaut* had long since been consigned to the locker of unsuccessful weapons. Now every sub could be a mine-layer through the simple substitution of mines for torpedoes. The Mark X Mod 1 contact and the Mark XII magnetic, both of them moored mines used to a limited extent in World War II, were launched through the torpedo tubes, as was the Mark 27 mobile mine.[1] That one, looking outwardly like a torpedo, traveled submerged under its own power on a gyro-directed course to sink to the bottom at preset range. It could not be placed as precisely as a moored mine, but it permitted the covert seeding of harbors or channels that were otherwise inaccessible.

Although we worked hard and developed many improvements in submarine minelaying, we knew that would never be a form of warfare popular with submariners, for it did not offer the satisfaction of direct engagement with the enemy and the knowledge of results achieved.

✳   ✳   ✳   ✳

The drastic postwar cuts in the defense budget were continuing; they required progressive reductions in force. In December of 1949 my division was swept up in a reshuffling of SubPac boats, and I was ordered to Washington for duty in the Office of the Chief of Naval Operations (Op-Nav). In the logistics division I was charged with monitoring the material readiness and maintenance of submarines, submarine tenders, and submarine rescue vessels from their construction to ultimate disposal. A collateral duty was to serve as a submarine representative to the Ship Characteristics Board (SCB). This was the staff agency through which the chief of naval operations (CNO) specified to the material bureaus the military performance requirements for ships, both new construction and conversions of older ones.

The executive member of the SCB was Capt. Victor C. Barringer, Jr., of Louisiana. He had been one of our instructors in ordnance and gunnery at the Naval Academy. Victor was a fine seaman, a dedicated destroyer sailor, and an articulate, charming southern gentleman. When I turned to him for definition of my SCB duties, he gave me a forty-five-minute exposition of how business was conducted in the "Puzzle Palace." He summed up as follows: "Young man, you've just come from duty at sea. You've been a division commander. You've drafted dispatches and even released them. You've written official letters and actually signed them. Here you mustn't be impatient. Draft your dispatch; write your letter; go up and down these corridors, and when you have a string of initials as long as an ensign's pecker, some admiral will sign it!"

It was advice that succeeding tours of duty in the Pentagon proved was all too pertinent. The initials referred to were those of officers heading the various "OPs" that had a responsibility or interest in the subject being processed. Such coordination could take days or weeks. The most effective officers knew not only the minimum length of initials required for a given subject, but also the sequence of concurrences most likely to beget other approvals and ultimate signature. It was also useful to know the idiosyncrasies of language upon which certain flag officers insisted. But most trying of all was the need to overcome the often parochial predispositions of some nonsubmarine administrative assistants guarding what they considered their admiral's prerogatives or best interests.

✶ ✶ ✶ ✶

But even as the realities of bureaucratic life ashore were being learned, it was a time of doubt and uncertainty, of deepening gloom and low morale in the Navy. Even while the war was in progress, the Army had established a study group to prepare its case for a single service with an Army-dominated general staff. Perhaps motivated by the Navy's initial lack of readiness to keep the sea-lanes secure against the U-boats, the Army would relegate the Navy to a simple transport and supply role. It failed to see the contradiction: Without a balanced force that included aircraft carriers, the Navy would be unable to maintain the freedom of the seas that was so vital to national, including Army, interests.

Promised separate status, the Army Air Force gladly supported the Army plan. Some of its most vocal but least thoughtful advocates even proclaimed that a Navy was no longer needed, that the atomic bomb and long-range bombers would keep the peace or decide all future wars.

The National Security Act of 1947 gave the Army Air Force status independent of the Army and centralized all three services in a national military establishment under a civilian secretary of defense. Two years later a further reorganization gave the secretary the new and broader powers he said were needed to enforce interservice cooperation.

In March 1949 President Truman appointed Louis A. Johnson to succeed James V. Forrestal as secretary of defense and gave him the mandate to reduce the defense budget. Without consulting either Secretary of the Navy John L. Sullivan or Chief of Naval Operations Adm. Louis E. Denfeld, Johnson canceled construction of the 65,000-ton aircraft carrier whose keel had just been laid. She was to be named *United States* and was essential to the Navy's plan to introduce larger and heavier high-performance aircraft in the fleet, a move the Air Force considered encroachment into its strategic bombing mission.

The interservice fight over unification and its underlying roles and missions swiftly grew more acrimonious. The section of his administrative staff that Admiral Denfield had charged to keep him informed of defense reorganizations and policy, and to prepare the Navy's analysis of their consequences, was OP 23. It was headed by Arleigh Burke. The most famous member of the Class of 1923, the daring combat leader of DesRon 23, was now the dedicated, uncompromising sailor in charge of OP 23.

Because of the nature of war at sea, the Navy has always emphasized decentralization of authority over the armed services. On the other hand, from its beginning the Air Force favored "unification" of the armed forces – a single service. The Navy opposed unification for both philosophical and pragmatic reasons. Opposition was philosophical in that the Navy abhorred the general staff system, which was suitable for armies but not for mobile, versatile, flexible naval operations. It was pragmatic in an almost paranoid fear of losing its essential air arm.

In the Navy's application of air power, aviation is not a separate entity; whether ship-based or land-based it is but one component, an essential element, of sea power. A naval aviator considers himself first and foremost a sailor, whereas flyers of the Army Air Corps thought themselves a breed apart from soldiers. That separatism and the extravagant claims of air power enthusiasts were part of the pressure for creating the third military service, the U.S. Air Force, coequal with Army and Navy. Once tied to a single weapon, the airplane, that Air Force has matured into a more flexible force of aircraft, ballistic missiles, spacecraft, and satellites, fully deserving separate status.

Historically, the Navy has never succeeded in explaining adequately to our nation, which is a huge continental island, the real need for a strong fleet, much less one that must include its own integral air power. Lacking that public understanding, the Navy's counter to the superficial logic of a "single service" and the siren song of quick and easy "victory through air power" seemed to be merely self-serving. The fight over unification quickly focused upon restoration of the now-deleted 65,000-ton aircraft carrier. The Navy's case for getting the funds and authorization for the canceled carrier resulted in an attack on the Air Force on three counts:

1. The fallacy of the single-service strategy of massive strategic bombing.
2. The immorality of using atomic weapons.
3. The deficiencies of the very costly B-36 intercontinental bomber, which it called "a billion-dollar blunder."

Seeking to end the interservice bickering, the House Armed Services Committee conducted a hearing and received the testimony of most of the Navy's wartime leaders: Admirals King, Nimitz, Halsey, Spruance, Kinkaid, and others. Every one of them, aviator or not, solidly supported the need for big carriers.

The press had come up with one of their catchy, attention-grabbing labels: "Revolt of the Admirals." Even the respected chairman of the Joint Chiefs of Staff, General of the Army Omar Bradley, sounded off to call Navy spokesmen "Fancy Dans who won't hit the line with all they have on every play unless they can call the signals." (He was one of those who believed there would be no more amphibious landings.) And when Secretary of the Navy Sullivan resigned, Chief of Naval Operations Denfeld and other officers were fired, and the Navy was ordered to cut its carriers to four, there was shock and dismay throughout the sea service. How could the history of sea power's importance to our country and the lessons of World War II be ignored at the same time that modern science and technology were augmenting the threat to our sea lanes and magnifying the contributions the Navy could make to national defense?

Morale in the Navy was low, especially among those fighting the "Battle of the Potomac" in the trenches of the Pentagon, enduring daily barrages of reporters' and cartoonists' gibes. A good many of us who were surface ship and submarine officers thought that our own aviators played too much the part of glamour boys and were as fiercely protective of naval aviation's priority within the Navy as the Air Force was of its claimed primacy in defense. Nevertheless, we had no doubt that the Navy added unique, essential capabilities to the nation's military power, and that aircraft carriers in proper number were essential. In the face of what was truly a threat to its existence as an effective fighting force, the Navy closed ranks and eyed warily what would develop under its new chief of naval operations Adm. Forrest P. Sherman, who was the first-ever aviator to hold the Navy's highest command. He came from command of the Sixth Fleet, but the fact that he was the choice of Secretary of the Navy Francis P. Matthews, whom the Navy considered a generally inept pawn of the despised Louis Johnson, was not in his favor.

Sherman was commanding officer of the aircraft carrier *Wasp* when she was torpedoed and sunk by Japan's submarine *I-19* in September 1942. He was a man of keen intellect and quiet determination, but there was some resentment of him in the Navy's higher echelons because he had not vigorously opposed the drive for unification. He had, in fact, worked closely and amicably with the brilliant Lt. Gen. Lauris Norstad of the Air Force in drafting the terms of the 1947 unification act. Those of us without personal knowledge of him were reassured by the fact that he had been the brainy strategist and plans officer for Admiral Nimitz during the final relentless drive on Japan. To me, a relatively junior commander, his caliber was indicated in the famous photograph of the Japanese surrender ceremony on board *Missouri*. The three officers standing behind Admiral Nimitz as he signed for the United States were Douglas MacArthur, William F. Halsey, and Forrest P. Sherman.

It was not long before the cool, confident leadership of our new CNO had us holding our heads high once more. To remove the doubts and misgivings that the public quarreling and unfavorable publicity of the past year had provoked about the Navy's future, Sherman chose the Naval Academy as the platform for his first major speech. He set forth his views on the role of the Navy and its future. As a former carrier commander he certainly understood the importance of naval aviation in projecting offensive power, but he stressed the need for a balance of capabilities, with emphasis on antisubmarine warfare. Loss of his own ship to a Japanese submarine and the alarming intelligence of the U.S.S.R.'s rapidly growing force of modern submarines gave conviction to Sherman's words. Neither the Army nor the Air Force could take issue with them.

But the event that made the whole untidy interservice quarrel moot was the explosion, five years sooner than predicted, of Russia's first atomic test bomb in 1949. There was urgent reexamination of our defense posture and recognition that all three services needed very substantial restoration of forces if they were to be credible deterrents to communist expansion or responders to aggression. Moreover, with U.S. monopoly of atomic bombs soon to be ended, the dreadful possibility of their use confounded our strategy. Both Army and Navy were pressing to include the new atomic firepower in their tactical weapons of gun, torpedo, depth charge, or mine.

Great secrecy shrouded the design and production of atomic weapons, euphemistically called "special weapons," but a start was being made in spreading knowledge of their awesome reality. At Sandia Base, Albuquerque, New Mexico, there was a one-week course for officers of all three services. The instructors, military officers themselves, were good, even brilliant, in their exposition of atomic weapons design, construction, and effects as then known. In the class convening in the spring of 1952, there were seven of us of various warfare or technical specialties from the Navy. On the Army side I can recall Col. Andrew J. Goodpaster. He was clearly an exceptional officer and later reached the highest levels of U.S. and NATO politico-military responsibility.

The question periods that followed each classroom session were revealing, not so much for the additional weapons information they yielded as for indicating the nature of training and postgraduate study existing in each service. When my Navy colleagues asked questions, they were generally technical ones concerning the physics and engineering of the terrible weapon. I felt vicarious pride in their obvious technical competence.

When the Army asked questions, I noted a significant difference. They asked difficult ones, such as, "What about the moral issue if we use atomic weapons again?" or, "Should we be influenced by world opinion?" or, "How will the potential use of atomic weapons affect the defense budget?"

As for the Air Force, their comments summed up generally as "Gee, what a big bang!"

These were superficial indications, of course, but the individual reactions did typify each service's characteristics at the time. The Air Force, youngest of the services, with many of its officers catapulted prematurely to senior rank, was still maturing, seeking an operational philosophy more meaningful than that of the utter destruction inherent in the mission of the Strategic Air Command (SAC). In the years ahead, however, as I was exposed to more and more Air Force officers of my own and higher ranks, I found that they generally possessed more postgraduate education than did their Navy counterparts.

The Navy was the most flexible and most highly technical of the services. It operated complex engineering plants and weapons systems required to cope with combat that could range from the bottom of the sea, to the surface, to the margin of continents, and to outer space. Deployed at sea for long periods, it was difficult for naval officers to sustain a personal program of advanced education. And when official assignment to postgraduate education did come, most likely it was concerned with thermodynamics, aerodynamics, electronics, and the like, not with economics, political science, philosophy, or other aspects of national life.

The Army and Air Force, less mobile in their peacetime training operations, more static in their basing, are able to spend more time in schools. The Army is exposed regularly, at home and broad, to the civil and social problems of local governments and necessarily has interest in political, fiscal, and psychological factors. In both peacetime training and postwar administration of conquered territory, it is involved in socioeconomic problems of the populace. The broad responsibilities of Gen. Douglas MacArthur in Tokyo and Gen. Lucius Clay in Berlin are modern examples. The Navy is spared this experience and burden. Its training and operations are conducted in the open reaches of the sea, far from public notice. Any territory that it is charged with administering is most likely to be a remote island.

It is not at all strange that several times in our history presidents have been chosen from triumphant generals but never from victorious admirals. The American home is conscious of the general who led its sons or husbands and brought them home in victory, not of the remote commander who fought battles, however important, at sea. In the years since the Korean War the names of MacArthur, Eisenhower, Westmoreland, and Haig have figured in our presidential politics, telling an interesting story of the unpredictable consequences of educational opportunity.[2]

This was brought home to me in June 1985, when our community of retired military officers in Pinehurst, North Carolina, invited Gen. William C. Westmoreland, USA (Ret.) to address us. He had terminated his suit against the Columbia Broadcasting Systems for its apparently libelous television portrayal of his conduct in command of all U.S. forces in Vietnam at the height of our involvement there. Outmatched in essential financial and legal resources, the general had finally to accept an inconclusive settlement of his case against the television media giant.

I had met Westy briefly during a visit to Vietnam in 1967 and respected him as a man of integrity and dedication worthy of his towering Army reputation. Now, both long retired, we could reflect on the twists of fate that service to our country can bring. Westy was a native of Spartanburg, South Carolina. A holiday in Europe, where he encountered midshipmen from Annapolis on their summer cruise, confirmed his desire to travel and see the world. To satisfy that urge he wanted to enter the Naval Academy. When he sought the necessary appointment from Sen. James F. Byrnes, the senator counseled that he go to West Point instead, saying that its curriculum was better and less technologically oriented. Westy gladly accepted the appointment and began the impressive career that took him from first captain in West Point's Class of 1936 to Army chief of staff from 1968 to 1972.

His story reminded me that Dwight D. Eisenhower had also wanted to go to Annapolis. At his home in Abilene, Kansas, his close boyhood friend was Edward E. (Swede) Hazlett, Jr. Hazlett entered the Naval Academy in 1911 and urged Ike to follow. In Ike's words, "I was not difficult to persuade – first, because of my long interest in military history, and second, because I realized that if I could make it, I would take the money burden entirely off my family."[3] He won his senator's competitive examination for an appointment, only to find that he would be overage, twenty-one, by entrance day and hence not eligible for the Naval Academy. He turned to West Point, and "the rest is history." In 1924, when Major Eisenhower was stationed in Panama, Lieutenant Hazlett was skipper of the submarine S-32. After his ship completed some repairs at the sub base at Coco Solo, Hazlett took his friend to sea for a dive in Panama Bay.

Had Ike gone to the Naval Academy, he would not have become supreme allied commander for the liberation of Europe, with all the subsequent accomplishments and honors that led to the presidency in 1953. Richard Nixon might not have been vice president at that time, or perhaps ever. The whole succession of U.S. presidents could have been different in timing and personality, with incalculable effect on Western Europe, NATO, and our country.

When I told that story to Admiral Burke, he said, "You know, Pete, when I was a boy in Colorado, I wanted to go to West Point."

I replied, "Arleigh, you missed being president."

A Naval Academy graduate did ascend to the presidency, but Jimmy Carter did so not through a military career but as a successful practicing politician. A second noncareer Navy alumnus, Ross Perot, aspired briefly to that office in 1992.

15

A UNITED NATIONS OPERATION

The precipitous demobilization of our forces immediately following the war did not take into account the new threat by an aggressive, expansionist communism. Alone of the major participants, the Soviet Union emerged from the war with a plan and a purpose, that of exploiting situations of weakness. At a time when her former allies were busily engaged in demobilizing and dissipating their vast military power, Russia maintained and even increased her military establishment. Under Joseph Stalin the tentative, suspicious, wartime cooperation of the U.S.S.R. with its Western allies gave way to outright deceit, disregard of agreement, subversion of lawful governments, violation of national boundaries, and plundering of occupied territories. It was the start of more than forty years of cold war worldwide between the communist bloc and the Western democracies led by the United States.

The conflict was rooted in the ideological differences between Western capitalist democracy and international communism. The West felt threatened by Stalin's massive land and air forces, and Russia persisted in her historic fear of invasion from the West. The Red Army aided and abetted communists in the takeover of Eastern European governments, inspiring Winston Churchill to warn of the danger looming behind what he named the "Iron Curtain." Meanwhile, to restore the economies of Western European countries devastated by more than five years of war, the United States established its Marshall Plan.

Because of its severe reduction in force, the Navy had kept only a token presence in European waters after the war. To support our ground and air forces in Europe, and to cooperate with U.K. Mediterranean naval units, our Eastern Atlantic and Mediterranean Force consisted of one light cruiser division, one destroyer squadron, two tenders, and occasionally one aircraft carrier for a month or two. However, in 1946, when communist rebels supported by Yugoslavia, Albania, and Bulgaria threatened Greek democracy, President Truman sent the battleship *Missouri,* the aircraft carrier *Franklin D. Roosevelt,* the cruiser *Little Rock,* and several destroyers to the Mediterranean as a mobile "police force" to give evidence of U.S. might and the determination to use it if necessary.

In 1947, when Russia began pressuring Greece and Turkey, President Truman offered those countries economic and military aid and declared it was U.S. policy to "help free peoples to maintain their free institutions and their national integrity against aggressive movements that seek to impose upon them totalitarian regimes."

The new Truman Doctrine required a more substantial and permanent demonstration of U.S. resolve. This led to establishment of the Sixth Fleet as the force in being, with constant presence in the Mediterranean. It became a force built around two aircraft carriers, sometimes augmented by a third.

As the United States sought to "contain communism" within its boundaries, Stalin took a bolder approach. In 1948 he set up a land blockade of West Berlin in order to force out the American, British, and French governing powers. The Western Allies responded with a massive Berlin Airlift, which, after eleven months, caused Stalin to lift his blockade.

On the other side of the globe, in 1949 Chiang Kai-shek and his Nationalist (Kuomintang) government, which the United States had supported throughout World War II, had been forced by Mao Tse-tung's communist forces to leave mainland China for Formosa (Taiwan). To prevent Red China's threatened expansion to the Pescadores Islands and Formosa, the United States turned again to the deterrent power of naval presence. Truman ordered the Seventh Fleet to the Formosa Strait, where it was also to block any Nationalist attack against the mainland.

In Korea, Japan's rule had ended with its capitulation after World War II, but the country was divided into the communist, Russian-dominated North and the democratic South, which U.S. forces occupied. North and South were unable to agree on a unified government, and after the United States withdrew its forces in 1949, the North Korean dictator Kim Il Sung moved to unify the country by force. He had Stalin's tacit approval and agreement to furnish material support and was emboldened by the fact that U.S. Secretary of State Dean Acheson had recently defined the U.S. "defensive perimeter" as including the Philippines and Japan but omitting Taiwan and Korea.

On June 25, 1950, North Korean troops invaded the South and Truman moved quickly to get U.N. Security Council approval for aid to South Korea. Because the U.S.S.R. was then boycotting the council, aid was promptly authorized, and the president ordered U.S. troops committed under General Douglas MacArthur's overall U.N. command.

Army, Navy, and Air Force all reacted swiftly to the demands of an unexpected war 6500 miles from our shore. Almost one million reservists were called to action. Ships that had been only recently placed in the reserve fleet due to Secretary of Defense Johnson's cost-cutting were hastily reactivated. But even before they could get into action General MacArthur used what forces the Pacific Fleet could make available. Five years after the end of the Pacific War there were still on-duty senior commanders with experience in the complexities of amphibious warfare and a supreme commander ready to exploit it. Fifty-seven amphibious operations, all successful, had been central to the success of MacArthur's campaigns in the Southwest Pacific.

In the war's boldest, most dramatic stroke, on September 15, 1950, MacArthur launched an amphibious assault at Inchon on Korea's west coast. By landing behind the enemy's lines and cutting supply routes, he reversed the course of U.N. action from desperate retreat to confident advance.

North Korea had no naval forces able to threaten our own, which had been augmented by British, Canadian, and Australian ships with token forces from Thailand and Colombia. United Nations sea power added mobility, flexibility, and firepower lacking in the enemy. The Sea of Japan, which only our submarines dared enter during World War II, was now a lake in which U.S. and Allied warships steamed at will. Operating close to land in support of ground and air forces, they were vulnerable to submarine attack. Our own subs kept clear; any submarine detected in the vicinity of our formations would be enemy, Chinese or Russian, should either of those countries risk enlarging the war. They were unable or unwilling to do so. United Nations sea power was the one element the enemy could not counter.

Our aircraft carriers, including at times one from Britain, supplemented the heavier bombing by the Air Force, but they were especially valuable in providing to the ground forces the specialized, close air support that Navy-Marine aviation had developed. Other ships, able to close the coast at will, gave night and day gunfire support to troops ashore. With a staying power that aircraft could not match, and under any conditions of visibility, they could deliver accurate, high-volume fire of projectiles varying from star shell to armor-piercing. Our control of the sea made possible rapid redeployment of forces, their evacuation or rescue when necessary, and steady resupply. It ensured that the vital supply lines from the United States, Japan, and the Persian Gulf stayed open.

The chief danger to our ships were the mines supplied to North Korea by Soviet Russia. Planted in harbors like Wonsan on Korea's east coast, mines sank four minesweepers and one tug, damaged five of our destroyers, and sank or damaged several South Korean supply ships. The mine – the "weapon that waits" in a form of underwater terrorism – takes a toll greatly out of proportion to its costs. Although not decisive by itself, mine warfare can delay, disrupt, or divert the thrust of amphibious operations as well as destroy shipping.

Although we had developed and stockpiled a variety of sophisticated bottom and moored mines of our own, and a variety of ships, planes, and submarines could be made available to plant them, we were not prepared to cope with even the simple mines that North Korea used against us. Mine countermeasures (MCM) did not get high priority in Navy plans. It has always been the unloved stepchild of our attack-oriented Navy. In competition for funds and personnel, it lost out to the more glamorous power-projection concepts. Our Pacific Fleet mine force had been disestablished after World War II, and the degaussing of ships to protect against magnetic mines was neglected. The uneasy rationale for this situation was that the harbors and channels of our NATO allies were much more vulnerable to enemy mining, and we could count on them to maintain capable minesweeping forces. However, those forces were positioned to cope with the threat to European ports, not remote Asiatic harbors. Only the United States, committed to freedom of the seas worldwide, was required to cope with threats to that freedom everywhere and in whatever form they took.

As it turned out, despite occasional proddings by the Congress, the Navy's lack of satisfactory preparation in mine countermeasures continued long after Korea. The Iran-Iraq War, followed in 1990 by the Persian Gulf War (Desert Storm) when relatively crude mines severely damaged U.S. warships, demonstrated anew the urgent need for a ready MCM force. In 1992 the secretary of the Navy and the chief of naval operations at last moved to place emphasis on that dangerous and difficult art, beginning with improved training in realistic exercises. The number of specialized ships and helicopters required to do the job properly has been specified. However, in the draw-down of forces now facing all the services, MCM will again have great difficulty maintaining adequate force levels and capabilities. With the Navy-Marine combat team now focusing on the littoral areas of a troubled world, mine countermeasures must be ready, quickly transportable to the scene of action, diverse, and effective.

✳ ✳ ✳ ✳

There was little opportunity or need to exploit the stealth of the submarine in Korea's limited war. The chief contribution of our subs was in covert photo reconnaissance and one commando raid against a North Korean supply route. *Pickerel* was sent to the steep east coast to make close-in periscope photos of possible landing sites that would give a raiding party quick access to Korea's single railroad line and its tunnels near Wonsan. Our transport submarine *Perch* used the information developed. She was fitted with a large, piggy-back hangar in which she carried equipment for an embarked amphibious assault team. On the U.N. operation she carried a team of British Royal Marines, who successfully carried out the raid and were withdrawn safely.

Our boats also kept careful periscope watch on the movements of Russian cargo and naval ships in and out of Vladivostok and on Chinese shipping. As they were then configured and armed, and lacking enemy naval opposition, the low power-value of diesel submarines in limited war was apparent. They could contribute only covert surveillance, minor commando raids, and minelaying.

In 1952, when I asked for command of the largest surface ship I could get, regardless of type, a friend highly placed in the Bureau of Naval Personnel tried to dissuade me. "Don't do it, Pete. You've got a good record. You've been in subs all along. You'll end up in the Service Force, and it doesn't get the kind of people you're used to."

It was true that most officers shunned duty in the Service Forces. They preferred assignment to the more glamorous, more exciting combat units like battleships, cruisers, or destroyers. The same attitude had prevailed in World War II when the relatively new Amphibious Force was exploding in size and importance, requiring great numbers of officers. In each case, BuPers generally detailed those it considered top-drawer officers to the first-line combatant ships.

In 1944 I had stalked Japanese shipping off the port of Takao, Formosa. It was there, eight years later, that I found my first surface-ship command. She was just the kind of juicy target every wartime submarine skipper yearned to come upon. She was the fleet oiler *Navasota*, 25,300 tons, 551 feet overall, a unit of the Navy's mobile, logistic support and replenishment force.

By 1952 Formosa had become Taiwan, and the city of Takao was Kaohsiung, a major base for Nationalist China's navy and marines. *Navasota* had come down from her usual operations in the Sea of Japan to refuel Seventh Fleet units that patrolled the Formosa Straits. The overnight railroad express had taken me from Keelung in the north to Kaohsiung at the southwest tip of the island, each wobble, bump, and jolt impressing more deeply on my sweating torso the pattern of the straw mat on which I lay. I was happy next morning to wait on the quay in the steamy August heat of the typhoon season for the captain's gig to pick me up. I could see the long, low silhouette of *Navasota* far out in the roadstead, blurred by the heat waves shimmering over the glassy sea.

Next day I relieved Capt. B. E. Lewellen, a fellow submariner since our prewar days in Pearl Harbor. In the Sea of Japan on August 13, 1945, in his submarine *Torsk*, Lew had sunk the last cargo ship to be torpedoed by a U.S. sub, the small freighter *Kaiho Maru*. The day after, just a few hours before the cease-fire, he torpedoed the final two ships to be sunk in the war, the small, 800-ton coast defense vessels *No. 13* and *No. 47*.

＊　＊　＊　＊

Unlike a conventional tanker, which transports bulk oil from point to point, the function of a fleet oiler is the underway replenishment of combatant ships in their forward operating areas. Just as the ammunition ships, stores ships, and the cargo ships delivered many tons of their hard goods by "highlines" rigged to warships steaming close alongside, so oilers would pump black oil, aviation gas, or diesel fuel through the heavy hoses strung between them and ships needing replenishment.

The capability for underway fueling of combat ships had been greatly refined and extended in World War II. It has been called the Navy's secret weapon and was truly a force-multiplier. As part of that system, *Navasota* was a water-borne community center, a seagoing filling station, a general store, a post office, and a bus terminal.

When *Navasota* left Kaohsiung to return to her normal base in Sasebo on Japan's island of Kyushu, we plotted uneasily the track of a developing typhoon curving northward from the Philippines. As we neared Okinawa, a message from the commander of the seaplane patrol force based there directed us to enter Buckner Bay and go alongside his flagship, the large seaplane tender *Pine Island* (AV 12), to refuel her. By the time we reached the harbor entrance, heavy, dark clouds and rain made visibility poor. The wind was gusting to forty-five knots, sending white-crested swells crashing against the harbor's ugly, encircling reef. The confines of the poorly protected roadstead was no place for a lumbering, deep-draft oiler in a storm; she could do her job better as she was designed to do it – underway on a suitable course.

By radio I reported that I would remain outside and refuel *Pine Island* when she came out. The reply ordered tersely, "Proceed into port." With extra lookouts stationed, the chains manned, anchors made ready, and radar sweeping carefully, we headed in cautiously. I tried to hide my rage but inwardly I seethed, "What is that stupid airedale trying to do? Does he want me to go aground? Does he want two ships damaged? Has he ever conned a big ship, any ship, in this kind of sea?"

In general, aviators had a reputation as poor ship-handlers. Just as with the rest of us, their first two years of sea duty had been taken up by rotating through their ships' various departments. After opting for aviation, however, they were preoccupied with flying and had very little opportunity to practice the art of ship-handling in close formations or under unusual conditions. For most, that would not come until a brief tour in command of an auxiliary ship. During our turnover of command, Lewellen had even cautioned, "Be careful of carriers when they come alongside. *Philippine Sea* banged into us, and sent another oiler into the yard for repairs."

As I conned *Navasota* carefully into the storm-torn bay, my mind was not eased by the sight of hulks rusting on the shallow reef. Not all were landing craft or supply ships stranded during our invasion of 1945. Would my own career founder on the same reef?

The unevenly gusting winds made 540-foot long *Pine Island* yaw in her mooring as we gingerly approached her starboard side. When we shot over our messenger lines and began to pass mooring lines, the sterns of the two big ships came dangerously close. "All back emergency! Right full rudder! Take in all lines!" I shouted.

A few feet away, across the narrow gap of water separating us, my classmate, Walter H. (Fig) Newton, watched anxiously as *Navasota* slowly slid aft and clear. He was chief of staff to the admiral, who remained discreetly out of sight, as did *Pine Island*'s own CO.

I would give it one more try. This time I eased further forward, well off *Pine Island*'s bow, and dropped my starboard anchor. Slowly veering chain, all the while using both screws and rudder to keep twisting our stern out, we came alongside *Pine Island* with only minor bumps, separated by all the fenders each ship could rig. As Fig and I waved to each other, relief showed as clearly on his face as it must have on mine. Never again would *Navasota* get her hoses connected so quickly, pump so strongly, and get clear so thankfully.

The Navy had seen the merit of giving future skippers of aircraft carriers not only more ship-handling experience but also exposure to ship-command responsibilities in general. It became policy to give them command of Service Force and Amphibious Force ships. Nonaviators, who were denied command of aircraft carriers in any case, grumbled that this reduced their own command opportunities.

Command at sea is every line officer's goal, the best training for and the best determinant of his readiness for leadership in combat. The number of ships being limited, officers wait in line to have their tickets punched as COs. As a consequence, command tours are too brief, seldom over one year. This barely gives a skipper time to learn his ship and his people, much less to combine them into a war-fighting machine. That coveted first command is not a time for risk-taking or for initiatives that fail. Too often it becomes a time for "keeping one's finger on his number," to play safe, to protect one's record and lineal seniority.

Ironically, we are coming full circle. Submarines once spent most of their time on the surface, and, like the destroyer force, took pride in the ship-handling experience they gave their junior officers. Now the surface is an artificial, dangerous place for a nuclear sub, which avoids it as much as possible. The erosion of ship-handling skills in confined waters is evident.

＊　＊　＊　＊

When *Navasota* raced back to Sasebo clear of the storm track, I found a harbor much like a small San Francisco Bay. It was the site of an important Japanese navy yard. Ships my torpedoes had sunk during World War II might well have sailed from here; some, only damaged, were certainly repaired here. It offered safe harbor in any weather, ready access to the coasts of Korea, and an adequate industrial base to supplement the underway logistic support of our Service Force. Its underground oil storage was the terminal for tankers that shuttled from the Persian Gulf and our own West Coast with black oil, diesel, and aviation fuels. This was our base. In the Allied Officers Club ashore we met and compared notes with friends from other countries of the United Nations that had committed naval forces to the war. Among them, Capt. G. G. O. (Gat) Gatacre of Australia and Capt. William (Bill) Landymore of Canada would, in time, become chiefs of their own countries' navies.

Every twenty days or so we would refill our tanks at the fuel depot in Sasebo and take on the stores, repair parts, mail, and replacement personnel for the combatant ships busy delivering bombs and shells on Korea. The first night out of Sasebo was always an uneasy one for skippers. Going north through Tsushima Strait into the Sea of Japan we had to run the gauntlet of hundreds of fishing sampans. As their dim lights bobbed and winked among the swells, it seemed as if we were in a swarm of fireflies. A collision would leave us unscathed, for we would simply brush the fragile wood-hull vessels aside, but we had no wish to make the lives of poor hard-working fishermen even more precarious.

Our ship could vary from a full-load draft of thirty-three feet to a ballasted condition of nine feet forward when empty. She would behave as two different ships. Fully loaded, we could have as little as six feet freeboard amidships. When we hit heavy seas, my own submariner's distaste for vainly tempting the power of the waves was confirmed. A loaded oiler ploughing a rough sea seemed to be virtually a submarine constrained to the surface for the sake of the top-hamper on its few feet of freeboard.

The least expensive, least complex parts of the ship – our huge tanks of sheet steel and their piping – were in the best environment. They rode submerged in the relatively still water below the lashing of the waves, which slammed mercilessly or built ice on the costly, sensitive elements of topside electronics, deck machinery, and rigging, not to mention personnel. More than once, as we beat into summer typhoon or winter storm, I wondered why we did not take the next step and put all of the ship underwater. A submarine oiler much larger and more efficient than *Guavina* was practicable.

* * * *

In the combat zone, days passed quickly. From dawn to dark, and sometimes at night, a procession of ships came alongside as we steamed on a steady course on the most stable heading we could find. Carriers came to our port side because their island (navigating bridge) was on their own starboard side. After we shot messenger lines over, the booms that supported the heavy fuel hoses were swung out and soon the two ships would be coupled together. For as long as five hours we'd pump bunker fuel and aviation gas to our thirsty customer. All hands turned to with a will, eager to help set daily records of gallons delivered, tons highlined, or personnel transferred from ship to ship.

With as little as forty or fifty feet of open water channeled between us, a carrier's flight deck and island would tower above us. We could look through her hangar deck, which sailors appropriately called the "bird barn." At the same time, destroyers would come and go to starboard. Over the highline rigged between ships we passed the cargo and personnel we had brought out for each ship or were passing along from previous customers. In return, our cargo deck would receive mail and homeward-bound officers and enlisted men.

Although carriers and destroyers, both voracious consumers of fuel, were our chief clients, occasionally a battleship or heavy cruiser had business for us. With enormous fuel capacity of their own, they rarely needed bunker fuel but did take drums of special lube oils, flasks of industrial gases, boxes of freight, and mail.

One of the tasks of an oiler as it refueled gunfire support ships was to take from them the empty brass cases of the fixed ammunition they had expended. The heavy cruiser *Los Angeles*, with nine 8" 55-caliber rapid-firing guns using cased ammunition, was one of those ships. One night, as *Navasota* held steady course and speed, *Los Angeles* came alongside to port and quickly coupled our replenishment hoses to her fuel manifolds. As the pumping operation proceeded, empty ammo cases, freight, mail, and personnel were also moving from ship to ship.

The executive officer of *Los Angeles* was my good friend and fellow submariner Capt. John S. McCain, Jr., who was also broadening his career by surface-ship duty. As our ships steamed through the dark night, Jack and I conversed via the telephone line rigged between the ships' bridges. According to Jack, "Last night a funny thing happened. We were giving star shell support to an Army outfit under attack. Their radio talker would give us the coordinates, and we'd send a salvo of star shells. Time after time the voice coming by radio to our speaker here on the bridge would say, 'Give us 'lumination.'

"We couldn't satisfy him. After every salvo he'd say, 'Give us more 'lumination.'"

"Finally the skipper got annoyed. He took the microphone and asked, 'Who am I talking to?'"

"This is Corporal Jones."

"Let me speak to an officer."

"They ain't no officers here. This is the front."

It was a story that my Army peers accepted with good grace in the friendly give-and-take of the burgeoning joint schools and joint staffs of later years.

∗ ∗ ∗ ∗

I was the only "trade school" (Annapolis) officer on board the *Navasota*. The eight others were men commissioned from enlisted ratings or young naval reserve officers. My executive officer, Commander Frank Cortese, was a former boiler-tender; my operations officer and navigator was Lt. Bill Brockman, a former quartermaster. My watch officers, young reservists like Bob Gianelli and Vince Alderman, were quick to learn, eager to take responsibility.

I followed submarine practice in ship-handling. As soon as I had checked myself out on the special maneuvering characteristics of our ship, I turned the ship-handling over to each O.O.D. in regular rotation. A commanding officer's task is not the repeated demonstration of his ship-handling skills, but the training and supervision of his junior officers, all the while being ready to intervene to avoid immediate danger.

Next I began what proved to be a particularly rewarding practice. I would invite, at random and by surprise, one of our warrant officers or chief petty officers to lunch with me in my cabin. I learned much about my ship and my men. And it paid dividends in another way. Not knowing when they'd get the skipper's invitation, all my leading men spruced up in dress and appearance, with a resultant ripple effect throughout the ship. It was not long before we could claim to be the smartest oiler crew in the fleet. So much for those who counseled against a command in the Service Force!

In the spring of 1953, one of *Navasota*'s exploits was publicized as an example of U.N. cooperation. Off the east coast port of Wonsan we received from our destroyer *Shelton* her position report and the urgent request, "Do you have medical operating facilities?"

We did. *Navasota* had been a commercial tanker built for long-distance, independent operations but conforming to certain Navy specifications prescribed in the event she would be taken over in wartime. She had an adequate operating room available for emergencies that could be handled by paramedical personnel. We had no doctor, but Chief Hospitalman G. N. Luke ably attended to our cuts and bruises and aches and pains.

At the time, *Anzac,* the Australian destroyer in which Gat Gatacre was both CO and squadron commander, was alongside taking a long drink of fuel. Telling Gat that I anticipated an operation on board but had no doctor, I asked if we could borrow his. Surgeon-Lieutenant Neil M. Baird, a Royal Navy Reserve officer from Glasgow, Scotland, was part of the Aussie destroyer squadron staff. He quickly came over to *Navasota* via highline. Meanwhile, as we proceeded with *Anzac*'s refueling, we gingerly turned both ships to head for *Shelton* far to the north. As soon as *Anzac* broke away, I ordered, "All ahead, full!" while Lieutenant Baird and Luke made ready for an unnamed operation.

When *Shelton* came alongside, her skipper, Comdr. P. Frazier, explained what was up. He had received an urgent call for medical assistance from the Republic of Korea marine garrison on the island of Yang Do, near Songjin, only a hundred miles from Vladivostok. *Shelton* was a destroyer divison flagship and carried a medical officer, Lt. (jg) James D. Lambing. When the patient, Cpl. Kang Chu Suck of the ROK marines was brought on board, Lambing quickly diagnosed the severe belly pains as appendicitis and needing operation promptly. Because of *Shelton*'s commitment to combat operations and her cramped, unsteady platform, she was not a good place for surgery. Hence the plea to *Navasota.*

Corporal Kang was lashed into his stretcher and swung outboard to *Navasota,* suspended from the highline that connected the two ships. Swinging wildly a few feet above seas that snarled and snatched at him, Kang had traded the familiar dangers of combat for unknown terrors. Should a man fall overboard into these icy waters, his time of survival could be no more than five minutes. In pain, helpless and alone, with no one able to speak his language, he was only a piece of war's flotsam. Salvaged by the mercy of allies, his life depended on the skills of foreign doctors.

Dr. Lambing came over in the regular highline chair, his battered bag of instruments at his feet. We now had two doctors and one patient. Kang was in great pain, and the two medics, one from Scotland, one from the state of Washington, quickly agreed that immediate surgery was required. Baird was senior, so he would wield the scalpel, but he said he did not like the U.S. government-issue surgical gloves.

The Canadian destroyer *Haida* came alongside just then for her share of black oil. In a few minutes we got from her a pair of British surgical gloves. The operation went well. A huge, purplish appendix was removed safely, and Kang was turned over to Chief Luke's care.

To get the doctors back to their own ships we passed them by highline to the destroyer *Brinkley Bass,* which was next to come alongside. All in all, a South Korean bellyache had involved a U.S. oiler, an Australian destroyer, a Canadian destroyer, two U.S. destroyers, a Scots surgeon, an American doctor, and British medical equipment. The patient survived. Ten days after his operation, Corporal Kang walked ashore in Sasebo to start the return to his unit.

✶   ✶   ✶   ✶

During four submarine war patrols in 1943 and 1944 close to Japan's shores I had searched her coastline countless times through my periscope, wondering what the real Japan was like beyond its rocky shore. Now, in a different kind of war, no longer needing or able to hide, I wanted to see more and learn more of our former enemy. I proposed to my boss, Rear Adm. Marion E. Murphy, Commander Service Squadron 3, that *Navasota* be permitted to visit Yokosuka. We would absorb the extra transit time in our upkeep period, and I would assure proper material maintenance and readiness. We made the visit, to the satisfaction of all save a few men who were becoming too attached to their Sasebo "girl-sans."

A later visit to Kure in the Inland Sea was even more thought-provoking. The pilot we picked up to transit the Strait of Shimonoseki had been a Japanese naval officer. In the passable English he had learned at their naval academy at Etajima, he told me he had been in six different ships during World War II, and our submarines had sunk each! Perhaps he had been the victim of one of my torpedoes from *Halibut.*

How inconsequential that seemed compared to what I saw when I drove the few miles from Kure to Hiroshima to see firsthand the devastation caused by one primitive A-bomb. The ugly reality of man's newfound ability to exterminate humanity was all around me. Only the twisted skeleton of one steel-reinforced, concrete building hinted of the major city that once stood there. Amid the rubble and ruin the Japanese were creating a memorial Peace Park, its centerpiece a simple, gleaming, white marble monument erected at ground zero. The saddest sight of all were the few survivors willing to display their terrible scars and burns.

Many times I have listened to and sometimes entered into debate about the necessity or morality of President Truman's decision to use the A-bomb to speed the end of World War II, when Japan was already defeated but would not accept that fact. In his judgment, use of the terrible weapon would actually save lives on both sides by preventing the slaughter that would accompany a full-scale invasion of Japan's home islands. I have witnessed the explosion of an A-bomb in the Nevada desert, have acquired rudimentary knowledge of the bomb's physics and effects, and have been involved in the development and production of our most effective nuclear deterrent system. Compelling as such cumulative experience can be, it is only when one has seen the reality of what even primitive A-bombs do that one comprehends the full horror and futility of their use. The evidence of Hiroshima and Nagasaki has been the true deterrent, staying the seemingly inexorable drift to nuclear Armageddon.

As with any successful new weapon, our monopoly of nuclear weapons was short-lived. The U.S.S.R. exploded its first test weapon in 1949. "The Bomb" was not used in the Korean War. When the United Nations forces under MacArthur drove toward the Yalu River boundary of communist China, the Chinese intervened with two hundred thousand "volunteer" troops, a force that ultimately grew to eight hundred thousand. President Truman believed that expansion of the Korean conflict risked escalation into a world war and was ready to engage in negotiations that could lead to peace. On the other hand, General MacArthur, intent on military victory, proposed bombing Chinese supply routes and depots.

When he issued a statement that suggested as much, counter to Truman's policy, the president called it insubordination and relieved MacArthur of all his commands.

While the resulting political fire-storm raged in the United States, both peace negotiations and combat proceeded in Korea. Finally, after two years, an armistice was signed in July 1953 and a demilitarized zone established, separating the two Koreas along virtually their original boundary, the 38th parallel.

The war had shown the unpredictability of events affecting the interests of the United States or its allies and the readiness of totalitarian regimes to take advantages of real or perceived weakness in U.S. military power or resolve. Misled by Dean Acheson's statement, and seeing only weak U.S. and South Korean forces at the end of a very long overseas supply line, Kim Il Sung had attacked.

The abrupt outbreak of war demonstrated anew that wars start at a time and place and in a manner of the enemy's choosing, not ours. Initially we can only react, making it all the more important that we maintain in-being, balanced, highly trained land, sea, and air forces with appropriate sea and air lift.

In the years following the end of World War II the United States placed too much reliance on strategic air power to deter or "win" a war, with consequent neglect of conventional forces. In trying to buy national security on the cheap, with minimal commitment of personnel, our foreign policy lacked the backup of flexible, credible, military power needed to make it effective. This was the lesson learned by the politicians, and for the next few years the United States would rearm. This was the most important outcome of the war, yet it was a principle often ignored.

The interdependence and mutual support of Army, Navy, Marines, and Air Force were apparent. Although the war was fought in a relatively confined geographic area, the special capabilities of each service were of critical importance in various phases of conflict. The amphibious assault capability of the Marines, the stubborn advance and ground control of the Army, the heavy bombing and air control of the Air Force, the precision bombing and close air support of carrier aviation, the Navy's sustained, accurate gunfire, its mobility for advance or withdrawal of ground forces, and its assurance of overseas supply – each was essential. At one time or another each was the crucial, dominant force in implementing a strategy or in responding to the ebb and flow of combat. Always the objective had to be the control or occupation of territory, not simply destruction.

For the Navy, the requirement to apply force in less than absolute terms, the need to keep the sea-lanes open to our forces and denied to the enemy's, demanded the existence and readiness of forces in which surface, air, subsurface, and land control (Marine) elements were integrated. Only their correlation on a continuous basis on the scene of action could assure control of the sea.

Beyond testing the individual services, the Korean War tested the reorganized Defense Department. It proved to be effective. With no large standing forces in-being after the hasty demobilization from World War II, it had quickly marshalled the nation's resources of men and material and coordinated their allocation to each service.

The importance of forward bases for any distant, continuing operation was shown. Only the ready availability of bases in Japan for air and ground forces made possible the timely and sustained reaction of U.N. land forces. On the other hand, Navy-Marine freedom from fixed bases gave them the ability to sustain a forward deterrent presence, as in the Formosa Strait.

Finally, the dramatic dismissal of General MacArthur confirmed the American tradition of civilian control of the military. No matter how brilliant the military commander, his strategy must conform to the national goals and political constraints specified by his own commander-in-chief, the president.

16

TRANSITION

A half century after submarines became a part of our Navy, command of a squadron – two divisions of four boats each – for one year, with the rank of captain, was as high as most submarine officers could rise in the hierarchy of their specialty. In 1950 there were eight squadrons. With just two submarine flag officer billets – ComSubLant and ComSubPac – very few submariners could aspire to those exalted positions. Thus it was gratifying to receive orders assigning me to command Submarine Squadron 7 at Pearl Harbor.

It was not easy to leave *Navasota* after a busy, rewarding year playing a small part in a war that would have been lost without the command of the seas that our Navy assured. My officers and men, so different in source and training from those in my previous commands, were every bit as dedicated, loyal, and efficient. It was during our ship's brief stay in Kobe that I said "good-bye and God bless" before flying back to Pearl.

In 1953, Submarine Squadron 7 was a good example of the uncertain transition phase in which the submarine force found itself. It had an odd mix of ships. Two of the three submarine hunter-killer (SSK) boats built in response to Swede Momsen's vision of large numbers of small, low-cost, antisubmarine boats were in the squadron; the third was operating out of New London, working with the Underwater Sound Laboratory. My six other boats were GUPPY conversions of World War II boats or standard fleet subs.

The skippers of the two SSKs – *K-2* and *K-3* – were Eric E. Hopley and Michael U. Moore, both of them energetic, imaginative young men who led their crews of three officers and thirty-three enlisted men to their best efforts in trying to prove the worth of the novel ships. Compared to the sleek, streamlined GUPPYs, the 765-ton K-boats were ugly ducklings. A large fairing projected from their bow, enclosing the many sensitive line hydrophones of the passive (listening only) sonar placed there to remove them as far as possible from the ship's own machinery noise. This sonar, designated "BQR-4," was an improved version of the system the Germans were installing in their Type XXI submarines at war's end.

By the standard of previous passive sonars, the performance of BQR-4 was phenomenal. Ten years before, off Japan, I had watched ships through my periscope, not 1500 yards away, and was unable to hear them. Now, submerged in one of the cramped, austere K-boats, I was amazed to be able to detect and track ships at a range of 105 miles! Submarines were a more elusive target, but these, too, were being detected at thousands of yards instead of hundreds as formerly.

The continuing research in Navy sonar laboratories, in university research centers, and in industry was producing advances in sonar technology, which in turn developed more data and knowledge of sound transmission in the sea. The existence of a deep sound channel in the ocean was found and exploited. This was the path of minimum sound attenuation that carried sound waves hundreds, even thousands, of miles into convergence zones recurring about every thirty miles. There was slow but steady input into the loop of theory, technology, and tactics. Advances in one field pushed each of the others. The sea was grudgingly yielding its secrets, and war at sea kept extending its reach.

Originally nameless when it was thought that large numbers of the class would be built, *K-1, K-2,* and *K-3* were later designated *Barracuda, Bass,* and *Bonita,* those names having been relinquished by their hard-working but unsuccessful predecessors. Despite their tantalizing demonstration of long detection and tracking ranges, the K-boats' radiated noise and frequent need to snorkel greatly reduced their effectiveness. The boats were under-powered, had poor endurance, and very poor habitability. The dream of efficient, small, mass-produced hunter-killer subs could not be realized. It had become clear that ever-larger, ever-costlier, more sophisticated sonars and fire control systems, demanding great amounts of electric power, were needed for the difficult job of sorting out high-performance submarines from all the sea's natural sounds. The K-boats had to be retired, but not before they and the fleet boats converted to SSKs had demonstrated that sub-versus-sub was a practicable tactic and a valuable addition to our total ASW effort. Thereafter, all our attack subs would have as their primary task the search for and destruction of enemy submarines.

The reason for our stress on the antisubmarine role was the ominous growth of the U.S.S.R.'s submarine force. Just as eagerly as the British and Americans, after the war in Europe the Russians had taken engineering data and reports of Germany's most advanced U-boats, along with any material they could retrieve from her devastated shipyards. They took the incomplete German aircraft carrier *Graf Zeppelin* and greedily loaded her hangar deck with captured sections of U-boats. As the hulk was being towed to Russia, it struck a mine and capsized, partly because of the overloading.

The U.S.S.R. copied the German technology and pressed on with the world's largest submarine building program. Between 1950 and 1958 the Soviets built about 235 subs patterned after the German Type XXI. It was estimated that their goal was a fleet of as many as 600 submarines, counting the obsolescent prewar types that had survived the defeat of Germany.

Lacking the full scope of naval power possessed by the United States and her allies, the submarine seemed to the U.S.S.R. a cheap, easy way to hold that power at bay. On land Russia had its belt of satellite states and the Iron Curtain. In their almost paranoid fear of invasion the Russians looked for a way to extend the Iron Curtain to sea. The submarine, traditionally the weapon of the inferior naval power, was well suited for such defensive use. But the buildup went far beyond defensive needs. The Soviet Union knew that in spite of Hitler's lack of appreciation of sea power, his U-boats came perilously close to severing Britain's lifelines. A Russian submarine fleet-in-being, many times the number of Germany's prewar force, could raise doubts in the Free World that Western sea power would be equal to the threat.

The Soviet shipbuilding program, emphasizing submarines, served notice that Russia would not repeat the error of Germany's naval strategy. Prior to both world wars, Germany, a land power occupying a position in the European peninsula similar to that of Russia in the total Eurasian land mass, initially tried to build a navy of surface ships able to overcome Britain's mastery at sea. By the time she recognized the futility of that effort, the astonishing success of her few U-boats showed how vulnerable were Great Britain's overseas lifelines. In both wars the German shift to full exploitation of submarine warfare came just a little too late to withstand the Allied ASW campaigns in the Atlantic.

On the other hand, following Pearl Harbor, the United States developed a navy around the fast aircraft carrier to carry the attack to the enemy as the best way to ensure command of the seas. Not being as dependent as Britain on overseas shipping, U.S. ASW capability was shaped to the defense of the carrier strike forces. However, ASW is the most complex form of naval warfare. It requires the coordination of effort by all elements of the Navy and integration of information from many sources: intelligence, hydrography, meteorology, operations analysis, and the like. Our submarines could make meaningful contribution to that effort only after major improvements in their sonars and weapons. It would then be possible to round out the composite ASW system and make it an air-surface-undersea team. That day was approaching.

There was growing acceptance, not only in the submarine force but also in the Navy's air and destroyer ASW forces, that ships operating in the very medium from which the enemy attacked could be well suited to detect and destroy him. Because of their stealth and their ability to operate in far forward areas, subs could be the forward extension of our overall antisubmarine system. By projecting aggressive ASW to the enemy's shore, they gave him an ASW problem of his own and forced the diversion of men, money, and materials from other programs.

✶   ✶   ✶   ✶

That was the rationale for the submarine in ASW when, after a year at Pearl Harbor, I turned SubRon 7 over to the innovative leadership of Dick O'Kane in July 1954 and headed for a new assignment at the National War College at Fort McNair in Washington, D.C. The ten-month course would be a welcome, mind-stretching experience in which I would share the company of my peers from Army, Air Force, Coast Guard, and Foreign Service. It was these associations, along with the exposure to national and international authorities in many fields, that made the course so valuable. The school is not a "war" college at all; it could more appropriately be called a "peace" college, covering all aspects of national security policy and strategic decision making, the better to understand how war can be prevented. Military power, its uses and limitations, is but one factor among the many that shape international relations.

In the relaxed, academic atmosphere of the college, the warm friendships forged with fellow students brought an appreciation of the mission of each service and of our professional interdependence. Even so, there would yet be years of contention and rivalry before full acceptance of the "jointness" in operations that the Congress and the secretary of defense had long been pursuing.

As we exchanged tales of peacetime and wartime experiences in our specialties, we gained understanding of the capabilities and limitations of each military branch and of the trends in new developments. Stimulated by the exciting news of *Nautilus*'s operations, our Army, Air Force, Coast Guard, and Foreign Service colleagues were particularly interested in what submarine officers could tell them of undersea warfare. Because we were the "silent service" during the war, and even in peacetime operated remote and hidden from them, they knew little of the submarine's accomplishments and potential. Because it was the one element of Navy-Marine power that was unique and did not compete with their own missions, they were very supportive of expanding the role of the submarine in ASW.

When I explained the operational advantages of increased depth in both attack and defense, I spoke with pride of *Tang*'s record-setting dive made just two years before. Col. Gladwyn E. (Pinky) Pinkston, USAF, thereupon asked, "How deep did you say, Pete?"

"Seven hundred thirteen feet."

"Aw, hell! I've flown deeper than that!"

"The hell you have!"

"Oh yes, I have! I've flown right over the surface of the Dead Sea."

Pinky was right. The Dead Sea is 1292 feet below sea level. How tellingly his exploit spoke of our slow progress in penetrating the ocean depths. This humiliation – being out-dived by a fighter pilot – rankled for years. I was determined to overcome it.

The Lockheed Aircraft Corporation had designed and built an undersea research vehicle named *Deep Quest*. This submersible, able to dive to 8000 feet, was operated by a crew of two and could accommodate two observers in very cramped conditions. *Deep Quest* and her surface transport craft, *Trans Quest*, were based in San Diego, California.

On October 28, 1968, during a visit to naval activities in the San Diego area as chief of naval material, I had a few hours free. When I learned that *Deep Quest* was available, I asked that she take me as deep as possible in the time available. The farther offshore we could get, the deeper the water would be, but proceeding out to sea was slow and I had to be back ashore by 1900. Within that constraint, Larry Shumaker, *Deep Quest*'s pilot, said he'd do the best he could.

When we reached our diving area outside San Diego's busy shipping lanes, Larry, his co-pilot, and I took our places in *Deep Quest*, cast off from *Trans Quest*, and started down. The afternoon's bright sunlight penetrated barely three hundred feet below the surface. Soon we entered the region of perpetual darkness and descended through eerie blackness. Aside from the dull green glow of our instruments, the only light was the bioluminescence of sea creatures through which we were sinking. As I peered out the small viewing port, it seemed that we were in a swarm of fireflies or in a midnight snowstorm with upward-swirling snowflakes.

When his depth-finder told him that we were nearing bottom, at this point 2450 feet deep, Larry said, "Stand by! I'll ease her down to about ten feet."

He slowed our descent and switched on the external flood lights. Lying on an air mattress with my face close to the thick viewing port, I eagerly anticipated the beauty and wonder of the bottom of the sea. Soon I saw it — my first object on the bottom of the sea! It was a Coors beer can! The neat triangular puncture in the top was clearly visible. The can seemed as bright and untarnished as it had been in the hand of the drinker before being carelessly tossed overboard from some ship or yacht.

I had accomplished my purpose. Not long after, as president of the National War College Alumni Association, I presided at our annual meeting. What a pleasure it was to have Brigadier General Pinkston in the audience as I told how I had finally purged myself of the humiliation of being out-dived by a fighter pilot.

But, to return to the War College in 1955, the Navy had announced that duty on a Joint or Allied staff was a desirable, if not essential, qualification for advancement. To that point, nineteen of my twenty-two years' service had been in submarine assignments; none of them, except the War College, was outside the Navy. Intrigued by the larger world of interservice and international military affairs, I asked for duty in the office of the Joint Chiefs of Staff (JCS) and was informed that was where I'd go in July 1955.

Suddenly the submarine detail officer in the Bureau of Naval Personnel called to say that signals were changed; I was to return to a submarine job in OpNav. Recalling Jimmy Fife's good advice, I did not protest strenuously. It turned out that Capt. Bernard F. (Barney) McMahon, Head Submarine Warfare Branch (OP 311), had become persona non grata to Rear Adm. Hyman Rickover. With the tremendous success of *Nautilus* strengthening his grip on the Navy nuclear propulsion program, Rickover was not about to accept what he deemed to be less than 100 percent enthusiastic support from the senior pro-submarine billet in OpNav.

A tough-minded, successful wartime skipper, Barney McMahon was a staunch supporter of nuclear power for submarines, but he was opposed to what he considered Rickover's intrusion into the seagoing officers' domain of operational control and personnel administration. If submariners resisted his increasing influence on submarine programs, Rickover would sometimes angrily call them "stupid operators who can't see the importance of what I'm doing for them."

In a letter to me after we were both retired, Barney summarized his feeling about Rick in a way that most submarine operational personnel would have agreed with.

> Without Rickover the timely and successful completion of his project would have been seriously delayed, with a chance of falling flat. He, along with assistants like Laney, Roddis, Dunford, Panoff, etc. should be given absolute and complete credit for its historic success.
>
> As a result of many conversations with present-day nuclear submariners, I still feel that we should have stuck to our guns at the very beginning of the operating period and should not have turned over so much operational and personnel control to the "Great White Father." Rick, I feel, would have eventually conceded (not very gracefully) and we would not now be faced with some problems that may turn cancerous.

Rickover's control of personnel entering the nuclear propulsion program, whether for surface ships or submarines, was absolute, both in their selection and training. He ostensibly had no authority over officers in submarine billets outside the nuclear power program, but his political clout on Capitol Hill made the submarine force commanders and the chief of naval personnel highly mindful of the benefits of cooperation. I supposed I had been "cleared" as to acceptability to Rick for, on graduation from the National War College, I was ordered to relieve Barney McMahon.

The head, Submarine Warfare Branch (OP 311), although only a captain's billet, was the senior pro-submarine post in OpNav. For my support I had an allowance of three officers and one female civil service secretary. To make up for our limited numbers, the submarine detail officer in the Bureau of Naval Personnel cooperated in assigning the branch the best and brightest officers available. Initially I had J. Sneed Schmidt, Charles W. Rush, and Robert D. McWethy. Bob McWethy, with operational experience in an icebreaker in the Arctic Ocean, was one of the first to recognize that region as a potentially important naval operating area and was pointing out that nuclear-powered submarines could dominate it. When an additional billet was authorized for OP 311, I chose Lt. Comdr. Robert L. J. Long. At one time our group of five included four who would reach three-star or four-star rank: Long, Jon L. Boyes, Marmaduke G. Bayne, and myself.

The relative importance of submarines to aircraft carriers in Navy plans and operations at the time was apparent in the fact that four of us did for submarines what it took 105 staff officers, including nine Marine Corps aviators, to do for naval aviation. We were the headquarters' focal point for all submarine operational matters and the central coordinating agency for all submarine plans and programs. This involved justifying the requirements for types and numbers of submarines within the Navy's total force levels; establishing performance requirements for new design and converted submarines; maintaining close liaison with the technical bureaus to enhance submarine readiness and capabilities (including their weapons); keeping abreast of research and intelligence affecting undersea warfare; working with BuPers for adequacy of personnel in numbers and training; and monitoring readiness of the two submarine forces and being their constant, responsive link to the policies of the chief of naval operations.

I had no quarrel with the numbers in our office; there was advantage in being a small, cohesive team able to act quickly. It was a reasonably fair allocation, in keeping with what each vehicle was then able to contribute to the Navy mission. There were no major Soviet fleets of warships or cargo carriers to be our targets; our sub-launched guided missiles were a very modest addition to naval aviation's atomic strikes; and our antisubmarine capability was, as yet, only an unproven concept.

There were, of course, many other submarine officers on duty in the Navy Department, but in jobs not directly concerned with submarines. They were informed on submarine matters through voluntary attendance at the Submarine Conference and were a valuable link to other offices of the department.

My immediate superior was the assistant chief of naval operations for undersea warfare (OP 31). This was the new title given to the "coordinator" billet that Rear Admiral Styer had first occupied. It was generally, but not always, filled by a submarine-qualified rear admiral. Rear Adm. F. B. Warder (dubbed "Fearless Freddy" for his wartime command of *Seawolf*) was en route to assume the OP 31 duties but had not yet reported when I took over OP 311.

The relatively low position of OP 31 in the departmental hierarchy was out of line with his great responsibilities, particular in ASW, a fact being alluded to by Congress and other critics. In May 1948 the National Research Council Committee on Undersea Warfare had reported to the secretary of defense that ASW was the "most pressing problem" facing the Navy and that there should be an authority adequately staffed "to concentrate the force of all present naval facilities" on the problem. To connote a more vigorous approach to the total undersea warfare problem, the new title of assistant chief of naval operations for undersea warfare was given to OP 31 in July 1948, and its staff increased from three to thirteen.

I was eager to get on with the promotion of my thinking on submarine warfare which the year at the National War College had stimulated. In the shipbuilding program for fiscal year 1956 was the nuclear-powered radar picket submarine SSRN 586, still unnamed. Ten attack-type diesel boats had been converted to radar picket configuration, and two more were built as such after the war, but SSRN 586 was to be a major advance. To accommodate the twin reactors, which were also part of Rickover's long-range plan for applying nuclear power to the Navy's major surface ships, the submarine had to be large. As the world's first multiple-reactor ship, she would be more important for her part in the development of multireactor technology than for her operational role as an early-warning radar picket for carrier task forces. She would be the world's largest submarine, 447 feet long, displacing 5450 tons. By virtue of her sea-keeping ability and power she was expected to deploy with fast surface forces.

Her cost was listed as $109 million, the costliest submarine yet built. Thanks to Rickover's collateral position as head of the AEC's Naval Reactors Branch, substantial additional costs for research and development did not have to be charged against the Navy.

Aircraft carriers were under continuous attack by critics as being too costly, vulnerable, and redundant. Whatever promised to enhance their survivability received support from the powerful air faction of the Navy, which had strong influence on the composition of the annual shipbuilding and weapons procurement programs. The submarine force as a whole was not an enthusiastic proponent of the SSRN 586, but it was happy to gain another nuclear submarine. If it had the support of our aviators, so much the better.

The weakness of the case of the SSRN, as I saw it, lay in the dichotomy of accelerating technology. Although nuclear power and Rickover's standards of engineering made possible a submarine of such size and phenomenal endurance, advances in other fields gravely threatened her ability to do her job. To carry out her mission she would be deployed some 600 miles ahead of a carrier strike force. There she would have to be on or near the surface, not only sacrificing her immunity from visual or radar detection but also inviting detection because of high-power radar emissions of her own. In an era of supersonic planes, air-to-surface missiles, and nuclear warheads, she would be very vulnerable without a means of defense. Further, it was not likely that we could ever have a sufficient number of such subs to make a meaningful contribution to carrier defense.

Even though the keel of SSRN 586 was not yet laid, there was no time to lose. In Admiral Warder's absence I wrote a highly classified memo to Rear Adm. Harry D. (Don) Felt, next up the chain of command and in charge of fleet operational readiness. He was a naval aviator, a forceful, able officer who went on to be commander of the Sixth Fleet, then vice chief of naval operations (VCNO), and finally commander-in-chief Pacific (CinCPac). He was small in stature, but a blunt, tough, demanding taskmaster who brought discomfiture to his peers and earned the antipathy, if not animosity, of his subordinates. Yet he could be generous as well. When he was VCNO in 1957 and I was unexpectedly selected for flag rank, he was the first to telephone congratulations.

In my memo I presented my reasoning and argued that the money for this one defensive unit would be better spent in creating a major modern offensive capability by building a nuclear-powered guided missile submarine of much greater capacity, speed, and endurance than all earlier ones, which were improvisations of diesel-powered boats that had been laid down as attack submarines. I proposed that we move quickly to change the military characteristics of SSRN 586 to those of a guided missile submarine, an SSGN, for the launching of Regulus II surface-to-surface missiles.

I knew the subject was sensitive and controversial, probably more so in OpNav than in Rickover's Naval Reactors Branch. Nevertheless, Rick could not be taken lightly on this issue. If "the operators" had specified a guided missile sub to begin with, he would have gone along, but to change now would bring highly publicized screams from Rick to the effect that "those stupid operators don't know what they want, and are interfering with my construction schedule." Not only that, to change the authorized shipbuilding program it would be necessary to go back before the Congress and the president.

My memo was promptly carried back to me by Capt. William D. Irvin, a fellow submariner who was Admiral Felt's administrative assistant. I was told that the SSRN issue was closed and that I should not rock the boat. I felt let down, piqued that what I considered sound views on a submarine matter were so cursorily dismissed by an aviator. I credited Don Felt with being as parochial an aviator as I was charged with being as a submariner. As I came more and more in contact with him, however, I grudgingly gave my respect for his ability and his devotion to the Navy's cause.

My sabbatical at the War College had kept me out of touch with Navy planning. I did not know that in 1953 the chief of naval operations had considered building a nuclear-powered guided missile submarine. Even before that, the strategic value of such a ship had been used as an additional argument in pressing for speedy development of a submarine reactor. However, the requirement for augmenting the air defenses of our carriers was apparently too strong to override, so that's where the advanced dual-reactor went.

My case was weakened by the fact that in the same building program with the SSRN was an SSG, diesel-powered, designed to launch Regulus I or II missiles. This meant that our most modern, Mach 2, atomic-armed missile would be launched from a horse-and-buggy-era ship. We had to find out from Rickover whether he could deliver on schedule the additional reactor that would be needed if we changed the ship's characteristics to specify nuclear propulsion. With no hesitation he replied affirmatively.

The new CNO, Adm. Arleigh Burke, was ahead of most of the Navy in thinking and planning for a nuclear Navy, so the chief problem was money – where to get the additional dollars that nuclear propulsion would cost. I was to learn that Rickover's estimate of costs for any reactor project he favored would be on the low side. Excess cost, or over-runs, were usually laid at the Bureau of Ships' door or blamed on design changes demanded by the operators. In this case, an estimated cost increase of $9 million for nuclear propulsion grew to some $20 million. Still, the logic for change was irrefutable, and the money was reprogrammed from lesser-priority projects.

My office was the one that recommended to the chief of naval operations and the secretary of the Navy the name that would be given to successive new construction submarines. In accordance with the policy recommended by the Submarine Conference, it would be chosen from the list of submarines that had won honors during the war and whose names were available by reason of loss or disposal. I so much believed in the importance of mating missiles with nuclear-powered submarines that when this first one so designed from the keel up was ready I took pains to have her named *Halibut* in honor of my own World War II torpedo-firing boat. Thus, in 1960 the first guided missile to be fired from a nuclear sub was launched by *Halibut*. The unarmed Regulus I missile flew 277 miles to its target.

* * * *

Rebuffed in my effort to transform SSRN 586 into a unit of enormous strategic firepower, I thought *Thresher* would be an appropriate name for a behemoth that would be required to expose itself frequently. (The thresher shark has a tail as long as its body. It flails it from side to side and slaps the water to frighten its prey.)

When he got wind of my plan, an irate Admiral Rickover telephoned to say, "Galantin, are you crazy? You can't give such a name to so important a ship! Suppose we had named *Nautilus* '*Sardine*'! What a travesty! You must not do this!"

When I remonstrated that a ship was not preordained to greatness, that what it did made its name famous and not the reverse, he brushed this aside. Skilled at invoking the power of the secretary of the Navy and of the Congress, his voice rose in shrill, impassioned invective, "Have you no God-damn public relations sense?"

Finally I said, "Well, Admiral, what do you think of the name *Triton?*"

"Good!" he said and down slammed his telephone.

Rickover had his own version of this exchange. To portray himself as the lonely voice of reason and progress in a benighted Navy, he was ever ready to fabricate. On October 20, 1958, soon after *Triton* was launched, he escorted Adm. Lord Louis Mountbatten through the ship at the builder's yard in Groton, Connecticut. Mountbatten recorded in his diary that "Rickover told me that the Navy Department, with typical lack of imagination, had christened this monarch of the deep by the ridiculous name of *Halibut,* but he arrived in time to discover this and managed to get the name painted out, and the fine name *Triton* substituted, before she was launched."[1]

Triton never paid off as a radar picket. Before long she was displaced in that role by aircraft carrying sophisticated radars and by missile-armed cruisers. She did fulfill her basic purpose and Rickover's intent from the start – to be the prototype for multireactor ships. The design and engineering talent that she nurtured were put to good use for the cruiser *Long Beach,* the world's first nuclear-powered surface ship, and for the aircraft carrier *Enterprise.*

Triton's enduring fame rests on her epochal voyage of 1960, when she circumnavigated the world underwater, traveling 36,014 miles. When Capt. Ned Beach ordered her to the surface off the East Coast, she had accomplished submerged in eighty-four days what it had taken Magellan's men three years to do by sail starting in 1519. Her voyage was the sole successful accomplishment of the several military and scientific feats that the Eisenhower administration had hoped to announce for their psychological effect prior to the president's summit meeting with Soviet Secretary General Khruschev in Paris.

17

TROUBLED WATERS

Arleigh Burke became chief of naval operations (CNO) in August 1955; he had been jumped over ninety-one admirals senior to him. Each of his five predecessors since World War II had served only two years in the Navy's top spot, but for Burke it was the start of six years of inspiring, demanding, innovative leadership in which he shaped the Navy's materiel and personnel to his vision of the needs of the future. His opposite number in the Royal Navy, with the title of first sea lord, was Adm. Lord Louis Mountbatten. They were good friends, both bold, aggressive destroyermen who had reached the top of the naval profession. Like Arleigh Burke, Lord Louis ("Dickie" to his intimates) had become almost a legendary figure for flamboyant wartime exploits. His destroyer HMS *Kelly* had survived striking a mine and being torpedoed, only to be sunk by German dive-bombers during the invasion of Crete. With other survivors he had clung to a life raft for hours while being strafed by German planes, an experience that he shrugged off with the words, "War is war."

But the two great seamen were in many respects unlike. Lord Louis was a patrician, of royal blood, related to most of the ruling families of Europe. Arleigh Burke, like all of us in the U.S. Navy, was plebeian; he was the descendant of immigrants, pioneer stock from Sweden. Mountbatten was effervescent and romantic; Burke was quiet, dogged, and pragmatic. Mountbatten loved publicity; he was admittedly vain. In his panache and what author Kenneth Rose called his "impregnable self-assurance" he was equaled only by Douglas MacArthur. In contrast, Arleigh Burke could be called reticent and unassuming.

Lord Louis's father had been first sea lord in 1914 while Britain was still the world's greatest sea power. It was the son's fate to preside over the Royal Navy in its twilight, but he did it with grace and style. With charm, persuasiveness, and the convincing record of his professional competence, he strengthened ties with our Navy. Ours could claim to be number one but, unlike the Royal Navy, we had never succeeded in securing public understanding of the importance of sea power to our nation.

Ever enamored by new technology and sensing the growing importance of undersea warfare, Mountbatten wanted above all to go to sea in *Nautilus* when he visited Admiral Burke in the fall of 1955. Earlier that year the United States and the United Kingdom had negotiated a Military Atomic Cooperation Agreement. Among other provisions it stated that "the U.S.A. may exchange with the U.K. such atomic information as the U.S.A. considers necessary for the development of the U.K.'s defense plans."

Both Admiral Burke and Rear Adm. Frank T. Watkins, Commander Submarines Atlantic, thought it fitting that Mountbatten should be the first foreign officer to embark in *Nautilus*. Unfortunately, Rear Admiral Rickover had another view. He did not consider a trip in *Nautilus* necessary for the United Kingdom's defense plans and believed it would be a dangerous precedent, leading to rapid erosion of our supremacy in nuclear technology. Exercising his political skills through his influential supporters in the Congress, he succeeded in preventing the trip.

Greatly embarrassed, Admiral Burke offered Mountbatten a visit to the next most significant ship in our submarine warfare program. *Albacore* was our hydrodynamic test vehicle, a highly streamlined submarine powered underwater by electric storage batteries, capable of speeds up to thirty knots. She was then operating out of Key West, Florida.

As head of the Submarine Warfare Branch of the chief of naval operations's staff, I was one of the small group that assembled at Washington National Airport in the frosty dawn of November 4, 1955, to fly to Key West with the two distinguished naval leaders. Mountbatten was fatigued by his heavy travel and social schedule, and as we flew south he laid down to nap in the bunk of the CNO's plane. A plane ride with Arleigh Burke, however, was never a time for his staff to relax; you were either briefing the admiral, exchanging ideas, or catching up on paper work. He was forever exhorting us to think, debate, evaluate, and plan.

On this occasion we were soon gathered around our new CNO while he drew us out on service problems as we saw them. Based on what I had observed in my two tours in the Pentagon, I volunteered that we had to be more ruthless in removing deadwood from our officer ranks, that too many were just sitting on their war records or were simply inept in departmental duties where planning, administration, and fiscal matters were so different from seagoing experiences. At sea their orders or commands would produce immediate action, but in Washington they could influence events only by the persuasion and logic of well-written papers or effective oral expression.

As in our first meeting in Boston several years earlier, Arleigh probably considered me just a brash young officer grinding an ax. Doubtless sensitive to his sudden elevation ahead of many able, accomplished flag officers, he replied that he did not see it as his role to eliminate officers who had performed well in war. Clearly, he did not agree with Field Marshall Bernard Montgomery's prescription: "An extensive use of weed killer is needed in the senior ranks after a war." In the next few years, however, I would see how his attitude toward this problem changed as he sought to make room for younger, more dynamic officers by encouraging the retirement of some whose time had passed.

We arrived in Key West in warm sunshine and embarked quickly in *Albacore,* where we were greeted by her captain, Comdr. Jon L. Boyes. Sliding smoothly through the clear, pale-green water of the harbor, our ship headed for the sea buoy and the dark blue of the Gulf Stream. As we proceeded to our diving area, lunch was served in the small wardroom. It was the usual submarine lunch for VIPs – steak and potatoes followed by baked Alaska, but it was unusual in the table conversation, which Lord Louis dominated with tales of his Mediterranean service and royal relatives.

I can still see his animated, ruddy face and twinkling eyes as he told why their young daughter, Pamela, on a visit to the United States, once had to spend a night as an immigrant on Ellis Island because of confusion as to her nationality. The immigration authorities were baffled by the fact that a supposedly English citizen carried a passport that seemed to make her a citizen of Spain.

It had happened this way. In the spring of 1929 the Mountbattens had sailed from Alexandria, Egypt, en route to England and Lord Louis's next duty station. The passenger liner paused at Algiers. Taking advantage of the chance to do some sightseeing, Mountbatten and the quite pregnant Lady Edwina took a small car. Because of primitive roads and her condition, they missed the sailing of their ship as it proceeded to Barcelona.

Although only a lieutenant, as a lord Mountbatten had an aide, who arranged passage in a small, uncomfortable craft to overtake their ship. As they crossed the Mediterranean to Spain, travel became increasingly difficult for Lady Edwina, but she was at last deposited safely in a hotel in Barcelona. During the night the aide called Lord Louis. "Come quickly! Lady Edwina's in difficulty."

Sure enough, she was in great pain with premature birth. Lord Louis was frantic and summoned all possible local help. Then a thought struck him, "I'll call my cousin in Madrid."

His cousin was King Alfonso XIII.

When the connection was made, Alfonso asked, "Where are you? What are you doing?"

"I'm in Barcelona. I'm having a baby! No! Edwina's having the baby! We need help!"

Help of every sort was soon underway, but the royal surgeon had difficulty getting access when he arrived. The king had ordered that a tight security guard be posted around the hotel.

✷ ✷ ✷ ✷

A ride in *Albacore* was, indeed, more exciting than one in *Nautilus*, which still had the hull form and twin shafts typical of conventional subs. As *Albacore* slipped easily through the Gulf Stream, Jon Boyes began the demonstration of his ship's capabilities with a brief explanation of her design and unique maneuvering characteristics. Using a grease pencil, he illustrated key points with diagrams on the stainless steel bulkhead in the battery compartment. Admiral Mountbatten never forgot the enthusiasm and conviction with which *Albacore*'s young skipper described his ship and put her through her paces, the ship heeling and turning, climbing and diving steeply in a way no other ship could. In my meetings with him years later he would always recall Jon Boyes with pleasure.

Late that evening, as we disembarked from our plane in Washington, I saw new evidence of the Mountbatten method and charisma. As we said good night, he recalled and thanked each of us in turn for some specific contribution or comment we had made during our busy trip. To me he said, "Captain, that was a good discussion of single screw versus twin screw." To another he said, "You made a good point on how speed compounds the ASW problem."

It was while we were in Key West that what was to prove the genesis of a significant development in Anglo-American relations took place. Ten years later, Mountbatten himself described what happened in a letter I received from him concerning the joint U.S.-U.K. Polaris program, which I will describe later.

I happened to be present on that historic day at Key West when Arleigh Burke was rung up from the Pentagon to say that the U.S. Air Force refused to cooperate with the U.S. Navy in producing an IRBM.

The CNO told me he had just given instructions for the Navy to go ahead and produce a missile with solid fuel which could be fired from submarines.

I was so deeply impressed by the idea that I asked if the Royal Navy could be associated with this in a small way; he agreed, and as you know we had a Commander, Royal Navy in the Polaris team almost from the beginning.

✶ ✶ ✶ ✶

At this time, in the public, the press, and the Congress there was enthusiastic support for submarines, occasioned both by our war record and by the remarkable performance of *Nautilus*. Despite continuing competition for a greater share of the defense budget, both Army and Air Force were advocates of fuller exploitation of the submarine by our Navy. It did not, at the time, seem to infringe on their missions, and neither cared to have anything to do underwater. This was so in February 1956, when I was one of an OpNav team sent to the Air War College at Maxwell Field, Montgomery, Alabama, to present Navy strategic concepts. My part was to explain the role of the submarine, and I began with the following anecdote from World War II.

Our Office of Naval Intelligence analyzed all aspects of the Japanese navy. When it came to personnel, ONI found that the officers and enlisted men of the Imperial Navy as a whole came on a properly proportionate basis from all the home islands of Japan. This was to be expected in a maritime nation. However, with respect to the Japanese submarine force, our analysts found a difference – submarine personnel came chiefly from one locality, the island of Hokkaido. That northern island has a generally rugged aspect of bleak and barren terrain, confirmed by my own countless periscope observations. It was that character of Hokkaido, said the intelligence experts, which caused the Japanese to choose their submariners from there. They reasoned that such surroundings produced "a breed of rugged simpletons ideally suited for the submarine service."

"What a strange way to select personnel," I said. "It's just as though we would take all our submariners from Texas."

A voice from the audience interrupted. "You can't do that! That's where we get our aviators."

When the laughter subsided, I pointed out that aviators and submariners do have much in common – both operate in three dimensions in a fluid medium, and both like to carry the fight to the enemy.

During my talk I described the guided missile submarine, its ability to remain hidden on station, to surface quickly, and to launch the Regulus missile armed with a nuclear warhead. At a preluncheon gathering, the subject came up again.

Maj. Gen. Orvil A. Anderson, USAF, was an ardent proponent of Strategic Air Command bombing concepts and a zealous advocate of Air Force claims against Navy and Army. Because of his rash, outspoken advocacy of "Preventive War," he had to retire from his post at the Air War College and was head of the Air Force Historical Foundation. I asked what his reaction would be to the following hypothetical situation: Guided missile submarines are deployed submerged off Murmansk, Vladivostok, Petropavlosk, and the like at the time of an aborted Geneva conference and imminent war. They need only a radio signal to surface and send their warheads on their brief flight. They would not have to be steamed there at the Navy's thirty knots or flown there at the Air Force's six hundred knots; they would already be there – a continuous, surreptitious deterrent. His reply was exactly this: "We'd better outlaw that Goddamn system!"

   ✶   ✶   ✶   ✶

The nuclear-submarine-guided missile combination was a politically attractive, militarily sound concept that received much support both from within and without the Navy. However, as is so often the case, the need for current readiness for unpredictable contingencies preoccupied Navy planners and absorbed most of the budget. The man responsible for that readiness, the CNO, could never move as fast and as far toward future capabilities as the proponents of new weapons and new technologies wished. I believe no one ever did a better job of balancing those competing demands than did Arleigh Burke. Had he yielded to the pressures for an all-out major buildup of our submarine-guided missile force, other more flexible capabilities would have been short-changed. And with the unexpected early advent of the fleet ballistic missile system, we would have been left with a bloc of expensive, obsolescent subs. Little did anyone know the speed with which the Polaris missile would be mated with the nuclear submarine to create a new order of deterrence.

Regardless of the virtues of the concealed, relatively invulnerable deterrent that our subs and Regulus could be, I felt strongly that for the next ten years our major submarine effort should be devoted to ASW. I reasoned that the submarine was only one of the essential, subordinate elements of our overall naval warfare system. To our ardent submarine proponents I pointed out, as was brought home during the Korean War, the shortcomings of the submarine in its inability to do many of the tasks that a modern navy had to perform. Neither was it ready to displace SAC and our carrier strike force in their deterrent role. Nevertheless, I was sure the submarine would be exploited to much greater degree in the tasks it was uniquely fitted to perform.

With Freddy Warder's approval, I tried to centralize submariners' thinking along these lines and present to the CNO a sound long-range program, one that embodied the views of the two submarine force commanders. This was the purpose of the Submarine Advisory Board we set up. It consisted of the director of the Submarine/Anti-Submarine Warfare Division of OpNav (OP 31), ComSubLant, and ComSubPac and would meet at least once a year.

However, it was not easy to enunciate and obtain loyalty to a submarine program that was consistent with overall Navy objectives and resources. Submariners tend to be individualists, independent and aggressive. They try to be intimately involved in the design and construction of their ships. They are quick to be critical of new designs and new concepts, as I had been of SSRN 586. Some were outspoken in their view that the submarine's capabilities were not being given adequate consideration in the Navy's top councils.

I counseled patience and persuasion and pointed out the harm being done by well-intentioned individual efforts to promote the cause of the submarine. To drive home the point, I had a sign painted and placed over the entrance to my office. On it were the words of Thomas Jefferson: "A good cause is often injured more by ill timed effort of its friends than by arguments of its enemies."[1]

I thought we were getting things back on the track when, on March 12, 1956, the too-aptly-named "Periscope" column of *Newsweek* magazine carried this item: "NAVY DEPARTMENT – Watch for new and highly publicized discontent among Navy's 'Young Turks,' unhappy over alleged traditional thinking of senior admirals who continue to plan in terms of aircraft carriers and destroyers. Young bloods contend the Navy can be supreme only with fleets of atomic-powered submarines."

The corridors in the Pentagon shook like a destroyer in heavy seas. The "senior admirals" viewed the article as evidence of disloyalty by submariners. I was quite sure that no submarine officer actively involved in our submarine planning had inspired the story. There were others, however, including some employed by industry, who openly talked of a "submersible SAC." They quoted Mahan's truism that changes in weapons come quickly, but new tactics come slowly; they must overcome the inertia of those trained in weapons that had been successful in the past.

The magazine's terse, two-sentence prediction only made more difficult the task of evolving a unified Navy, one in which the special qualities of its diverse elements were integrated into a balanced whole. I had been stressing the contributions our submarines could make in ASW and in guided missile warfare. Their ability to operate concealed in forward combat areas not tenable by our surface forces gave individual units a high power value. In no way could they do the job alone, but they could greatly further the Navy's primary mission, which was to retain control of the seas for ourselves and our allies and to deny it to the enemy.

I had reason to stress ASW. In World War II my submarine, *Halibut,* had contributed to the substantial part our submarines played in the victory over Japan. Later, as a division and squadron commander of submarines, in exercises against surface task forces, I saw that our boats were too easily penetrating ASW screens. Time and again enthusiastic young submarine skippers would report short-range torpedo attacks against our heavy warships, sometimes even flaunting close-in periscope photos. Too often the attack would be written off by a fleet umpire as not being conducted under the realistic conditions and tactics that would pertain in war.

This led to a personally distressing incident in the spring of 1956. Admiral Burke had called a late-afternoon meeting with all his staff captains, more than a hundred of us, with no flag officer present. Delayed by a JCS meeting in the so-called tank, and showing the strain of the punishing workload he set for himself, he had no time to organize his thoughts but spoke forcefully off-the-cuff. The thrust of his remarks was the large part we had to play in shaping the Navy to the needs of the future. Always frank and direct, he was critical of us, saying that we were not giving him the support he needed. He declared that we refused to take responsibility, that we passed problems up the line, many of them to him personally, rather than make a decision ourselves. How our individual decisions taken in any significant matter could survive in the Pentagon maze of multilayered, overlapping responsibilities was not explained.

After the CNO let off steam for a while, he invited questions. From his answers to the few innocuous queries and from the meeting itself I noted that his attitude toward personnel had hardened since the brief discussion I had with him during the flight to Key West seven months before. I tried a question of my own. "Is the Navy taking full advantage of new methods and new weapons in performing its primary task – ASW to keep the sea lanes open?"

Recognizing me, he retorted, "I suppose you mean why don't we use more submarines?"

"No, sir, but I know what submarines can do to our Navy, so I believe we should put more into ASW." (I had in mind not only the war records of German and U.S. subs but also the vastly increased potential of nuclear submarines.)

In answer he said we should not turn loose of proven weapons, that we had to have all the answers to a problem before making major changes, and that "we must not kill somebody else's baby to keep one's own alive."

It was apparent that calling ASW our primary task had provoked him, but I sensed no animus. However, the next day Rear Adm. Harry (Savvy) Sanders told my boss, Rear Admiral Warder, that four captains had separately told him, "Galantin irritated Admiral Burke and made him angry." Sanders said he thought highly of me and my work, but that perhaps my tactics were wrong and that I might "get better results other ways." He went on to mention that Carl Holden, a very fine officer, was initially passed over simply because he "kicked up too big a wake."

I could not believe that Admiral Burke would resent initiative and frank discussion of Navy problems. And events proved that I was right. He was too big a man, too great a leader. In the numerous but brief meetings I would have with him, there was never undue criticism or annoyance with well-reasoned positions; more often there was encouragement.

A case in point was the $10 million project put forward by the Bureau of Ships (BuShips) for the modification of *Albacore.* She was our experimental, unarmed, diesel-electric hydrodynamic test submarine. Operations in her original configuration had produced important data for the design of larger, even higher speed, attack submarines, but there was much more to be learned. It would be very helpful to our submarine designers to test alternate systems of underwater control, such as a cruciform set of stern-diving planes, and to determine safe limits for high-speed maneuvers and the possible need for speed brakes. Admiral Burke asked that we consider giving *Albacore* a combat capability as well. In a lengthy session I presented as strong a case as possible for the changes to be made and for the benefits of keeping *Albacore* as an experimental vehicle dedicated to BuShips' needs. If the ship was given a torpedo-firing capability we would gain one attack boat of very limited capability and lose flexibility and operational time needed for the exploration of new design concepts. The CNO deferred decision but said, "Don't give up. You have a lot of good reasons. I just want to be sure you've considered all possibilities." We soon were able to go ahead with the proposed changes.

✴   ✴   ✴   ✴

Great as were the advances being made in submarine capabilities at this time, destroyers and aircraft, fixed-wing and helicopter, those primary agents of ASW, were also acquiring new tools and greater efficiency. The same was true in the Soviet navy. It was important that we not be satisfied with the depth reached by *Tang.* I had gone to sea in boats of the O-, R-, S-, and V-classes and various models of fleet submarines, as well as *Tang, Nautilus,* and *Seawolf.* In pro- and antisubmarine exercises I had seen the great advantages of deeper operations, but throughout a spectrum of designs whose construction spanned thirty-seven years, we had progressed only from 150 to 700 feet in operating depth. Most convincing of all, in my own combat operations in *Halibut* I had often longed for the safety and flexibility of maneuver of greater depth, even when exceeding the official "safe" operating depth.

But going deeper was not simply a matter of increasing the thickness of hull plating. Any increase in the weight of hull would have to be compensated by reduction in size or payload. Improved steel of greater strength-to-weight ratio was required. Furthermore, many components and fittings would need to be redesigned, with consequent weight and space penalties. All this would add considerably to the cost and difficulty of construction.

Broadly speaking, the submarine's ability to reach great depths is analogous to the airplane's ability to reach great altitude. Actually, the ability to operate at great depth is an even more important operational asset for the submarine than is great height for the plane. Large in bulk, limited in speed, the stealthy submarine benefits greatly from the freedom of maneuver granted by increased operating depth. In addition to the extra margin for recovery in case of operational casualty or battle stress, the greater volume of ocean made accessible enhances the submarine's concealment and greatly complicates the enemy's search task. The deeper it can go, the better the submarine can seek out the ocean layers that give it the best acoustic paths for detecting and tracking targets. Conversely, on the defensive it can take fuller advantage of thermal or salinity gradients and make the problem for enemy weapons much more severe.

The extra sinking time required for free-falling weapons such as bombs, depth charges, and ahead-thrown rockets virtually eliminates them as a threat to deep submarines. To cope with deep submarines that have, as well, the increased speed and unlimited endurance of nuclear power, costly and complex homing weapons – in effect, miniature unmanned submersibles – would have to be developed.

Having said all that, the analogy with aircraft must not be carried too far. For example, whereas the higher the airplane flies the less inhibited it is by terrain, the opposite is not true for the submarine. The deeper it goes the more its movements will be constrained by bottom topography. Nevertheless, because of the great advantages accruing from operation at greater depth, it was important that we be able to go much deeper than 700 feet.

Admiral Burke listened sympathetically to our arguments, but he insisted on more than generalized, seat-of-the-pants judgments before approving the complex and costly engineering effort required. We had to get factual scientific validation of the benefits of going deeper. Fortunately, this was before the heyday of systems analysis. I doubt that our problem, so dependent as it was on operational experience and military judgment, would have withstood the emphasis on cost. How do you quantify safety, concealment, and flexibility?

We did have within the Navy Department the Operations Evaluation Group (OEG), which had proven its worth in wartime operations analysis. Headed by Dr. Jacinto Steinhardt, it was made up of civilian scientists and mathematicians who applied their methods to rational analysis of strategic and tactical problems. Our task was assigned to Erwin Baumgarten and completed by L. S. Pocinki, who spent much time discussing submarine warfare with all of us in OP 311: myself, Sneed Schmidt, Bob McWethy, and Charlie Rush. Meanwhile, I had been stressing to Rear Admirals Mumma and Morgan, and to Capt. James S. Bethea in BuShips, the importance of being able to go deeper. They were already working with the steel industry to develop reliable sources of HY-80 (high-yield, 80,000 p.s.i.), a stronger, lighter steel suitable for welding and able to withstand the cyclic stresses peculiar to submarine operations, but they were understandably cautious.

A fortuitous coincidence may have advanced our cause. In the spring of 1956, I went to Portsmouth, England, to speak at an antisubmarine conference. My subject was "A Concept for the Use of Submarines in ASW." In port at the time was the U.S.S.R's cruiser *Ordzhonikidze*. With two escorting destroyers she brought President Bulganin and First Secretary Khruschev on an official visit to England. I was able to inspect the ships closely from dockside and from a boat trip alongside, and was impressed not only by their shipshape appearance but also by evidence of good construction and up-to-date armament.

In London I had lunched with Rear Adm. T. Inglis, RN, Director of Naval Intelligence. The evening before he had attended the Admiralty dinner honoring the senior Russians. I was surprised to hear him say that the talk Khruschev gave, entirely without notes, was one worthy of Churchill. In his speech Khruschev asked, "What are cruisers like *Ordzhonikidze* good for in this day of thermo-nuclear weapons?"

"They're good to carry high-ranking official on visits to friendly countries," he told his audience and offered to build similar ships for Britain. It was a clever ploy to undermine confidence in surface fleets while Russia was busy expanding her own. She already had the world's largest submarine force.

My return to Washington was via Paris, where I spent one night in the Hotel George V. Who should I meet in the elevator but Rear Adm. Armand Morgan, concluding his European tour of shipyards and inspecting progress in hydrofoil boats. Armand was assistant chief of BuShips for ship design and research. He was a brilliant, articulate engineering duty officer who had graduated at the head of his 1924 class of 523 midshipmen. During the war he had been in charge of all submarine material maintenance and improvement in BuShips, in effect being "Mr. Submarine" in the bureau. He had maintained close, effective liaison with the submarine force commanders in their continuing demands for technical refinement and improvement.

In his room, relaxing with a whisky, there was plenty of time to answer his questions, "Now tell me, Pete, why do you need to go deeper? What good reasons are there?" I did my best to give them.

In February 1957 the OEG study, *The Effects of Increased Submarine Test Depth,* was completed. It concluded: "Since submarine survival is appreciably improved by increased test depth which can be provided at modest cost, test depths to at least 1,300 feet are recommended."[2]

✳ ✳ ✳ ✳

By this time it was clear that nuclear-powered submarines of adequate performance would have to be considerably larger than our diesel boats, but there had been much debate over size. Definition of the characteristics, or performance requirements, of a new class of subs, a necessary preliminary to including it in the annual shipbuilding program, was not a matter left solely to experienced submarine officers. Much time and energy was spent in justifying design features to nonsubmarine officers who occupied key positions in the chain of approval. Victor Barringer's friendly advice of years past – that I needed a string of initials of a certain length before an admiral would sign any letter – came often to mind.

Many officers, including some submariners, believed that to be successful a submarine had to be small. In part this idea had credibility because it was always the belief of greatly respected Adm. Thomas C. Hart from his early days as director of submarines in 1918 to his influential position as president of the General Board as late as 1942. In addition, the unhappy histories of large submarines, among them the U.S. *Nautilus I, Argonaut,* and *Narwhal,* the French *Surcouf,* and the British *M-1,* were recited.

It was finally accepted, however, that a submarine, like any ship that was given adequate, reliable horsepower, could be as large as necessary to perform its function. In this respect it was helpful to point to the pride of the fleet, our newest aircraft carrier *Forrestal*. In order to operate aircraft that were themselves more advanced, more capable, larger, and heavier than their predecessors, she had to be larger than earlier carriers and displaced 76,000 tons.[3]

✶ ✶ ✶ ✶

Even as such great technical progress was being made, the climate of discord and suspicion highlighted by the "Periscope" item in *Newsweek* was exacerbated by the unexpected retirement of two distinguished submariners. This drew much public attention, as well as the concern of top Navy officials that widespread defections might be in the offing. Was the traditional esprit de corps of the silent service crumbling?

In the spring of 1957, within one month of each other, Capt. Richard H. O'Kane and Capt. Chester W. Nimitz, Jr., requested retirement. Dick, my *Argonaut* shipmate and our consummate submarine attack skipper, had won the Congressional Medal of Honor when in command of *Tang I* and had survived ten brutal months in Japanese prison camps. Chester, the rangy, outspoken son of our five-star fleet commander-in-chief in World War II, had performed brilliantly both as a junior officer and in command of his own boats, *Haddo* and *Sarda*.

Hanson Baldwin, a Naval Academy graduate and the respected military analyst of the *New York Times*, had noted the trend of early retirements among able, experienced naval officers, and he made the cases of O'Kane and Nimitz the subject of a widely read column. Chester was out of reach at sea in command of the submarine tender *Orion*, but Dick was on duty in Washington. He had relieved me as ComSubRon 7 in Pearl Harbor in 1954, but now sat unhappily behind a desk in the Pentagon, where Baldwin reached him by telephone.

Baldwin's article concluded, "Pay is a factor, an important factor, but it is by no means the major factor. Unnecessarily frequent changes of duty, too narrow an interpretation of service loyalty, and above all the absence of a sense of a job worth doing and well done have too often stultified the most energetic and the most ambitious."

As variously repeated, certain remarks attributed to Dick could be construed as a statement of support for the "single service," a concept that is anathema to the Navy. Storm signals were hoisted. Admiral Burke was furious over this apparent disloyalty. I was told by one of his assistants that the admiral wanted to get to the bottom of why these two successful and famous submariners chose to retire at this time. He wanted more than the sterile reasons they put in their official requests. The task of interviewing my colleagues was assigned to me.

Dick O'Kane was a pragmatic innovator, impatient with routine and scornful of any rigidity in planning or procedure. In a Pentagon assignment that was little more than clerical, updating an interior communications manual, he was completely miscast. In his words, "What I have accomplished in one year could be done in one month."

Chester Nimitz gave as his reason for early retirement the fact that forthcoming educational expenses for his three daughters would be too heavy to meet on a Navy captain's pay, and he wished to start a career in industry while still young enough to build a future.[4] However plausible, this begged the question of how the many dedicated naval officers serving in the surface Navy who were without the benefit of submarine or flight pay could manage the same problem.

After twenty years of commissioned service one could retire and receive retainer pay of 50 percent of his base pay. In 1957 this meant $358 a month to a captain. In addition, the Navy and Marine Corps had another benefit. To those who had earned a combat decoration, legislation governing retirement gave the privilege of promotion to the next higher rank on the retired list. Captains could thus retire with the rank of rear admiral. They received no increase in pay on that account, but there were intangible psychic rewards in bearing the "tombstone" rank in civilian pursuits.

Dick and Chester qualified for both benefits, but I was certain that their decisions were prompted by disenchantment with peacetime Navy duty, whereby many experienced officers, accustomed to high responsibility and command at sea were relegated to dull administrative chores ashore. Men with the vigor, initiative, and daring of O'Kane and Nimitz, qualities that had made them good submarine officers, could not be happy and productive in such an environment. Such events only made more difficult the integration of an orderly submarine program within the Navy's overall requirements.

18

THE RICKOVER EQUATION

Abrasive, *b*rilliant, *c*ontentious, *d*edicated, every letter of the alphabet – all the way to *z* for *z*ealot – led to some word of praise or blame appropriate to Hyman Rickover. In many years of acquaintance and professional association I would use them all.

Hyman George Rickover was born in Poland in 1900, and came to the United States at the age of six. His family settled in Chicago, where his father was a tailor. Young Rickover was not an outstanding student in Chicago's public schools, but a steadily improving one, with great self-discipline. His motivation to enter the Naval Academy in June 1918 was simply the desire to get a good education that was otherwise beyond the reach of family resources. At any rate, the hard-working young man attracted the attention of his congressman and received an appointment to the Academy. His intensive, self-imposed individual study to prepare for the entrance examination was early proof of the personal responsibility and accountability he would forever stress.

Rickover's record at the Naval Academy was undistinguished, with no significant activity in sports or other extracurricular events. He kept pretty much to himself, concentrating on academics, and graduated in the upper quarter of the 539 in the class of 1922.

The class had seen the Navy drawn down severely from the wartime level that existed when they became midshipmen in 1918, and the U.S.-sponsored Washington Naval Conference was in the process of making further drastic reductions in heavy cruisers and battleships. It established a capital ship tonnage ratio: United States, 5; Great Britain, 5; Japan, 3; and 1.6 each for France and Italy. Thus, in 1922 prospects for a rewarding long-term naval career were not good. A fourth of the class chose to resign on graduation.

Rickover stayed in. His first assignment was to the destroyer *LaVallette* in San Diego, followed by two years in the engineering department of the battleship *Nevada*. In both ships his greatest satisfaction came from studying, operating, and improving the efficiency of the engineering plants. Next came postgraduate instruction at Columbia University, where he earned a master's degree in electrical engineering. When he was ordered to the battleship *California* in a repeat of the job he'd already held in *Nevada*, he volunteered for duty in submarines. As a twenty-nine-year-old lieutenant, he was considered too senior to be eligible, but after the intercession of a former commanding officer he was accepted.

After Submarine School, in June 1930 Rickover was assigned to *S-48*. She was one of the last four S-boats to be built; already in operation were *V-1*, *V-2*, and *V-3*, leading the way in search for a successful fleet boat. *S-48* was notorious throughout the submarine force for having sunk in Long Island Sound during her builder's trials in 1921, as well as for her chronic engineering problems.

Rick was apparently a competent submariner. Within a year he became executive officer of *S-48*, next to the skipper the most important position on board, largely responsible for the efficiency of the ship as a whole. Shortly after, he was declared "qualified to command submarines," a designation not awarded lightly. However, his three years in *S-48* were destined to be his only submarine operational experience.

After shore duty in a Navy materiel office, he went to sea again as assistant engineer officer of the battleship *New Mexico*, the first of six turboelectric power battleships. (After the Washington Treaty, six others of the same design were canceled while under construction, and one was sunk as a gunnery target.) In *New Mexico*, Rickover's passion for engineering efficiency became even more evident, and the style of his leadership was apparent in the resentment that his abrasive, intolerant manner provoked in his enlisted men and fellow officers. Nevertheless, for three years in a row his relentless, intense commitment won *New Mexico* first place for battleships in engineering proficiency and the right to paint a huge red *E* on her smokestack.

In 1937 he was given command of USS *Finch*, an old, decrepit minesweeper on the Asiatic Station. Appalled by her materiel condition, he instituted a vigorous corrective program. Here again his hypercritical, seemingly abusive treatment of personnel caused resentment. After only three months in what would be his only ship command, Rickover was assigned duty in the Cavite Navy Yard in the Philippines. Perhaps sensing dubious success should he pursue command at sea, a sine qua non for any line officer aspiring to promotion and higher command, and also responding to his fascination with engineering, he had requested transfer to the ranks of line officers restricted to engineering duties only and designated engineering duty officer (EDO).

When Rickover returned to the United States in 1939 for duty in the Bureau of Ships, the prospect of war in Europe had impelled Congress to authorize a shipbuilding program to enlarge the Navy greatly. Before long he was in charge of the bureau's electrical section, with great responsibility and authority over the electrical systems that were so crucial in every type of ship. With his customary disdain for established procedures, intense attention to detail, readiness to take responsibility, and unrelenting pressure on self and subordinates, he made his section probably the most effective in BuShips and earned from the deputy chief of BuShips, Rear Admiral Mills, the support that would lead to his control of the Navy's nuclear propulsion program.

In 1947, when Mills designated him his special assistant for nuclear matters, the "office" that was assigned to Rickover was a barren room, once a women's toilet, on the fourth floor of the Navy Building on Constitution Avenue. Blanked-off piping still protruded from the flimsy walls of the "temporary" structure built in 1918's wartime emergency. He had no secretary, nothing to work with except Mills's moral support. As the saga of his career unfolded, Rickover proudly used that office as a symbol of his uphill fight to triumph over opposition and circumvent "the system" he held in such contempt.

When he was placed in charge of the bureau's Nuclear Power Branch in 1948, he had overcome his start in a staff position that carried no responsibility for technical developments in BuShips, and, in the face of adamant opposition by many of its senior officers, he took charge of the Navy's participation in the Atomic Energy Commission's ongoing nuclear power projects. He moved quickly and vigorously. He astutely established himself in the AEC as chief of the Naval Reactors Branch in its Reactor Development Division. He would then use the authority and responsibility of either agency, Navy or AEC, in a reinforcement or cross-ruff, as needed, to advance the mission that obsessed him: to bring into being a nuclear-powered Navy, with the initial application to be in a submarine. It was a tactic he exploited with Machiavellian skill, using it to ignore or override the authority of his ostensible seniors in the chain of command as he consolidated his control over every major aspect, personnel included, of the Navy's nuclear power program.

In large meetings he was deferential, low-key, and deceptively mild. It was in the one-on-one personal relations that he frequently became abusive, caustic, and profane. I was past the point where I was eligible for consideration as a "nuke," to be trained in nuclear technology under his direction and to command a nuclear submarine, so I was never subjected to the notorious interview in which he frequently browbeat and humiliated candidates before making his Olympian judgment as to their fitness for the nuclear program. Rickover shrugged off all criticism of his personnel selection method and refused to change, saying it was his way, the best way, to probe young men's character, motivation, and potential. He declared that he was looking for officers who were not hampered by conventional thinking and who were genuinely interested in the technical challenge of nuclear power.

Although the Rickover interviews were viewed widely as capricious and irrational, there was a guiding principle. An important objective was to uncover and reject any candidates showing a tendency toward the unimaginative, go-by-the-book type of thinking that he so disdained and to find those whose motivation was driven more by intellectual interest in a new technical field than by the furtherance of their career by being in the right spot at the right time. His means of determining this often seemed bizarre; seemingly excellent candidates were often rejected, whereas others were unaccountably accepted. He encouraged the idea that the interview was to be feared and that the candidates would be nervous and so less liable to hide their true natures under the questioning and browbeating. He abhorred the notion that there were "right answers" to some of his more frequently used questions. Anyone who appeared to have been briefed as to what to say was given short shrift.

Unscientific and subjective as his screening method was, it brought to nuclear-powered submarines and surface ships officers and enlisted men who were highly motivated, superbly trained in the technology of nuclear propulsion, and, in general, loyal to their stern taskmaster. Most would acknowledge that his challenge to excel, to perform at the highest level, and to be held accountable made them better naval officers.

In the early years, before there was a pool of nuclear-trained officers working their way up to command, Rickover was screening individuals not only for technical training but also to command the new ships. One of the best of them, William E. Sims, now captain, USN (ret.), was one of the first three to be chosen to command a Polaris missile submarine, the *Theodore Roosevelt* (SSBN 600). In his judgment, "Rickover was the best thing that ever happened to this navy, but we don't need another." Because the Bureau of Naval Personnel nominated their best candidates for his interview and selection, its regular detailing system would doubtless have identified the same officers for ships of such importance. However, it is questionable whether they would have been as loyal to Rickover, and that was of great importance to him in maintaining control over the performance standards he demanded for ships and personnel of the nuclear Navy – which was soon being called "Rickover's Navy."

In this context, perhaps *loyal* is not the right word. Rickover never sought personal loyalty. Indeed, from the start of his commissioned service upon graduation from the Naval Academy in 1922, his record was that of an intensely hardworking, unprepossessing, noncharismatic officer who violated accepted norms of leadership and wanted respect not for personal traits but for what he had accomplished. Engineering excellence was his Holy Grail: to use the laws of physics for society's benefit, humanity must be obedient to them through the excellence of the engineering by which they are applied.

It was to find officers who were, or could be made, loyal to that principle that Rickover used his interview system. Preliminary quizzing by some of his key staff was followed by the climactic confrontation with Rickover himself in which technical matters never came up. As the nature of his interview became known, another motive was clear: Rick's purpose was to establish his dominance, to leave no doubt in a candidate's mind that if he entered the nuclear program he must conform to Rickover's standards and not to those of his previous training when conflict or uncertainty arose.

Of his own experience, Sims said, "After my interview I walked out knowing that I had failed, and I was happy to be out of it. I called the submarine detail officer in BuPers and said that he would have to send someone else, because I wouldn't work for the son-of-a-bitch even if I had been selected. He laughed and said, 'What are you talking about? You've been selected, and you're in the program.' I soon realized that I had not understood what the purpose of all the procedures was. . . . When Leonard Erb, an outstanding naval officer, fine submariner, and a very intelligent man, came in to be interviewed, I was the third man in the room. When the interview was over, Len was so down I felt he could have walked out the door without opening it and not even bump his head. He was very depressed over failing the interview. After he had left the room, Rickover turned to me and said, 'That is one of the best guys we have ever brought in.'

"I answered, 'You wouldn't know it from anything that was said in the last fifteen minutes.'

"Rick's answer was, 'Watch him work now. He'll be great.'"

Significantly, Rickover designated Erb for a special challenge – to be commanding officer of the *Abraham Lincoln* (SSBN 602), first of the three SSBNs that would be built in the government shipyard at Portsmouth, New Hampshire. It was the yard of whose management and performance he was particularly critical.

It was ironic that the man who never commanded a submarine, and had command at sea for only three months, became the sole arbiter of those who would head up our most advanced and complex ships. That he chose well is proven by the roster of his selectees who reached the highest positions in the Navy. Four of the last five chiefs of naval operations are products of the Rickover process, and a remarkable number of his graduates have risen to three- and four-star rank. Numerous others, after retirement from the Navy, have filled important national and industrial leadership positions, among them President Jimmy Carter.

Few can recall ever hearing Rickover praise an officer or enlisted man, or even a civilian engineer of his organization. His basic brand of leadership was the lash of immensely hard, sustained work and of perfection unattained. Yet this ruthless, friendless, driven man could be caring and compassionate. When the child of one of his skippers-in-training died tragically, it was he who comforted the grieving father with readings from the Bible.

Much as I disliked Rickover's often abusive treatment of personnel and his Machiavellian operating techniques, I admired his engineering accomplishments. From my wartime experience and postwar operations I was convinced that nuclear power was essential for our submarines if they were to contribute significantly to our nation's sea power. Perhaps for that reason, and the fact that in four successively senior assignments in the Navy Department I was concerned with fuller exploitation of the submarine in our Navy's mission, I enjoyed generally friendly relations with the caustic genius who had such unswerving commitment to personal responsibility and excellence.

When I took up the first of those assignments in 1949, I was among those whose support he wanted and whom he tried to keep informed of progress – but never of problems – through technical briefings by his staff or, on special occasions, by himself. I was one of a party he conducted to Bettis Atomic Power Laboratory near Pittsburgh in 1951 to visit the plant urgently constructed for the production of pure zirconium. Because of its unique nuclear characteristics, this rare, costly, highly corrosion-resistant metal was needed in quantity for the reactor core and fuel elements. It was my first exposure to a Rickover sales technique: flattering personal attention to a customer or interested official and the gift of a small memento. In this case, we each received a small, bright and shiny piece of zirconium rod.

As he grew in accomplishment and power, the little favors became more notable and more eagerly accepted. At a ship's commissioning, the sponsor of a nuclear submarine would receive, along with a graciously worded note from the admiral, a small, carefully crafted model of "her" ship. Sometimes a tiny bottle of water collected by a submarine at the North Pole would be bestowed on a key supporter. Letters written on board a nuclear-powered ship or submarine during sea trials or demonstrations would be dispatched to influential officials who contributed in some way to its success.

He was particularly careful to keep members of Senate or House committees before which he had to appear well informed. Aware that favorable publicity was mother's milk to ambitious politicians who were ever eager to be identified with popular, successful programs, especially if they brought money and jobs to their districts, he praised, flattered, or cajoled them liberally. His loyalty to those whose support in the Congress had been important extended to the point that he over-rode policy and succeeded in naming, posthumously, new attack submarines for Rep. William H. Bates of the Joint Committee on Atomic Energy (JCAE), Glenard P. Lipscomb of the Appropriations Committee, L. Mendel Rivers of the Armed Services Committee, and Sen. Richard B. Russell.

Such tactics were viewed by most of the line seagoing community of the Navy and Rickover's own engineering colleagues as self-serving, part of his scheme to establish himself before the Congress as the Navy's sole authority on nuclear power. As time went on, it was apparent that he would allow no one on his staff to attain the stature, prestige, or authority that would make him a logical successor to Rickover himself. Several brilliant and capable engineering officers were either shunted aside or forced out. Some others left of their own choosing when it was clear to them that extended duty in Rickover's shop violated the duty rotation policy that applied to advancement in both the seagoing and EDO communities.

Rick was not hesitant to declare that no one else could bring nuclear power technology to the Navy successfully and that it was essential that he remain in control. He would point out that nowhere else in the Navy, or in the AEC or private industry for that matter, was there the same strict accountability to which he held himself, his staff, and his contractors. He maintained that only he was fully aware of the complexities and dangers inherent in the new technology and totally committed to achieving and sustaining the highest possible safety, reliability, and operational excellence.

He knew all too well that the mutual antipathy that marked his relations with most senior operational and engineering duty officers meant that to maintain his position he needed the support of powerful men in the Congress. Notable among them were Senators Brien McMahon of Connecticut, Henry M. Jackson of Washington, John O. Pastore of Rhode Island, Clinton P. Anderson of New Mexico, and Representatives Sidney R. Yates of Rickover's home district in Chicago, Illinois, Chet Holifield of California, and John W. McCormack of Massachusetts. It was these men, and others with nationwide reach and influence, who would come to his aid in the major crisis of his career.

By 1951 Rickover had been a captain for nine years and, with the nuclear program well underway, could reasonably look forward to being selected for promotion to rear admiral. However, that year's selection board of nine senior admirals, including three of his own EDO category, passed him over. Now he was convinced that the traditional, conservative Navy was against him, that it resented any officer, regardless of achievement, who did not conform to its hidebound standards of conduct and leadership and operate by the book. He was certain that "the system" would never accept him and that he would have to circumvent it, not just to get higher rank but because he was the only man who could successfully bring nuclear power to the Navy.

The law governing promotion to Navy flag rank provided a second chance in the annual selection process, but anyone who was passed over twice had to retire when he had thirty years of commissioned service. Thus, when Rick again failed of selection in 1952, he faced retirement.

Aware of the great controversy and resentment that Rickover and his methods caused, even before the second failure members of his staff had mounted a campaign to prevent his forced retirement. Clay Blair, Jr., an ambitious, aggressive young reporter for *Time-Life*, was given material explaining the importance of nuclear power in submarines and stressing Rickover's important role. Blair's "inside" stories dramatized and gave national publicity to supposed intra-Navy dissension and vindictiveness. More important, three of Rickover's most senior engineers went to key members of the Senate Armed Services Committee to stress the importance of retaining him.

The controversial issue was resolved by political pressure from important senators who had been impressed by Rickover's achievements and by Congressman Yates. Yates went so far as to introduce a bill that would require the Navy to include three civilians in its selection boards. When the Senate Armed Services Committee, chaired by Leverett Saltonstall of Massachusetts, held up the promotion of the thirty-nine captains who had been selected and called for an investigation of the selection process, the Navy gave in.

To make Rickover eligible for consideration by the 1953 selection board, Navy Secretary Robert B. Anderson convened a special board in 1952 to select engineering duty only captains for retention on active duty for a year. Its precept specified that one had to have nuclear power qualifications that only Rick possessed. The 1953 rear admiral selection board, guided by a similar precept, then selected him for promotion.

∗   ∗   ∗   ∗

While he freely bullied and ridiculed junior officers entering his program, Rickover used subtler tactics in denigrating the senior officer community. In congressional testimony, in speeches and articles he would flaunt his superior technical expertise and breadth of intellectual attainment. He was a master in playing off one agency or official against another by implying that differences existed between them while he moved swiftly and independently on his own path outside routine channels. He delighted in keeping off-balance the operational and administrative commanders whose prerogatives he was engaged in annexing. He even went so far, in 1959, as to tell one of his aspiring skippers, "See what reaction you get by announcing that I want to become CNO." He knew very well that this would never be, but his sly tactic did generate some consternation and confusion.

Small wonder then that evaluations of his character and accomplishments produced emotional, exaggerated outbursts. One of his Naval Academy classmates who reached high rank said, "The only thing wrong with Rickover is that when they circumcised him they threw away the wrong piece." At the other extreme, Rep. George P. Miller of California observed, "As far as I'm concerned, I want to stand at the foot of the pedestal on which you will eventually be placed, and bow to you."

Among the stalwart Rickover allies on Capitol Hill, Chet Holifield, a thoughtful, influential member and alternating chair of the JCAE, was probably the most active and effective on his behalf. His evaluation of the admiral went far to explain the unprecedented rapport between a maverick military officer and the Congress. "Of all the men I dealt with during my public service, at least one will go down in history: Admiral Hyman G. Rickover, the father of the nuclear navy. His creativity and strength were not with the Navy but with Congress; we had extremely high confidence in him for assuming full responsibility and delivering on his commitments. He was completely open and honest and never tried to palm something off on us." Yet even before Congress Rickover was not above intimating that his efforts to bring the benefits of nuclear power to the Navy were opposed by "the operators" and that he had to drag the Navy "kicking and screaming" into the twentieth century.

There was indeed a reluctance by chiefs of naval operations, secretaries of the Navy, and key officials in the Office of the Secretary of Defense (OSD) to include in annual shipbuilding programs as many nuclear-powered ships or submarines as Rickover was prepared to deliver and argued for in the Congress, but that was chiefly for budgetary and national security reasons. The Navy chiefs are responsible for the Navy's readiness to meet diverse potential threats around the globe and unpredictable contingencies that require a balance of forces with varied capabilities. The increased costs of nuclear-powered ships and their highly trained crews – about 50 percent more – meant that there could be fewer ships for the hotly contested dollars in a given year's shipbuilding budget. Thus, the quantitative need for ships of various classes sometimes overrode the qualitative advantages bestowed on major warships by nuclear power.

For many defense officials, when there was no clear and readily understood military advantage of nuclear power, as there was for the submarine, the fiscal imperative was overriding. This was the case in the fierce Navy-OSD debate over nuclear power for aircraft carriers, when the assistant secretary of defense (systems analysis) held stoutly that "the nuclear power issue is primarily a budget allocation question."[1]

To Rickover must go credit for so quickly and effectively transforming scientific concept into pioneering reality when the AEC's prototype plant for *Nautilus* became operational in 1953. His enduring fame rests on creation of *Nautilus,* made possible by his superb engineering, intensive training of personnel, and the minutely detailed and disciplined management of the government-industrial development and production infrastructure he brought into being.

When *Nautilus* got underway for the first time in 1955 from the outfitting pier of her builders, the Electric Boat Division of General Dynamics Corporation in Groton, Connecticut, Rickover was on the bridge alongside Comdr. Eugene P. (Dennis) Wilkinson, whom he had carefully chosen to be her first commanding officer. Dennis was not a product of the Naval Academy, but of the University of Southern California. In Rickover's eyes, this was an asset. Dennis had considerable wartime experience as a junior officer in submarines and had risen to command of *Wahoo* (SS 565), one of the few advanced, fast-attack, conventional submarines built after the war. He had a solid grasp of nuclear technology from his postwar assignment to Argonne National Laboratory. He personified Rickover's insistence on detailed technical training and full understanding of hazards, actual or potential, associated with atomic energy. When he sent his simple but profoundly significant message, "Underway on nuclear power," on January 17, 1955, it signaled a new era in sea power.

The shoreside prototype's sustained performance and the sea trials of the new ship and her revolutionary propulsion system were proof that Rickover had given her a level of engineering reliability, safety, and performance unmatched by any other project. More than that, the successful development and application of the pressurized water reactor laid the groundwork for the nation's and the world's commercial electric nuclear power program.

Throughout 1955 and 1956 *Nautilus* continued her dramatic performance. While she set records and made headlines, her sibling, *Seawolf,* plodded along her unspectacular but also highly important path. Instead of pressurized water, her reactor used liquid metal (sodium) as its heat transfer agent. Delayed in completion because of potentially dangerous leaks in her steam superheater, she commenced operations in 1957, ably skippered by one of our most imaginative, innovative, foresighted young officers, Comdr. Richard B. Laning. She was the first nuclear sub to embark for a cruise a president of the United States, Dwight D. Eisenhower. And in 1958 she carried out tests in which she was first to remain completely shut off from the atmosphere for sixty days while she traveled 13,700 miles.

There were those who doubted the practicability of nuclear power at sea, citing cost, complexity, risk of accident, and training problems. It would take more than successful solo runs to convince them. The opportunity to do so came swiftly. In early 1957 pleas came from the Pacific Fleet to let them see the "wonder ship" and to test their tactics against her. Admiral Burke was sympathetic to Adm. Felix Stump (CinCPacFlt) in his desire to receive *Nautilus.* Rear Admiral Rickover, however, was strongly opposed. In the ensuing dispute, Secretary of the Navy Thomas S. Gates would not intervene; he viewed the issue as an operational matter best left to the CNO. At this time I was on duty in the Pentagon as head of the Submarine Warfare Branch (OP 311). OP 311 was not directly involved in submarine operations but was charged with planning submarine warfare readiness. It was the link between the afloat submarine force commanders and the Navy Department. I had the task of justifying the proposed Pacific deployment.

Soon Rickover's office was on the telephone. He never wasted breath in idle chatter and never beat around the bush. After his usual curt "Hello," Rick said, "Galantin, I hear you're trying to send *Nautilus* to the Pacific. I never heard of such a stupid thing! I want to see you!"

"Why, yes, Admiral. I'll come right over."

Shortly after, in his cluttered, unpretentious office in one of the even shabbier buildings behind the thirty-eight-year-old "temporary" Main Navy Building on Constitution Avenue, I faced the frail, deceptively mild-appearing titan of nuclear power technology. The conversation started calmly enough, but as always in those days Rick soon raised his voice to

express conviction that "the operators" didn't know what they were doing, were interfering with his careful plans to do what was best for the
submarine service, and that the operating schedule for *Nautilus* was best
left to him. After interjecting some comments that were ineffectual in
stemming his wrath, I said, "Well, Admiral, there's only one reason I know
for that ship not to go to the Pacific, and that is if you tell me she's not
reliable."

His bright, clear, blue eyes seemed to shoot sparks, and his face flushed.
Shaking his finger at me, he shrilled, "Galantin, the art of greatness is to
keep the unexpected from happening!"

I came away from our meeting believing that Rick was going to fight
to maintain his complete control over *Nautilus*'s operations. He was always ready to go outside normal channels, to go over the heads of his
departmental superiors to achieve his ends. However, as it turned out, I
had said the one thing that would tie his hands. I had identified him with
his product and cast suspicion on what he cherished above all – excellence
of technological performance. Absolutely dedicated to the principle of
personal responsibility, he could not appeal to the Congress without
implying his own fallibility.

More than anyone else he was aware of the unfamiliar dangers inherent in the use of atomic energy and the probabilities of weaknesses or error
in the first large-scale practical demonstration of the complex engineering he was pioneering. "The art of greatness is to keep the unexpected
from happening." What a fine aphorism! It was his way of saying, "Why
take a chance when you don't have to? We're pushing the state of the art,
and can't be sure what may happen. We can lose far more than we gain,
and might set the program back for years."

It was a point of view I did not share at the time. Some years later when,
as director of the Special Projects Office, and then as chief of naval material, I, too, had responsibility for some complex and dangerous technology, I came to a full appreciation of that same concern and its wisdom.

But Rick wouldn't say that *Nautilus* was unreliable. Admiral Burke
stood by his guns, and in the spring of 1957 she was ordered to the Pacific
for training and fleet familiarization. Once that decision was made, Rickover was the best man on our side. He did everything needed to prepare
her for this new test and to plan for contingencies. From New London
the ship steamed submerged to Panama, transited the canal, then resub-
merged for the long passage to San Diego. On this voyage of more than
5200 miles, all but 126 were underwater. When I asked Wilkinson how

many work requests for repairs he had to submit on arrival in San Diego, he replied that he had put in just one.

"What was that for?"

Pausing while he scratched his cheek in his characteristic country-boy fashion, he replied, "Oh, we had no printing press, and that was for printing some public information handouts."

From San Diego, *Nautilus* went up the coast to San Francisco and Seattle, where, on June 18, 1957, Dennis turned over command to Comdr. William R. Anderson. By then Rickover had chosen Wilkinson for another important assignment, to be skipper of the first nuclear-powered surface ship, the cruiser *Long Beach.* In 1970, with the rank of vice admiral, Dennis became Commander Submarine Force U.S. Atlantic Fleet, in charge of the most potent undersea force in the world. Meanwhile, Bill Anderson, the same who had been exec of *Tang* when we made the historic deep dive, retired from the Navy in 1962 to conduct a winning campaign for election to the Congress as representative from his home district in Tennessee.

∗ ∗ ∗ ∗

In the Pacific, in a busy period of providing target services and familiarization demonstrations to thousands of personnel, hundreds of Navy aircraft, and almost a hundred ships, *Nautilus* showed a collateral benefit of nuclear-powered submarines: the ability of one ship to provide ASW target and training services that would have required the concurrent use of several fossil-fueled submarines.

Retracing her course, by the time she returned to New London *Nautilus* had steamed 18,256 miles, most of them submerged, free of major difficulty, at an average speed of 16.9 knots. Coming as soon as it did, her deployment gave confidence for an even more amazing exploit the following summer.

Deployed once more to the Pacific, ostensibly to provide target services to the fleet, she made a secret effort to reach the North Pole. Forced to turn back because of ice conditions in the shallow Chukchi Sea, she retreated to Pearl Harbor. On July 23, 1958, she sailed once more with the announced purpose of carrying out submerged tests. Instead, after diving she headed north from the sun and sand of the Paradise of the Pacific and set course for the fog-shrouded, rocky Aleutian Island chain. Passing through it and the Bering Strait, she chose a different route through the Chukchi Sea and entered the Arctic Ocean. Proceeding submerged across the top of the world and under the ice, *Nautilus* reached the North Pole on August 3, then continued until she surfaced off Portsmouth, England, nineteen days and 8146 miles from Pearl Harbor. Any other ship would have had to travel 10,700 miles.

The remarkable performance of *Nautilus,* and the nationwide adulation for her creator, greatly strengthened Rickover's position. Members of Congress who had over-ruled the Navy and insisted on his promotion to rear admiral in 1953 now basked in the dramatic confirmation of their wisdom. Surely the Navy would want to reward its modest, unassuming, brilliant, irreplaceable officer with promotion. In October 1958, Hyman Rickover was promoted to vice admiral.

With an impregnable political base, Rickover now went about creating virtually a Navy within a Navy, one accountable to him as much as to the chief of naval operations. His complete control over the selection and training of officers and enlisted men for the nuclear propulsion program, his absolute control over reactor design and engineering, and his intense concern for safety made this possible. The AEC, through its Reactor Safeguards Committee of distinguished scientists and engineers (its first chairman was Dr. Edward Teller), had statutory responsibility for the safe operation of nuclear reactors. As chief of the commission's Naval Reactors Branch, Rickover was charged with overseeing the safe operation of reactors in the fleet. The safety measures he prescribed and rigidly enforced gave him authority over reactor plant safety and ships' operations that even the CNO would not challenge in peacetime.

At this stage of his ascendancy Rickover seemed to glory in controversy and to seek contention and conflict, apparently confident in his power. Frequently he turned problems that were capable of straightforward resolution into pseudo-crises. In public discussion he remained cool, soft-spoken, and frequently deferential. He was often brilliant in speeches and articles on many subjects, notably on the sad state of education in the United States, particularly in science and engineering. In private, he could become heated, profane, and vitriolic, glorying in humbling his juniors.

As much as I could, I avoided dealing personally with Rick, either by telephone or in person. I wanted to escape entanglement in his political machinations and needless arguments that would undermine my ability to be an objective spokesman in the numerous other issues that submarines faced in OpNav at that time. I think he realized the problem and generally followed the same course after the meeting in 1955 when he sought to impress me with the wisdom of his long-range plans for nuclear submarines. Our point of contact was Comdr. James F. Calvert, a truly outstanding officer assigned to Rickover's office for training prior to taking command of *Skate* (SSN 578). She was our third nuclear boat, had a reactor of 7500 shaft horsepower instead of the 15,000 of her predecessors, and in March 1955 was the first submarine to surface at the North Pole.

Those of us who were beyond the redemption of Rick's infamous interview and college of nuclear knowledge were not spared scorn and ridicule. He delighted in casting "the operators" as obtuse bad guys who "couldn't see the big picture" and had "no God-damn political sense." Once he told me, "You operators have great bravery in battle, but you lack moral courage in these peacetime jobs. You do only what will please your bosses."

He knew what our problems were in OpNav. Naval aviation dominated Navy planning and strategic thinking. It watched uneasily the steady rise in funds going to nuclear submarines and eyed nervously the submarine's intrusion with cruise missiles into naval aviation's jealously guarded share of the nation's strategic warfare capability. But Rick sneered at this reality of Pentagon life. "Don't you know there are certain facts of life? One is that the entire aircraft industry is a lobby for and promotes air power. No aviator criticizes an airplane. If it has wings, it's good." He went on to say, "You submariners are prone to criticize submarines or features of their design simply because they don't include all your own ideas, or are too new. You should be like aviators, and support every new boat."

Rickover's objective was not merely the advancement of our submarines' military capabilities. He envisioned a modernized Navy whose major warships would all be nuclear powered. To achieve that goal he could be devious or direct, flexible or unyielding, as the situation in the Pentagon or the Congress warranted. To the Submarine Conference of May 31, 1955, he stated, "I think you all know from previous discussions I am violently opposed to a ship with a single reactor of any kind. I think there ought to be two. I think a nuclear submarine is too valuable to depend on one source of power supply."

This was said at the time when *Nautilus* and its prototype plant in Idaho were operating successfully; the second nuclear submarine, *Seawolf*, was under construction but its prototype plant was encountering delays; and two boats of the smaller Skate class were already authorized for construction, with more to follow. Each of these had a single reactor. But this was also the time when the AEC's prototype for a twin-reactor plant was under development but a ship to utilize it had not been authorized. The next year's shipbuilding program did contain the radar-picket submarine *Triton,* the first twin-reactor ship. She was followed at yearly intervals by the cruiser *Long Beach* (two reactors), aircraft carrier *Enterprise* (eight reactors), and cruiser *Bainbridge* (two reactors).

I considered Rick's surprising comment to be a political statement intended to promote the cause of multiple-reactor ships, but many years later I asked Milton Shaw if there was another explanation. Milt was an early member of Rickover's team and became a key man on his senior staff, in charge of reactor development for submarines, surface ships, and commercial application.

Shaw thought the comment was a sincere expression of Rickover's concern at the time. In spite of the success being demonstrated by *Nautilus* and the plans to proceed with the single-reactor Skate class, he said, Rickover shared the uneasiness of senior engineers in the reactor development community about reliance on a single reactor. Difficulties being experienced with the liquid-metal cooled reactor prototype plant for *Seawolf,* and with many other AEC reactor programs, may have been a factor. During this pioneering stage, scientific knowledge and theory were not precise enough to overcome tremendous concern about the unknowns that could arise in the engineering and operation of reactors. Driven by Rickover, all of Code 1500 (the designation of his Nuclear Power Division in BuShips) felt a great responsibility to really know what they were creating. One thing they did know: They wouldn't find in one ship's short-term experience the assurance they wanted. They would need a cumulative record of operating and maintenance experience. These concerns underlaid the great emphasis on prototype testing and the "brute conservatism" philosophy that was the hallmark of Code 1500's engineering. It brought Rickover recurring criticism for fighting off ideas that were "not invented here." However, it also brought an unparalleled record of engineering reliability and safety in both submarine and surface ship nuclear propulsion.

Both Shaw and Rickover believed they were fortunate that the military benefit of nuclear power in submarines was so compelling. It meant that the all-important first application would be in a vehicle whose personnel were already imbued with the very high standards of discipline, engineering excellence, and operational safety that all nuclear applications required.

It was critically important both to Rickover and the submariners that this application be successful. Unless freed from dependence on the atmosphere, the submarine's future role in our Navy would be very limited. And if the submarine installation was not successful, it would be many years before the Navy would get nuclear power for its surface ships or the nation could have confidence in commercial nuclear power plants.

As it was, Rickover's record of success was such that it brought promotion to four-star rank in 1973. This came as the result of pressure from his powerful supporters in Congress who claimed that passage of the bill authorizing the Navy's Trident missile submarine program was in jeopardy if this ultimate recognition of Rickover's accomplishments and stature was not forthcoming.

Because he reached the Navy's statutory retirement age of sixty-two in 1962, Rickover had been able to remain on active duty only because of the successive two-year presidential extensions he orchestrated through his admirers on the Hill. As the years went by, he became increasingly obdurate, disregarding or circumventing the policies and directives of his superiors, the chiefs of BuShips, naval material, and naval operations, the secretary of the Navy, and the secretary of defense.

Apart from the issue of his flouting of superior authority, I believe Rick overstayed his time. In later years he was not receptive to new ideas in nuclear technology or management. He had grown ultraconservative, fiercely protective of what he had created, great as it was for its time. Through his constant ridicule of Navy education and leadership, he had become a divisive, arrogant force. The needs of the overall Navy meant nothing to him. His sole consideration seemed to be his own aggrandizement and assurance of continuous use of his Reactors Branch in developing nuclear plants for the expanding "Rickover Navy."

From 1948, when Rick was first put in charge of the Navy's nuclear power program, until his forced retirement in 1982, there were seventeen secretaries of the Navy and twelve chiefs of naval operations. Several secretaries explored the means of retiring him, but he had acquired such formidable support on Capitol Hill that not even presidents would risk the political fallout of retiring a national godhead against his will. Not until many of Rick's congressional supporters had passed from the scene was the carefully prepared plan of the young (forty-one years old) Secretary of the Navy John F. Lehman, Jr., supported by our oldest president, Ronald Reagan, seventy, able to force Rickover's retirement over his bitter protests. He was eighty-two and had served on active duty continuously for sixty years. By that time, 169 submarines (SSN, SSRN, SSGN, and SSBN), four carriers (CVN), and nine cruisers/frigates (CGN and DLGN) – all nuclear powered – had either been completed or authorized for construction.

THE ULTIMATE DETERRENT

In the 1948 Key West Agreement on service roles and missions, the Air Force was assigned responsibility for development of intercontinental ballistic missiles (ICBMs), and the Army was allowed to proceed with development of the 1500-mile intermediate-range ballistic missile (IRBM). The Navy was given no role in the evolving realm of ballistic missile warfare. It pursued its program for the delivery of cruise missiles from mobile, seaborne platforms, cruisers as well as submarines.

A cruise missile needs the atmosphere for flight support during its transit to target at fixed or variable altitudes. Its course to where it dives on its target is controlled by a preprogrammed guidance system that may be supplemented by on-board sensors of various kinds. On the other hand, a ballistic missile is launched verti-cally. Its rocket motors boost it above the atmosphere on the bearing of its target, much as a shell is propelled from a gun. Its on-board, prepro-grammed guidance and control mechanism then releases its warheads at proper points for free-fall to their targets.

The system we deployed in 1954 used the submarine as launching plat-form but from a surfaced position, and the missile was the subsonic cruise missile Regulus I. When *Tunny* deployed with two nuclear-armed mis-siles the combination was, in effect, our nation's first intercontinental missile system. She and succeeding guided missile submarines covered important targets on Russia's Pacific flank. Planning proceeded to intro-duce the supersonic Regulus II and to follow that with Rigel or Triton, which were even more advanced cruise missiles.

By 1955 there was mounting concern over Soviet advances in ballistic missiles. The heavy-lift rockets she was developing, coupled with the atomic (fission) or hydrogen (fusion) bombs she had already tested, posed a serious threat to the United States. The oceans were no longer our pro-tective moat; we could be subject to nuclear blackmail.

President Eisenhower's Science Advisory Committee, specifically the Killian Committee on Technological Capabilities, saw the seriousness of the situation and urged priority development of both ICBMs and IRBMs. Most important from the Navy's standpoint, the committee also stated that a need existed for a sea-based ballistic missile.

At this time the use of solid propellants was confined to forward-fir-ing rockets and to short-duration, jet-assist, take-off thrusters. Only liq-uid fuels could produce the thrust needed for ballistic missiles able to carry atomic warheads to a meaningful range. The Air Force had under development its Atlas and Titan ICBMs and the Thor IRBM. The Army was seeking approval to develop Jupiter, its version of a shorter-range IRBM.

When Arleigh Burke came on board as CNO in August 1955, he quickly resolved the Navy's doubts about its need for ballistic missiles. The other services were approached about the feasibility of a joint venture to de-velop a 1500-mile missile that could be launched from fixed sites but could go to sea as well. The Air Force was not interested, but the Army, although fearful of the complications added by Navy requirements, agreed. The joint project was approved by the Eisenhower administration in Novem-ber 1955.

For its part, the Navy was not enamored by the prospect of huge

115,000-pound, 65-foot-tall Jupiter missiles with liquid propellant being installed onboard ships. Liquid fuels were, of course, used in other shipboard applications, but in this case the more volatile fuels and their complex stowage and pumping problems would greatly complicate shipboard operation and safety.

The Navy's goal was to have the Jupiter missile deployed in surface ships in 1960, and possibly in submarines by 1965. A submarine could be designed that would carry the monster missiles, but even a boat of 8500 tons could carry only four of them. What the Navy wanted most was a solid-fuel missile, which would not only greatly reduce shipboard hazard but also provide much shorter response time and be suitable for submarine use.

To manage its responsibilities in the joint Army-Navy program, the Navy set up its Special Projects Office (SP), which reported directly to the secretary of the Navy, independent of the existing material bureaus. Of profound importance to the program was Admiral Burke's choice for Rear Adm. William F. (Red) Raborn, Jr., to be its director. Given unprecedented authority and responsibility, Raborn applied his ebullient personality, great energy, uncommon organizational skill, and rare scientific and political acumen to his enormous task. Although not a factor in his selection, there was a dividend to his assignment. If the Navy's sea-launched ballistic missile project was successful, it would take over much of the carrier-based atomic strike mission. Raborn was a naval aviator; success in his challenging assignment would make the shift more palatable to naval aviation.

The Army was notified that the Navy's primary goal was a solid-fuel missile armed with a lighter-weight atomic warhead. Once that was attainable, we would go either our own way or welcome the Army as a partner. To both Army and Air Force the solid-fuel rocket seemed a long-term prospect, but by mid-1956 Navy contractors had demonstrated its feasibility, albeit still of very large size.

That same summer the Navy sponsored a "summer study" of the "growing Russian submarine menace," to be made under the auspices of the National Academy of Sciences, whose Committee on Undersea Warfare was chaired by Dr. Eric Walker, the dynamic and articulate president of Pennsylvania State University.

Whenever used, the summer study method received amused comment and some caustic criticism from those constrained to work long hours in Washington's summer heat, but it was an effective way to focus top scientific minds on complex defense problems. It was not hard to attract top-drawer scientists from universities, laboratories, and industry by giving them, in effect, a summer vacation at government expense at an attractive site. In 1956 the locale was Nobska Point, Woods Hole, Massachusetts, on Buzzards Bay.

Navy sponsors of the study envisioned a straightforward analysis of U.S.S.R. submarine capabilities and of U.S. ASW concepts to cope with that threat. The scientists were not content simply to extrapolate from the Navy's standard mode of ASW, however, and the study took an unexpected turn. Looking at the trend in technology that had already produced the atomic bomb and *Nautilus*, the study gave a strong boost to prosubmarine concepts.

On August 25 Admiral Burke went to Woods Hole to receive a preliminary briefing on Project Nobska. Flying with him were his aide, Comdr. Thomas R. Weschler, an outstanding destroyer officer who would later work for me in the Special Projects Office, and four of us in OpNav who were concerned with both pro- and antisubmarine warfare: Rear Admiral Warder, Capt. Sidney D. B. Merrill, Capt. Cyrus C. Cole, and myself. The director of Woods Hole Oceanographic Institution and of Project Nobska was Dr. Columbus O'D. Iselin. His low-key presentation of "The Implications of Advanced Design on Undersea Warfare" gave an alarming assessment of the potential threat of Soviet nuclear-powered ballistic missile submarines. As he developed his thesis, the logic was inescapable: the United States must make greater use of the submarine in both strike and ASW missions.

A month later, at the National Academy of Sciences in Washington, D.C., Dr. Walker's committee of distinguished scientists and educators presented the conclusions of Project Nobska to Admiral Burke and most of his top-level staff. To the dismay of carrier strike-warfare zealots, the committee made a very good case that submarines could provide the cheapest, most effective means of naval strategic nuclear weapons delivery. It went on to recommend that the Navy make a reappraisal of its research and development efforts to channel them more directly in support of its primary mission – sea control, meaning greater emphasis on antisubmarine warfare.

Project Nobska had suggested that one means to reduce the Soviet missile threat was to force the diversion of Russian resources by deployment of a strong U.S. nuclear submarine force armed with ballistic missiles. This was another version of the "give 'em an ASW problem of their own" strategy that our submariners were pushing. We already had the nuclear-powered submarine; the problems lay in the missile, its warhead, and the associated technologies of fire-control, guidance, and navigation.

The key to breaking the logjam of technology that constrained prompt development of a fleet ballistic missile (FBM) was Dr. Edward Teller's question at Nobska, "Why are you designing a 1965 weapon system with 1958 warhead technology?" By thus highlighting the steady trend in nuclear warhead design (and in other technical areas as well), the feasibility of a submarine-based FBM at an earlier date became apparent.

In December 1956 the Navy was authorized to proceed at highest priority on its own solid-fuel, 1500-nautical-mile IRBM program and bowed out of the Jupiter program. The name chosen for the new seagoing missile was singularly apt – Polaris. From time immemorial that North Star has guided mariners.

In organizing his lean technical and managerial team of outstanding military and civil service personnel, one of Red Raborn's most inspired decisions was to bring on board as technical director Capt. Levering Smith. Levering had served sixteen years as a line officer, nine of them at sea in surface ships but had become an ordnance engineering duty only (OEDO) specialist, the Navy's officer most capable of coping with the manifold uncertainties of the rapidly evolving rocket technology. Aside from the complexities of the missile itself, there would be a host of complex subsidiary systems, many of which would require development or outright invention. It would be Levering's job to direct and coordinate a massive assault on existing technologic barriers. The only parts of the revolutionary undersea weapon system that were straightforward extensions of proven technology were the submarine, which was in the capable hands of BuShips' engineers, and the nuclear-powered propulsion system, which was utterly controlled by Rear Admiral Rickover.

Under Smith's chairmanship there was established a Steering Task Group (STG). It was essentially a brain-storming group of senior representatives of each of the major subsystem contractors. Their task it was to establish minimum acceptable performance goals for all major system components. Dr. William F. Whitmore, the first chief scientist of the Special Projects Office, suggested only half-facetiously that the criterion for designation of STG members should be, "The senior guy who will be fired if this thing doesn't work." Among those so designated were Dr. C. Stark Draper of the M.I.T. Instrumentation Laboratory, Willis M. Hawkins of Lockwood Missiles and Space Company, Dr. Harold Brown of the AEC's

Livermore Laboratory, Dr. Werner R. Kirchner of Aerojet General Corporation, and Dr. George Mechlin of Westinghouse Corporation.

★ ★ ★ ★

Submariners were notably absent in the decision-making process of the program. This was to be expected, for the Navy's pre-Polaris concept called for surface ship launching, and missile programs in the Navy Department were chiefly under the cognizance of the deputy chief of naval operations for air (OP 05). They were implemented by his supporting technical agency, the Bureau of Aeronautics (BuAir). A few submarine officers were in subordinate positions in the Navy's missile hierarchy, notably Capt. F. Worth Scanland, Jr., and Comdrs. W. P. Murphy and W. E. Sims.

In the Submarine Warfare Branch (OP 311), which I headed, there were three officers in addition to myself, all grossly overburdened. Busily engaged in promoting the ASW capability of our submarines and trying to build a meaningful guided missile force, we were not vociferous advocates of the new weapon system, which it seemed would be many years in the making. Nevertheless, as the representative of the director of submarine/antisubmarine warfare (OP 31), Rear Adm. F. B. Warder, it was my task to set forth to the Steering Task Group the views of the submarine professionals who would ultimately operate the FBM system.

Conditioned by my *Argonaut* and wartime submarine experiences, I knew that the most reliable weapon system was the simplest one. The FBM system would be the most complex, most technically advanced that the Navy had ever adopted. That made it imperative that we ensure its operability under all conditions it might encounter if it was to perform its deterrent function successfully. If ever a system deserved to be called a technological audacity, this was it.

Two aspects of the system were of particular concern to submarine operators: one was the size of the submarine, and the other the mode of launch – would it be from the surface or submerged?

The volume and length of ship space devoted to propulsion were fixed, based as they were on the proven nuclear-powered propulsion system used in attack submarines. The determinant of ship tonnage would be the size of the missile compartment needed to carry the desired missile load.

The size of the missile itself was not yet fixed; we knew only that it would be about 20 feet long; 4½ feet in diameter, and weigh about 30,000 pounds. With that knowledge, BuShips' preliminary designs showed that boats with missile tubes varying in number from 4 to 48 were technically feasible. In fact, the missile capacities, from 2 to 32, would have little effect other than on the length of the ship. The larger number of missiles appealed to some scientists and cost analysts; it produced a more cost-effective ship, that is, one that could put more missiles on station per dollar invested.

To those who would have to operate the ship and be responsible for its constant readiness, a lesser number gave greater assurance of a "mission effective" ship, one that offered greater assurance of readiness and hence a more credible deterrent. After all, once a nuclear exchange began, deterrence would have failed, and "victory" through numbers of missiles was meaningless. And, in keeping with the thrust of the Nobska report, if a given total missile inventory was dispersed in more smaller ships, an enemy's task of locating and countering them would be magnified. Further, if a ship was lost or off the line for any reason, we would lose less of our capability. System costs, however, would unquestionably be higher: More high-cost subs and crews would be needed. A balance would have to be struck.

When it appeared that thirty-two would be the magic number for ballistic missile submarines, I requested a recess. In an adjoining room I huddled with my submarine operator assistants and our BuShips' submarine designers, Capt. Jim Bethea and Comdr. Harry Jackson. We could not fault the balance sheet logic of numerical analysis, but years of operational experience with ships, weapons, and men, all elements individually and collectively imperfect, sent storm warnings to seamen and urged a more conservative approach. No submarine of the size contemplated had ever been built. The largest subs had all been cranky in submerged operation, especially near the surface and in only moderately rough seas, a fact I had regularly experienced in *Argonaut.*

Like the airplane pilot, the submarine skipper must make decisions based on information relayed by sensors and instrumentation. Many a flight or dive has been aborted by perceived, even though nonexistent, danger. The proposed quantum jump in sub size and complexity would be similar to leaping from the first jet aircraft to the jumbo jet.

Returning to the STG deliberations, I stressed that what was essential in this deterrent weapon system was military utility, the assurance of continuous high reliability and readiness. From the operators' viewpoint, a ship sized for thirty-two missiles would not be likely to meet that requirement. We preferred a ship of about 5900 tons that could carry sixteen missiles.

At this point Levering Smith, chairman of the STG, shrewdly called for a secret ballot, asking each member to write on a slip of paper the number of tubes he thought would be best. In this way he hoped to avoid having members committed to defend a number. He found that although one person opted for twelve, the number twenty-four would have won had the issue been put to a vote.

Influenced by his own seagoing operational experience, Levering was reluctant to over-ride the operators' judgment, and he adjourned the session. Meeting separately with Raborn, he reviewed the situation and recommended that sixteen be adopted. Not only were our forty-one Polaris subs built to that standard, but the British, French, and some Russian models all followed suit. Years later, Bill Whitmore would twit me, "Pete, when you came up with sixteen, that was like throwing a dart and then drawing the bull's eye around it."

At any rate, sixteen remained the standard until development of the Trident missile and the need to replace the aging, early SSBNs. *Ohio* (SSBN 726), launched in 1979, was the first of a new class of 18,700-ton subs, each with twenty-four missile tubes.

The second problem involving operational experience was the question of surface versus submerged launch of missiles. The initial concept for a surface ship installation of ballistic missiles, to be ready by January 1, 1960, had given way to a submarine version that was to be ready by January 1, 1965. This would be a 1500-nautical-mile missile (Polaris A-2) capable of submerged launch. There was to be an interim 1200-nautical-mile (Polaris A-1) submarine capability, using surface launch, ready in 1963.

Some persons argued that once a boat fired a missile it disclosed its position and might as well be on the surface. That would simplify ship control and weight compensation as missiles were launched. The submarine design included a bulky gyro stabilizer to minimize ship's roll, but for those who had for years experienced the contrast between the often stormy ocean-air interface and the calm beneath the waves, it seemed wise to provide the most stable platform possible. After all, it was a submarine weapon being designed; why not from the start take full advantage of the nuclear sub's ability to stay submerged, where the waters were relatively still, to provide a concealed, all-weather capability?

As submarine operators we wanted the operational benefits of submerged launch, but we were not familiar with the numerous technical problems that entailed. We knew only that the Germans had experimented with launching short-range missiles from submerged U-boats and that our own Navy had conducted an inconclusive test off Key West in launching small dummy missiles while submerged. There was no evidence that a missile as large and as heavy as that being designed would be hydrodynamically stable when ejected underwater. Before it could penetrate the air-water interface, it would be subjected to the force of water flowing over the launch tubes. If the rocket motor was ignited while still underwater, there might be further instability or even detonation of the missile, with damage to the submarine. This uncertainty dictated ignition only after the first-stage motor was above the surface, where the missile would commence its programmed ballistic trajectory through the atmosphere and beyond.

Red Raborn and Levering Smith were noncommittal. Their years of sea duty in surface ships made them appreciative of the advantages of submerged launch. However, they were responsible for the implementation of whatever system was decided upon, and their task was already monumental in scope and complexity.

The civilian engineers and scientists who would have to find solutions to the known or perceived problems of developing a safe, reliable, underwater launch system were understandably cautious. Brilliant in their own technical fields, they had little or no experience of the sea. All were greatly interested in the nautical debate and the effect it could have on the system elements for which they were responsible.

I could not give scientific data to support the case for submerged launch, but in one session on the subject I gave an analogy: "For thirty-five years we've been doing the reverse – dropping a missile at high speed out of the air, flat on its belly, and asking it to run accurately just below the rough surface. That's the torpedo. What's so difficult about going the other way? Why can't we shoot a missile to the surface from a slow, steady platform, pierce the interface vertically in a second, and be on our way?"

Stark Draper spoke up, "By God, that's right!" Elaborating on my simplistic example, Stark led the way to discussions and analyses that supported underwater launch, both as a sound operational concept and as an attainable technological goal. This was a typical Draper reaction. Although acclaimed and honored worldwide as the "Father of Inertial Guidance," he deplored being called a scientist. He called himself "just a greasy-thumb mechanic." To him every advance in science or triumph of engineering was merely another milestone on the endless path to greater achievement.

The Navy is particularly indebted to Dr. Draper and the M.I.T. Instrumentation Laboratory.[1] His development of the gyro-stabilized Mark 14 gunsight during World War II gave our surface ships more effective defense against swarming Japanese air attacks. Soon he extended the same principle to aerial gunnery. Next he made space navigation and missile guidance possible through developing the refined inertial guidance systems required for both Navy and Air Force. The Ships Inertial Navigation System (SINS), which he developed for our nuclear submarines, freed them from the need to get frequent position (navigation) information from above the surface and helped make them true submarines.

But perhaps Doc Draper's most lasting contribution to our Navy lies in the many officers we sent to be his graduate students at M.I.T. He kindled their imagination, fortified their knowledge, bolstered their patriotism, and instilled a lifelong challenge to excellence.

✶ ✶ ✶ ✶

Because as its least vulnerable segment the Polaris FBM system was so important to our national strategic deterrent policy and had so many technical problems to overcome, it was subject to more than the usual high-level review and critique. At its inception, President Eisenhower required a monthly report of progress, and Admiral Burke had to be kept informed weekly. He had cautioned that Navy funds and technical talent were not unlimited and that numerous other desirable programs were being placed in jeopardy. If an insurmountable problem was identified, it had to be acknowledged at once – and the project canceled.

Here again Levering Smith was the indispensable man. His personal absolute integrity and honesty were the foundation of his scientific and engineering excellence. In whatever forum he was called to testify, whether in our own internal Special Projects status reports, in higher-level Navy Department program reviews, in Office of the Secretary of Defense technical analyses, or before pertinent House or Senate committees, he never hid or minimized a problem or a failure – and there were many – in our urgent development and production programs. His characteristic soft-spoken, agonizingly deliberate and detailed analysis invariably gave confidence that problems would be solved and program goals achieved.

* * * *

In April 1957, the President's Science Advisory Committee, chaired by Nobel prize-winner Dr. Robert A. Milliken of the California Institute of Technology, was given a status report by the Polaris steering committee. The day-long give-and-take with many of the nation's top scientists was highly encouraging. An interested observer was Charles A. Lindbergh. He did not speak during the meeting, but during recesses quizzed me about submarine operations. I was struck by his youthful appearance and friendly, candid manner. He said, with a smile, that he had been exposed to the "battleship admirals" years ago, and that in his opinion we had their counterpart in "carrier admirals." He believed that the Navy was not capitalizing adequately on its mobility and advocated more use of the seaplane because of its heavy lift capability and access to the indestructible airfields that oceans, rivers, and lakes provide. I mentioned our Seamaster experience, but he still thought the seaplane was worth giving up one carrier to develop. In one respect he was farsighted, for he went on to say that "the prime dangers now are peripheral wars."

* * * *

The original Navy operational requirement for the FBM specified a 1500-mile missile capable of submerged launch to be operational in 1965. However, in October 1957 the U.S.S.R. launched its *Sputnik*, the world's first earth-orbiting satellite. The dramatic and unexpected demonstration of Russia's potential military exploitation of outer space caused consternation in the United States. Sooner than expected, any part of our country could be the target of ballistic missiles. To thwart temptations for such attack, we needed a foolproof system of deterrence, one that would convince any aggressor that his own attack would be followed by his certain destruction, and the more rapidly the better.

There was urgent reevaluation of U.S. missile and space programs. Progress already made with Polaris showed that if a reduced-range, 1200-mile missile was acceptable, the submarine system could be placed in operation by November 1960. With that as the new goal, the construction lead time of the submarine to be used became critical. To save as much time as possible, the nuclear attack submarine *Scorpion*, already on the building ways, was cut in two and a 130-foot missile section inserted in her midsection. The ship was renamed *George Washington*.[2] Construction of two other Polaris submarines, *Patrick Henry* and *Theodore Roosevelt*, was started at the same time.

Distressing to the Navy as a whole was the loss of support for a second nuclear-powered aircraft carrier (CVAN) at that time and the shift of funds into the rapidly expanding Polaris program so favored by the Congress. Although the FBM system was still in its unproven development stage, there was talk of building six, nine, even twelve SSBNs in the next two years. It was implied that there would be supplementary funds, but there was no assurance of this. Consequently, when sources outside the Navy talked of building a total of thirty-nine SSBNs, the Office of the Chief of Naval Operations suffered a mild state of hysteria for fear that all other programs might be starved out.

Our aviators were understandably worried about the effect this would have on the future of the big carriers. There were renewed charges that the submarine community was free-wheeling and not conforming loyally to Navy policy. That policy, of course, called for promoting and advancing the capabilities of carrier-based aviation.

The construction of *George Washington* brought the submarine to a size that just a few years before had been deemed colossal. She and her four sister ships each displaced 5900 tons. The emergency-improvised construction of this class, however, and the prudent installation of redundant equipments, resulted in ships that were too cramped and crowded, particularly in their living accommodations. Given time to refine the design and exploit operational experience, BuShips designed the next class to be thirty feet longer, a thousand tons heavier, and deeper-diving. Of this design, the Ethan Allen class, five ships were built, but growth did not stop. To the last thirty-one boats, fifteen feet in length and a hundred tons were added to bring the LaFayette class to 425 feet and 7000 tons.

While building of *George Washington* went forward, the development and testing of the missile and all related subsystems proceeded. Working at forced draft under the friendly prodding of Red Raborn's leadership, the Navy bureaus and contractors discarded the usual methods of weapon system development and procurement. Not only did Polaris have topmost national priority, but also, and of equal importance, Special Projects controlled and managed its total budget in funds segregated from the rest of the Navy's. What once seemed fantasies of technology became realities, directly on schedule. Reliable submerged navigation, a solid propellant, submerged launch, fire control from a moving platform to targets

1200 miles away, and accurate missile guidance were only the major achievements. All had to be devised and engineered in the knowledge that they had to be compatible with the human factor – capable of being maintained and operated by men isolated beneath the seas for sixty days or more at a time.

To get maximum return from the great investment in the subs and their missiles, and to take advantage of their practically unlimited nuclear fuel, the ships are deployed for a greater period of time than it is reasonable for a single crew to sustain. For this reason, each SSBN has two crews, a Blue Crew and a Gold Crew. While one is on patrol with its ship, the other is in its home port undergoing recuperation and refresher training preparatory to its next patrol.

✶ ✶ ✶ ✶

At the end of 1959, two events of great significance for the Navy and for submarines occurred within five days of each other. On December 30, our first ballistic missile submarine, *George Washington* (SSBN 589), was placed in commission at Groton, Connecticut. It had been only three years since we grappled with the design of the ship and her revolutionary weapon system, aware of the urgency of our task.

The second event was the commissioning of *Halibut* (SSGN 587) at Mare Island, California on January 4, 1960. She would carry three Regulus II cruise missiles in her large hangar compartment, but would have to launch them from the surface. Never mind that *George Washington* and her ballistic missiles made *Halibut* already obsolescent; the worth of missile-armed submarines for sustained deterrence or for projecting power over land was accepted. In time, cruise missiles more advanced than Regulus II would give all attack submarines that capability without having to surface.

✶ ✶ ✶ ✶

On July 20, 1960, *George Washington,* cruising submerged off Cape Canaveral, Florida, successfully launched the first full-range Polaris test flight. Three hours later a second missile was sent on its way to another successful splash-down far down the Atlantic Missile Test Range.

It was a historic event, even more significant than the first launch of an aircraft from a ship at sea. In the new era of nuclear deterrence, the submarine, hidden beneath the sea, would become the nation's primary, ultimate strategic deterrent, able to strike targets anywhere on earth.

The Navy-industry accomplishment was a triumph of cooperation in what has been called an "adventure in partnership," wherein programmed development, scheduled invention, and concurrent production were the order of the day. However, an often overlooked but major factor in the success of the revolutionary system was the fact that the Navy had sixty years of submarine experience, with a long tradition of persistent innovation, resolute operation, and effective maintenance.

Sea-based ballistic missile deterrence became a reality on November 15, 1960, when *George Washington* deployed from Charleston, South Carolina, under the command of hard-driving, blunt-speaking, cigar-smoking Comdr. James B. Osborn. Once in deep water, the ship proceeded submerged to an area in the North Atlantic from which the arching trajectories of her missiles could reach targets far inside Russia's borders. As she roamed randomly and silently within a sea area the size of Texas, no one ashore, not even her operational commander, Commander-in-Chief Atlantic Command, could know exactly where she was at any time. Lacking an outright emergency, the submarine would keep absolute radio silence, transmitting no signals to betray her presence. Meanwhile, via her submerged antennas she constantly monitored the VLF broadcasts beamed over the Atlantic from the lofty towers of the naval radio stations at Annapolis and Balboa, Canal Zone.

But this first patrol of *George Washington* was a time of uneasiness. Time and again the Soviets had shown readiness to use force to serve their ends. They had shot down planes on peaceful missions and had brutally invaded small, defenseless nations. Most submariners were confident that *George Washington* could not be detected and attacked – she had her own torpedo tubes for defense – but there was a school of thought that held that the Russians would go all out to destroy and discredit this first undersea deterrent patrol. If she failed to return, who could be able to say from what cause she was lost? Was it enemy attack beneath the sea, or simply another in the long list of peacetime submarine disasters? While we awaited the outcome of that pioneering patrol, *Patrick Henry* sailed to augment the lonely, silent watch beneath the sea that has been maintained in growing numbers ever since.

Sixty-seven days after she sailed, *George Washington* emerged from the deep and returned to New London. She had been submerged sixty-six days and ten hours. Unlike our World War II patrols, when we had to dive and surface innumerable times to recharge batteries and fix position, she had made only one dive and one surfacing.

∗ ∗ ∗ ∗

As that first deterrent patrol demonstrated, it was not essential to forward-base such long-range, long-endurance submarines. However, in view of the limited number of boats and the relatively short range (1200 miles) of the Polaris A-1 missile, a more efficient operation in terms of target coverage could be attained by reducing the time of transit to deployment areas. We did not need a fixed base on foreign soil, with attendant political, psychological, and fiscal problems. All we needed was a submarine tender in a quiet, sheltered anchorage readily accessible from the North Atlantic.

In spite of demonstrations and propaganda by Ban-the-Bomb organizations, the British government granted the United States the right to use the Holy Loch in Scotland as the replenishment site for our first squadron of FBM submarines. Considering both domestic and international political factors, this was a courageous decision.

It is said that the Holy Loch, across the Firth of Clyde from Gourock and Greenock, was so named because a ship ballasted with earth it had brought from the Holy Land had foundered there. This normally calm, deep inlet where the Highlands meet the sea is a favorite holiday spot for Scots and English. It was there in early 1961 that we deployed USS *Proteus* (AS 19) to tend and refit the submarines that would operate from there. This was the same *Proteus* that had been present in Tokyo Bay at the Japanese surrender in 1945, and which I had helped inactivate in 1947 and place in reserve in the Thames River at New London. Who could foresee that when I next set foot on her deck in 1961 it would be in the Holy Loch, Scotland, as rear admiral, director submarine/antisubmarine warfare, and that 21"-diameter torpedoes would be puny toys alongside the 54" missiles she issued to her new breed of submarines?

The U.S. presence in the Holy Loch was greeted by well-organized, peaceful "Yank-Go-Home" protesters, many coming from as far away as London. But not many Scots cared for the idea of Sassenachs intruding in their territory and voicing sentiments they did not share. When large, white letters reading "POLARIS SPELLS DOOM" appeared on the seawall near Ardnadam Pier, one canny Scot, with a single stroke of the brush, corrected it to read, "POLARIS SPELLS BOOM."

The boom manifested itself in various ways. Perhaps the most lasting and constructive was in marriages. In the first two years of *Proteus*'s stay in the Holy Loch, more than forty Scots women wed American sailors. At a reception of local dignitaries during one of my visits, I mentioned this to Isabel Ross, the lady Provost of Dunoon. With a smile and twinkle in her eyes, she replied, "Admiral, you're taking all our naughty girls away."

✶ ✶ ✶ ✶

On March 8, 1961, *Patrick Henry* (SSBN 599), under command of Comdr. Harold E. (Hal) Shear, came alongside *Proteus* to be the first FBM submarine to receive her upkeep and tender support overseas. (Thirteen years later, Hal Shear, with four-star rank, would be commander-in-chief of U.S. naval forces in Europe, with headquarters in London.)

On the surface, alongside *Proteus,* the upper portion of *Patrick Henry*'s tall, vertical rudder protruded from the water, seemingly detached from the sub because of the tapering of her underbody from the maximum beam amidships. On a dreary, wet day a young man scrambled from a boat to the top of the rudder and sat hunched in the rain, forlorn and lonely, looking like a primitive sea creature protesting the desecration of his abode. Quickly he became the focal point of a newsman's dramatic picture, one that was widely published around the world. He was one of the group, three men and a woman, who occupied a tent pitched on nearby Strone Point as resident atomic bomb protesters, highly alert to photo opportunities. When the cold, bedraggled young man was removed from his perch, he was asked why he did what he was doing. He replied, "I get eight pounds a week for this" – from a London newspaper.

Here was early evidence of the same easy manipulation of audiovisual journalism that would reach new heights (or depths) during the war in Southeast Asia. All too often news is treated as a commodity in the commercial competition of news media, who excuse their excesses by pious declarations of the "public's right to know" and the sanctity of the First Amendment.

When I asked Admiral Shear whether he could verify the forgoing incident involving his ship, he wrote:

We were met by a group of Ban-the-Bomb-ers who tried to block off the Holy Loch with a small flotilla of canoes, kayaks, and rowboats. Their escapades that day, and in the following weeks, got a lot of publicity throughout the British papers, but it was largely of nuisance value and they never really caused us any problem. For the most part, the local Scots did not participate and held the protesters in disdain. A number of the protesters were brought up from Southern England and paid to demonstrate. This we established conclusively as time went on. One day, one of them tried to board the *Proteus* by climbing up the anchor chain and was washed off with a fire hose. Another day one climbed up on the rudder of *Patrick Henry* and sat there to have his picture taken so that it could appear in the press, which it did. By the time that little event had occurred, I was embarked on a Polaris lecture tour throughout Europe, which you sent me on.

Throughout this period of Ban-the-Bomb demonstrations, which lasted for several months to a greater or lesser degree, the Scottish police and the Royal Navy cooperated 100 percent with us and we never had anything more than a few minor incidents. I recall that one day forty or fifty of them lay down in the street and approach to Ardnadam Pier, such that when we came ashore and landed at the sea wall, we had to step over their prostrate bodies. Again, this got some attention in the press, but it was entirely passive and was nothing more than a nuisance. On the morning of our arrival from our first patrol, I was asked to give a press conference in the wardroom of *Proteus*, at which there were more than a hundred newsmen from all over the world. One of the press reporters was from *TASS* in Moscow. He asked question after question, all of which were easy enough to answer, until eventually, the other newsmen got tired of his hogging the limelight and shoved him aside. As you may recall, we experimented in those early patrols with several college courses, sponsored by Harvard and the University of Maryland. We had the first of these courses sponsored by Harvard, consisting of a taped lecture series, and those who completed it actually obtained college credits. The first course was a political history course entitled "An Analysis of Revolution" which analyzed all revolutions, including the American, French, and Russian. In one way or another this course and subject came out during the press conference. This sent the *TASS* reporter completely into orbit, to find that American Polaris sailors were studying the art of revolution, and he asked me question after question, much to the glee of the other reporters.

The 1961 European "lecture tour" Hal Shear referred to was part of U.S. diplomatic efforts to reassure our NATO allies that our Polaris submarines were commanded by mature, carefully chosen, highly trained and disciplined officers who were keenly aware of their responsibilities in the deterrent retaliatory force entrusted to them. The commanding officers, accompanied by wives, whom we sent on these official visits to NATO capitals were Hal Shear, Bob Long, and Larry From.

Rear Adm. James Fife, Jr., Commander Submarine Force Atlantic Fleet, 1948. (U.S. Naval Historical Center)

Change of command, Submarine Squadron 7, Pearl Harbor, July 1954. Author (at microphone) and his successor, Capt. R. H. O'Kane. (U.S. Navy photo)

Adm. Arleigh A. Burke, 1955. (National Archives)

USS *Nautilus* is welcomed to New York City, August 25, 1958, after her historic undersea voyage from Pearl Harbor through the Aleutians and underneath the North Pole into the Atlantic Ocean. (National Archives)

Nautilus is inspected by three submarine officers who had much to do with winning World War II. Left to right: Vice Adm. Charles A. Lockwood, Fleet Adm. Chester W. Nimitz, and Adm. F. S. Low. (U. S. Naval Historical Center)

USS *Seawolf*, underway in 1957. America's second nuclear-powered submarine, she had a liquid sodium-cooled reactor. (General Dynamics Corp.)

USS *Skate* on the surface at the North Pole, March 17, 1959, the first submarine to accomplish the feat. (National Archives)

Rear Adm. Hyman G. Rickover emerging from the engine-room hatch of *Nautilus*, 1958. (National Archives)

Author, with fingers crossed, assuring President John F. Kennedy that inert warheads fired off Cape Canaveral would fly perfectly to target in the Atlantic Test Range. Aboard the observing ship *Observation Island* are (left to right) Capt. R. O Middleton, Rear Adm. V. L. Lowrance, Kennedy, the author, and Maj. Gen. Ted Clifton. The photo was taken on November 16, 1963, six days before Kennedy was assassinated in Dallas. (U.S. Navy photo)

THE WHITE HOUSE
WASHINGTON

19 November 1963

Dear Admiral Galantin:

The Polaris firing I witnessed from the USS OBSERVATION ISLAND on 16 November was a most satisfying and fascinating experience. It is still incredible to me that a missile can be successfully and accurately fired from beneath the sea. Once one has seen a Polaris firing the efficacy of this weapons system as a deterrent is not debatable.

Thank you very much for allowing me to see a Polaris firing. Certainly, those of us who saw it are more conscious of the professional competence of our naval forces.

Would you please express my appreciation to the Commanding Officer and crew of the USS ANDREW JACKSON for their splendid performance.

With best wishes,

Sincerely,

JOHN F. KENNEDY

Rear Admiral I. J. Galantin, USN
Special Projects Officer
Main Navy
Washington, D. C.

President Kennedy, with glasses, watches as a Polaris missile is launched by USS *Andrew Jackson*, November 16, 1963. Rear Adm. Lowrance stands alongside. (U.S. Navy photo) Insert: Letter from President Kennedy to the author.

USS *Patrick Henry* maneuvers to a berth in the Holy Loch, Scotland, 1963. The submarine tender USS *Hunley* is in the background. (U.S. Navy photo)

USS *James Monroe,* with all missile doors open, alongside USS *Andrew Jackson,* 1964. (U.S. Navy photo)

Radar picket submarine USS *Triton* underway with all radar masts and periscopes housed, 1960. The hull form is typical of submarines that must operate much of the time on the surface. At 6670 tons, she was the world's largest submarine at the time. (National Archives)

Launching of USS *Sea Devil,* Newport News, Virginia, October 6, 1967. Her sponsor was Virginia Galantin. (Newport News Shipbuilding and Drydock Co.)

Admiral Lord Louis Mountbatten (National Archives)

Aboard HMS *Resolution*, Great Britain's first Polaris submarine, after the successful firing of her first missile, February 15, 1968. Left to right: author, Commander M. C. Henry, RN; Vice Adm. Sir Hugh Mackenzie, RN; Capt. Charles Shepherd, RN; and Rear Adm. Levering Smith, USN. (U.S. Navy photo)

Author at periscope, USS *Henry L. Stimson,* March 17, 1968. (U.S. Navy photo)

THE FUTURE OF
NUCLEAR-POWERED SUBMARINES

In World War II, U.S. antisubmarine warfare capability, honed in the severe challenge by U-boats in the North Atlantic, had little difficulty coping with Japan's misdirected submarine campaign. Our losses to air attack, including those to the sacrificial, human-guided kamikazes, were more severe. That turn of events in the Pacific, which the Navy always considered its primary theater of operations, influenced postwar planning and budget allocations. Strike warfare by fast carrier task groups, with their necessary shield of air defense, received top priority at a time when the Soviet submarine force was the major and mounting threat to our oceanic coalition and its command of the seas. If an inadequate ASW capability was acknowledged and a major increase requested in its funding, it would imply increased vulnerability of aircraft carriers and undermine the Navy's case for them even though it was a good case. A strong, two-ocean force of aircraft carriers, deploying high-performance planes, is essential for command of the seas, for manifold maritime tasks, and for the extra dimension it brings to joint military operations worldwide.

By 1956 the apparent inadequate attention to ASW led to growing criticism by the Congress, the Office of the Secretary of Defense, and the media. And when Gen. Earl E. Partridge, USAF, Commander-in-Chief Continental Air Defense Command (CinConAD), asked for a briefing on the Navy's ASW capability, specifically our ability to cope with the threat of Russian guided missile submarines, the Navy read his request as only another more subtle effort to divert the Navy from emphasis on air strike into concentration on ASW.

Admiral Burke directed that Rear Admiral Warder (OP 31) form a team to make the presentation. Headed by Warder, the team included the following captains: Ralph C. Styles, who covered intelligence; John S. McCain, Jr., our apostle of sea power, who extolled mobility and dispersion; myself, who gave an appreciation of submarine warfare; and Sidney D. B. Merrill and Ray Pflum, who covered surface and air ASW.

After careful rehearsals, modifications, and final clearance by our top naval hierarchy in the Pentagon, there evolved a favorable picture of our ASW capabilities. Thus prepared, we were sent on a succession of visits to give our presentation to the senior Navy commanders in Norfolk, Pearl Harbor, San Diego, San Francisco, and Seattle. This was to ensure that the Navy spoke with one voice on antisubmarine warfare.

In these preliminary bouts it seemed that the senior aviators, men who had played a large part in the great accomplishments of carrier aviation in World War II, wanted to minimize any implied threat to carrier task forces. They pointed out that only one Japanese submarine ever sank one of our fast carriers. That was at the battle for Guadalcanal in 1942 when *I-19* sank *Wasp* with three torpedo hits.[1] On the other hand, younger flag officers, those who might have to cope with the attacks of large numbers of modern submarines, were receptive to a more realistic assessment. They preferred a clearer recognition of the magnitude of the threat, the complexity of ASW, and the need for more funds, forces, and effort in that field. Aware of the generally inept employment of Japan's submarines, they were more impressed by the fact that our own boats had sunk one battleship, nine aircraft carriers, twelve cruisers, forty-six destroyers, numerous smaller Japanese naval craft, and heavily damaged many other warships, carriers included, despite our very inferior torpedo. Yet that fact was not permitted to cloud the generally rosy picture we gave of our ASW readiness and capability. The perceived, if not real, domestic threat by Congress and the Air Force to the Navy's essential air arm took precedence over the threat by a foreign enemy.

In February 1957, our team went to Colorado Springs and put on our show before General Partridge and his senior staff. We had a most attentive audience, and General Partridge seemed as advertised: highly intelligent, objective, and dedicated. He said that he was reassured to have, for the first time, "so comprehensive a picture of the measures Navy takes to cope with the submarine menace." As to the submarine guided missile (SSG) threat, he gathered that there was no serious present danger inasmuch as an enemy would not be likely to apply an inadequate force prematurely. After successfully side-stepping what it considered a probable attack on its air strike capabilities, the Navy then reverted to usual practice and gave lip service to ASW through unrealistic, too brief, limited training exercises against obsolescent subs.

Antisubmarine warfare has a time dimension of its own. There must be intense, patient, persistent effort by every applicable means to detect the stealthy opponent at great range, then localization and attack as promptly as possible against a swift, silent, maneuvering enemy. In their operations with the fleet, *Nautilus* and *Seawolf* demonstrated how much nuclear-powered submarines outclassed the antisubmarine tactics that were successful against diesel-powered, air-breathing submarines. With no need to conserve electric power, in boats that were free to run as fast and for as long as they wanted, the two innovative, aggressive skippers were delighted by the flexibility they had in attack. Dennis Wilkinson in *Nautilus* and Dick Laning in *Seawolf* had little trouble attaining excellent torpedo-firing position using an occasional periscope look, or making no periscope exposures at all and using passive (bearings only) sonar for target information. Their dramatic successes with the outmoded sonars, obsolescent fire control systems, and obsolete torpedoes available to them disclosed the severity of the new ASW problem.

In Dick Laning's words, "We both found that a certain ASW complacency required that we do things with a certain flair and even shock value to get their attention to the enormity of the ASW problem we would face. When a HUK [hunter-killer] group commander in the wash-up [postexercise critique] would deny that the carrier had been sunk, we would show pictures of the carrier's screws and views into the hangar deck. Wilkinson even fired green flares [denoting torpedo attack] which landed on the carrier deck."[2]

Bewildered at first by the amazing capabilities of their elusive new targets, the best minds of the surface ASW forces began to devise new tactics. It was apparent that early detection of attacking subs, as far from a task group or convoy as possible, was essential. With no above-water target for visual or radar contact, that detection would have to be by fixed, passive sound surveillance barriers, by sophisticated air-dropped sonobuoys, or by the passive sonars of mobile, underwater search vehicles - nuclear submarines themselves. The high-frequency airborne radars that had been instrumental in defeating the U-boats would no longer be relevant, although the high-speed, long reach of specially configured ASW planes, helicopters, or drones would be invaluable in extending the search and attack range. To develop and procure the sophisticated aircraft and target-seeking weapons required would take years and billions of dollars.

The Commander Destroyer Force Atlantic Fleet (ComDesLant) arranged a demonstration of a promising new "standoff" tactic in which a destroyer that had contact on a sub would vector its helicopter to a drop point for its homing weapon. In April 1957 I was included in a group of senior officers from the Pentagon and the Bureau of Aeronautics who embarked in the new destroyer leader *Norfolk* (DL 1) at Norfolk, Virginia, for two nights and a day to witness the new tactic.

Seawolf, which had been placed in commission just twenty-one days before, would be the target for *Norfolk* and the modern destroyers *Mitscher, Forrest Sherman,* and *Cromwell.* I was concerned that she had been committed to an advanced exercise after so little time for shakedown and training. There was no need to be. Dick Laning had seen to it that during her building period *Seawolf's* torpedo attack team used the shore-based attack trainers at Sub School more than did all other subs of the Atlantic Fleet combined.

As our screening destroyers searched vainly for *Seawolf* with their active, pinging sonars, first notice of her presence came from the wakes of torpedoes streaking for *Norfolk*. Of the five exercise torpedoes set to run under their target, I watched three pass right under the ship. It was only fair to note that *Seawolf* was then probably the victim of a homing torpedo dropped by the helicopter attracted by the torpedo wakes. Clearly, the outcome of such an encounter would depend on who made first detection, who maneuvered most effectively, and who attacked first. The advantage to the nuclear-powered submarine in these factors was obvious.

From *Norfolk* our party transferred to *Seawolf* to observe Dick Laning and his sharp, proud crew make repeated attacks on the surface units before racing submerged to New London.

✶ ✶ ✶ ✶

Not long afterward, I received orders transferring me to New London to be chief of staff for Rear Adm. C. W. (Weary) Wilkins, ComSubLant. Weary was the most unassuming, kindly, considerate flag officer I had known, and it would be a real pleasure to work with him. I had wanted a change from the many years of submarine duty on my record, at sea and ashore, especially after the last two trying years in the Pentagon. However, recalling Jimmy Fife's advice, I did not protest. After all, the new job meant at least a year out of the high-cost Washington area, with the added benefit of submarine pay.

Then came a stunning development; the closely held list of those whom the annual selection board had chosen for flag rank was published. On it were Thomas H. Moorer and myself, the first unrestricted line officers of our class of 1933 who would be promoted to rear admiral.

Tom then moved steadily through the Navy's top operational commands in the Mediterranean, the Pacific, and the Atlantic. He was clearly being groomed to be the leading candidate for chief of naval operations in a few years. Greatly admired within the Navy and highly regarded in top political circles, Tom was nominated for that position by President Richard Nixon in 1967 and quickly approved by the Senate. He performed brilliantly, both as CNO and subsequently as chairman of the Joint Chiefs of Staff from 1970 to 1974.

As for myself, the choice assignment to New London had to be forgone. In September 1957 I was sent overseas to a joint NATO assignment as deputy chief of staff, logistics and administration, for the Commander-in-Chief Allied Forces Southern Europe (CinCSouth) in Naples, Italy.

As I was winding up duties in OP 311, the Naval Institute in Annapolis asked me to write for its *Proceedings* magazine an essay titled "The Future of Nuclear Powered Submarines." I thought my submarine days might well be over, there being only three billets, ashore and afloat, earmarked for a submarine-qualified flag officer, and I welcomed the chance to set forth my views on the subject that was causing such misunderstanding and divisiveness.

It was timely to do this. Two recent events had caused an uproar in OpNav and fueled Admiral Burke's anger. First, there were allegations that a young submarine officer had persuaded the editor of *The Reader's Digest* to cancel a favorable story about aircraft carriers. Next, retired Adm. Daniel E. Barbey had written an article titled "Let's Build the New Deterrent Force Now," which was published as the magazine's lead article in its January 1958 issue. Admiral Barbey was not a submariner, but a distinguished senior officer, architect of our modern amphibious warfare force. His organization, training, and command of amphibious forces for General MacArthur's campaigns in the Southwest Pacific had been brilliant. Newsmen called him the "founder of modern amphibious warfare."

True to his forthright, decisive character, Barbey argued strongly for immediate buildup of a nuclear submarine force armed with Regulus missiles to take over the aircraft carrier's nuclear deterrence role. The strategy he presented to such a wide readership was strikingly similar to that which many submarine officers had been advocating within the Navy, and the chief of naval operations was convinced that Admiral Barbey's article was written by a submariner. No names were cited, but I was among the usual suspects. I had been a prewar shipmate of Dan Barbey when he was first lieutenant of the battleship *New York* and admired his friendly, hardworking, strong leadership of junior officers, but had never had contact with him thereafter. Actually, Arleigh Burke supported the building of a submarine-based guided missile force, but at a more deliberate pace that later events proved to be wise. By 1964, when the Regulus program was canceled, we would still have only four SSGs and one SSGN.

Beset by pressures from the competing factions of our own service and by continuous Air Force efforts to minimize full development of naval aviation capabilities, Admiral Burke was convinced that "all submariners are disloyal to him and to the Navy, that they have embarked on a very subtle and deliberate campaign to take over the Navy, much as the naval aviators attempted right after World War II."[3]

Part of the problem was the fact that the billet charged with both submarine and antisubmarine warfare readiness, that of a relatively junior rear admiral, was so low on the OpNav totem pole. Submarine-qualified flag officers of greater seniority who had the ear of the CNO had not served in submarines since before the war and were not current on submarine technology, operational concepts, and capabilities.

One submariner who did have direct access to the CNO was the dynamic and forthright Rear Adm. Lawson P. (Red) Ramage. He was one of the first two young captains to be "deep selected" for flag rank. Admiral Burke had chosen him to be his special assistant, not for submarine matters in particular but as a trouble-shooter in general. Red did his best to convince Arleigh that fears of the very small minority of the Navy who were submariners being disloyal were baseless. Ninety percent of operating submariners were junior officers on sea duty, and all other commanders, captains, and admirals were spread far and wide in billets where they had little or nothing to do with submarine matters and were in no position to undermine his programs.

In the calm of Naples, far removed from intra-Navy bickering and interservice jealousies, my thoughts flowed easily to paper. I hoped they would help remove from "naval officers qualified in submarines" the stigma of free-wheeling disloyalty. In June 1958 the lead article in the *Proceedings* was my rationale for the nuclear submarine's role in our Navy. Before its publication my essay was circulated among the top echelons of OpNav, where it received overwhelming approval. Were I writing it today, I would change little of its nontechnical, conceptual thinking and enlarge chiefly on the use of nuclear-powered submarines in deterrence, in what the late Sen. Henry M. Jackson termed "the fourth dimension of warfare – ballistic sea power."

From the point of view purely of ship construction, the installation of a nuclear power reactor for the propulsion of ships could have been made more easily in a surface ship than in a submarine. That it was applied first to the submarine is simply recognition that of all types of naval ships the submarine had most to gain from this revolutionary power source. It meant not simply an extension of current capabilities; more than that, it transformed an intermittent submerged capability into a continuous one. Freed from its tie to the atmosphere, the submarine could now operate for virtually unlimited periods below the zone of most probable detection. It would be essentially a new weapon system, the only one that combined mobility with concealment. It changed the submarine's traditional mode of warfare from "ambush" to "chase" and exploited the oceans of the world not just as a fluid plain for movement but as a vast zone of three-dimensional operations. I reasoned that more and more of the manifold tasks of naval power would be performed by nuclear-powered submarines as the efficiency of underwater movement and the military advantages of concealment were exploited. However, that very concealment inhibits it to some extent in influencing action on the surface of land or sea. The objective of war is control of the land, on which all power ultimately depends. The nuclear submarine can influence that control chiefly through interdiction of seaborne movement, naval and commercial, and through massive attack (or threat of attack) on land positions of power.

Although a nation is sovereign over its land areas, and its airspace is similarly inviolate, beyond its narrow territorial waters there is a vast region that knows only the sovereignty of sea power. Nuclear propulsion makes it possible for submarines to add greatly to that power, but it does not make surface forces obsolete. As Fleet Admiral Nimitz stated, "What determines the obsolescence of a weapon is not the fact that it can be destroyed, but that it can be replaced by another weapon that performs its functions more effectively."

The nuclear submarine cannot perform all the functions of the aircraft carrier that a variety of manned aircraft and the diversity of their weapons make possible. It is but one element, an essential and powerful component of the integrated, flexible weapons systems of air, surface, and subsurface forces that comprise modern naval power. Operating concealed in waters untenable by surface forces, it is the forward extension of that power.

✷　✷　✷　✷

When Admiral Warder became commander of the Submarine Force Atlantic Fleet in 1957, Rear Adm. Charles E. Weakley, a very able, highly regarded destroyer officer, relieved him as OP 31. However, there was continuing criticism in the Congress, in scientific groups, and the press of what seemed the Navy's inadequate organizational structure to plan and monitor its ASW program. The U.S.S.R. was building a submarine force of such size and sophistication that it threatened the U.S. control of the seas that was essential for our own security and for the survival of our overseas allies. Furthermore, the shift to nuclear power and the introduction of Polaris meant that the portion of Navy resources going to submarine-related programs was growing rapidly.

Considering all these factors, in 1960 Admiral Burke made a change. Charlie Weakley was designated assistant chief of naval operations for antisubmarine warfare (OP 001), reporting directly to the CNO and charged most strongly to get drastic improvements in ASW. Aided by a small staff, he was to coordinate the efforts of the many Navy agencies involved in ASW. At the same time, the OP 31 billet, still with its dual responsibilities, was returned to a submarine officer, Rear Adm. Lawrence R. (Dan) Daspit.

Charlie Weakley and Dan Daspit were much alike. Both were proven combat leaders, highly respected in their warfare specialties, each of thoughtful, scientific bent. In command of *Tinosa* during World War II, it was Dan who brought back convincing evidence of the defective contact exploder in our torpedo warheads and prompted its urgent redesign. He had methodically fired fifteen torpedoes at a 19,000-ton Japanese tanker after carefully conning his boat to ideal, close-range firing positions. Hit after hit, eleven in all, were duds.

There was a too frequent turnover in the OP 31 billet, five in six years, a fact that was receiving pointed criticism from Congress, the Office of the Secretary of Defense, and the media. Red Ramage had relieved Dan Daspit in that spot at the end of 1959, and I took over from Red in January 1961. My own tenure was short; in a year I was designated to head the Polaris Special Projects Office. However, the new CNO, Adm. George W. Anderson, finally rationalized the situation and split the job into the two functional areas that were unique to the Navy – submarine warfare and antisubmarine warfare – so that they could be given the vigorous, detailed attention each required. I became solely director of submarine warfare, and Rear Adm. J. N. Shaffer, an experienced destroyer sailor, took over the ASW responsibilities.

Congress was seeking an even more highly placed, central ASW authority. In its 1961 report, the House Armed Services Committee (two of its most influential members were Gerald Ford and Melvin Laird) stated:

The Navy has failed to push undersea warfare programs with sufficient vigor. Except for the indefatigable effort and obstinacy of one man we probably would not now have the nuclear powered submarine which in itself, in the attack version, is one of the best antisubmarine weapons. The nuclear powered submarine has proven to be one of the major accomplishments of this generation. The marriage of the atomic submarine with the Polaris fleet ballistic missile promises to give us one of the greatest deterrent weapon systems yet devised. Both of these accomplishments have been notably successful because management at a crucial stage was divorced from the stagnation of the usual bureaucratic organization and procedures. Studies made of our antisubmarine warfare efforts indicate that both organizational and inspirational action along similar lines is required. The Navy says that it is giving antisubmarine warfare its highest priority rating, yet there is no indication of dramatic or dynamic leadership in this field. The development work in this area is not being divorced from control of the semi-autonomous bureaus in the Navy Department. Until a single manager similar to that provided for the Polaris ballistic missile system, with delegated responsibility and the full backing of top officials, is established, it is doubtful that antisubmarine warfare will attain the goals so urgently required. The Committee recommends that such action be taken immediately.[4]

When the Navy did not follow this advice, the committee, with some asperity, made identical comments the next year. It seemed not to understand that the all-powerful, centralized, focused management appropriate to single-purpose development and procurement projects such as reactors and Polaris missiles was not applicable to a warfare systems as all-encompassing as ASW. Virtually every element of naval air-surface-undersea power is directly involved in or supports ASW. What was lacking was frank acknowledgment of the submarine threat, priority given to its solution, adequate commitment of assets, and emphasis on sustained, realistic training for all our air, surface, and submarine forces involved.

The pressures from the Office of the Secretary of Defense and the Congress continued, and in 1964 the Office of Director ASW Programs was established in OpNav "to exercise centralized coordinating authority over all ASW planning, programming, and appraising." A very strong-minded surface warfare officer, Vice Adm. Charles B. Martell, was assigned to be, at least in title, what the Congress wanted, a "Czar of ASW." However, he did not have authority to override the claims of the air, surface, and submarine platform sponsors and to allocate resources and priorities. The position would change in title and scope under succeeding CNOs and Navy secretaries.

Progress in ASW was always constrained by the Navy's need to maintain the mix of forces required to cope with its wide range of missions and tasks. Indeed, not until 1986 was there unequivocal acknowledgment of the great threat that newer Soviet subs presented to U.S. surface ship operations, both naval and commercial. The CNO, Adm. Carlisle A. Trost, himself a submariner, declared that "ASW is Priority One," a commitment that held until the apparent end of the Russian high-seas threat when the Soviet Union collapsed.

ALLIES

After World War II, the United States committed itself to the policy of collective security. This centuries-old principle sought to substitute the deterrent and complementary forces of an association of legally pledged states for the dangerous, unbalanced forces existing among individual states. Its adoption and avid promotion by the United States, so different from her attitude after World War I, was recognition of our country's changed strategic position. Faced by continuous Soviet intransigence and obstructionism, the United States turned more and more to bilateral and regional security arrangements, a procedure consistent with the charter of the United Nations.

A list of these treaties and the number of nations included in each is impressive evidence of the scope of commitment undertaken by the United States:

North Atlantic Treaty	sixteen nations
Australia, New Zealand, U.S. (ANZUS) Treaty	three nations
Rio Treaty	twenty-three nations
Philippine Treaty	bilateral
Japanese Treaty	bilateral
South Korea Treaty	bilateral
Southeast Asia Treaty	bilateral
Formosa Treaty	bilateral

The forty-four separate nations that joined with the United States in these treaties are located on six continents across the world's major oceans. Forty-one of them front on the sea; the three that do not are Luxembourg (in NATO) and Bolivia and Paraguay (under the Rio Treaty). Even so, these three are entirely surrounded by countries that are in the same collective security organization and are themselves accessible from the sea. In addition, the United States entered into military assistance agreements with numerous other countries. These did not bind us to go to war, but implied a moral obligation to do so. In sum total, the United States committed itself to defend or assist some sixty-four nations.

It is clear that the collective security system tied together by the mutual defense pacts listed, as well as by the U.N. Charter, is heavily based upon sea power, specifically on the ability of U.S. naval power to ensure the projection of the industrial and military might of this nation to the shores of its allies. So basic is this understanding that the forces allied in opposition to the designs of the U.S.S.R. were called the "Oceanic Coalition," tacit recognition of the unifying, strengthening influence of sea power. As Walter Lippmann said, "The Atlantic Ocean is not the frontier between Europe and the Americas. It is the inland sea of a community of nations allied with one another by geography, history, and vital necessity."[1]

Reversal of the historic U.S. policy of avoiding permanent alliances meant that sizable American land and air forces had to be stationed in allied countries from Asia to Europe, and the Navy would have to keep strong, balanced task forces deployed continuously near areas threatened by communist takeover. The great burden of keeping open the sea lanes of support to all these forces clearly defined both the U.S.S.R. naval strategy and the U.S. need to defeat it through sea control.

* * * *

From the end of World War II through 1992 there were 240 crises that threatened world peace or the interests of the United States or its allies. In 202 of these, U.S. naval forces were involved, with most of the incidents occurring in the Third World.[2] In almost every case the first question asked was, "Where are the carriers?" – tacit recognition that naval power has the continuing ability to "carry the signs and symbols of international law and order." This historic role of naval power, essentially a symbolic act of diplomacy, is magnified by the attributes of modern naval power: mobility, flexibility, concentration of power, and continuity of presence. With the progressive loss of overseas bases for U.S. land and air forces, it is the one constant of U.S. influence and resolve.

The examples of the Sixth Fleet in the Mediterranean since 1946, and of the Seventh Fleet in the Taiwan area since 1949, are evidence of the continuity of naval power and of the force it may be for maintaining peace and stability in critical areas. That it is a deterrent when its objectives are defined and stated is clear from the restraint imposed on Russia's attempt to dominate Greece and Turkey and on China's threatened expansion to Formosa (now Taiwan). The policy of containment of communism could not succeed without the "over the horizon," mobile presence of our fleets giving assurance to friends and foes alike of U.S. power and resolve.

When NATO's military command was activated in 1951 under Gen. Dwight Eisenhower as Supreme Allied Commander Europe (SACEur), the Sixth Fleet was committed to its support, supplementing U.S. ground and air forces stationed in Europe. Through it, the Navy became a principal player in the Cold War.

In 1957 the commander-in-chief of NATO's southern command, Allied Forces Southern Europe (CinCSouth) was the kindly, southern-bred Adm. Robert P. Briscoe. He was a respected sailor of the old school, a man of deep humanity, well-liked throughout his polyglot area of command. CinCSouth's superior commander was SACEur, Gen. Lauris Norstad, USAF, headquartered in Paris. Deputy supreme commander was British Field Marshall Bernard L. Montgomery. His often acrimonious remarks, denigrating U.S. generals' leadership in battle and deploring General Eisenhower's overall command of the Allied armies, fueled a swirling controversy in the media over the relative competence of American and British field commanders. He even said of Eisenhower, "Ike had simply no experience for the job. As a field commander he was very bad."

NATO's conventional forces strategy was dependent upon backup of U.S. nuclear weaponry, and the United States had established at Oberammergau, West Germany, a school to give its allies some familiarization with those weapons. In November 1957, as the senior American in the one-week course. I took my lunches with the senior "other national," Gen. Hans Speidel from West Germany. He had been chief of staff to the "Desert Fox," Field Marshall Erwin Rommel, and had faced Montgomery as well as American generals in battle. I asked his opinion of Monty's criticism.

Although Rommel had lost to Monty in the crucial battle of El Alamein in Egypt, as much because of British air and submarine interdiction of his seaborne supply lines as for tactics, Speidel replied, "We never had great difficulty with Montgomery. We knew how he fought. He would make a massive buildup of men and material, then smash ahead once more. The ones who gave us the most trouble were Bradley and Patton; we never knew where they would go or when."

Hans Speidel was a highly educated man, a Ph.D. who spoke excellent English and with whom it was easy to exchange ideas. That was not always possible in Allied Forces Southern Europe headquarters in the town of Bagnoli just west of Naples. We were staffed by U.S., U.K., Italian, Greek, and Turkish military, with a French general on board in liaison status. The men and women of all the military branches of the six nations wore twenty-four different uniforms and spoke five different languages. English and French were the official NATO languages, but there were times when Italian, Greek, or Turkish were useful. This was especially true in my billet, whose responsibilities for logistics and personnel administration required frequent contact with our host country's military and civilian officials.

Shortly after my arrival, Generale di Divisione Aldo DeMarco, Italian army, reported as deputy chief of staff for plans and operations. Neither of us spoke a word of the other's language, and we undertook to help each other overcome that shortcoming. The method we used was not that promoted by Berlitz. Our primary texts were the daily newspapers *Herald-Tribune* and *Il Mattino,* which we supplemented by practice on each other and on any unwary bystander on social occasions. Once we reached the level of *la storiella* (storytelling, preferably a bit bawdy), we made rapid progress. By 1959 we were reasonably proficient in each other's mother tongue.

In June, President Celal Bayar of Turkey visited the Italian government in Rome, then came to Naples for an official call on CinCSouth, who included in his NATO command substantial elements of Turkish ground, sea, and air forces. Among the official functions incident to his visit was a reception hosted by the senior Italian military commander in the area, Ammiraglio Francesco Ruta, who held both the national command of the Tyrrhenian region and the Central Mediterranean NATO Command (CoMedCent). Admiral Ruta's reception was on the terrace of the historic *Ammiragliata* in Naples, close to and overlooking the busy harbor dominated by Mount Vesuvius to the east. (Admiral Lord Nelson looked on the same scene 160 years earlier when he dallied there with Lady Hamilton).

At anchor in the harbor and exciting comment for her graceful lines was the Turkish presidential yacht *Savarona*. The trim, white-hulled craft with steam drive and a clipper bow had been designed by the famous American naval architect William Francis Gibbs and was the largest yacht of its kind ever built. Constructed for Mrs. R. M. Cadwalader of Philadelphia, she had been built in Denmark in the late twenties. However, luxury yachts requiring a crew of ninety-two went rapidly out of style, and *Savarona* was put up for sale. Purchased by the government of Turkey, she was used both as the presidential yacht and as a training ship for midshipmen of the Turkish Naval Academy.

The reception was another good occasion to practice my Italian. Pointing to the beautiful *Savarona,* I said to Aldo, "Ecco la nave scuola."

General DeMarco asked, "What did you say, Pete?"

I repeated my simple Italian sentence, "Ecco la nave scuola."

Now Aldo's eyes twinkled, and he asked, "Don't you know what 'nave scuola' means?"

"Certamente. 'Nave scuola' significa 'school ship.'"

To this Aldo promptly replied, "Oh, no, no, no! In Italiano 'nave scuola' means a smooth, round bottom on which young officers get experience."

I was surprised that this euphemism came from a soldier rather than a sailor. However, it is so much in keeping with the good-humored, quick-witted, volatile Italian character that it was apparently accepted by all the services. In such ways is unification of the armed forces advanced.

Not all interservice differences were so smoothly resolved. It was to protect further the Navy's right to the top command of AFSouth against the covetous reach of the Air Force that Adm. Charles R. (Cat) Brown was designated to relieve Bob Briscoe. Unlike his predecessor, he was a naval aviator. Command of the U.S. Sixth Fleet deployed in the Mediterranean was reserved for a three-star aviation admiral, and it was in that command that Cat Brown had very ably conducted the peacekeeping landing of U.S. Marines in Lebanon in 1958. The Sixth Fleet was the most powerful and most versatile force that would be available to CinCSouth in the event of a war involving NATO. For such an emergency, some of the plans and directives of CinCSouth were controversial. The several nations, ours included, and their various armed services all sought to promote their special interests through their own interpretations. In his conferences with his principal subordinate commander, the colorful, fun-loving Admiral Brown was incisive, calm, and poised, an excellent commander.

* * * *

Italians are keenly aware of the importance of the sea, not only in the history of their own country but also to the success of the NATO enterprise. And their pride in the great part their countryman, Enrico Fermi, played in developing controlled chain reaction of atomic energy made them especially responsive to *Nautilus*'s feats. The city of Genoa had established the annual International Congress of Communications, at which she awarded gold medals for outstanding accomplishment in science, the arts, and technology. In October 1958 Bill Anderson, skipper of *Nautilus,* came to Genoa to receive the Christopher Columbus Prize for Communications, and I was asked to shepherd him and his wife through the impressive ceremony.

In his opening remarks in the beautiful hall of the ancient Palazzo San Giorgio, the mayor noted "the dizzying pace of progress. Hardly a year has passed since Admiral Rickover was awarded the same prize by which we now honor Commander Anderson for his legendary deed, the sub-polar passage of *Nautilus.*"

In his response Anderson remarked that it was no wonder that Genoa, one of the oldest maritime communities of the world, had produced an explorer like Columbus. To the Italians' satisfaction he went on to say that, in one sense, the voyage of *Nautilus* under the North Pole had its beginning right there in Genoa several centuries ago. In the conclave of many notable Europeans, Bill Anderson was the star, modest but sure of himself, a great credit to the United States, the Navy, and the submarine service.

* * * *

Duty in CinCSouth headquarters did not involve direct contact with the Italian submarine service, but I did enjoy friendly relations with officers of that branch, some of whom had served in World War II. The most modern sub they operated was the former USS *Barb*, renamed *Enrico Tazzoli*, which had been transferred to Italy in 1954 in our Foreign Military Assistance Program. Later, Italy would receive eight more of our diesel boats.

My growing familiarity with the strategic importance and unusual characteristics of the Mediterranean increased my respect for the submariners of any nation who fought there. Almost completely land-locked, dependent on steady inflow of water from its Atlantic and Black Sea outlets as well as from rivers, the Mediterranean is subdivided by peninsulas and islands into several lesser seas. Each of these relatively confined basins can be continuously and closely monitored by air or surface patrols from numerous nearby bases. In addition, minefields in the straits and shallow areas make transit extra hazardous.

Germany had deployed U-boats to the Mediterranean to attack Britain's line of sea communications to Alexandria, to Malta, and to North African ports supporting Montgomery's Eighth Army. Important sinkings were made, but U-boat losses were disproportionately high. Of the sixty-two boats that were sent to the Mediterranean, forty-eight were lost. Britain had similar experience. Of the total of seventy-six submarines she lost, forty-five went down in the Mediterranean. A submariner's life expectancy in that area was little more than twelve months!

Our own large World War II subs, designed for long surface transits and for only intermittent submergence in an ocean fifty-six times the area of the Mediterranean, would not have fared well in the Mediterranean. The nuclear-powered attack and ballistic missile boats that we deploy there today can do so in combat only because of continuous, silent submergence and their sophisticated sonar, navigation, and communication systems.

The Italian submarine force had indifferent success in its wartime operations in the Mediterranean and the Atlantic, but it had long experimented with the use of small, specialized underwater assault teams for penetrating the numerous harbors ringing the Mediterranean that were used by the British. Even before the Japanese developed a similar capability, the Italians had evolved four modes of sneak attack from the sea: (1) *midget submarines* of twelve and thirty tons; (2) *explosive motorboats* carrying one or two torpedoes and manned by a single operator; (3) *guided torpedoes,* twenty-one feet long, three feet in diameter, and controlled by two men who rode them underwater; after placing the detachable warhead in position, the crew would try to ride the torpedo back to safety (the Japanese *kaiten* concept differed in that its crewman was expended with the warhead); and (4) *limpet mines* to be attached by specially trained frogmen.

All of these relied to some degree on the support of conventional submarines, either for transport, navigation, communications, or recovery. Although they influenced the course of naval action in the Mediterranean, they were not a decisive force. Their greatest success came in December 1941, when three of the manned torpedoes penetrated Alexandria Harbor and sank the British battleships *Valiant* and *Queen Elizabeth* and a large tanker.[3]

Germany, Japan, and Britain also developed special-purpose, miniature submarines. They did not use them in the same diversity and extent as Italy did, but it is to the British that I credit what I consider the most calculating, sustained heroic action of undersea warfare in World War II. In Naples I had the opportunity to say so to one of the principal participants.

In January 1959 the aircraft carrier HMS *Eagle* visited. On board I was delighted to meet and chat with Capt. B. C. Godfrey Place, RN. The slight, smallish man, soft-spoken and always in tight control of himself, was chief-of-staff for British Flag Officer Aircraft Carriers, embarked in *Eagle*. I recalled that another HMS *Eagle*, in New York Harbor in 1776, had been the target of a primitive submersible's attack.

As a young lieutenant who had already made a name for himself in submarines, Place was captain of *X-7*, one of the midget, 27-ton submersibles designed for the specific purpose of penetrating Alten Fjord as far as Kaa Fjord in Norway, where the German battleship *Tirpitz* was hiding, supposedly safe from air, surface, or submarine attack. The X-craft were forty-eight feet long and about six feet in diameter, with both diesel and battery power. They had a crew of two officers and two enlisted men. Outboard were slung two huge mines weighing about two tons each.

In September 1943 six X-craft were towed, each by a submarine, from their remote training base in northwest Scotland about a thousand miles to a point about fifteen miles off the Norwegian coast. Only four arrived there able to continue the operation. The temporary passage crews were replaced by attack crews, and the four remaining craft started their separate, intricate, deadly dangerous two-day journey up the complex fjords, submerged by day.

Acting independently, *X-6* and *X-7* succeeded in avoiding mines, surface patrol craft, lookouts, antisubmarine nets, and booms to come under *Tirpitz*. Both were detected and badly damaged so that they had to be scuttled, but not before they placed their mines under their target. The four men of *X-6* were picked up by the Germans and had the unique satisfaction of being on board *Tirpitz* when the four underwater charges detonated. Soon after, Place and his second officer were also rescued. *Tirpitz* was heavily damaged in her machinery spaces. Not for six months could she move to another harbor, where she survived repeated air attacks until November 12, 1944, when she was finally sunk.

Place of *X-7* and Lt. Donald Cameron of *X-6* were each awarded the Victoria Cross. When I asked Place why so successful and honored a submariner had chosen to shift to aviation, he replied, "Well, after the war and all that submarines had done, I couldn't see much of a role for them. I thought that naval aviation had a brighter future and I wanted to be a part of it."

I could understand his reasoning. His answer was reminiscent of the situation facing U.S. submariners after World War II. I had seen our own postwar fumbling to find a meaningful mission for our submarine force, and one of my junior officers who fought the war with me in *Halibut* had also made the transition to aviation. John M. Barrett became one of the very few officers who was qualified both as a submariner and an aviator and was entitled to wear both insignia. Such choice, once made, generally precludes a return to submarines, but Jack surmounted that, served in important submarine billets, and reached the rank of rear admiral.

Ironically, by 1959 the Royal Navy's Fleet Air Arm was in a period of retrenchment and curtailment, never again to be a dominant naval force, while nuclear power and the Polaris missile were to extend vastly the capabilities and responsibilities of the Royal Navy's submarine service. However, Captain Place's reply partly answered a question that had long puzzled me: Why did the Royal Navy contribute so much to naval aviation, yet so little to submarines?

Historically the submarine has been the weapon of choice for an inferior navy in challenging Britain. This demanded her best naval thinking to counter it, not to advance its capabilities. Perhaps the words of the revered Lord St. Vincent, Admiral Jervis, still carried weight. In 1805, commenting on Prime Minister Pitt's interest in Robert Fulton's submarine experiments, he said, "Pitt was the greatest fool that ever existed, to encourage a mode of war which they who commanded the seas did not want, and which if successful would deprive them of it."

Except for X-craft, the miniature submarines designed for a limited, special purpose, we received no technologic improvements applicable to U.S. submarines. On the other hand, U.S. carrier aviation benefited enormously from British initiatives. Not only was the turbojet aircraft engine an RAF development that we eagerly adopted, but the mirror landing system, the ejection seat, the steam catapult, and the angled-deck also all came from Britain.

Could our successes with carrier aviation in the Pacific war have made us complacent? Perhaps the luxury of great sums of money to buy quantitative advantage dulled the edge of our qualitative thrust. Unable to pour vast sums into naval aviation projects, the British spent more thought on analysis and technologic innovation.

By 1957 the bits of information reaching NATO regarding performance by *Nautilus* and *Seawolf,* and Soviet Russia's massive submarine program, were so tantalizing in their implications for a potential renewed Battle of the Atlantic that in 1958 NATO established in La Spezia, Italy, an antisubmarine operations research and development center under the cognizance of the Supreme Allied Commander Atlantic (SACLant), who was also CincLantFlt, based in Norfolk, Virginia. In addition, the NATO Defense College in Paris expanded its consideration of submarine warfare. I was asked to lecture to each six-month class on "The Capabilities of the Modern Submarine." There were severe restrictions on nuclear information that could be released to our allies, but it was easy to make an interesting case for the forthcoming revolution in sea power. There was particular interest in the deterrent role that the nuclear submarine, armed with ballistic missiles, would play.

When it came time to return to sea duty, I arranged that Comdr. James F. Calvert (later vice admiral) take my place as lecturer on nuclear submarine matters. This he could do with authority and finesse; he was commanding officer of *Skate,* first of a new class of nuclear submarines and first to surface through the ice at the North Pole.

My departure for duty at sea came at the end of 1959. In 1960, the Sixth Fleet, under command of Vice Adm. George W. Anderson, was organized in two task groups, TG 60.1, commanded by Rear Adm. Robert E. Dixon, and TG 60.2 under my command. Each was comprised of one aircraft carrier, approximately a dozen destroyers, a heavy cruiser, and, at times, a submarine. A destroyer tender deployed to a convenient harbor was available for material support when needed. Bunker fuel and aviation gasoline were brought to the combatant ships by fleet oilers. Other specialized underway replenishment ships brought food, supplies, and ammunition from bases on our East Coast. Sometimes ships of the amphibious force, with combat-ready Marine battalions embarked, joined the fleet for NATO exercises or for a persuasive show of U.S. force. After a normal six-month deployment, each task group would be relieved by a similar group and would return to the United States.

The fleet was a mobile, versatile, effective warfare system, well suited to give continuous, convincing evidence of U.S. power and resolve. No one saw all of this fleet at a time. The two task groups operated separately, with their carriers, the centerpiece of their formations, protected by antisubmarine and air defense screens. As commander of Task Group 60.2, I was embarked in my flagship, USS *Newport News,* a handsome 21,500-ton heavy cruiser. She and her sister ship, the Sixth Fleet flagship *Des Moines,* had nine 8" 55-caliber guns mounted in three triple-gun turrets. However, in its continuous state of evolution, adapting new technology and new weapons to their uses at sea, the Navy was installing surface-to-air guided missiles, Terrier, Tartar, or Talos, in selected cruisers and destroyers.

We had already developed missiles for delivery of antisubmarine weapons against submarines many miles distant. These were the ASROC for destroyer use and SUBROC for our hunter-killer submarines. At the same time, we were pressing the development of long-range, surface-to-surface guided missiles for surface ship use. Accurate fire by major caliber guns would still be required, chiefly in amphibious assault, but the speed, accuracy, and long-range of rocket-propelled warheads would greatly extend the area of the fleet's influence. As always, similar missiles in enemy hands would complicate a defense that was already under stress to defend against air and submarine attack. However, as each six months brought a different group of ships, more and more armed with missiles, and improved radars there was slow but steady increase in the fleet's power.

As each task group engaged in a series of air defense, ASW, and air strike exercises, it roamed the length and breath of the Mediterranean and made many port visits in a ceaseless demonstration of the peaceful exercise of naval power in "presence" or "suasion." In May 1960 my task group anchored in the harbor of Cannes on the Mediterranean coast of France. This was at the time of President Eisenhower's visit to Paris for the summit conference with Premier Khruschev of the U.S.S.R., Prime Minister Macmillan of the United Kingdom, and President DeGaulle of France. Part of the U.S. strategy for the summit was to face the Russians with convincing evidence of our technologic superiority. *Nautilus,* of course, was already world-famous for her subpolar transit, but in 1959 she and *Skate* had returned to the Arctic and demonstrated the SSN's unique ability to operate under or through the ice on Russia's northern flank. Even more dramatic was *Triton's* submerged circumnavigation of the globe, conceived in haste to fit the summit schedule but concluded successfully on March 10, 1960. The plan to exploit her dramatic feat to the hilt was overtaken by the immense furor of Khruschev's announcement of May 5 that the U.S.S.R. had shot down one of our very-high-flying U-2 spy planes.

Bungled U.S. diplomacy failed to placate an angry, truculent Khruschev, and on May 17 he scuttled the Paris summit. That evening my wife and I were guests at an official function attended by numerous notable Europeans. In the course of the formal dinner party, an officer from my flagship twice brought messages just received from the commander of the Sixth Fleet. All eyes were on me as I read the decoded texts and did my best to seem unconcerned. When it was apparent that I would not leave, one could almost hear a collective sigh of relief. But more positive evidence of the trust placed in our forces overseas, of the psychological effect they have, came from my dinner partner. "When the news from Paris came today, we wondered whether you'd sail away. And tonight we watched to see whether you'd turn on your lights. How good that you stayed!"

Such firsthand evidence confirmed that the Sixth Fleet was a force for peace and stability. When we resumed our cycle of exercises at sea, it was with sharp awareness of their importance in being prepared for the unexpected.

The coming of summer, with its abatement of winds that mixed the waters of the Mediterranean, complicated our ASW exercises. To assess the problem through the eyepiece of a periscope and the ears of submarine sonar, I embarked in our submarine *Sennet* (SS 408) in Barcelona. She was a conventional diesel-powered boat that had fought against the Japanese in World War II but would now simulate attacking our surface ships as they headed for Pollensa Bay in Mallorca. Opposed only by our normal screen of destroyers, *Sennet* had no difficulty gaining position undetected 1500 yards abeam of the carrier *Franklin D. Roosevelt.* The 7° negative temperature gradient from the surface to one hundred feet depth helped shield *Sennet* from detection by sonar, just as similar sonar conditions had helped our boats in wartime attacks off Japan.

The ASW measures that could be deployed to the Mediterranean in the event of a hostile submarine campaign there are far superior to those that had caused the very heavy losses of both British and German submarines in World War II. If on the scene in time and experienced in the unique hydrography of the Mediterranean, they would exact a similar toll of boats like *Sennet*. However, modern quiet diesel or nuclear-powered subs that gained access to the Mediterranean would be a severe challenge to any fleet seeking to maintain sea control.

✳ ✳ ✳ ✳

Aside from the submarine threat, our control of the sea faced the growing challenge of Russia's surface navy. It was a navy in transition from a coastal defense force to a blue-water, high-seas fleet. In the face of an inglorious naval tradition and a history of maritime failures, the same psychological urge that drove the U.S.S.R. to proclaim preeminence in scientific discovery and invention impelled it to demonstrate its right to superpower label through a navy capable of challenging U.S. sea power.

The Soviets were aware that the entire defense structure of the NATO alliance rested on sea power, on the ability to keep open the sea lanes from North America. They did not forget that sea power, as applied in World War II by the U.S. and Allied navies, kept Russia alive by keeping open the sea lanes to Murmansk, to the Persian Gulf, and to her Pacific ports for delivery of the immense quantities of munitions and supplies she needed. The mobility and precise attack of carrier strike forces, the surprise and power of amphibious assault, and the demoralizing stealth of submarine attack were not lost on the Russians even as they were desperately withstanding the blows of German land power.

✳ ✳ ✳ ✳

In 1955, only ten years after the defeat of Nazi Germany, the Federal Republic of Germany had been admitted to the North Atlantic Treaty Organization and was engaged in rebuilding her navy, one that was denied the use of submarines and restricted to coastal self-defense. Nevertheless, facing the ominous buildup of Soviet Russia's navy, it could contribute significantly to NATO's naval forces in the Baltic and North seas.

With a fifteen-year hiatus in naval experience, West Germany turned to veterans of her World War II navy to lead and train a new generation of seamen. In a NATO-approved program, on two separate occasions in the spring of 1960 groups of German officers, twenty in one, nineteen in the other, embarked in ships of the Sixth Fleet for two weeks of training. Not surprisingly, because so much of Germany's wartime naval effort had belatedly been concentrated in submarine warfare, many of our visitors were former submariners. They were the fortunate survivors of the U-boat campaign in which thirty-two thousand of the thirty-nine thousand men who took part were lost. These were men whose training, discipline, and determination could have drastically altered the course of World War II had Hitler and the German High Command had the same appreciation of sea power as did Churchill and Roosevelt and their military commanders. What thoughts must have filled the minds of these sailors, recalled to duty in the Mittel See, on board ships of the nation whose sea power had been so crucial for the defeat of Nazi Germany?

Each group was led by a flag officer, men who had commanded important surface ships during the war. Flotillen-admiral Hans Meyer, one-armed veteran of both world wars, lean, austere, reserved, had been commanding officer of *Tirpitz* when she was badly damaged by the X-craft attack. Flotillen-admiral Wolfgang Kahler, towering, outgoing, and articulate, had been gunnery officer of the battleship *Gneisenau* during her daring escape from Brest in company with the battlecruiser *Scharnhorst* and the heavy cruiser *Prinz Eugen*. Despite the constant British air and sea surveillance, the ships slipped out of harbor undetected. They withstood every attack by air and sea that the British could throw against them and fought their way up the English Channel to temporary refuge in German waters. Later, Kahler commanded the cruiser *Emden*.

Most prominent among the younger German officers was Kapitan-zur-See Otto Schuhart. The dynamic, self-confident, tough submariner was commander of *U-29* in one of the war's earliest and very important actions. On September 17, 1939, in his tiny sub patrolling in the western approaches to the English Channel, Schuhart resolutely pushed home an attack on the aircraft carrier HMS *Courageous* in spite of her escort of four destroyers. Hit by two of the three torpedoes that Schuhart fired at close range, *Courageous* sank with the loss of her captain and 518 of the crew.

Another who fought in the Atlantic, but in its distant, western reaches, was Rolf Ruggeberg. In command of *U-513* in the summer of 1942, he had patrolled off Newfoundland, where he sank ore carriers and other important targets.

But one who gazed over the sparkling, deep-blue water of the Mediterranean with even longer thoughts of what might have been was Frans-Georg Reschke. In command of *U-205*, he had operated in these very waters. *U-205* had joined with *U-81* in locating a British task force in which were two aircraft carriers and a battleship. On November 13, 1941, *U-81* torpedoed the carrier, HMS *Ark Royal*, which sank the next day as she was being towed to Gibraltar. Later Reschke sank the British cruiser *Hermione*, which was operating in support of Britain's Eighth Army, then fighting its way along the North African coast.

There was little doubt that fifteen years after the close of World War II the submarine still posed a major threat to surface forces. If it exploited its traditional ability to take the initiative, even the conventionally powered diesel submarine could inflict intolerable losses. How much more severe the problem would be when an enemy's subs had nuclear power or some other form of air-independent propulsion.

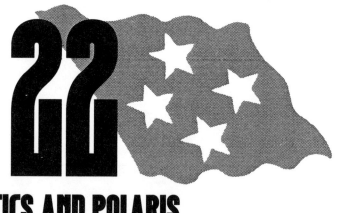

POLITICS AND POLARIS

It was inevitable that the advent of ballistic missiles, and their impact on strategy and on the force levels and budgets of all the services, would extend and intensify the differences between Air Force and Navy. In its earlier, bitter controversy with the Air Force, contrasting the flexibility and precision of carrier-based air strikes with the massive destruction of B-36 bombings, the Navy had unsuccessfully argued that the Air Force strategic warfare concept was immoral and unsound. For its part, the Air Force resented what it considered Navy intrusion into its strategic mission.

By 1958, when steady progress in Polaris development made its early deployment seem assured, the rivalry erupted anew.

Comparative analyses of ICBM and SLBM systems were made, and Air Force supporters began impugning the technical feasibility of Polaris and the costs of a fleet ballistic missile (FBM) system. Ironically, the limitations of the initial Polaris missile – its lesser accuracy, shorter range, and smaller payload – required Navy acceptance of the massive destruction role it had previously decried. At the same time, because of Minuteman's greater accuracy, longer range, and greater megatonnage, the Air Force adopted some of the Navy's earlier arguments and stressed its role in a counterforce, damage-limiting strategy.

The rivalry did not arise in the development and procurement agencies – the Navy's Special Projects Office and the Air Force's Ballistic Missile Division (BMD). Rear Admiral Raborn's relations with the head of BMD, Lt. Gen. Bernard A. Schriever, were friendly, even cooperative, in important technical areas. Engaged in the management of complex, costly technology, each respected the problems and efforts of the other. After I relieved Red Raborn in February 1962, I enjoyed the same relationship. Polaris and Minuteman were each better because of the competition for technological achievement and exchange of technical information. The real rivalry came at the level of our program sponsors in the headquarters of the Air Force chief of staff and of the chief of naval operations. That is where budget allocations were made, force levels determined, and command and control issues debated.

In presentations to the secretary of defense, in testimony to congressional committees, in questions planted with committee staffs and in news stories leaked to favored reporters there were aspersions about accuracy of the SLBM, its cost effectiveness of megatons delivered, its communication problem, and its invulnerability.

It is true that due to its mobility the early SLBM system had an inherent error in accuracy. ICBMs could be launched from silos whose exact geographic coordinates were known. However, the same geographic exactitude that aided Minuteman made it the bull's-eye for the U.S.S.R.'s counterforce attack. On the other hand, SLBMs were fired from a moving platform whose computed position could be a hundred yards or more in error. For the least vulnerable of our deterrent systems, the one that could not be targeted and that guaranteed massive retaliation, this was acceptable.

For all strategic systems, the link to the National Command Authority had to be reliable and assured. The Air Force could rely on protected hard-wire communications to its silos. The Navy had to use its standard very low frequency (VLF) radio transmissions. Comparisons of the two systems missed the central issue: Was the ability to exercise command and control of a military force consistent with and appropriate to the mode of operation of that force? To a force in danger of preemption before it could be brought into play, instantaneous reception of communications is essential. To a force in no such danger, one that can be activated with deliberation, a different system is adequate. The submarine has traditionally operated and been controlled by a redundant, one-way, receive-only communication system. This war-proven system is effective even when the submarine is under water.

The stations that broadcast these signals were "soft," vulnerable to attack, but we added a more powerful, more efficient VLF station at Cutler, Maine, and, as Polaris patrols expanded worldwide, built others in the state of Washington and in Australia. To further assure communications survival and efficiency, specially configured aircraft are airborne around the clock, alert for signals from the National Command Authority and ready to retransmit by VLF to SSBNs submerged in either hemisphere.

Now, even greater redundancy is in place. Land-, air-, sea-, and space-based radio communications provide continuous linkage to strategic missile submarines across the full spectrum of frequencies available in VLF, ELF (extremely low frequency), HF (high frequency), and UHF (ultra-high frequency).

An effective strategic deterrent system has to be immune to surprise attack, but both of the land-based systems – the manned bombers and the ICBMs – were vulnerable to preemptive strike by their own kind. This fact led to urgent and very costly measures to improve their utility. The bombers were dispersed to more bases; some were kept in flight at all times. The ICBMs were placed underground in hardened silos, but even this could not ensure Minuteman's survival as a deterrent. Plans were made to supersede or supplement the silo system by either a rail-mobile system (Peacekeeper) or a road-mobile system (Midgetman).

Ironically, as higher-performance bombers and missiles became less vulnerable through such measures, they were perceived to pose a greater threat to an enemy's equivalent forces, resulting in an uneasy, destabilized situation that tempted a preemptive strike. On the other hand, the submerged SSBN with its missiles is not targetable by an enemy's bombers, ICBMs, or ballistic missile submarines and is in no danger of destruction by them. It does not pose a first-strike threat, but remains a credible, deliberate, retaliatory deterrent.

As for invulnerability to antisubmarine warfare measures, we must acknowledge that history records the continuing interplay of offense and defense, the temporary superiority of one or the other through technologic progress. Do the vastness and complexity of the oceans in which SSBNs hide give them immunity? Claims are advanced that science will make the oceans "transparent," but the periodic, detailed reviews by the CIA, the Defense Science Board, and other scientific study groups can find no plausible prospect for many years to come for an ASW breakthrough that would remove the concealment of submarines roaming the world's oceans.

The claims of potential vulnerability of the SSBN are especially ironic coming from those who operate in a medium that truly is transparent yet advocate continuing construction of supersophisticated, vulnerable, and enormously expensive bombers for that medium.

A small example of this competition came in 1962 when I testified before the Senate Armed Services Committee, of which Stuart Symington of Missouri was an influential member. When the National Security Act of 1947 established the Air Force as a separate military service, Symington was appointed the first secretary of the Air Force. He was so completely taken in by the "Victory through Air Power" school that he believed a strong Army and Navy were superfluous. In the Navy's eyes, he was an unscrupulous promoter of the "single service."

During my testimony I described the submarine's mode of operation, and he pounced on the low speed of a submarine as compared to the speed of a bomber. "Isn't that very slow? Doesn't that make the submarine vulnerable?"

"Sir, the submarine has a great advantage. The airplane has to close its target. It can be detected visually, by satellite, by radar, by infra-red, by sound. The submarine lies fully submerged at great range from its target. It can be detected only one way – by sound – and by going slow it puts out very little sound."

"Thank you, Admiral. I have no further questions."

As he learned more and more of the system, Senator Symington became a firm supporter of Polaris, but within an Air Force-dominated triad of ICBM, bomber, and submarine.

In 1959, even before the first Polaris submarine had been completed and deployed, the Air Force sought to integrate the fleet ballistic missile system into a single U.S. Strategic Command that would direct both the Strategic Air Command and the Navy's FBM force. It argued that because the Polaris missile had no naval function to perform, and because the submarine was merely another launching platform, there was no reason for Navy control. At this time, joint operations by the Armed Services were still in their infancy, and the Navy, suspicious as always of Air Force motives, resisted.

There was logic in the Air Force position, except for the fact that submarines are unique vehicles; there is no experience in their operation in the commercial world or in any military service other than Navy. By stressing the special factors of the maritime environment, of submarine personnel training, and the necessary close coordination with ASW forces, all within an existing and proven command structure, the Navy was able to retain operational control.

Two factors worked to the Navy's advantage in this issue. First, submarine operation is an arcane subject, both for the Air Force and the Congress, and, second, there was unparalleled political support for Polaris. The FBM program was established by the Republican administration of President Eisenhower, acting in response to intelligence warnings of Soviet Russia's capabilities and the recommendations of eminent scientists. Congress has the responsibility to oversee the military and to exercise control through its appropriation of funds. Acting always with an eye to enhancing their already formidable prospect for reelection, members of Congress frequently distort the balanced development and procurement program submitted by the secretary of defense by directing changes purely for partisan advantage or constituent benefit. In this case, with national security in jeopardy, Congress welcomed the opportunity to spend large sums on a program with great political sex appeal. It quickly perceived the advantages of the FBM system's military invulnerability, climbed on board its scientific and industrial bandwagon, and gave it political invulnerability as well.

The major industrial corporations involved in the development and production of the fleet ballistic missile system added their own considerable political clout. They included Aerojet General, General Dynamics, General Electric, Hercules Powder, Hughes Aircraft, Lockheed Missiles and Space, Newport News Shipbuilding, Northrop, Sperry Gyroscope, and Westinghouse, among others. And as the FBM program was expanded and accelerated, the network of subcontractors extended into every state in the Union.

Although the Navy's programmatic and management control of the Polaris system was secure, it was undeniable that there had to be centralizing planning and coordination for strategic deterrence or strategic warfare. The former secretary of the Navy, Thomas S. Gates, was secretary of defense. In what he considered the most important decision he made in that office, in 1960 Gates created the Joint Strategic Target Planning Staff (JSTPS), located at SAC headquarters at Offutt Air Force Base, Omaha, Nebraska. It developed the Single Integrated Operational Plan (SIOP), which, coordinated with our allies, specified and assigned priority to targets for all strategic atomic weapons. The JSTPS was headed by an Air Force general with an admiral as vice director. Initially a naval aviator filled that billet because of naval air's sizable role in strategic warfare plans, but as submarine participation grew, the position has gone to an admiral with prior duty in the SSBN force.

About the same time, responding more to the importunities of the submarine community and to advocates of the FBM system in the Congress than to the lukewarm support of the rest of the Navy, Secretary Gates elevated the rank of the Commander Submarine Force Atlantic Fleet to vice admiral. The only other time submarines had so ranking a commander was in World War II, when Charles A. Lockwood, Jr. was ComSubPac.

✳   ✳   ✳   ✳

In his 1960 presidential campaign John F. Kennedy made unjustified claims that the Eisenhower administration had tolerated a "missile gap" between our forces and those of the Soviet Union. When he took office in 1961 he promptly stepped up the size and pace of the Polaris program, first to twenty-nine boats, then to forty-one, even before his secretary of defense, Robert S. McNamara, had fully applied his five-year Planning, Programming, Budget System (PPBS) and its underlying weapon system analysis. However, when it was placed in the context of the nation's overall Strategic Retaliatory Forces, Polaris withstood critical analysis of its cost effectiveness in the role of deliberate response/assured retaliation.

President Eisenhower had approved the start of the Polaris program; President Kennedy greatly expanded it and was the first to contemplate its possible use. By October 1962 – the time of the Cuban missile crisis and the eyeball-to-eyeball confrontation with Soviet Premier Khruschev – we had deployed seven SSBNs, a total of 112 missiles. Under the nuclear deterrent shield of Minuteman and Polaris, the naval "quarantine" of Cuba was successful in forcing the removal of Russian missiles that threatened the United States from Cuba. The Kremlin paid the penalty for having a second-best navy, but it promptly accelerated its naval building program to overcome that weakness.

Of great importance to a strategy of deterrence, and a factor in the increasing part being played by the SLBM in that strategy, is the ability to monitor constantly the readiness, reliability, and accuracy of the system. In 1962 a complete test of the Polaris system was conducted in Operation Frigate Bird. *Ethan Allan* (SSBN 605) was sent to the Christmas Island test area in the South Pacific for that purpose. She was the first submarine designed as an SSBN from the keel up and was larger and deeper-diving than the first five. I had participated in her test dives and had the utmost confidence in her skipper, Comdr. Paul Lacy (later rear admiral). Paul was an exceptional naval officer, a man who combined great technical knowledge with outstanding operational competence and leadership.

On May 6, 1962, cruising submerged in the remote reaches of the South Pacific, *Ethan Allen* received the radio command to launch a Polaris missile. Erupting from the silence of the sea, the A-1 missile arched skyward and roared to conclusive atomic detonation on target.

Of greater importance than *Ethan Allen*'s dramatic demonstration was the operational test procedure established by Secretary McNamara. He was willing to spend what was necessary to know at all times how reliable and accurate a system he was buying. (What a welcome change from the debacle of the Navy's pre-World War II torpedo program!) In this test procedure, one of the submarines deployed far at sea is recalled on a surprise basis, replaces a warhead with an inert load, then returns to patrol and awaits the signal to fire into the missile test range. Costly though it is, the recurring procedure gives measured, factual data about system reliability and accuracy.

Secretary of Defense McNamara had been in office more than two years before he witnessed a demonstration of the FBM system. We had long tried to have him embark in one of our SSBNs to witness a test firing, and the delay was a tribute to our project. We presented no problem that provoked his personal attention, and he held the Polaris program in high regard.

In July 1963, after a full day's work in Washington, McNamara, Secretary of the Navy Fred Korth, Rear Adm. John H. Maurer (who had relieved me as OP 31), and I flew to Patrick Air Force Base near Cape Canaveral, Florida. Up early next morning for a 5:30 helo flight to the Cape, we embarked in *Lafayette* (SSBN 616), where we were joined by Gen. Maxwell D. Taylor, chairman of the Joint Chiefs of Staff. Levering Smith had preceded us to the Cape to ensure that all was in readiness. The ship was under command of Comdr. James T. Strong, skipper of the ship's Gold Crew, but Comdr. Patrick J. Hannifin, later vice admiral, skipper of the Blue Crew, was also on board to assist in briefing our important visitors.

As we cruised beneath the surface of the Gulf Stream, removed from the pressures and demands of his Pentagon office, Secretary McNamara revealed a personage quite unlike his reputation. Surrounded by the fine young officers and enlisted men typical of the submarine force, he showed himself to be much more affable and receptive than his usual press characterization. In frank and searching wardroom discussions on the essence of deterrence and the reliability of weapons systems, he was patient, painstaking, and polite. Nevertheless, it was clear that most military officers would have heavy going in debate with him. His databank mind spewed facts and figures, revealing the penchant to derive decisions statistically, with insufficient regard for experience or imponderables.

The firing of two A-2 (1500 nm) missiles went exactly on schedule, and they performed flawlessly. Afterward, in the little talk he gave over the ship's announcing system, Secretary McNamara was most complementary of the crew's performance and stressed the importance that President Kennedy and he placed on Polaris's role in our overall deterrent system. It was, he said, the one weapons system that did not create problems for him. The secretary's military aide, an Air Force colonel, was heard to mutter good-humoredly, "Who the hell wrote that speech for him?"

As we ran submerged back to Port Canaveral, Levering and I were in the wardroom with Secretary McNamara discussing the status of the A-3, the third-generation, 2500-nm missile we were developing. The fact that the same subs could carry and launch from the same tubes the successively larger and heavier A-1, A-2, and A-3 missiles greatly interested the secretary. When I mentioned that we had growth potential for a still larger missile, he was immediately intrigued. "How is that possible?"

Levering explained how the uncertainties of missile size and weight in the original, urgent development had made it prudent to leave ample room in the missile launch tubes.

"If you'll come aft to the missile compartment, sir, we can show you," I said.

Opening one of the tube access doors, I pointed to the excess shock mitigation measures designed into the launching tubes. Now that we were working with missiles of known size and weight, and because depth charge attack on any SSBN was extremely unlikely, we could apply to the missile the same shock mitigation standard applied to other subsystems. This meant that a missile 74" in diameter (compared to 54" for previous missiles) could be accommodated in the existing missile tubes.

The fact that the great capital investment already made in our forty-one boats could be further exploited with a more advanced missile appealed at once to Secretary McNamara in his constant quest for cost effectiveness. This hands-on demonstration was helpful in getting approval, in 1965, for development of the Poseidon missile. Three feet longer and thirty thousand pounds heavier than A-3, Poseidon carried twice the A-3 payload and with much improved accuracy.

✳   ✳   ✳   ✳

On October 27, 1963, I was on board *Andrew Jackson* (SSBN 619) for the first submerged launch of the new A-3 Polaris. It was a complete success, and I sent the following message to the White House: "On 20 July 1960 USS *George Washington* reported Quote Polaris from out of the deep to target perfect Unquote. Today Old Hickory's namesake reports to you: *Polaris A-3* from out of the deep to any potential target on earth. Perfect."

There was no reaction, official or otherwise, to this important accomplishment. A little afterthought would show that it was not politically smart to associate an achievement of the current Democrat administration with President Eisenhower's initiative.

However, this was prelude to an unforgettable, poignant experience. President Kennedy would be visiting NASA activities at Cape Canaveral on Saturday, November 16. Special Projects was asked what kind of Polaris demonstration the Navy could give him on the same day. At first it seemed we could do no more than a briefing on A-3 in our missile hangar because we had no missile ready for even a shoreside pad launch, and no ship was in port. However, *Andrew Jackson* was at sea en route the deep, quiet waters of Tongue of the Ocean in the Bahamas for acoustic measurements, and she had four A-2 missiles on board. We turned her around and offered a realistic firing near the Cape.

I joined the presidential party when JFK arrived in midmorning of the bright, sunny day. After touring the launch complex, we were briefed on Project Gemini by astronauts Gordon Cooper and Gus Grissom, then on the moon program and the Saturn missile by Dr. Wernher Von Braun. Following a brief helicopter tour of NASA facilities on Merritt Island, we headed out to sea, where *Observation Island* awaited us. She was the surface ship used in development and test of our special navigation equipment.

During the thirty-mile flight it was my turn to brief the president privately, while Sen. George Smathers of Florida, Dr. Robert Seamans and Dr. Kurt Debus of NASA, and Maj. Gen. Leighton Davis, USAF, Commander Atlantic Missile Range watched our overwater flight from the adjacent compartment.

Presidents, like everyone else, wonder how, from a moving platform beneath the sea, we can hit a target thousands of miles away. This was the chief subject of his questions as we winged offshore. The main point I tried to make was the high confidence that could be placed in the SLBM system because of its survivability and our continuing realistic test firings at sea.

After his Marine helicopter settled on *Observation Island*, the president was piped on board in traditional Navy fashion. The lean, youthful commander-in-chief seemed fully at ease. Slipping off his jacket, he donned the dark-blue Navy windbreaker on which had been sewn the colorful insignias of *Observation Island* and *Andrew Jackson*. As he handled a pair of heavy Navy binoculars, it was apparent he was a sailor, at ease and comfortable in familiar surroundings.

Andrew Jackson would launch her missile on receipt of the command from the president – a mini-rehearsal for horror – an event that must never become reality. With the order to fire radioed to the silent black hull 1200 yards to starboard but invisible beneath the sparkling surface, we waited anxiously during the final two minutes of countdown. Would there be a misfire? Would the missile fly right, or would it take off in some crazy pattern?

At T-20 seconds I was surprised by word of an unplanned "hold." With fingers crossed, trying to appear unconcerned, I had to ad-lib various possibilities to the president. The countdown soon resumed, and suddenly a missile leaped from the sea. A roar like a dozen jet engines numbed our minds, and the missile climbed its arc into the sky as if trying to escape from the white plume that trailed it.

The president was thrilled by the sight and sound of the missile as it climbed its trajectory down the Atlantic Missile Range. Success of the impromptu demonstration of our system was convincing evidence of the readiness and reliability of the sea-based deterrent, and he spoke a congratulatory message by radio to the still-submerged *Andrew Jackson*, calling the event "an excellent demonstration – wonderful!" Then he boarded his helo and flew ashore to a weekend at his house in Palm Beach before proceeding to Dallas, Texas.

In Washington six days later, in my office in the Munitions Building on Constitution Avenue, I was reading the letter just received in which he complimented our performance. Suddenly my aide burst in. "Turn on the TV! The President's been shot!"

The young, vibrant, smiling sailor president who, just a few days before, was with us in *Observation Island,* confident in his leadership, proud of his Navy, had been assassinated by a maniacal ex-Marine.

✳ ✳ ✳ ✳

In 1964 the Special Projects Office was concluding successful development of the A-3 missile (it deployed in September) and was engaged in studies of a follow-up missile, B-3. However, more and more we were hearing, "When will SP join the Navy?"

The Navy's traditionally organized and managed agencies, from Op-Nav to the separate material bureaus, still harbored jealousy and even resentment toward the Special Projects Office and its direct line to the secretary of the Navy. They envied the comprehensive management authority, the separate, sacrosanct funding, and the over-riding priority that SP exploited. The future of our mature, highly motivated, experienced team, with its record of success in managing complex technology, was in doubt. There was no assurance that B-3 would be authorized and funded for development. It was, in fact, superseded by C-3 (Poseidon), but the go-ahead for that and its new multiple independent reentry vehicle (MIRV) did not come until 1965.

After the *Thresher* disaster in April 1963, Secretary of the Navy Paul Nitze designated a study group to review Navy needs and capabilities for operations in the deep ocean. It was headed by Oceanographer of the Navy Rear Adm. Edward C. Stephan. As the study proceeded, a logical fit with SP's proven development ability was apparent. I had long argued for submarine operation at deeper depth and had happily seen a significant step in that direction in the design of *Thresher* and follow-on attack submarines, as well as in *Ethan Allen* and subsequent Polaris subs. However, the McCann Rescue Chamber, first used to rescue *Squalus* survivors in 1939 and dependent on mooring a submarine rescue vessel (ASR) accurately over the sunken boat, could not be used at the new depth.

When the Deep Submergence Systems Program was approved, its chief task was development of six (later reduced to two) deep submergence rescue vehicles (DSRVs), which can rescue personnel from a disabled submarine that was almost as deep as its collapse depth. By this time I was chief of naval material and, with the secretary of the Navy's approval (SP still reported directly to him), I assigned the project to SP rather than to BuShips, which coveted it as well. Designated as project manager was SP's civilian chief scientist, Dr. John P. Craven, a brilliant and enthusiastic proponent of deep ocean technology.

The project was difficult, not only in its structural challenge but also in the very complex maneuver control function. Once more we turned to Stark Draper and his Instrumentation Lab at M.I.T. to solve a control problem that was more complicated than guiding a space capsule. In the vacuum of outer space there are no currents to contend with, and visibility is unlimited. Radio and television communications bring constant advice and support from ground stations. On the contrary, in inner space the DSRV must grope blindly in dark currents thousands of feet beneath the surface, constantly adjusting position and attitude.

Today the fifty-foot-long, air-transportable DSRVs stand ready with trained operators to be air-lifted wherever needed or carried piggy-back to the scene of disaster on a nuclear sub. Once the stricken sub is located, the DSRV descends, fixes itself over one of the sub's escape hatches, and takes aboard as many as twenty-two survivors at a time for return to the surface.

★   ★   ★   ★

Red Raborn had done a masterful job of organizing the complex development effort for Polaris and managing its production. He had wisely frozen in their billets the team of expert line and engineering duty officers he had assembled for SP commencing in 1955. When I relieved Red in February 1962, some in the staff were restive, fearful that prolonged duty in one billet, however glamorous or important, was hurting their chances for promotion. This was a particular problem for unrestricted line officers (such as I was), and I was sympathetic. Personnel policy at the time called for them to progress through a diversity of assignments, some as brief as one year, as they sought to be qualified for the challenges of higher naval command. In my own case, I had fretted that almost continuous assignment to submarine billets, ashore and afloat, would jeopardize promotion.

SP had assembled a splendid team of outstanding civil servants, in both engineering and fiscal-administrative disciplines, who gave it the continuity and stability needed. With that backup, I preferred to have on the staff the energy and enthusiasm of fresh thinking rather than the uneasiness and the understandable career concern of some old hands. Good as the original team was, the Navy was not so poor in talent that replacements could not be made safely. A program of such national importance, visibility, and success was a magnet for good people. I was sure that we would find many officers ready to demonstrate that they could carry on our project as effectively as the superb team Red had chosen. So in my first year as director, I permitted the relief of almost 30 percent of our officers and had an orderly replacement program thereafter. There was one vital exception: Levering Smith remained continuously in SP for almost twenty-two years.

When it came time in 1965 for me to move on to be chief of naval material, the CNO, Adm. David L. McDonald, asked my views on my replacement. He was considering three submariners, all splendid officers and good friends of mine. Rather to his surprise, I demurred. "I think the job should go to Levering. He can handle it. The organizational and promotional days are past; operational procedures and relations with the fleet are well established. What we need now is follow-through on the U.K. program, and detailed attention to the tough Poseidon development that is in the works."[1] Dave McDonald agreed, and Levering capped his great career with twelve years as director of the Special Projects Office (later designated Strategic Systems Project Office).

This was my first step to cope with a worrisome situation as I looked ahead to the challenges of my new job. The Navy was losing too many of its technical specialist officers (EDOs, AEDOs, OEDOs) just as they were reaching the peak of their engineering and managerial capabilities. We were suffering a sort of "brain drain." This was partly due to the lack of senior flag officer billets to which our specialists could aspire. These disciplined, highly trained officers, experienced in management, were attractive to industry and the commercial world and readily found important positions in civil life. The increasingly technical and complex Navy would benefit if we could use the talents of outstanding specialist officers for a longer time.

From its start, I wanted the FBM system to be as simple and reliable as possible, but I knew that the many uncertainties in our totally new system justified some redundancy. When operational experience verified that certain equipment and procedures were not needed or were overly redundant, we removed from earlier ships (and eliminated from those under construction) such mechanisms as the bulky gyro stabilizer, the complex, costly navigation periscope, one of the three Ships' Inertial Guidance Systems, as well as lesser equipment and instrumentation. The pneumatic missile-launching system was replaced by a simpler steam launching system. The space, weight, and dollars saved through these changes were put to better use in improved maintenance ability and habitability.

To replace old patterns of administration was a more difficult problem. Vice Adm. Elton W. (Joe) Grenfell was ComSubLant. He was the only man to have commanded both Atlantic and Pacific submarine forces; with the rank of rear admiral he had previously been ComSubPac. In his wartime command of *Gudgeon,* and in later assignments, he personified the aggressive, independent spirit of submariners. Fiercely proud of submarine force accomplishments in the war, including uncovering and solving torpedo deficiencies, he was wary of dependence on shore-based bureaucracy. In his view, Polaris missiles were just another weapon – "Issue it to us, and we'll do the rest." I disagreed with Joe. In concept of operation and system complexity, the SLBM was and is totally unlike anything the submarine force had known. Its readiness and reliability are vital to our national interest, and its command line runs all the way to the president. Careful analysis and use of technical data collected on the submarines' long deterrent patrols is essential.

Gradually I won Joe over. His initial antipathy to SP gave way to realization that some factors could not be adequately monitored and controlled by the personnel and resources belonging to the forces afloat. There had to be continuous, intimate collaboration between the developer and producer, SP, and the seagoing operators, SubLant and SubPac. In addition, unforeseen emergencies, with need for urgent technical support and special funding, made full and frank cooperation essential. It was not unlike the relationship between the submarine forces and Admiral Rickover's Nuclear Reactor Division (Code 1500) in BuShips, but I believe we achieved it with notably less trauma.

★ ★ ★ ★

In 1990, long after my own retirement, deployment of *Tennessee* (SSBN 734) with Trident D-5 missiles brought a new dimension to our national strategy of deterrence and retaliation. However, unlike the earlier decision to limit each Polaris SSBN to sixteen missile tubes, cost effectiveness and annual operating costs were given undue weight. The system reliability established by the Polaris and Poseidon boats, the greatly improved silencing (stealth) of the Trident submarines, and their freedom to roam the oceans at much greater range from their targets (4500 miles) were used to justify a lesser number of boats (eighteen instead of forty-one), each carrying a greater number of launch tubes (twenty-four instead of sixteen).

Such a concentration of assets means that at a given time a greater proportion of our deterrent/retaliatory force will be nonavailable for various reasons, and we will lose flexibility of operations. It also means that as we face the uncertainties of turbulent international relations and future Strategic Arms Reduction Talks (START) we will be hampered by loss of flexibility in negotiations.

Advances in submarine and missile technology and changes in international relationships, I believe, make a fundamental reexamination of nuclear deterrent strategy desirable. Reliance on the triad (ICBM-SLBM-bomber) is no longer necessary. Among the factors that make a less redundant, less costly, less vulnerable national strategic deterrent system practicable are improved missile accuracy, MIRV warheads, greater missile range, more reliable communication links, ethical considerations that stress counterforce rather than countervalue targeting, and negotiated strategic arms reductions.

Because our ballistic missile submarines are the most survivable and most economical leg of the present triad, they are the keystone of our nuclear deterrence system. Their stealth and readiness to deliver multi-azimuth reprisal circumvent enemy defenses. Furthermore, the submarine-based Trident D-5 missile, as accurate as a silo-based ICBM, can be more continuously monitored by realistic operational tests and has reliable command and control communications. With no real threat to its long-term invulnerability, the SLBM remains our primary strategic deterrent. As future strategic arms reductions are negotiated, it is probable that the SLBM alone will constitute our nuclear deterrent, thereby removing from our land the bull's-eye for preemptive counterforce strike.

On the other hand, the ICBM, whether in fixed silos (Minuteman), rail-mobile (Peacekeeper), or road-mobile (Midgetman), has questionable survivability and faces growing public opposition, for both psychological and fiscal reasons.

If the manned bomber is retained for the near-term as the backup to the SSBN, a choice can be made between the B-1 and the B-2, the so-called stealth bomber. Each is under attack as too costly and too vulnerable, but cost must be a secondary consideration if a true national defense requirement is being met. Because the B-1 has some flexibility for other missions, it may be the preferred supplement.

For the B-2, the real questions to be answered are: What is the B-2's mission? What essential task can it perform that can't be done as well and at less cost by other means? Would manned aircraft of such extremely high cost and very limited numbers be risked against Third World countries, which are acquiring sophisticated air defense weapons?

The capability of manned aircraft to contribute to victory by strategic warfare is increasingly constrained. They must cope with vastly improved methods of surveillance and detection and a variety of ever "smarter" weapons that can be launched against them. Moreover, manned military aircraft, both Navy and Air Force, operate near human biologic boundaries to the control and meaningful application of air power. Pertinent technology may be applied in increasingly sophisticated form to provide greater speed, stealth, or payload, but we must evaluate total system costs more thoroughly, taking into account other needed capabilities that might otherwise be denied us.

* * * *

In 1992 the consolidation of strategic deterrent commands advocated by the Air Force more than thirty years before was implemented. Going beyond mere target coordination of all U.S. strategic forces, bombers, ICBMs, and SSBNs were integrated into a U.S. Strategic Command that superseded the Strategic Air Command. Commander-in-chief of the new joint command, initially an Air Force general with a Navy vice admiral as his deputy, will come alternately from Air Force and Navy. By this time joint commands for operations of U.S. military forces were well established, and the fleet ballistic missile system (armed with the Trident missile) was the most important of our strategic deterrent systems. The SS-BNs carried 50 percent of the strategic warheads in the U.S. inventory, and they achieved this at a cost of only 25 percent of the Defense Department's total budget for strategic warfare.

THE SPECIAL RELATIONSHIP

In 1957 the British government decided to develop and maintain an effective nuclear deterrent. To that end it undertook the development of an airborne missile – Blue Steel – that was to be the armament for Vulcan, Victor, and Valiant bombers in their deterrent role. Difficulties with the missile led to the decision to develop a surface-to-surface ballistic missile – Blue Streak – and a suitable nuclear warhead. However, the realities of development and deployment costs, an unfavorable geographic situation, and attendant political and psychological factors caused Britain to abandon Blue Streak in 1960 in favor of the U.S. Skybolt missile. This was to be a nuclear-armed missile with a thousand-mile range, to be launched from bombers at standoff range of their ground targets. To be in production in 1964, it would extend the life of Britain's bomber force.

As part of the quid pro quo for Skybolt, the United States received basing rights at Holy Loch, Scotland, for U.S. ballistic missile submarines. The British received from the United States the promise that they could purchase Polaris missiles for their submarines if they so chose.

The apparent trend toward separate European national nuclear weapon systems caused much concern in the U.S. administration. In an attempt to divert France from its independent course, the United States even made a tentative offer to sell France nuclear-powered submarines of our most advanced class. Partly because of Rickover's determined opposition and the power of his political allies on the Hill, the offer was withdrawn. In any case, President Charles DeGaulle insisted that France would create it own national nuclear force.

In a further effort to head off such proliferation, the United States offered to sell Polaris missiles to its European allies. As land-based, medium-range ballistic missiles (MRBMs) they would provide NATO with a counter to probable Soviet nuclear blackmail. There were no takers.

In August 1960, Robert Bowie, previously head of the State Department's Policy Planning Staff, suggested a bolder plan. He proposed a NATO multilateral force (MLF) of Polaris-armed submarines manned by mixed, international crews. Nothing came of this plan either, but in May 1961, the new president, John F. Kennedy, incorporated it into a U.S. commitment to NATO of five Polaris submarines. The mixed-manning idea was startling to the conventional military thinking in all nations, especially in its application to nuclear-powered submarines, where intimate, harmonious personnel relations and instant, correct action are essential.

In the United States there was a particularly formidable roadblock in the person of Rear Admiral Rickover, who reluctantly accepted the feasibility of mixed-manning but strongly objected to the risk to national security. Our primacy in nuclear propulsion would be jeopardized, and operational procedures of our own Polaris force would be disclosed. These factors were of concern to the Joint Committee on Atomic Energy, whose support would be needed to get congressional approval.

By 1962 the submarine MLF was abandoned and a non-nuclear surface ship version substituted in planning. Cruising the high seas in a random pattern within range of potential targets, the surface MLF would be under NATO command and would supplement the U.S. and British national deterrent forces. The ships were to be built in Europe, but the missiles and complex subsystems would be furnished through our Special Projects Office.

From the beginning of his term as secretary of defense in 1961, Robert McNamara stressed the need for a sound planning, programming, and budgeting system to manage the enormous complexities of national defense. A key element in this trinity was the formalized application of systems analysis to the problems of choosing strategies and their related weapon systems. No other technique became so emotional, so divisive among military officers and their civilian colleagues in the Office of the Secretary of Defense, as did this one. The practitioners of the art of weapon system analysis defended it as being "quantified common sense," but the military community in general condemned it as "downgrading the military" and substituting computers for military judgment and operational experience.

Strengthening the case of the system analysts as they applied their "rational economic analysis" to Skybolt and its place in U.S. nuclear weapons strategy was the continuing success being demonstrated by both the land-based Minuteman missile and the sea-based Polaris. By the fall of 1962 the United States had expended $500 million on Skybolt and had only a lengthening series of test failures to show for it. It was small comfort to the Air Force that when Skybolt was found wanting in the analysis of its capabilities and costs and was canceled, so too was the Navy's plan to install Polaris missiles in the nuclear-powered surface cruiser *Long Beach* (CGN 9).

As the United States and Britain inched toward some form of cooperative undertaking that would substitute Polaris for Skybolt, there was not much enthusiasm in the Navy Department. In Special Projects we were proceeding under forced draft to meet a demanding schedule. The administration emphasized its determination to close the much publicized real or imagined "missile gap," and Polaris was a key element in that plan.

By December 1962 we had completed only ten SSBNs; thirty-one more had to be delivered by December 1966. All the while, the new, complex Polaris A-3 was under development. Chief of Naval Operations Adm. George W. Anderson also pointed out that whatever progress had been made toward acceptance of a multilateral force as a substitute for individual national forces would be all but wiped out by a bilateral U.S.-U.K. program.

Cancellation of Skybolt caused a major political storm in England. Prime Minister Harold Macmillan had regarded Skybolt as a mark of

Britain's "special relationship" with the United States. The abrupt, unilateral cancellation set off a major uproar in Parliament and the press, which led to the meeting between President Kennedy and Prime Minister Macmillan in Nassau, Bahamas, in December 1962. The resulting Nassau Pact called for creation of an international nuclear deterrent force and invited France to join as a partner. Four principal points were made:

1. The United States would sell Polaris missiles to the United Kingdom, but the United Kingdom would provide its own warheads, as well as design and build its own nuclear-powered submarine launching platforms.
2. The United Kingdom agreed that the resulting system would be part of a NATO nuclear deterrent force. However, she retained the caveat that supreme national interest could justify other use.
3. The United States agreed to match the British contribution to NATO by "at least equal U.S. forces."
4. The United States offered to sell Polaris missiles to France under the same conditions.

In spite of the offer, DeGaulle persisted in his policy of independent action, and by 1969 France completed *Le Redoutable*, the first of its five SSBNs.

The Conservative government in the United Kingdom moved quickly to follow up on the terms of the Nassau Pact. It invited a U.S. team to visit London in January 1963 to confer with British authorities about negotiations that would be required to produce the Polaris Sales Agreement. The team was comprised of W. W. Rostow, chairman of the Policy Planning Council, State Department; Paul Nitze, assistant secretary of defense (international security affairs); Henry Owen of the State Department; and myself, as director special projects, Office of the Secretary of the Navy.

There was much ferment within the Royal Navy at the time of our visit. British naval aviators, like those in the U.S. Navy, considered that the survival of the Royal Navy as an effective fighting force depended upon the continuing availability of up-to-date strike carriers. The interservice rivalry in Britain was intense as Navy and Air Force competed for the funds each considered essential to implement its role in national defense. Each feared that, within the total defense budget, there would be funded either the Royal Air Force's new fighter-bomber or the Royal Navy's new aircraft carrier, but not both.

The Royal Navy was divided over the prospect of introducing yet another complex, costly weapon system – Polaris – at this juncture. It voiced the same fears the U.S. Navy had in 1956 and 1957 – that the heavy commitment of funds and skilled personnel to Polaris would unduly weaken the traditional balanced-force concept.

However, with the Skybolt fiasco to overcome and the decision made to persist in building a national nuclear deterrent, the Conservative government pressed on with Polaris. Rear Adm. H. S. (Rufus) Mackenzie, later Vice Admiral Sir Hugh, and I were promptly designated our nations' joint project officers to bring into being a British force of four SSBNs. Like myself, Rufus was a sea-going operator beached for duty in the equally rigorous but even more measurable arena of management.

While being loyal both to the spirit and the letter of the Polaris Sales Agreement that Secretary of State Dean Rusk and British Ambassador David Ormsby Gore had signed in Washington on April 6, 1963, I could permit no interference with our own urgent Polaris program. Another sensitive issue was the security of information about our nuclear submarine projects in general. The British had no experience in the operation of nuclear subs. The United States had cooperated with our important ally by selling them a 15,000-shaft-horsepower reactor for *Dreadnought*, their first nuclear-powered attack submarine, which was nearing completion. Their negotiators sought authority to obtain continued access to information that was more closely related to our nuclear submarines than to the Polaris missile system. They argued that it was the sense of the Nassau Pact that a Polaris sales agreement would include all necessary authority for establishing a fully operational U.K. SSBN force, and that such information was a part of the total package.

We did not need Rickover's furious opposition to this point to stand firm. The final agreement stated: "This Agreement does not, however, authorize the sale of, or transmittal of information concerning the nuclear propulsion plants of United States submarines."

Part of the urgency attached to the U.K.'s program was a result of the waning political fortune of Prime Minister Macmillan's Conservative party. In the next few months he would have to call a general election, and polls were already giving Harold Wilson's Labour party an edge. The deputy leader and vice chairman of the Labour party was George Brown. He was expected to be either foreign minister or defense minister in a Labour government. Always outspoken, he said that if his party gained office all efforts to maintain an independent nuclear deterrent would be abandoned.

During his visit to Washington in June 1963, with the approval of my superiors, I invited Brown to come to my office, where we could give him a status report on the British program. What he wanted to learn was how certain we were that Polaris A-3 would be a success. The Conservatives, still in power and bearing responsibility, had already done their best to get assurance on that point, and I so advised Brown. However, my technical director, Capt. Levering Smith, presented a more convincing case. He reviewed the performance of each of our A-3 developmental flight tests to date, sixteen in all. I think Brown was convinced, as we were, that A-3 would indeed be a success, and the specter of another Skybolt fiasco was dispelled.

In Britain, responsibility for the development and procurement of aircraft, missiles, and nuclear weapons for the armed forces lay in the Ministry of Aviation (MOA). However, because of the intimate connection between submarine design and the Polaris missile, the Royal Navy worked directly with our own in procurement of the missile. The MOA remained responsible for the nuclear warhead.

The head of the MOA at this time was Julian Amery, son-in-law of Prime Minister Macmillan. I had first met Amery in March 1960, when I was in Cyprus with my flagship, USS *Newport News*. We were both guests of Governor Sir Hugh Foot at a luncheon in Government House, Nicosia. Amery, then under secretary of the Colonial Office, was negotiating terms of the treaty by which Cyprus was to become an independent nation and member of the Commonwealth.

In 1964 Amery visited the Special Projects Office and some of our field activities to obtain firsthand information on the A-3 missile. He had a reputation for being if not actively anti-American, then at least greatly suspicious of U.S. economic imperialism. I did my best to assure him that the deal our heads of government had made was mutually beneficial.

At a dinner in the Fairmont Hotel in San Francisco, with Cyprus once again torn by bloody fighting between Greeks and Turks, we reminisced about the negotiation period in 1960 and compared notes of our evaluation of His Beatitude, the Archbishop Makarios. In the course of the evening, Julian Amery said that he had aspired to be an officer of the Royal Navy. "When I was eleven I put my name down for Dartmouth. I wanted to be a sailor. Then my father took me to the House of Commons to meet Lloyd George. The Prime Minister asked what I wanted to be. With great pride, I told him I wanted to be in the Navy. He said, 'Humph, if it's piracy you want, pikes and cutlasses, blood on the decks, and walking the plank, *this* is the place for you!'"

In October 1964 the Labour party won election as predicted. Harold Wilson replaced Alec Douglas-Home, who had succeeded Macmillan in 1963, and the foreign minister in the new cabinet was my erstwhile visitor George Brown. With a majority of only four seats in Parliament, it would clearly be difficult for Labour to carry out some of its campaign pledges, including that to renegotiate the Nassau Pact. A sobering fact was that in addition to economic disruptions in Britain the costs of canceling Polaris contracts already in force would total $52 million. By January 1, 1965, this figure would be $80 million. Not surprisingly, the program was continued.

During my semiannual visits to London to confer with Admiral Mackenzie and review progress, I called not only on the senior U.S. naval authority, the Commander-in-Chief U.S. Naval Forces Europe (CinCUSNavEur), to keep him informed, but also on the senior British officials, civil and military, concerned with the international program.

The first lord of the Admiralty, counterpart of my own civilian superior, Secretary of the Navy Fred Korth, was always near the top of my list. With the change of parties in power and the restructuring of the Defense Department, the first lord became minister of state for navy. In quick succession I had the pleasure of calling on Lord Carrington, Lord Jellicoe, Christopher Mayhew, Joyce Cary, and David Owen as they followed in that historic office. My visits to the first three were especially memorable. Each of them told the same anecdote on my first meeting with him.

In the office of the first lord stood a handsome cabinet of dark, polished wood. At some time during our conversation, each of the distinguished public servants said, "Admiral, do you see that cabinet? Do you notice that crack in the lower right-hand panel? A predecessor of mine did that. He kicked it in a fit of rage when he couldn't get the admirals to do what he wanted."

"Who was that, sir?"

"Winston Churchill."

Others on my calling list, not solely for reasons of protocol but because they were men of influence and conviction in Defense Department affairs, were Admiral Lord Mountbatten, Chief of Defense Staff (CDS), and Sir Solly Zuckerman, Chief Scientist Ministry of Defense.

Sir Solly confided that even as things looked good for the survivability of Polaris submarines he was despondent over the prospect of ever achieving a meaningful antisubmarine warfare capability against nuclear submarines. Two world wars had driven home the fact that no other form of warfare was more important to Britain, and he was not sure that U.S. attention to ASW matched the new threat. He was more confident of a counter to the ballistic missile in the form of other missiles and hoped for close collaboration with us in the field of penetration aids for Polaris. (These were decoys and masking techniques to enable the actual warheads to avoid interception and destruction.)

Privately I shared Sir Solly's concern about ASW. Our own country's economic well-being and ability to project military power required a ready, effective ASW capability, which I knew we did not have, against modern submarines. However, I did not want to be disloyal to our Navy position, even to an ally, and I replied only that our head start in nuclear submarines gave us a big lead in learning to counter them.

During one of our chats Sir Solly pushed a button on an intercom and said, "CDS, CDS, Galantin is here."

"Good. I'll be right down."

In a few minutes Lord Louis strode in. His erect bearing, handsome features, and lively, inquiring mind always added a dynamic presence to any gathering. Recalling with pleasure our ride in *Albacore* when she was the world's fastest submarine, he inquired about Jon Boyes, who was her skipper at the time. I could tell him that Jon continued to play an important part in developing our submarine capabilities.

Mountbatten was always interested in my evaluation of the progress being made in their Polaris program. I was impressed by the competence and enthusiasm of their design team. Although they followed generally the same submarine design as our own, they incorporated some innovations and improvements made possible by the more deliberate schedule they could follow. Their boats had six torpedo tubes; ours had four. Their boats also had modified living spaces. The most apparent outward difference was location of the diving hydroplanes in the conventional position on the bow rather than elevated on what we called the "sail."

Dependent as it was on shipyard facilities and previous practice, their shipbuilding procedure was somewhat different from ours. It included some ingenious time- and cost-saving techniques. In the U.S. program, we were working under the constant tyranny of our schedule. First, our goal was to get the earliest deployment of the sea-based deterrent with the A-1 missile. Next, it was to reach a building rate of one Polaris submarine (SSBN) a month, an astounding peacetime effort. In the British program, the strategic urgency did not exist, but the internal political situation, the national spotlight on the controversial program, and the direct cost consequences of schedule slippage made close adherence to the mutually agreed schedule very important.

As our meeting ended, Mountbatten said, "We've decided on a submariner for our next first sea lord. What do you think of that?"

Surprised by this confidence, I could say only, "Congratulations, sir!" which gave him great amusement.

It was Admiral Sir David Luce to whom he referred. It is an interesting footnote to naval history that both Admiral Luce of the Royal Navy and Adm. Louis Denfeld of the U.S. Navy were submarine officers who headed their navies at times when naval aviation was under severe criticism as an overly costly, redundant element of national defense forces. When it was decided in 1966 to end the role of the large aircraft carrier in the Royal Navy, Admiral Luce resigned in protest, as did Navy Minister Christopher Mayhew.

On September 15 of that same year, Rufus Mackenzie and I were in Barrow-in-Furness for a historic event – the launching of *Resolution,* Britain's first ballistic missile submarine and her fourteenth ship to bear that name. It was less than three and a half years since we had been charged to create a force whose firepower exceeded that of every ship and plane in Britain's long maritime history. By 1970, when *Renown, Repulse,* and *Revenge* joined their sister ship, Britain's national nuclear deterrent was in full force.

SPINDRIFT

Since 1900, when *Holland* was built, four naval shipyards and thirteen private shipyards have produced submarines. Initially only the private, commercially oriented yards were engaged in that specialized construction, but when it was apparent that Electric Boat Company (EBCO) was seeking to monopolize submarine design and construction, in 1915 the Navy made Portsmouth Naval Shipyard its own submarine design and construction agent. As the primitive submarine designs evolved steadily into larger, more complex craft, they required special shipyard facilities and specially trained workers for their construction, and the weaker corporations faded from the scene. By 1957, when the high-priority Polaris fleet ballistic missile subs (SSBN) were superimposed on the ongoing buildup of nuclear-powered attack boats (SSN), only two naval shipyards (Portsmouth and Mare Island) and two private yards (EBCO and Newport News Shipbuilding and Drydock Company) were qualified to take on the additional workload.[1] All of them responded magnificently.

EBCO had a long, sometimes contentious relationship with the Navy Department, but Newport News had not built a submarine for our Navy since 1909. It had earned its reputation at the nation's premier builder of surface ships. At the entrance to its shipyard was a large granite boulder to which was affixed a bronze plaque proclaiming the words of the company's founder, Collis P. Huntington:

> We shall build good ships
> At a profit if we can
> At a loss if we must
> But always good ships

As director of the Special Projects Office in charge of the fleet ballistic missile program, I had numerous occasions to praise the company for its commitment and the fourteen splendid SSBNs that it subsequently produced. Nevertheless, I was realistic enough to know that only a profitable company could continue to produce "good ships."

A few years later, when Newport News was acquired by the giant conglomerate Tenneco, the new management lost little time in removing the bold commitment to excellence. At that time I was chief of naval material, with oversight of all our shipbuilding programs, but I could only chide the company. It continued to build good ships.

The year 1963 was one of hectic shipbuilding activity for the Special Projects Office. We had been directed to build a total of forty-one SSBNs, complete with support facilities for crew training, ship maintenance, supply, and rework of missiles. The entire force was to be operational by 1967, with its strategic subs based in Holy Loch, Scotland, Rota, Spain, Guam, Marianas Islands, and Charleston, South Carolina. That meant a shipbuilding rate that would be unprecedented for such complex ships. In what we called our "Boat of the Month Club" we launched twelve SSBNs in 1963. On June 22 we launched three: *Tecumseh* in Groton, Connecticut; *John C. Calhoun* in Newport News, Virginia; and *Daniel Boone* in Mare Island, California. A fourth boat, the attack submarine *Flasher,* followed *Tecumseh* down the ways in Groton to bring to four the number of nuclear-powered subs launched in a single day!

Seizing on this exceptional day to publicize the urgency and importance of our task, my innovative and energetic public information officer, Comdr. Ken Wade, tried mightily to have me participate in each launching ceremony. Although the events would take place on opposite coasts, Ken had worked out a plan in which I would be rushed to airports under police escort, then sped by Navy jet to the next stop. Unfortunately, he had no more luck than did King Canute in rolling back the tide. Ships are launched at slack water, and his plan had to conform. We could not quite pull off the public relations blitz, and I settled for the trip to Mare Island and *Daniel Boone*.

★ ★ ★ ★

During the nine thousand years that men have used the sea for sustenance, trade, conquest, or defense, and during which the ship has evolved into the many forms it has today, there developed rituals, customs, and traditions unmatched in any other field of human technology. Throughout a ship's life – from keel-laying to launching to commissioning to underway operations to final disposal – there are customs, even superstitions, that are still preserved. In the Navy, three events are marked by a formal ceremony: the laying of the keel, launching, and commissioning. In addition to patriotic rededication, they can bring enlightenment and even humor.

It is a much-sought-after honor to be the principal figure at such an occasion. Politicians, ever hungry for visibility and publicity, crave it for obvious reasons, and the Navy is not above cooperating with senators or members of Congress whose committees are key to the passage of legislation affecting the Navy. In addition to these, the list of participants includes presidents, wives or daughters of presidents, cabinet officers, ambassadors, labor leaders, educators, governors, or persons distinguished in almost any walk of national life.

In modern shipyards the keel-laying of a warship is barely recognizable as that event, as a lofty crane swings a prefabricated modular segment into position, yet some of the ritual survives. On the morning of December 3, 1962, the keel of *Sam Rayburn* (SSBN 635) was laid at the Newport News Shipbuilding and Drydock Company. Lyndon B. Johnson, then vice president, a fellow Texan and devoted disciple of the late speaker of the House, performed the ritual. It was a raw, chilly morning when the official party and spectators assembled at the building ways on the mist-shrouded bank of the James River. Like most others on the scene, I was gently stamping my feet, crinkling my toes, and flexing my fingers to keep the chill off as we listened to the vice president's brief remarks pertinent to Sam Rayburn. When he concluded, LBJ pronounced the traditional words, "I declare this keel well and truly laid."

I still recall the surge of warmth when the retired admiral standing next to me said in a stage whisper, "Ah, that's what my wife used to tell me when I was a young man."

The most colorful of the ceremonies is the launching, when the woman who is sponsor smashes a bottle of champagne against the bow and gives the ship her name. While a prominent official delivers a patriotic speech or even, on occasion, one of international significance, the sponsor nervously awaits her cue, mentally rehearsing her swing of the heavy bottle and the words, "In the name of the United States, I christen thee _____."

Sponsor for *Daniel Boone* was the gracious and attractive Peg Wakelin, wife of the assistant secretary of the Navy for research and development, the Hon. James Wakelin. Their sons, two young college men, attended, and I asked if they'd like to join me in riding the ship down the ways. Both were eager to share this exhilarating experience, which would be the first for me as well.

As soon as I concluded my brief remarks in the ceremony, the young men and I were escorted to the space reserved for us on the bow of the unfinished ship. While Secretary Wakelin gave the principal address, we stood within lifelines, awaiting the smash of the ceremonial bottle that would send the ship sliding down the inclined ways into the harbor amid cheers, music, and tooting of whistles. When we took our places I noted that we were next to two men of about my age dressed in black clerical garb. Speaking to the tall, lean men of open, friendly countenance, I remarked pleasantly, "I guess you're here because that's Christian Brothers champagne being used."

"Yes. How did you know? I'm Brother Timothy, and this is Brother Jonathan."

Brother Timothy was the expert cellarmaster of Christian Brothers Winery in the Napa Valley, not far from Mare Island. Many of our ships probably received their baptism with the special good omen of their bubbly, and no doubt another Christian Brother, John P. Holland, the "Little Professor" from Liscannor, Ireland, looked down approvingly as a descendent of his brainchild slid down the ways in Vallejo, California.

Another memorable occasion was the launching of *Sturgeon* (SSN 637) on February 26, 1966, at Groton. Luella Dirksen, wife of the Republican senator from Illinois, was sponsor. I was myself from Illinois and had met the Dirksens on other occasions, so I knew them for the warm-hearted, kindly, unassuming persons they were. However, Everett Dirksen did enjoy using his voice. Its distinctive deep tones and slow delivery were recognized nationwide when television carried the "Ev and Charlie Show," the weekly news conference by which he and his opposite number in the House, Minority Leader Charles Halleck of Indiana, sought to balance the Johnson administration's publicity by giving their Republican party's minority viewpoint.

At the sponsor's dinner in the Lighthouse Inn in Groton, we expected to be favored with some senatorial remarks. To our surprise, the senator resisted all efforts to "say a few words." He insisted that the evening honored his wife alone, and he would do nothing to divert attention from that.

Finally, in keeping with the good-humored, lighthearted ambiance of the occasion, our host, J. William Jones, president of the Electric Boat division where *Sturgeon* was building, stood up with a copy of sheet music in his hand. "Senator, this is one time we've done our homework. I have here a piece of music entitled 'Chinese Love Song.' One of its joint composers is E. McKinley Dirksen. Could that be you?"

Surprised by this foray into his past, or perhaps because our relations with mainland China at the time could hardly be called a love song, the Senate minority leader took the floor. "Yes, I'm the one."

Tossing the tousled locks that political cartoonists liked so much, he rumbled in his bass voice, "When I was a young man I was interested in the theater. I did a bit of acting and composing. Let me tell you how we came to use that title. I came from a wonderful town in Illinois, in Tazewell County, on the bank of the Illinois River. It was founded in 1839. The ladies of the town didn't want just any name; they wanted a special name. A committee was appointed to find the right name. The way they did it was to take a globe of the world and they followed the equivalent parallel of latitude," he repeated, rolling out in his inimitable style, "the equivalent parallel of latitude, until they came to China. There they came upon the name Pekin. One of the ladies said, 'That's a lovely name. Why don't we choose that?' And that's why my town is named Pekin." Enchanted by his story, rapt by his delivery, we applauded at length as the orchestra rendered "Chinese Love Song."

The following year there was a launching of special interest to me. As chief of naval material from 1965 to 1970 with the rank of admiral, I was shown on organization diagrams to be Vice Admiral Rickover's superior officer, but, realistically, I referred to him as my "senior insubordinate." We were often in communication as he continued his controversial crusade to apply nuclear propulsion to all major warships of the surface Navy and was a constant critic of management practices other than his. As we finished a business conversation by telephone late one evening – routine office hours meant nothing to him – I said, "Rick, we've worked together many years, but now our names will be entwined forever."

Always blunt and to the point, he shot back, "Why?"

"Well, next week my wife is launching the submarine named for you."

Strangely at a loss for words, and knowing very well that ships were never named for living people, he paused considerably. "What do you mean?"

"Don't you know? Ginny's the sponsor of *Sea Devil*."

Taken aback, he said at last, "Well, you delete the word *Sea* and I'll accept the compliment."

I really intended my remark as a compliment appropriate for the man who stressed that "the devil is in the details" and coped with them better than did anyone else.

Sea Devil (SSN 664), an attack submarine built by Newport News Shipbuilding and Drydock Company, was launched on October 5, 1967. On that brilliant fall day, my devoted, loyal Navy wife smashed the ritual bottle of champagne on *Sea Devil*'s prow, and the sleek black hull slid smoothly into the sun-dappled James River.

Sixteen years later, in the same shipyard, Rickover was given the unprecedented honor, while still living, of having a ship named for him. On August 27, 1983, his wife Eleonore launched the attack submarine *Hyman G. Rickover* (SSN 709). The sixty-one other ships of her class are all named for cities of the United States.

QUIETER, DEEPER, FASTER?

The keel for *Nautilus* had been laid in June 1952, with *Seawolf* following in September 1953. The uncertainties about what the performance of these revolutionary ships might be meant that we had to continue construction of diesel-electric boats to meet the needs of the fleet. Even while the nuclear-powered ships were under construction we commenced work on conventional diesel-powered subs: two radar picket subs (SSR), three guided missile subs (SSG), and three attack boats (SS). The latter were the culmination of our conventionally powered submarine designs; *Barbel, Blueback,* and *Bonefish* used the single-screw propulsion and advanced hull form that *Albacore* had pioneered. The last diesel-powered boats we built, they joined the fleet in 1959.

Once *Nautilus* and *Seawolf* demonstrated the astonishing performance and reliability of nuclear-powered submarines, there was no turning back. Nuclear power became the sine qua non for submarines of our Navy. Some designs fell short of hoped-for operational performance, but the military advantage of being a true submarine of continuous stealth was so compelling that we would build no other type. Some critics claimed that lower costs, the need for greater numbers, and the superior quiet of diesel boats when operating on their batteries justified building some diesel-powered boats. However, submarine operators argued that the numbers of Soviet Russia's submarines and their steadily improving capabilities could only be overcome by submarines of continuous, not intermittent, high performance. Unspoken but real was their concern that if they accepted the lesser-cost boats a cost-conscious Congress would shortly buy no others.

Save for the liquid-metal (sodium-cooled) reactor produced for *Seawolf*, all Navy reactors have been extrapolations of the pressurized water-cooled reactor in *Nautilus*. The sodium-cooled reactor was sound in principle and offered benefits in nuclear and thermal efficiencies in conjunction with steam turbines. However, for shipboard application there were major disadvantages: the intense residual radiation levels of sodium as reactor coolant and the hazards of fire and violent chemical reaction should molten sodium contact water or steam. The associated metallurgical and engineering problems were severe. When cracks developed in tubes of *Seawolf*'s steam superheater, that unit was bypassed, allowing the ship to operate safely at 80 percent of its designed power. After two years of successful operation of *Seawolf*, Rickover abandoned the liquid-metal design as less favorable than pressurized water for military application, and her original reactor was replaced by one using the water coolant.

Seawolf was quickly followed by four boats of the Skate class, which had 7500-shaft-horsepower reactor plants. Next were six boats of the Skipjack class, using an improved model of *Nautilus*'s 15,000-shaft-horsepower reactor. Thanks to their streamlined, single-screw, *Albacore* hull form, they were the world's fastest submarines.

While submariners kept pressing for ever more capable combat subs, quieter, faster, and deeper-diving, Rickover was exploring alternative reactor concepts, not only those conceived in his own shop but also some others being studied in AEC laboratories. He remained convinced that for military, mobile application his form of nuclear technology, specifically the pressurized-water reactor, was superior. Disdaining the allure of exotic reactors that existed only on paper, he fought off every proposal for alternate design by sound engineering analysis or, when necessary, by ridicule or political influence. The rigid control Rickover exercised over all Navy-related nuclear power development, fortified by the unarguable success of his product, meant that our operational concepts were hostages of his nuclear power technology and the propulsion variants he proposed.

A weapon system whose unique and major advantage is concealment cannot exploit its immunity to visual or radar detection if it reveals its presence by noise emission while submerged. For what was being accepted as our submarines' primary mission – to seek out and destroy enemy submarines – quiet operation is especially important. The great advances in oceanographic knowledge, sonar performance, and acoustic signal processing made since World War II made it essential that our submarines be as silent as possible as they cruise underwater, not only to get maximum performance from their own sonar systems but also to minimize risk of detection by enemy sonar and attack by homing weapons. The submarine, in the words of the title of that fascinating and widely read book about World War II undersea action by my friend and longtime colleague Edward L. Beach, must truly *Run Silent, Run Deep.*

A major contributor to the radiated noise of our boats was the reduction gear through which the power of the high-speed turbine was transmitted to the propellor shaft. By the latter part of World War II, when diesel engines were our primary power source, we had substituted slow-speed, heavy-duty electric motors for the reduction gears in all new construction submarines. However, for greater propulsion efficiency in our nuclear-powered subs, reduction gears were again in the power train from the high-speed turbines.

Those of us on the operational side of submarine warfare, enthusiastic about the great potential of our newly attained true submarines, were insufficiently aware of the many uncertainties associated with nuclear power that were influencing Rickover and his engineers. We pressed for a smaller, quieter boat that could be effective in ASW and economical enough to build and operate in greater numbers. All prior ASW experience showed that whatever the system employed against so elusive a target – be it surface ship, submarine, aircraft, sono-buoy, or mine – the greater the number, the more likely success.

It was, of course, advantageous to keep size down for a number of reasons, including cost and numbers of crewmen. To find the optimum attack submarine we had to approach our goal from two sides, paying in dollars and tons for speed on the high side while giving on speed for a smaller, relatively economical boat better suited for ASW.

Rick responded eagerly to any requirement that would enable him to advance the art of nuclear reactor design and construction. On May 31, 1955, speaking to the Submarine Officers Conference, he estimated that for a submerged displacement of no more that 1500 tons, a reactor providing 2000 shaft horsepower would give a speed of about 15½ knots. In actuality he chose Combustion Engineering Corporation to develop a 2500-shaft-horsepower plant for what was to be a ship of about 1600 tons, using electric drive in place of reduction gears. So eager was he to get on with that next link in his family of water-cooled reactors that he called me at home on a Sunday to get assurance that the CNO's shipbuilding program would include the new ship.

I could not give it. When I wouldn't give the assurance he sought so that he could proceed more quickly, he wanted to know who could.

"No one. You'll get the answer as soon as Admiral Burke decides on the total building program."

For the first time he included me in "those stupid operators" before slamming down his phone.

The new ship, named *Tullibee* for the World War II submarine that had been sunk by the circular run of one of her own torpedoes, was authorized in the 1958 shipbuilding program and completed in 1960. Unfortunately, the goal of 1600 tons displacement could not be met; the final design required 2640 tons. She was, indeed, our quietest submarine to date, but, like the diesel-powered SSKs, she proved to be too slow and too cramped in volume for all the sensors, weapons, and habitability needed in a good ASW sub.

By the start-up date of *Tullibee*'s reactor in 1960, seven separate designs of submarine reactors were in use or under construction. The trend was for ever larger, bulkier ships, requiring larger, more powerful reactors. Better said, the larger, more powerful reactors that Rickover offered required larger, bulkier submarines to be wrapped around them.

There was one exception, the nuclear-powered research vehicle *NR 1*, 136 feet long and 400 tons in displacement, which would have a crew of five and room for two scientists. It was conceived by Rickover in 1964 as a long-endurance, deep-diving submersible that would complement the Navy's recently established Deep Submergence Systems Program (DSSP). His proposal of *NR 1* was not motivated solely by a desire to advance undersea research and technology. In the growing national awareness of the importance of the productive use of the sea, he saw a justification for another reactor, a means to establish the lower end of his growing family of them.

There would be no military function for *NR 1,* and it would be hard to justify including it in the naval shipbuilding program, so Rick wanted all the support he could get from the operational side of the Navy. As usual, he minimized developmental problems and cost. In January 1965 I was director of special projects, in overall charge of DSSP, when he asked that I assist in gaining the support of the CNO, Admiral McDonald. When Rick came to our brief meeting he was accompanied by Dennis Wilkinson, who by then was a rear admiral in the submarine warfare billet, OP 31, which I had left in 1962. Dennis was carrying a wooden, full-scale mock-up of the proposed pressurized-water reactor, its volume little more than that of a Pentagon waste basket.

The project deserved support not for potential benefit to combat submarines, but for its great assistance in undersea research and engineering and possible utility for clandestine recovery of Soviet missiles, torpedoes, and other ordnance. Both Admiral McDonald and Secretary of the Navy Paul Nitze approved of this development, and it was authorized for construction outside of the regular shipbuilding appropriation.

My special interest – to have our submarines operate at depth greater than the seven hundred feet of the *Tang* (SS 563) class – was rewarded in 1958 when the keel of the lead ship of a new nuclear-powered class was laid. *Thresher* (SSN 593) was built in the government shipyard at Portsmouth, New Hampshire. She used the same 15,000 shaft-horsepower reactor as did the fast Skipjacks, but her various improvements made her almost 800 tons bulkier. BuShips designed her to operate at the depth recommended by our 1957 Operations Evaluation Group study, using the stronger steel, HY 80. The design, albeit of routine steam turbine-reduction gear drive, also emphasized sound-quieting.

Rickover agreed with the need to go deeper, but he only grudgingly accepted the silencing measures that BuShips prescribed for some elements of the power plant. He never took kindly to features of improved design that other agencies proposed when they impinged upon his own propulsion plant design or construction schedule. His own proposals for silencing were of grander scope, involving the entire power train or the nuclear reactor itself, as in *Tullibee, Narwhal,* and *Lipscomb.*

Thresher was a success, deeper-diving than any of her predecessors, not as fast as the Skipjacks but somewhat quieter and with a much improved sonar system, the BQQ 2. This was a large spherical array mounted in the ship's streamlined bow in order to be far removed from the ship's own noises. This required relocation of the torpedo tubes to amidships, two on each side angled slightly outboard, and limited the speed at which torpedoes could be fired. The compromise of combat potential by reducing the number of torpedo tubes from six to four was made to keep ship size down in order to avoid further loss of speed.

After *Thresher* operated for about a year, testing and evaluating her new capabilities, including dives to the increased operating depth, she returned to Portsmouth for her delayed postshakedown repairs and maintenance. Nine months later she went to sea for routine sea trials. On the morning of April 10, 1963, she submerged for a deep-dive test. At or near her test depth, a casualty, possibly a leak from a sea connection, caused the loss of electric power and the shutdown of her reactor. Unable to drive the ship upward by power in normal manner, the CO probably ordered main ballast tanks blown by high-pressure air. For unknown reason, possibly because expansion of the air caused ice to form in the blow valves, insufficient air reached the tanks, and *Thresher* sank ever deeper. When the enormous sea pressure shattered her hull, her wreckage littered the ocean floor at 8400 feet. The 129 men on board were lost.

When we received word of *Thresher*'s disaster, I was in Annapolis in the Naval Academy's Mitscher Hall conducting a Polaris Navy-Industry Team program review. In keeping with his evangelistic management style, Red Raborn had initiated these reviews for which the chief executives of the major corporations on our industrial team would come to Washington. I had continued the practice but added my own touch. I wanted these senior partners in our top-priority project to concentrate their attention on Polaris, not to go looking for other business in the Department of Defense or to spend their time lobbying on Capitol Hill.

There is no better place than the Naval Academy to see and sense the Navy's historic ability to adapt to its environment the most advanced technology of the day. As we had progressed from sail to steam, from coal to oil, weapons had kept pace, from muzzle-loading cannon, to rifled guns, to armor-piercing projectiles, to torpedoes, to aircraft and guided missiles. Now we were taking the rocket-propelled ballistic missile to sea in nuclear-powered submarines.

Amid our discussions of technical problems, of performance goals and test results, of cost and delivery schedules, *Thresher*'s loss came as a chilling reminder of human costs should our commitment to excellence be wanting. Led by Dan Kimball, chairman of the Aerojet-General Corporation and a former secretary of the Navy, the industrialists who were present quickly pledged funds to provide scholarships for the children whose fathers were lost in *Thresher*.

Thresher's tragedy, and the inability to determine the definitive cause, led to searching examination of submarine design, construction, and operation. The resulting comprehensive "Sub Safe" program included more rigorous inspection of material and workmanship, redesign and replacement of some components and piping systems, and improved training and operating procedures.

This was a very costly, time-consuming process, applicable in varying degrees to all submarines, whether operational, under overhaul, under construction, or still on the drawing boards. The hundreds of millions in cost was unbudgeted and would have devastating effect on other shipbuilding projects. Fortunately, because of the national emergency that had occasioned our program and in recognition of the many difficult development and engineering problems we had to resolve, once the Navy had committed its available funds to the start of the project the Congress had been generous in its annual funding of the Polaris program. By our eighth year, with many of our early problems solved and operations at sea proceeding satisfactorily, we had accumulated a substantial surplus that, with some trepidation, I released for the all-important Sub Safe program.

Nevertheless, in spite of the best efforts of submarine constructors and operators, the danger inherent in undersea operations was demonstrated anew in May 1968. *Scorpion* (of the less deep-diving Skipjack class) disappeared with all hands as she was crossing the Atlantic submerged, homeward bound from the Mediterranean. Her hulk was eventually located in very deep water some four hundred miles from the Azores. Other, lesser accidents, not resulting in loss of ship, add their own compelling evidence to the need for utmost commitment to excellence by builder and operator alike.

Thresher and the thirteen others of her class (improved by Sub Safe) that were built during the next six years gave us the deeper operating depth we sought, but the penalty for their larger, more effective sonar and improved quieting was increased size, hence loss of speed.

The BuShips submarine design division was not always just a passive collaborator with Rickover's nuclear power division. It had conclusively shown with its design and construction of *Albacore* that it, too, was capable of innovative, bold engineering. It redesigned one of the Threshers to get greater propulsion efficiency and quieter operation. *Jack* (SS 605) used the same S5W reactor as the others but eliminated the reduction gears by use of a direct-drive steam turbine that drove two coaxial contra-rotating shafts and propellors. Her increased cost, size, and mechanical complexity prevented exploitation of her design, but the concept may yet prove useful.

Eager to get on with the buildup of our attack submarine force and strongly supported by Rickover and his allies in Congress, we pressed on with thirty-seven of the "improved" Sturgeon (SS 637) class, which were also designed around the S5W reactor. Unfortunately, the improvements resulted in a still larger sub further reduced in speed over the Threshers.

Besides the progressive loss in speed, the space and weight required for ever-larger, more efficient sonars, improved quieting, advanced weapons, sophisticated fire control, and navigation systems resulted in attack submarines that were more cramped and crowded than our World War II boats. As BuShips and submarine operators studied how best to redress the situation, Rickover offered a new approach to the quieting problem.

Since 1956 he had been studying and doing developmental engineering on a reactor that would use the natural flow of convection instead of the relatively noisy main coolant pumps to circulate the hot pressurized water. (At high speeds the pumps would still be required.) In 1962 Rickover and his engineers, notably Robert Panoff and Theodore Rockwell, briefed us on the new system and urged construction of a submarine to exploit it. Most submariners were enthusiastic about the new approach to quieting and glad to commit one ship to it in the 1964 shipbuilding program.

That ship was *Narwhal* (SSN 671), completed in 1969. The 15,000-shaft-horsepower reactor performed as advertised, but again the ship had grown in size, to 5390 tons, and lost speed. Her tactical performance was not good enough to justify committing a class of submarines to that design, and no more of her type were built.

The rapidly growing menace of Russia's submarines, both in numbers and operational performance, confirmed ASW as the primary mission of our own attack subs. The first Soviet nuclear-powered boat was completed in 1959, four years after our *Nautilus,* but, unlike the United States, which undertook a deliberate program of building a limited number of differing classes of nuclear submarines, the U.S.S.R. quickly began construction of larger blocs of nuclear boats. She knew that defense of Europe and other areas vital to the West relied on U.S. control and use of the seas. The best way to defeat that control was by large numbers of submarines. To that end she continued building diesel-powered boats even as she accelerated the building of nuclear-powered torpedo attack subs (SSN), guided missile subs (SSGN) to attack our surface fleets, and ballistic missile land attack SSBNs.[1]

This heavy building program meant that by 1972 she had a total of almost 350 submarines, about a hundred of which were nuclear. We had a total of ninety-nine nuclears, forty-one of which were the original Polaris strategic deterrent boats (SSBN), and fifty-eight were torpedo attack boats (SSN). We still operated a few special purpose diesel boats, but these were gradually being retired. Our goal was an all-nuclear force of ninety SSNs and eighteen SSBNs of a new class to carry the heavy, long-range Trident missile. These numbers, modest in relation to Soviet Russia's, were rationalized on the assumption that we would have a continuing advantage in quality of submarine technology and quality of submarine personnel. However, the Russians had already produced boats that were deeper-diving and faster than our best. Only in quietness of operation did we still have the edge, and it was fast eroding. We needed continued stress on silent operation, as well as great improvement in speed, but as usual the Navy's specification of performance requirements for nuclear-powered ships was hostage to Rick's control of nuclear propulsion technology. There was extended debate between the Office of the Secretary of Defense and the Navy about how best to attain high-speed submarines when Rickover proposed a renewed effort in silencing as well as separate development of a high-speed sub.

✶ ✶ ✶ ✶

In 1965, after I turned direction of the Special Projects Office over to Rear Adm. Levering Smith, I became chief of naval material, in relief of Vice Adm. William A. Schoech. The CNM coordinated, but did not command, the efforts of the Naval Material Support Establishment (NMSE). This was the comprehensive, nationwide technical and logistic support structure for the Navy. It was made up of the four material bureaus – the Bureau of Ships, Bureau of Naval Weapons,[1] Bureau of Supplies and Accounts, and Bureau of Yards and Docks – and all their associated laboratories, shipyards, and maintenance activities.

Unlike the Army and the Air Force, the Navy Department had a bilinear organization. This meant that the CNM reported not to a military superior but to the secretary of the Navy, the civilian head of the Navy Department. Thus there were two separate lines of authority, one for military planning and administration by the CNO and one for the management of all development, production, and procurement by the secretary. In 1955 that structure had become even more complex with creation of the Special Projects Office, which also reported directly to the secretary.

I knew that organizational changes by themselves do not guarantee better performance and better products, but three years' experience as director of the Special Projects Office, working with the separate bureaus, disclosed certain symptoms and clues that could be traced to organizational deficiencies. I wished to strengthen a total system approach to weapon development and acquisition and to emphasize lifetime logistic support and maintenance. To that end I reshaped the four loosely coordinated material bureaus into six functional system commands reporting to the chief of naval material.[2] After months of study and debate, with the approval of the CNO, Adm. David L. McDonald, Secretary of the Navy Paul Nitze, Secretary of Defense Robert S. McNamara, and the concurrence of the commandant of the Marine Corps, Gen. Wallace M. Greene, Jr., the NMSE became the Navy Material Command in March 1966. The most significant change was to abandon the historic, bilinear organization and give the Navy's top military commander a clear line of authority over his technical support agency.

The position and responsibilities of Rickover remained the same in the Naval Ship Systems Command as they had been in BuShips. However, he minced no words in criticizing what he considered to be my useless, bureaucratic reshuffling.

In 1967, to better justify its needs for ships with specific performance capabilities and to cope with the increasingly critical views of Secretary McNamara's systems analysts which were challenging its own strategic concepts, the Navy established its own division of system analysis in OpNav (OP 96). A particular warfare community could advocate a new weapons system, ship, or plane, but OP 96 would make the final evaluation of need, cost, and capabilities in the context of total fleet requirements. Thus, in theory, Rickover's proposals for nuclear-powered ships would have to survive the objective scrutiny of two weapons systems analyses as well as review by the chief of naval material, procedures he excoriated as no more than wasteful, time-consuming criticisms of his superior technical knowledge and military judgment. He turned to his powerful, astutely cultivated supporters in the Congress and induced the Senate Armed Services Committee to hold hearings on the state of the nuclear submarine program. As usual in that forum, Rickover's views prevailed.

The "quiet" submarine he proposed would have turbo-electric drive as in *Tullibee,* but on a much larger scale, using the 15,000-shaft-horsepower reactor (instead of 2500) to power the resulting 6480-ton attack submarine. This provoked great controversy among senior naval officials as well as among submariners. Secretary Nitze asked searching questions about the wisdom of building a large, slow, albeit quieter submarine whose high cost and specialized nature would very likely make her one of a kind. I was supportive of the technology to be gained for possible future application but cautioned that the cost was very high and would probably increase. In time, because of the critical importance of finding the best means of quieting new construction submarines, both Admiral McDonald and Secretary Nitze supported Rickover's plan and succeeded in getting Secretary McNamara's approval for construction.

General Electric, the corporation best qualified to design and manufacture the large, unique main motor required, refused to do so. It pleaded prior commitment to other work but actually did not want to get involved in a probable one-shot project whose technology would have no commercial application. Moreover, from its extensive experience with Rickover's methods of technical supervision and contract enforcement, G.E. foresaw acrimonious relations, with severe management and cost implications. The impasse required the intervention of Secretary Nitze, who chose the presidential yacht *Sequoia* as the site for a conference with Fred Borch, chairman of G.E. On a hot summer evening we cruised down the Potomac in quiet comfort. With his exceptional intellectual powers and excellent grasp of technical factors, Nitze presented the Navy's case so effectively that Borch agreed to reconsider his company's position – provided that safeguards were provided against undue intrusion by Rickover.

The electric-drive submarine *Glenard P. Lipscomb* (SSN 685) was completed in 1974. She was named for the late member of the House Armed Services Committee who had been one of Rick's strong supporters. As predicted, she was quiet and costly but too slow to cope with high-speed Soviet subs or to be an effective screen for surface battle groups. She remained the only one of her kind.

By 1967 our carrier battle groups faced dual threats – the rapid build-up of a Russian surface fleet armed with sophisticated surface-to-surface missiles and the growing numbers of nuclear submarines able to dive deeper and run faster than ours. To help cope with these dangers to the centerpiece of U.S. naval power we needed a substantial building program of improved subs. Our fastest submarines were the six boats of the Skipjack class completed in 1961, able to make thirty-one knots. After them came eight different designs of submarines; six were single, special purpose boats – *Triton, Halibut, Tullibee, Jack, Lipscomb,* and *Narwhal* – and two were attack subs of the Thresher and Sturgeon classes, which would total fifty-one boats.[3] Not one of these ships was as fast as *Skipjack;* all had sacrificed speed for one reason or another – to accommodate the reactor Rick specified, to attain needed volume, to dive deeper, or to improve quieting.

In January 1968 an episode at sea dramatized and gave urgency to our problem. Our nuclear-powered aircraft carrier *Enterprise,* en route from California to Hawaii, was trailed by a submerged Soviet nuclear sub. As *Enterprise* progressively increased speed to her maximum of thirty-one knots, the submarine kept pace. This proof that even the older November-class Russian subs could match the sustained speed of our most advanced carrier caused consternation in the CIA, the Office of the Secretary of Defense, the Navy, and Congress.

Rickover seized the moment to put forward his solution. It was a brute force response in the form of a 35,000-shaft-horsepower reactor, more than twice the power of those used in previous designs. He had for years fought off all proposals, whether by U.S. industry or the Navy's own Office of Naval Research, to develop smaller, lighter reactors, possibly using heat transfer agents other than water. Once more it would be Rickover's reactor and propulsion system that would determine the size and speed of the submarine. The large volume required to accommodate the weight and space of the reactor and propulsion system greatly limited the maximum attainable speed. Both the Navy and the Office of the Secretary of Defense were opposed to a design that, at double the cost, would have only a slight speed advantage over existing U.S. subs and none over Russia's best. However, we were not ready with a viable proposal that could overtake the support Rickover had already generated on the Hill.

Nevertheless, Capt. Donald H. Kern, submarine designer in the Naval Ship Systems Command (NavShips), which was the new title for BuShips in my restructured Naval Material Command, had undertaken exploratory studies of possible alternative nuclear sub designs. He believed that by using the natural circulation reactor and twin propellors on a centerline shaft he could produce a lighter, faster, quieter, less costly submarine. I thought well enough of his effort to be briefed on it and requested my new superior in the revised unilinear chain of command, CNO Admiral Moorer, for a private meeting to learn if he would support what would be a highly politicized clash with Rickover. Tom replied that he was very occupied with Vietnam War problems in the Joint Chiefs of Staff "tank," but that I should brief his vice chief, Adm. Bernard A. (Chick) Clarey, who would then report to him.

Chick was a good friend and fellow submariner whom I highly respected. In our pre-World War II days at Pearl Harbor he had been a junior officer in *Nautilus* (SS 168) at the same time I was in *Argonaut* (SS 166), and our paths of submarine duty crossed frequently thereafter. During the war Chick commanded *Pintado* (SS 387). For her outstanding record of ships sunk in bold attacks under his excellent leadership *Pintado* was awarded the coveted Presidential Unit Citation. And I am ever-grateful for the assistance Chick gave me when *Pintado* escorted my severely damaged *Halibut* 1500 miles to Saipan after the near-fatal depth-charging my boat had undergone.

In the quiet of a Saturday morning in the Pentagon, with the help of a few simple diagrams, I outlined the possibilities. We both knew that pursuing them would bring a stormy confrontation with Rick, as well as delay the buildup of our attack submarine force. Much more detailed concept formulation and design studies would be required, but I felt sure that if we were willing to challenge Rickover's proposal with a sound case for smaller, faster, less costly subs, the secretaries of the Navy and defense would support us. Such a case was not ready and was sure to receive Rick's furious opposition. Tom Moorer soon sent word that the issue was moot.

A panel of experienced nuclear submarine commanders was soon assembled by the CNO and charged to design a fast submarine using the new, large reactor Rickover proposed. Under strict security and in a demanding schedule they soon learned that the giant reactor and propulsion system required so large and heavy a submarine that there was no hope of significant improvement in speed. They could find no compensatory reductions or removals of systems without unacceptable loss of combat capability. Directed to use the 35,000-shaft-horsepower reactor and to wrap a fast combat submarine around it, there was only one way to give it speed just a knot or two above that of *Skipjack*, designed fourteen years earlier. The weight of the ship had to be drastically reduced, and that had to come out of the hull. The lighter-weight hull meant that the designers sacrificed much of the increased operating depth we had worked so hard to attain and had proven in the Thresher class. Instead of a design to fulfill an operational concept, we had a design to justify preordained engineering. And this time the penalty for so long tolerating Rickover's monopoly of mobile reactor design was degradation of the combat capability not of one experimental boat but of a whole class of ships, sixty-two subs of the so-called SSN 688 fast-attack Los Angeles class. Some of them will be in service well into the twenty-first century. Fortunately, they have not had to be tested in combat against enemy submarines and weapons that can run faster and dive deeper.

In an attempt to redress some of the shortcomings of the 688s, the last thirty-one boats were modified and designated the "Improved 688 class." However, within the constraints of their basic hull structure, it is not possible to back-fit greater speed and greater depth. The improvements are in the sonar and fire control systems and enhanced Tomahawk cruise missile capability. The installation of twelve vertical launch tubes for Tomahawk in the ballast tank space outside the pressure hull leaves the four torpedo tubes free for their basic purpose and gives the boats a formidable land-attack capability as well.

These features exhausted the margin for further improvements needed to cope with the methodical technologic advances of new classes of Soviet submarines. Accordingly, in 1983 the Navy undertook a costly research, development, and design program for what would be the most advanced submarine in the world. It is designated *SSN 21* – the submarine for the twenty-first century. Her primary task would be to seek out and destroy enemy submarines. Her name is already chosen – *Seawolf* – honoring her two famous namesakes, *SS 197* made famous by World War II exploits of Freddie Warder and *SSN 575*, our second nuclear-powered sub operated so effectively by Dick Laning.

EPILOGUE

Physically exhausted after ten consecutive years in Washington in three demanding assignments, on June 30, 1970, I turned my job as chief of naval material over to my very able deputy, Vice Adm. Jackson D. Arnold, cleared out my desk, and retired from the United States Navy. During forty-one years in uniform I had seen it develop from the battleship Navy of the early 1930s into a finely tuned, flexible instrument of national power and prestige, constantly serving our nation's interests around the globe. The submarine service in which I chose to specialize in 1935 now constituted the world's chief deterrent to global strategic aggression, for the only potential foe capable of attacking us knew all too well that our response would be certain, overwhelming, and, until the moment of launching, virtually undetectable.

I had no complaints and every reason to take satisfaction. I had served in peace and war, risen from midshipman to four-star rank, worked alongside many fine shipmates and colleagues, and made many dear friends. When I reported for duty aboard USS *New York* fresh out of the Naval Academy I was twenty-three years old and unmarried. Now Ginny and I, married thirty-five years, had three children. (In 1994, as I write this, we have been married for fifty-nine years, and there are six grandchildren as well.)

I have seen sea power develop in ways that would have been almost inconceivable to even the most forward-looking naval planners of an earlier day and have been privileged to play a part, however modest, in that development. Naturally enough, I have some thoughts on what it has all meant – and what might lie ahead.

In World War II, submarines of Germany and the United States had a major, near-conclusive impact on the war's outcome. The United States came out of that conflict with submarines that, however useful against Japan, were obsolescent, outclassed by the Allied ASW measures that had been developed and applied, chiefly in the Atlantic, to defeat Germany's U-boats. There was no longer an enemy who could challenge us at sea, and we had the time and the money to explore various roles for our boats.

Subsequently, when Soviet Russia undertook its massive submarine building program, new U.S. technology in sonar, weapons, and nuclear propulsion revitalized our submarines, which became the primary agents of our antisubmarine and strategic deterrent missions. Through many years and many designs they have evolved into the very large, and very costly, subs of the Los Angeles and Trident classes. They were designed to counter Soviet high-performance subs and surface ships, or to be an unassailable, ever-ready strategic deterrent.

✷ ✷ ✷ ✷

Ironically, the end of the Cold War finds us once more searching for a mission for our attack boats. The Clinton administration has approved the construction of three submarines that are expected to be the most capable undersea combat vehicles ever built – the Seawolf (SSN 21) class. This decision was justified not in response to an operational requirement but as an interim measure to preserve a submarine construction and support base pending the design of submarines more consistent with fiscal and strategic reality.

In the new era of lean defense budgets and drastic reduction of forces from those required by the bipolar, super-power confrontation, the submarine must do more than make incremental improvements in its performance of covert undersea missions of deterrence, attack, and intelligence collection. Too often the reasons put forward to justify additional submarine construction have been simply product improvement items: enhanced stealth, greater speed and endurance, deeper depth, and greater weapon variety and capability. These operational characteristics do not address the basic issue: What essential function of national defense does the submarine perform better and more economically than can any other agent?

Because the *Trident* submarine (SSBN) provides strategic deterrence more effectively and at less cost than can other systems, it is secure in its role as our nation's primary strategic deterrent. This is true today when nuclear-tipped missiles still menace our country and may be even more so should Trident submarines be armed with more flexible conventional missiles.

On the other hand, because the *Seawolf* attack submarine (SSN) can not justify its complexity and high cost in the face of a diminishing high-seas submarine and surface threat, the attack submarine needs redefinition of its mission and performance requirements.

Pertinent to this problem is the fact that the historic importance of ocean transport is magnified by the economic interdependence of modern industrialized nations, as well as by the logistic requirements of potential peacekeeping and regional conflict missions. Two world wars have convincingly demonstrated that even limited-performance submarines are a major threat to sea transport. And had they been used against us in the Korean, Vietnam, Gulf, or Desert Wars, the ensuing problems and costs would have been tremendous. To quote from a report by the director of Naval Intelligence, "Aside from the United States and the CIS [Commonwealth of Independent States], some 40 states collectively possess nearly 400 submarines; about half of these submarines belong to our allies, friends, and true neutrals."[1]

In more than ninety years of U.S. submarine development and operation, the progress of technology has so enhanced the submarine's unique capability to operate unseen and unsupported in a variety of roles that the nuclear-powered sub is now an essential element of our total naval warfare system. But the inexorable march of science and technology continues, as well for potential enemies as for the United States. Now that we are free from Rickover's rigid control of propulsion technology, it is time to supplement his legacy. However, we must not again allow design of the engineering plant to dictate the mission of a submarine. Even here, form must follow function. We must design and produce submarines that are more efficient, more capable, and more cost effective in performing appropriate roles in our revised national military strategy.

There must be rigorous analysis of the submarine's strengths and weaknesses, identifying useful capabilities it can contribute to naval or joint task forces. Instead of emphasizing independent operations by single attack submarines of general-purpose design, we must explore the capabilities of specialized submarines which are made possible by the great advances in production technology, computerized control, sonar, weapons, and communications. Just as we experimented with a variety of submarine designs in the 1940s and 1950s, it is timely to do so again. What better way could there be to maintain and enhance, on a competitive basis, submarine design and production capability? We may even find that nuclear propulsion is not essential for every mission, as in regions were ASW is rudimentary at best.

We must avoid the pitfall of justifying the need for submarines merely by cataloging the many tasks they are capable of performing. In 1964, as part of our Advanced Sea Based Deterrent Study Group, the Special Projects Office organized a strong team of scientists and engineers. During discussion of the value of deep-ocean technology to our nation, the wisest remark came from Dr. Charles C. Lauritzen of the California Institute of Technology. After listening quietly to many positive, supportive comments, he said that for years he had been on the President's Scientific Advisory Committee (PSAC). Each year they heard the Air Force give lengthy justifications for some new airplane, including a dozen reasons why it should be funded and developed. (I hasten to add that the same could be said of some Navy programs, submarines included.) "But the President and the Secretary of Defense don't want a dozen reasons. They want one reason."

What is the compelling reason for enhancing our submarine capability? Aside from freedom of movement on the sea that the United States has historically upheld, the oceans increasingly provide the food, energy, and materials needed by many nations, whether for economic well-being, peace-keeping, or defense. The singular requirement is clear; to maintain its primacy of power and leadership, the United States must control and use the inner space of the sea. It is there, in waters that are both dark and deep, that world supremacy can be wrested from us or further strengthened. Our presence and authority there are required absolutely. For that, as the only system that combines concealment with mobility and endurance, the submarine in various forms and applications is essential.

APPENDIX A: ABBREVIATIONS

AA	Antiaircraft
AEC	Atomic Energy Commission
AO	Oiler (a fleet auxiliary)
ASR	Submarine rescue vessel
ASW	Antisubmarine warfare
BB	Battleship
BuAer	Bureau of Aeronautics
BuOrd	Bureau of Ordnance
BuPers	Bureau of Naval Personnel
BuShips	Bureau of Ships
BuWeps	Bureau of Naval Weapons
CDS	Chief of Defense Staff (in United Kingdom)
CinCLantFlt	Commander-in-Chief Atlantic Fleet
CinCPacFlt	Commander-in-Chief Pacific Fleet
CinCPOA	Commander-in-Chief Pacific Ocean Area
CinCSouth	Commander-in-Chief Allied Forces Southern Europe
CinCUS	Commander-in-Chief U.S. Fleet (before World War II)
CNM	Chief of Naval Material
CNO	Chief of Naval Operations
CO	Commanding officer
ComCruBat	Commander of Cruisers Battle Force
CominCh	Commander-in-Chief U.S. Fleet (during World War II)
ComNavGruChina	Commander Naval Group China
ComSubLant	Commander Submarine Force Atlantic Fleet
ComSubPac	Commander Submarine Force Pacific Fleet
ComSubRon	Commander Submarine Squadron
ComSubSoWesPac	Commander Submarines Southwest Pacific
CV	Aircraft carrier, conventional power
CVN	Aircraft carrier, nuclear-powered
DD	Destroyer, general purpose
DesDiv	Destroyer Division
DSRV	Deep submergence rescue vehicle
ELF	Extremely low radio frequency (below 10 kHz)
GUPPY	Greater underwater propulsive power
ICBM	Intercontinental ballistic missile
IRBM	Intermediate range ballistic missile
J.O.O.D.	Junior officer of the deck
JSTPS	Joint Strategic Target Planning Staff
MAD	Magnetic anomaly detector
MIRV	Multiple independently targeted reentry vehicle
MLF	Multilateral force
MRBM	Medium range ballistic missile
NASA	National Aeronautic and Space Agency

NATO	North Atlantic Treaty Organization
NMSE	Navy Material Support Establishment
OEG	Operations Evalution Group (in OpNav)
OpNav	Office of the Chief of Naval Operations
OP 31	Director Submarine-Antisubmarine Warfare Division
OP 311	Head, Submarine Warfare Branch
OP 433	Head, Submarine Branch, Fleet Maintenance Division
OSD	Office of the Secretary of Defense
OTC	Officer in Tactical Command
PC	Patrol craft
PCO	Prospective commanding officer
RADAR	Radio detection and ranging device
SAC	Strategic Air Command
SACEur	Supreme Allied Commander Europe
SACLant	Supreme Allied Commander Atlantic
SACO	Sino-American Cooperative Organization
SCB	Ship Characteristics Board
SecDef	Secretary of Defense
SecNav	Secretary of the Navy
ServFor	Service Force
SLBM	Submarine-launched ballistic missile
SLCM	Sea-launched cruise missile
SLO	Submarine liason officer
SONAR	Sound navigation and ranging, underwater
SPO	Special Projects Office
SS	Attack submarine, diesel-powered
SSBN	Ballistic missile submarine, nuclear-powered
SSG	Guided missile submarine, diesel-powered
SSGN	Guided missile submarine, nuclear-powered
SSK	Hunter-killer submarine, diesel-powered
SSN	Attack submarine, nuclear-powered
SSO	Submarine oiler, diesel-powered
SSPO	Strategic Systems Project Office (successor to SPO)
SSR	Radar picket submarine, diesel-powered
SSRN	Radar picket submarine, nuclear-powered
START	Strategic Arms Reduction Talks
StratCom	Strategic Command (successor to SAC)
SubPac	Submarines Pacific Fleet
SubSoWesPac	Submarines Southwest Pacific
TDC	Torpedo data computer
UHF	Ultra high radio frequency (300,000 to 3,000,000 kHz)
VHF	Very high radio frequency (30,000 to 300,000 kHz)
VLF	Very low radio frequency (10 to 30 kHz)
X-craft	Midget submarine for harbor penetration

APPENDIX B: HAZARDOUS DUTY PAY

In the spring of 1939, in a period of less than thirty days, each of the three major democracies lost a fine ship, two of them just off the building ways. Three submarines went to the bottom. Our *Squalus,* England's *Thetis,* and France's *Phenix* had sunk in areas widely spaced around the world. Were these disasters, coming so quickly on one another, really accidents, or were they the result of a sinister international plot?

The tragic events began on May 23 when the United States lost *Squalus,* a brand-new boat, during her sea trials. Under command of Lt. Oliver F. Naquin, an experienced, respected submariner, *Squalus* had made a number of successful dives following her construction by the Portsmouth Navy Yard in New Hampshire. Air for the ship's diesel engines was drawn through the main engine air-induction valve, a large, hydraulically operated valve located under the platform ("cigarette deck") just abaft the periscope shears. It was the failure of this valve to close as the boat dived that caused the disaster. Tons of sea water poured through the open valve, flooded the engine rooms, and carried the ship to the bottom, 242 feet down, in the trial area off Portsmouth near the Isle of Shoals.

By slamming shut the heavy watertight door leading aft from the control room, the flooding was confined to the after portion of the submarine. Of fifty-nine men on board, thirty-three in the forward part of *Squalus* remained alive, sealed in her hull on the sea floor. After the stricken sub was located, the submarine rescue vessel *Falcon* moored over her. With four round trips of her rescue chamber, she brought all survivors, including the skipper, to safety. It was not until September 13 that *Squalus* herself was raised with the use of lifting pontoons. Overhauled by the navy yard in eleven months, she was renamed *Sailfish* and went on to compile a splendid combat record in World War II.

Just nine days after the loss of *Squalus,* the newly commissioned British submarine *Thetis,* also making a test dive, sank in Liverpool Bay off England's western shore when a torpedo tube door was inadvertently opened to sea. She had on board 103 men, of whom ninety-nine were lost. This was the worst disaster in submarine history to that time.

Then, just a few days later, in Cam Ranh Bay off Indo-China (now Vietnam), the French lost *Phenix;* seventy-one men died in her.

To leap ahead thirty years, with the disappearance of nuclear-powered *Scorpion* in 1968, the macabre coincidence of 1939 recurred: Once again three submarines were lost within a short time of each other. On January 25, 1968, the former British submarine HMS *Totem,* renamed *Dakar* and operated by the Israeli navy, was en route Portsmouth, England, to Haifa, Israel, when she disappeared near Cyprus with her crew of sixty-nine men. Two days later the French *Minerva,* nearing her home port of Toulon, sank without a trace, taking with her a crew of fifty-two. USS *Scorpion,* proceeding home across the Atlantic at high speed submerged from deployment in the Mediterranean, vanished in May with her crew of ninety-nine.

Once again international tensions of cold war and potential conflict inspired dark suspicions. Laymen muttered of intrigue and hostile action and revived stories of sailors' superstitions. But when *Scorpion*'s shattered hulk was found in October in water more than ten thousand feet deep, four hundred miles southwest of the Azores, no foul play was deduced.

Such disasters, suffered by all nations that operate submarines, dramatically portray the hazard of undersea operations. Public emotion runs high, particularly when there are survivors trapped in the sunken hull. There is a special, horrified fascination in the plight of seamen who trusted technology and their own skills to live and work in the dark, wet world beneath the sea. From pulpit and press come welcome prayer and thoughtful editorial, as well as newsprint drama. Well-meant suggestions and demands for investigation pour in to naval authorities and the Congress, while the slow, arduous work of search and rescue proceeds.

On December 17, 1927, *S-4* was surfacing off Provincetown, Massachusetts, when she was rammed by the U.S. Coast Guard destroyer *Paulding*. *S-4* sank in 102 feet of water. When a diver reached her, he determined that six men were still alive, but they could not be rescued in time.

Typical of the emotional reaction to such remote, unseen tragedy is the poem entered in the *Congressional Record* of April 9, 1929, by Representative Canfield. It was written by his constituent John Alvin Garrett, of Rising Sun, Indiana.

Submarine "S-4"

Nigh fathom twenty sunk they lie,
awaiting rescue or to die,
entrapt inside a submarine.
With death approaching on the scene,
the crew compose their minds with dice,
more for the pleasure than the vice.

We pass along upon our way
to seek the pleasures of the day,
or rack the brain with one concern,
to make today a good return
with wealth employed to sell or buy
while valiant men thus bravely die.

Condemn a Cain by court's decree,
we sue the courts to set him free;
and here we pause with sombre grin
to scan the daily bulletin
and read the news with scarce a sigh,
when such brave men with honor die.

A heavy sea does now prevail,
a timely rescue soon must fail;
the air consumed, they gasp for breath,
and faint, and then succumb to death;

and at half mast Old Glory waves
in mourning for these valiant braves.

It has long been recognized that within every military service there are certain tasks and duties that are more rigorous or hazardous than the norm of military life and should be compensated by a higher rate of pay. Indeed, as technology makes it possible for humans to operate in ever more hostile environments, or under greater and greater stress, the list of extrahazardous duties lengthens.

Within the U.S. submarine service there was never an effort to promote extra pay for the hazards involved or to increase it as time went on. However, as the discomforts and dangers of submarine duty became more apparent, administrative action by the Navy Department and some congressional initiative evolved a submarine pay policy that now seems appropriate and equitable.

Prior to 1928, officers received no additional pay for duty in submarines. On the other hand, enlisted men serving in subs were given extra pay of $5 per month, plus $1 for each day during any part of which they were submerged in a submarine, with the maximum allowable of $20 per month. Under this concept, the greater part of additional pay for duty in submarines was based on the hazards and discomforts of an individual day's submerged operations. However, it was also based on the deleterious effect on clothing caused by duty in the tiny, crowded, gasoline- or diesel-powered boats, almost continuously damp and foul-smelling. (It was not true that all submariners were spoiled; they only smelled that way.)

Submarine pay for officers was initiated by Congress in 1928, and was established at 25 percent of their base pay. At the same time, submarine pay for enlisted men was continued as additional pay of from $5 to $30 a month, based primarily on their rating and their submarine qualification and not on the number of days submerged.

The impetus for submarine pay for officers came from Fiorello La Guardia, then U.S. congressman from New York. In December 1927 he embarked in *S-8* at New London and proceeded to Provincetown, Massachusetts, where *S-4* had been sunk by collision, with the loss of forty men. Experiencing the discomforts of constant wet, piercing cold and sensing the ever-present hazard of duty in the small, crude, underpowered boats of that day, he was amazed to learn that there was no extra compensation for those factors.

It was another congressman from New York, Rep. W. Sterling Cole, who was instrumental in the next change in submarine pay. The Act of August 4, 1942, established sub pay for both officers and enlisted men as 50 percent of the base pay for their rank or rating. This raised submarine pay to the same rate as flight pay for naval aviators. No doubt acceptance of this standard was hastened by the fact that, with the start of wartime submarine operations in 1941, we were increasingly sensing the tragedy of submarines "overdue and presumed lost." During World War II, out of every thousand American submariners who sailed on war patrols, 220 lost their lives, a percentage of loss higher than for any other branch of U.S. military forces.

In spite of the historic and legislative background of submarine pay, it, or at least the administration of its payment, came regularly under scrutiny and criticism by congressional committees or the comptroller general. Unlike flight pay, which was payable even though the officer or enlisted man was not attached to an operational unit but maintained his proficiency through training flights, submarine pay was discontinued to personnel when they went to nonsubmarine duty. This was readily accepted by the submarine service and is the rule today.

A difficult situation arose in 1950 when the General Accounting Office took exception to submarine pay that had been paid to officers and enlisted men serving in administrative and training capacities on the staffs of submarine operational commanders. These were afloat commands for submarine divisions and squadrons as well as for their superior submarine force commands. Personnel serving in such assignments could not perform their duties effectively if they were embarked in submarines as continuously as those engaged in actual operation of the boats. In addition, it was critical that all persons assigned to those necessary and important duties in support of the afloat commanders be as competent and experienced as possible, not penalized with a reduction in pay when ordered to the operating staffs.

Nevertheless, the fiscal watchdogs interpreted the law as narrowly as possible. From their viewpoint, no one was entitled to the extra pay for submarine duty for any day in which he was not physically on board the sub. The concept of pay for extrahazardous duty was not questioned; what was challenged was the legality or propriety of submarine pay for those whose duties did not require them to serve continuously on board. The GAO even recommended that the amounts disbursed to those in the staff assignments be recouped by checkage of the pay of those concerned. In my own case this would have been $9,347!

To help resolve the problem in as equitable a manner as practicable, Vice Adm. James Fife, Jr., who had recently commanded Submarine Force, Atlantic, and in 1950 was deputy chief of naval operations (OP 03), appointed a committee of submarine officers, myself among them. We were charged to look into the alleged abuses and to make recommendations as appropriate. We were particularly sensitive to the fact that then, as now, the bulk of submarine pay went to enlisted men. At that time 7,881 enlisted men and only 962 officers received some $6.5 million in submarine pay. This was one-third of 1 percent of the annual pay received by all Navy personnel.

Any reductions made were likely to fall most heavily on those who would feel it most, with severe impact on family standard of living and the education of children. Nevertheless, among our recommendations was one calling for a careful screening of all staff billets. Only those whose proper performance required regular and frequent participation in submarine operation would be entitled to submarine pay. What a wrenching task it was to single out on carefully structured, close-knit staffs jobs which, once on a par, were now declared to be somewhat less equal.

With the revised procedures placed in effect, and with the strong support of Secretary of the Navy Francis P. Matthews, the auditors' case was successfully rebutted, and submarine pay has remained on a sound and equitable basis ever since, although not without review and statutory revision from time to time.

The advent of nuclear-powered submarines brought changed patterns of operations. The introduction of the Polaris blue and gold concept of 1959, in which each fleet ballistic missile submarine had two complete crews that alternately took their ship to sea on their long, deterrent patrols, made it necessary once again to enact legislation so as not to penalize the "off" crews during their periods of recuperation and training.

It was natural that a subject as sensitive as pay would be the subject of wry humor during the uneasy periods of investigation. In the early 1950s, the Senate Military Preparedness Subcommittee, which had been Harry Truman's stepping stone to the vice-presidency, was chaired by Lyndon B. Johnson. His investigators compiled data along the same lines as had the General Accounting Office. Not bothering to work through the chain of command, they went directly to the chief yeoman in charge of personnel records at the Submarine Base, New London.

The hard-bitten chief, a man with many years of duty in submarines, was among those who might have to forfeit sub pay. This was the time of the Korean War and recurring appeals for blood donors. The chief had previously donated blood for those wounded in the bitter fighting, but he responded again, grumbling all the while, "They keep taking my blood, and now those sons-of-bitches want to take my sub pay!"

In a short time, so the story goes, the flask of his blood arrived in the battle zone. Just in time, a Navy hospital corpsman crawled to a badly wounded Marine lying on a fire-swept hillside. Hanging the container of blood from the rifle he stuck in the ground, he transfused the vital fluid to the wounded man. As the fresh blood seeped through the Marine's arteries, his eyes opened, his lips moved, he painfully muttered through clenched teeth, "I won't fight unless I get submarine pay!"

But it was not only enlisted men who could jest about sub pay. The matter of pay for extrahazardous duty and pay for proficiency came under the scrutiny of Secretary of Defense Robert S. MacNamara in his constant search for cost effectiveness in the defense budget. He suggested that the sums all services were paying to maintain flying proficiency among their pilots were excessive, not just because of pay but because of the procurement, maintenance, and operating costs of the many training aircraft required. He pointed out that most of the senior flying officers whose flight proficiency was being maintained would never be called upon to fly in combat or in the increasingly complex aircraft being introduced.

After much study and debate, adjustments and revisions were made, chiefly in the area of entitlement to flight pay. Shortly thereafter, I escorted Secretary of Defense MacNamara to Cape Canaveral in July 1963 to embark in USS *Lafayette* (SSBN 616) to witness the firing of Polaris missiles. When we returned to Washington the next day, I sat facing him in the military Jet Star plane as we flew over the Navy section of Andrews Air Force Base preliminary to landing. As we made our turn over the field we could see lined up the numbers of small, light, twin-engine craft that naval aviators on duty in the Washington area flew regularly on their proficiency flights. Looking me in the eye, absolutely deadpan, Bob Mac-

Namara said, "I'm so grateful submariners haven't insisted on miniature submarines to maintain their proficiency."

It was reassuring to get even that small bit of humor from that remarkable but controversial man.

NOTES

CHAPTER 1: BATTLESHIP PRELUDE

1 More recent examples of this fact of warship life are the battleships *Iowa, New Jersey, Missouri,* and *Wisconsin.* Built as long ago as 1940 and decommissioned after World War II, they were activated for the Korean War, laid up again, then after modernization of electronic systems and weaponry rejoined the fleet commencing in 1984.

2 Contrary to popular belief, the Navy gets most of its commissioned officers from sources other than the Naval Academy. In 1992 only 920 of 5348 total accessions were from USNA.

3 Quoted in *Time,* June 4, 1934.

CHAPTER 2: IN THE BEGINNING

1 Submarines of any size, then as now, were called "boats" rather than "ships." This custom derives from the early designs of submarines, which were so small that they could carry few men and were not capable of extensive cruising. In fact, for some transoceanic voyages they were, like boats, simply hoisted on board a transport ship and carried to their destination.

2 Letter dated April 25, 1939, from Adm. Thomas C. Hart to Comdr. James Fife.

3 Twenty years later, just prior to our entry into World War II, seven of the aged, decrepit O-boats were reactivated for use as Submarine School training boats.

CHAPTER 3: SCHOOL DAYS

1 These procedures are no longer required. Today's submariners are trained in more modern escape techniques, using the Steinke hood, free ascent, or the deep submergence rescue vehicles *DSRV-1* and *-2.*

CHAPTER 4: RUBE GOLDBERG WAS HERE

1 *Argonaut,* the V-4 of Willie's superstitions, served long and well for all her shortcomings until, in action against the Japanese off Rabaul Island in 1943, she was lost with all hands. The 105 men in her was the largest number we lost in one submarine during the war. Two men on board, my shipmates from 1936 to 1940, Chief Gunner's Mate Charles J. Cerrinack and Chief Radioman Lawrence D. Leland, had served in her continuously since they, too, assembled in the commissioning detail as young seamen in 1928.

CHAPTER 5: SPIES

1 At that time, because of their longitude about 40° west of California, the Hawaiian Islands used a "sun time" 2½ hours earlier than the West Coast's.

2 Midway through the war, change was made to various shades of gray to minimize visual detection when on the surface at night.

3   Perhaps the Japanese observed or learned of this test to extend the reach of naval aviation. In March 1942, two of their submarines, *I-15* and *I-19*, refueled two "Emily" seaplanes at French Frigate Shoals. The planes then flew on to an unsuccessful nighttime bombing of Oahu.

4   Rear Adm. Edwin T. Layton, USN (Ret.), *"And I Was There"* (New York: William Morrow, 1985), 54.

CHAPTER 6: HEADING FOR WAR

1   In Navy parlance, a "head" is a toilet, and in older submarines its contents were discharged to sea by air pressure.

CHAPTER 7: LESSONS IN WAR

1   U.S. Fleet Antisubmarine Summary, 1942.

2   Antony Preston, *Sea Power* (London: Phoebus Publishing, 1979), 197.

3   An excellent account of this sorry chapter in U.S. naval history is Michael Gannon's *Operation Drumbeat* (New York: Harper and Row, 1990).

4   Vannevar Bush, *Modern Arms and Free Men* (New York: Simon and Schuster, 1949).

5   After the war we learned that Japan had indeed planned an attack on Panama Canal, but the attempt was never made. The submarine *I-401* had been designed for the specific purpose of destroying the canal. She displaced more than 5000 tons and had a deck hangar to carry three seaplanes, whose mission it would be to bomb the canal's vital points.

6   Rod Rooney was the only one of our group who did not survive the war. He was lost when his *Corvina* (SS 226) was torpedoed by a Japanese sub.

7   Capt. Jospeh F. Enright, USN, with James W. Ryan, *Shinano!* (New York: St. Martin's Press, 1987), 11.

CHAPTER 8: DUDS AND DEPTH CHARGES

1   *Maru* is the Japanese word appended to every merchant ship's name, signifying its character.

2   Naval History Division, Officer of the Chief of Naval Operatons, *U.S. Submarine Losses, World War II*, fifth printing (Washington: Government Printing Office, 1963), 54.

3   Vice Adm. Charles A. Lockwood, USN (Ret.), *Sink 'Em All* (New York: E. P. Dutton, 1951), 92.

CHAPTER 9: CRESCENDO

1   In 1941 U-boats sank more than two million tons of shipping; in 1942 more than six million.

2   When the war started there was a total of fifty-one U.S. submarines in the Pacific; six were obsolescent S-boats, and eleven others were on the West Coast undergoing overhaul, modernization, or training.

3 Japan was far behind in her Navy's use of radar. All her major warships were not fitted with radar until June 1944.

4 John D. Alden, *U.S. Submarine Attacks during World War II* (Annapolis: United States Naval Institute, 1989), 57, 66.

5 Atsushi Oi, "Why Japan's Antisubmarine Warfare Failed." In *The Japanese Navy in World War II*, 2d ed. (Annapolis: United States Naval Institute, 1986), 388.

6 Oi, "Why Japan's Antisubmarine Warfare Failed," 396.

7 Alden, *U.S. Submarine Attacks during World War II*, 147.

8 Samuel Eliot Morison, *History of U.S. Naval Operations in World War II*, vol. 12: *Leyte, June 1944–January 1945* (New York: Little, Brown, 1958), 333.

9 Dr. John Hoyt Williams, "Leyte Gulf, 1944: A Periscope View," *The Retired Officer* (Oct. 1984): 33.

CHAPTER 10: RICE PADDY NAVY

1 By war's end, our submarines rescued a total of 504 aviators downed at sea. One of them was Navy Lt. George Bush, who was picked up by *Finback* after he parachuted from his crippled plane near the island of Chichi Jima.

2 T. H. White and Annalee Jacoby, *Thunder Out of China* (New York: William Sloane Associates, 1946), 150.

3 Vice Adm. Milton E. Miles, USN, *A Different Kind of War* (Garden City: Doubleday, 1967), 567.

4 A commander in rank when he was sent to China in 1942, Miles was promoted successively to captain, commodore, and rear admiral while Commander, Naval Group China.

5 Howard L. Dutkin, *Soldier, Patriot, Financier* (Washington: Acropolis Books, 1971), 103.

CHAPTER 11: END OF WAR

1 Walter Raleigh, *The War in the Air, 1914–1918* (London: Clarendon Press, 1922).

2 Joint Army-Navy Assessment Committee, *Japanese Naval and Merchant Shipping Losses* (Washington: Government Printing Office, Feb. 1947).

3 Out of a total of 863 U-boats that became operational, the Germans lost 630 at sea.

CHAPTER 12: LET-DOWN

1 *Report of the Secretary of the Navy*, 1945.

2 Of all the men who sailed on submarine war patrol, 22 percent were lost. This was the highest rate of loss suffered by any branch of our armed forces.

CHAPTER 13: WHERE DO WE GO FROM HERE?

1 General Board letter No. 420-15 (Serial No. 280), dated Feb. 6, 1946.

2 *Report of Submarine Conference*, May 18, 1949, 11.

3 *First Preliminary Characteristics for Submarine (Nuclear Powered), Shipbuilding Project No. 64,* March 1950.
4 The cost of the hydrogen peroxide to run a German Type XXVI boat for its endurance of six and one-half hours was $200,000!

CHAPTER 14: SEX AND THE SINGLE SERVICE

1 When the use of Roman numerals to identify successive models of weapons became cumbersome, new weapons were designated in Arabic numerals.
2 Even more recently, professional politicians of both major parties eyed hungrily the voter appeal of Gen. Norman Schwartzkopf and Gen. Colin Powell.
3 Dwight D. Eisenhower, *At Ease: Stories I Tell to Friends* (New York: Doubleday, 1967).

CHAPTER 16: TRANSITION

1 Philip Ziegler, ed., *From Shore to Shore: The Tour Diaries of Earl Mountbatten of Burma, 1953–1979* (London: Collins, 1989), 30.

CHAPTER 17: TROUBLED WATERS

1 Letter to James Heston, May 20, 1826.
2 *Thresher* (SSN 593), completed in 1961, was the first boat built to the new standard. Sadly, she was lost with all hands on the postoverhaul dive in 1963, but for reasons other than hull failure.
3 Today's Trident submarines of 18,750 tons displacement carry twenty-four Trident D-5 ballistic missiles, each weighing 130,000 pounds.
4 The soundness of his personal planning is shown by the fact that when he retired from his civilian career he was chairman and chief executive officer of Perkin-Elmer Corporation, one of our leading high-tech firms.

CHAPTER 18: THE RICKOVER EQUATION

1 Alain C. Enthoven, *Systems Analysis and the Navy* (Annapolis: Naval Review, U.S. Naval Institute, 1965).

CHAPTER 19: THE ULTIMATE DETERRENT

1 In 1969 the laboratory was renamed the Charles Stark Draper Laboratory after its founder and guiding genius.
2 U.S. subs had historically been named for creatures of the deep or else simply given a class letter and serial number. Because they were built in a time of national emergency and were so important to our defense, the large, new, strategic missile submarines (still called "boats") were named for men who had won our freedom or had helped preserve it. To be sure, as the list grew to forty-one, a few could be faulted for not wholly meeting that criterion, and the taint of politics was detectable.

CHAPTER 20: THE FUTURE OF NUCLEAR-POWERED SUBMARINES

1 At the Battle of Midway Island in 1942, *Yorktown,* already severely damaged by air attack, was sunk by a Japanese submarine's three torpedo hits. In 1943, near Makin Island in the Gilberts, the escort carrier *Liscome Bay* was sunk by one torpedo from *I-175.*
2 Capt. R. B. Laning, USN (Ret.), "The Seawolf: Going to Sea," *Naval History* (Summer 1992): 55.
3 Personal letter from Rear Adm. L. P. Ramage, dated Dec. 31. 1957.
4 Rep. Gerald R. Ford became president in 1974, following the resignation of Richard M. Nixon; Rep. Melvin R. Laird was secretary of defense from 1969 through 1973, during the Nixon administration. House of Representatives, 87th Cong., 1962, *Report of Appropriations Committee,* 15.

CHAPTER 21: ALLIES

1 Walter Lippmann, *U.S. Foreign Policy* (Boston: Little, Brown, 1943), 135.
2 James L. George, *The U.S. Navy in the 1990s* (Annapolis: U.S. Naval Institute, 1992), 62.
3 A good account of Italy's naval assault teams is given in chapter 14 of Comdr. Marc' Antonio Bragadin's *The Italian Navy in World War II* (Annapolis: United States Naval Institute, 1957).

CHAPTER 22: POLITICS AND POLARIS

1 The Joint U.S.-U.K. Polaris Progam was initiated by the Nassau Agreement of December 1962 reached by President Kennedy and Prime Minister Macmillan.

CHAPTER 24: SPINDRIFT

1 Two other private yards, Ingalls Shipbuilding Company and New York Shipbuilding Corporation, would build a total of fifteen SSNs.

CHAPTER 25: QUIETER, DEEPER, FASTER?

1 The name of the Bureau of Naval Weapons resulted from the amalgamation of the Bureau of Aeronautics and the Bureau of Ordnance.
2 The six system commands were: Naval Ship Systems, Naval Air Systems, Naval Ordnance Systems, Naval Electronic Systems, Naval Supply Systems, and Naval Facilities Engineering.
3 The forty-one ballistic missile submarines may be disregarded because high speed was not important in their mission.

EPILOGUE

1 Statement, Director of Naval Intelligence to Seapower, Strategic, and Critical Materials Subcommittee of House Armed Services Center, 4 Feb. 1992.

Index

ADM. I. J. GALANTIN, USN (Ret.), was born in New York City in 1910 and grew up in Illinois, where he attended Maine Township High School in Des Plaines. He won a competitive examination against thirty-one other applicants for a senatorial appointment to the U.S. Naval Academy, which he entered in 1929. At Annapolis he captained the fencing team and was intercollegiate champion in 1933, the year he graduated and was commissioned an ensign. After two years in the battleship Navy, he commenced a career that was chiefly in submarines, ashore and at sea.

In World War II he commanded the submarine *Halibut* and was awarded the Navy Cross, three Silver Star medals, and the Navy Unit Commendation. In 1945 he flew over the Hump to Chungking, China, for duty as submarine liaison officer.

In subsequent assignments he commanded a division of submarines, a squadron, was head of the submarine branch in the Navy Department, head of the submarine warfare branch, and director of the Submarine/Antisubmarine Warfare Division. While director of the Special Projects Office of the Navy, developing the Polaris missile system for submarines, he was also U.S. project officer for the Joint U.S.-U.K. Polaris Program. From 1966 until his retirement in 1970, he was chief of naval material, with the rank of four-star admiral. He is also the author of *Take Her Deep!* (1987).